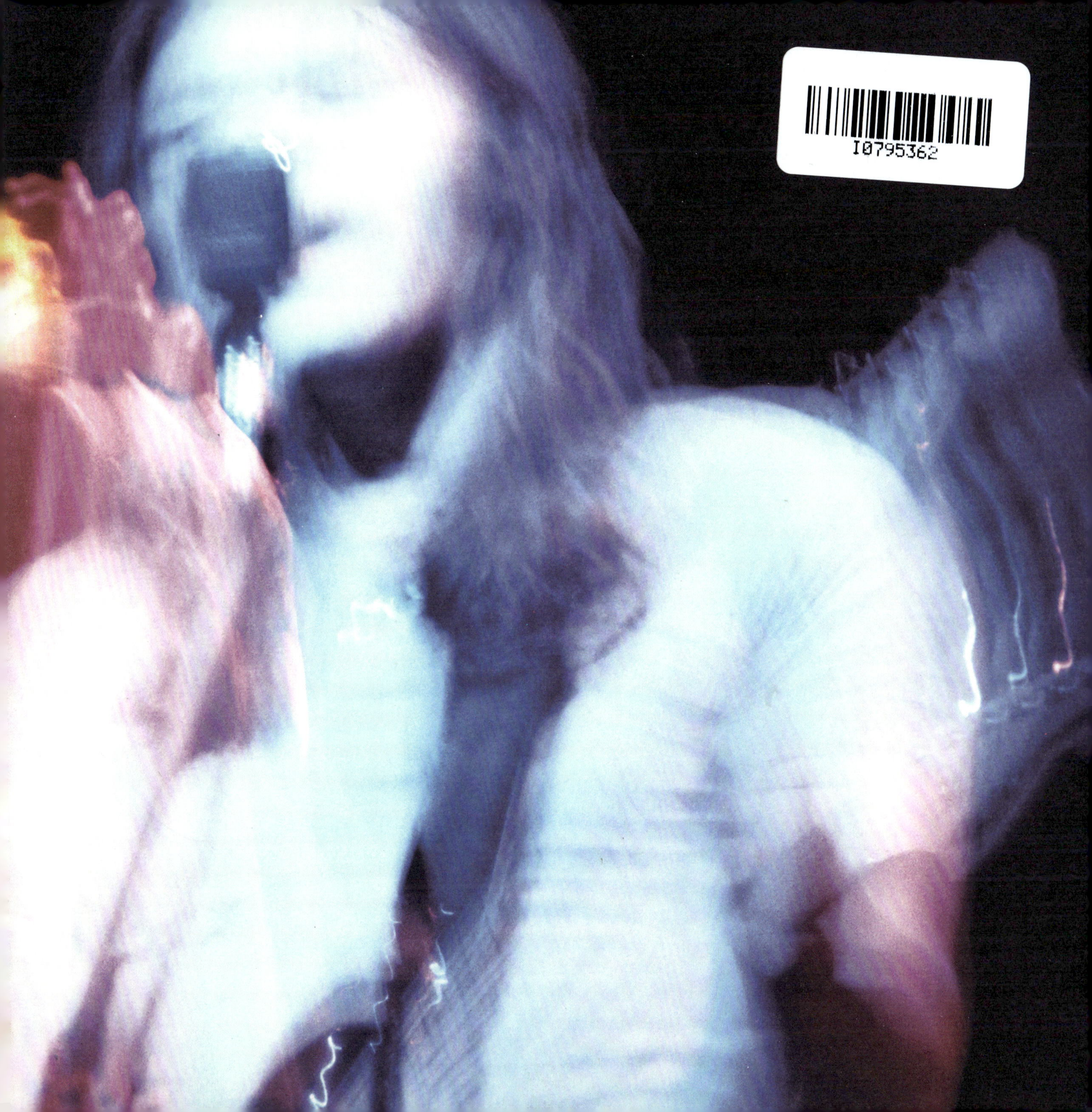

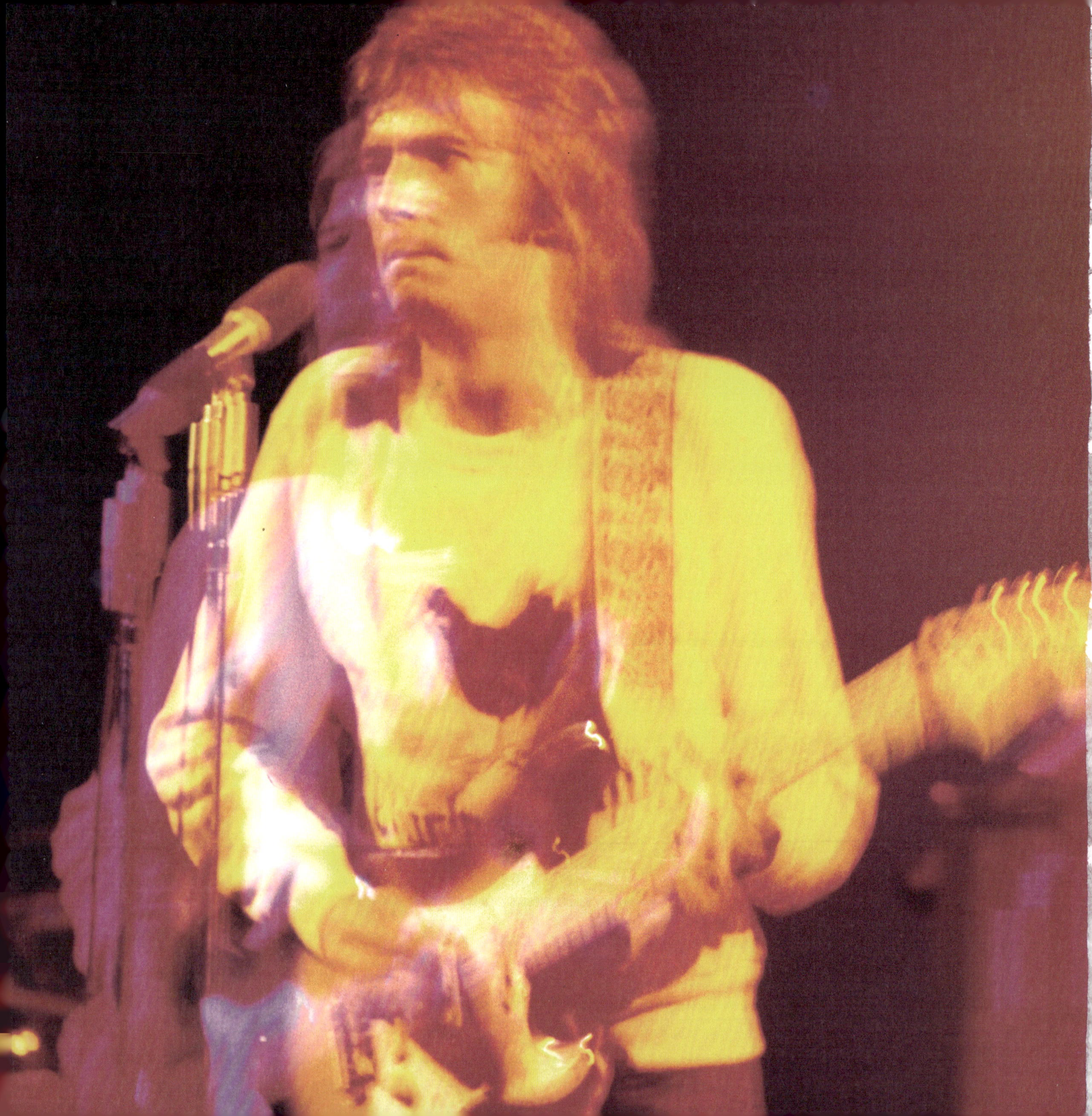

HURRICANES OF COLOR

THE PENNSYLVANIA STATE UNIVERSITY PRESS
UNIVERSITY PARK, PENNSYLVANIA

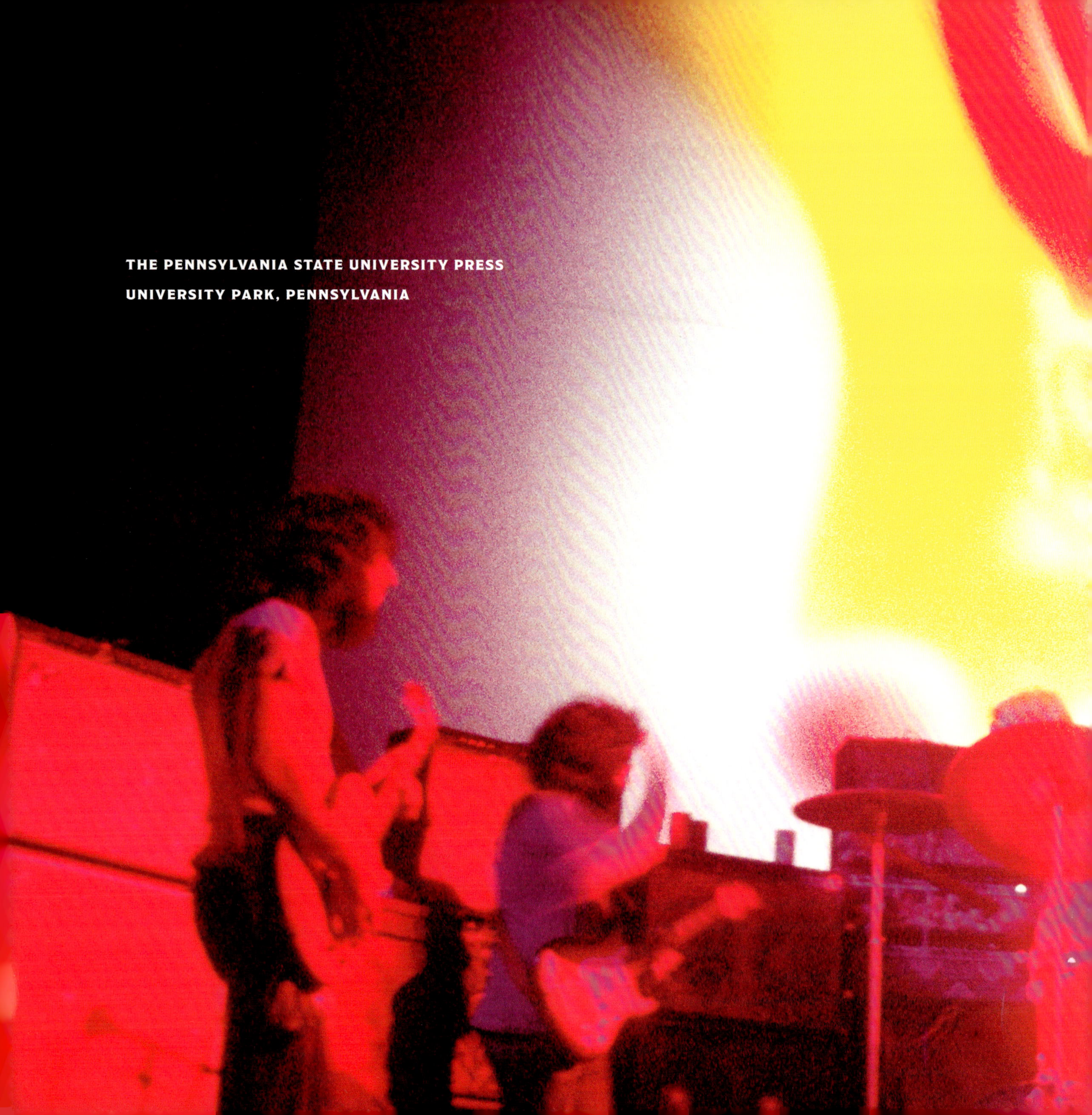

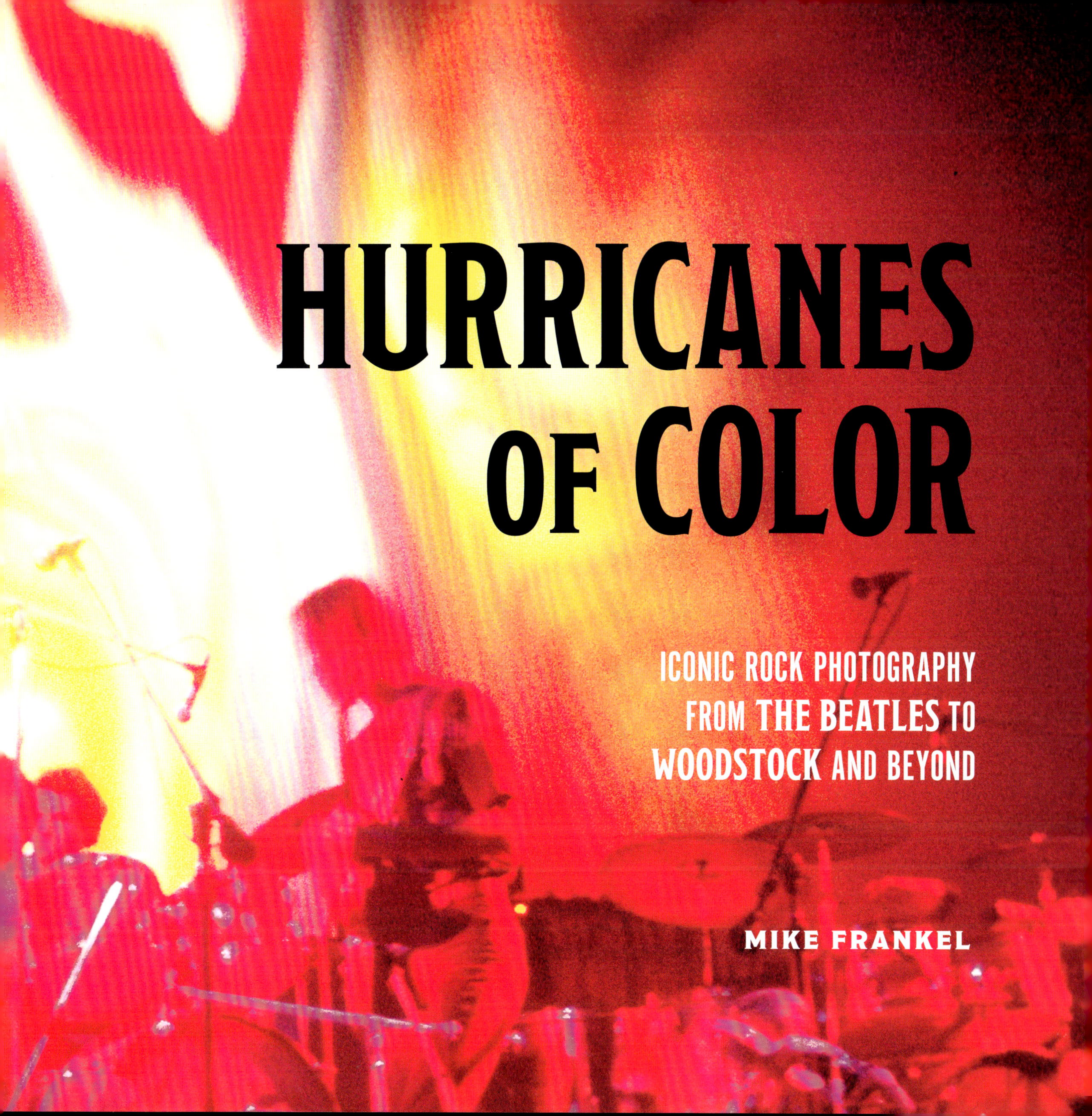

HURRICANES OF COLOR

ICONIC ROCK PHOTOGRAPHY FROM THE BEATLES TO WOODSTOCK AND BEYOND

MIKE FRANKEL

This is a work of creative nonfiction. The events are portrayed to the best of the author's memory. No names have been changed, no characters invented, no events fabricated. This text is a memoir. It reflects the author's present recollections of experiences over time. This work depicts actual events in the life of the author as truthfully as recollection permits and/or can be verified by research. All persons within are actual individuals; there are no composite characters. Any conversations and dates of images all come from the author's recollections and dated original 35 mm slides. The conversations are not written to represent word-for-word transcripts. Rather, the author has retold them in a way that evokes the feeling and meaning of what was said, and in all instances the essence of the dialogue is accurate. The opinions expressed within this book are the author's own and are exercises in "freedom of expression."

Library of Congress Cataloging-in-Publication Data

Names: Frankel, Mike, author.
Title: Hurricanes of color : iconic rock photography from the Beatles to Woodstock and beyond / Mike Frankel.
Other titles: American music history.
Description: University Park, Pennsylvania : The Pennsylvania State University Press, [2024] | Series: American music history | Includes bibliographical references.
Summary: "Explores the author's career and evolution as a photographer during the turbulent 1960s, including his experimental photographs of some of the most significant concerts and artists in rock history"—Provided by publisher.
Identifiers: LCCN 2023036670 | ISBN 9780271094861 (cloth)
Subjects: LCSH: Frankel, Mike. | Rock musicians—Portraits. | Rock music—Pictorial works. | Portrait photography. | Photography, Artistic—20th century.
Classification: LCC ML87 .F77 2024 | DDC 781.66022/2—dc23/eng/20230814
LC record available at https://lccn.loc.gov/2023036670

Printed in China
Published by The Pennsylvania State University Press, University Park, PA 16802–1003

10 9 8 7 6 5 4 3 2 1

The Pennsylvania State University Press is a member of the Association of University Presses.

It is the policy of The Pennsylvania State University Press to use acid-free paper. Publications on uncoated stock satisfy the minimum requirements of American National Standard for Information Sciences—Permanence of Paper for Printed Library Material, ANSI Z39.48–1992.

Endsheets: (front) Jorma Kaukonen and Jefferson Airplane, Winterland, December 1969, and Roger Waters and David Gilmour, Fillmore East, September 1970; (back) Eric Clapton and Bobby Whitlock, Fillmore East, October 1970, and Buddy Miles, Fillmore East, June 1969. Additional credits: title page, "Dark Star" jam, the Grateful Dead with Peter Green and Mick Fleetwood of Fleetwood Mac, Fillmore East, New York, February 1970; page v, Lillian Frankel and Mike Frankel circa 1952 (left), Noah Nathan Frankel circa 1942 (right); page vi, David Bowie, Radio City Music Hall, February 1973; page viii, Jerry Garcia and Bob Weir the of the Grateful Dead, Fillmore East, New York, May 1970.

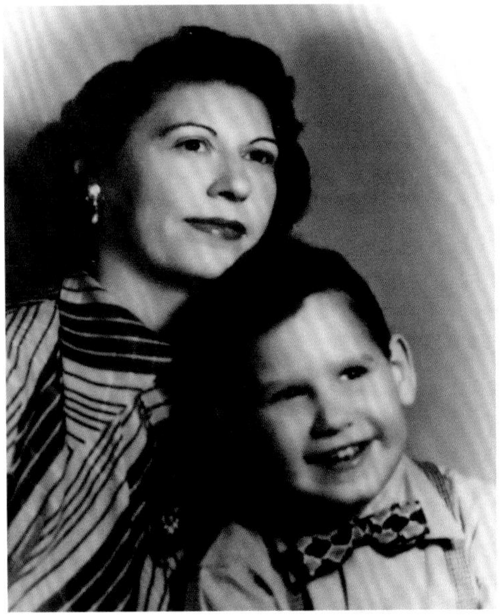 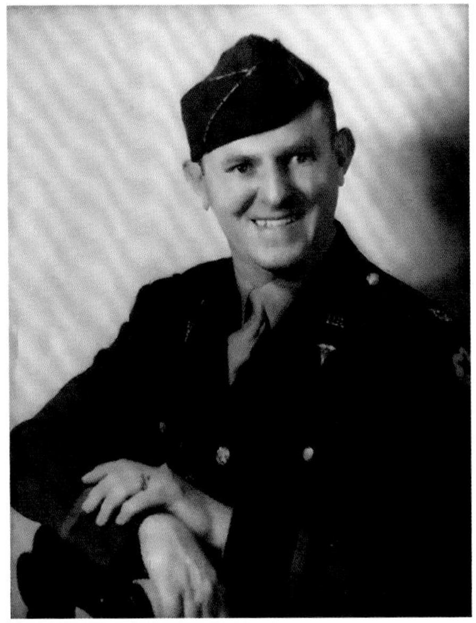

DEDICATED TO LIL AND NATE

No finer, nurturing, and empathetic
humans have ever walked planet Earth!

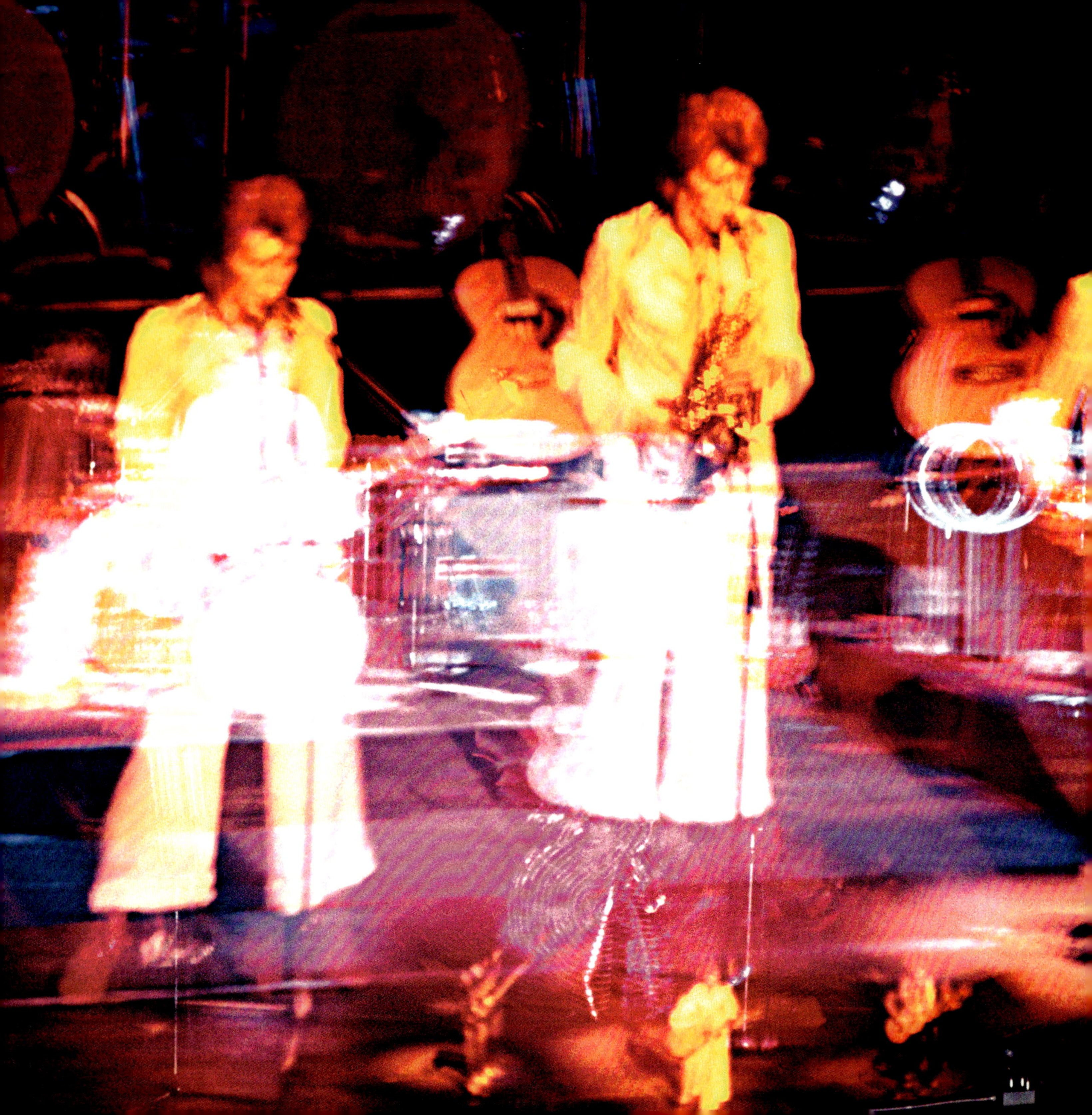

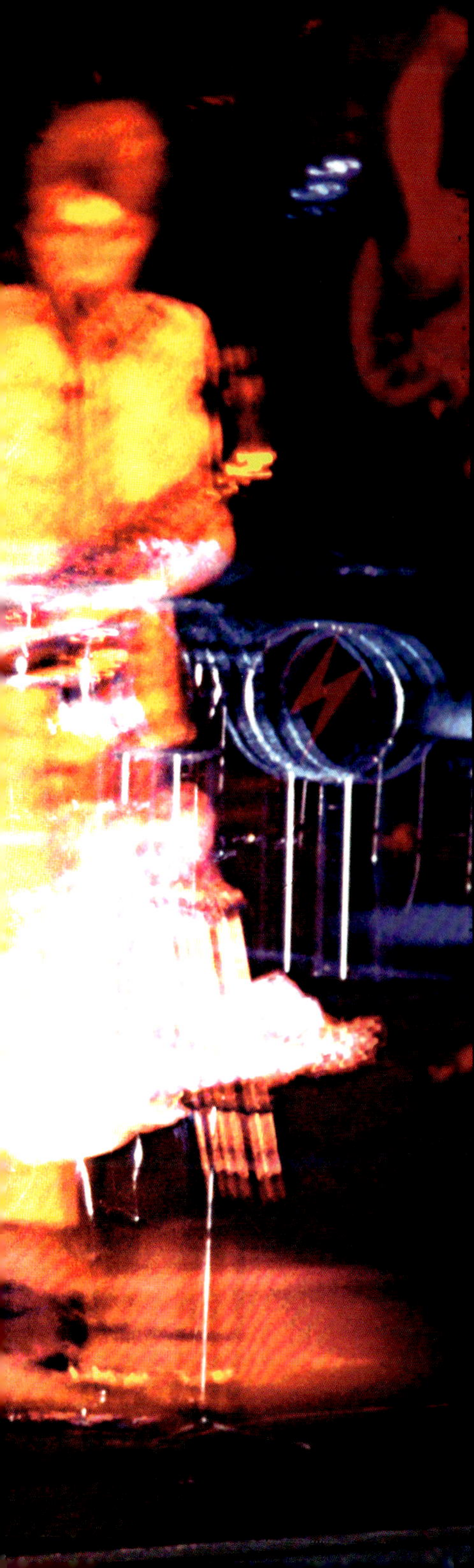

CONTENTS

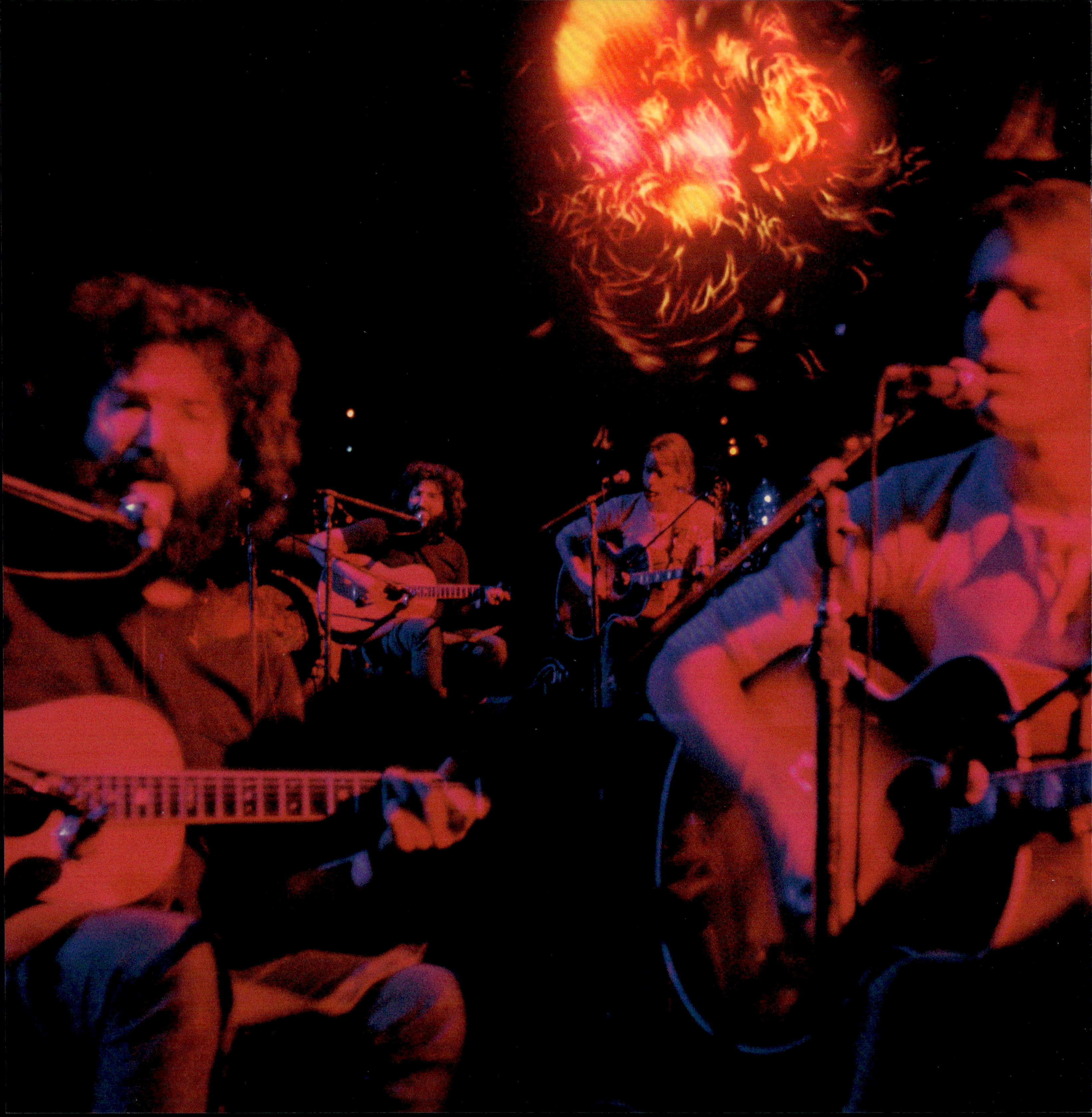

FOREWORD

Hurricanes of Color, a Fusillade of Style

Kenneth Womack

Mike Frankel's life and work as a photographer affords us with a powerful catalog of images that captures the rock era's progress from black-and-white into color, from the low culture of popular music into the upper echelons of pop art. Along the way, his personal story also came into focus, imbuing him with new senses of identity and purpose even as his creative practice as a working photographer began to take flight.

Frankel's innovative portfolio ranges across rock's pop explosion in the 1960s through its mass-market proliferation in the 1970s and beyond. At its heart, *Hurricanes of Color: Iconic Rock Photography from the Beatles to Woodstock and Beyond* brings this paradigm shift vividly into life. Frankel's lens not only memorializes this period of intense change, but does so with increasing experimentation and panache. Take, for instance, his photographs of the Beatles in Philadelphia in September 1964. As with the period in which they were taken, the photos are appropriately staid—formal, even—befitting the preternaturally conservative mood of the times. The Beatles' American onslaught, which had begun back on February 9 when seventy-three million viewers tuned into their legend-making performance on *The Ed Sullivan Show*, was still on its maiden voyage. But change was clearly in the air, and, as the photos in this book so profoundly reveal, it was hurtling forth with a vengeance.

Frankel's photographs from Philly's Convention Hall that September capture the inherent discontinuity between the Beatles' presence at their customary pre-show press conference and, later, at the concert itself. A thirty-three-year-old fixture on the city's cultural and sports scenes, Convention Hall, with its imposing Art Deco façade, was already obsolete. Indeed, the Beatles would be one of the last major acts to perform at the twelve-thousand-seat arena. In 1967, the sleek new Spectrum would open in South Philly, in the process ushering in the possibilities of a more dynamic, modern concert experience.

The contrast between the spectacle of the press conference and the Beatles' concert is remarkably telling. In particular, Frankel's photographs capture the intensity of the Fab Four's media-friendly embrace. His lens affords us with a rare window into the interplay among the participants: first, the Beatles, who spar in equal doses among themselves as well as during their interactions, often mocking and humorous, with the media. And then there is the spate of local dignitaries vying for face time in the immediate vicinity. Working the periphery of the press conference is the increasing police presence associated with the Beatles' peculiar brand of fame—the kind that sends young girls into hysterics and, in turn, the assembled hordes into a frenzy. For the Beatles, the endless parade of press conferences made for a shrewd investment. Having fomented "good press" in their early days would prove to be essential to the Beatles' survival. In fact, just a few years later, the media would go relatively easy on them in the wake of the publicity crisis associated with John Lennon's ill-advised remark about the band being "bigger than Jesus Christ."

When it came to the concert itself, Frankel later recalled being ushered from the lion's den of the press gaggle into the even greater and more fearsome lair of Convention Hall. Before he knew it, the photographer had been "swept away with the other press and camera people down a very short hallway and deposited right in front of the stage!" Frankel's photographs record the striking contrast between the events on stage and the melee unfolding among the audience behind the press pool, where all hell was breaking loose. Clad in their neatly tailored suits, the Beatles ripped through a carefully choreographed, twelve-song set. By this point, their movements—even their song introductions—had become robotic. Any of their original flair had been drained out of their stage show with the onset of an omnipresent Beatlemania. For all the fervor associated with their visit, Beatles concerts were decidedly brief affairs. By the time that they launched into "Long Tall Sally," their traditional closing number, fewer than thirty minutes had passed since they first alighted the Convention Hall stage.

As a working photographer with a penchant for rock and roll, Frankel would shortly begin capturing the rapid cultural shifts roiling at the heart of popular music. The Beatles' Philly performance would prove to have little in common with the concert experiences that awaited Frankel in the coming years. His understandable fascination with Jefferson Airplane and his attendant photographs of the Bay Area group would exemplify the movement from Middle America–friendly concerts from the likes of the Beatles into the full-blown psychedelia of the late-1960s rock rave. Having been produced with the aid of his Nikon F camera, Frankel's photos of the Airplane would underscore his well-honed technique of capturing increasingly kinetic imagery on film.

Jefferson Airplane would prove to be central players in terms of Frankel's evolving aesthetic, as he painstakingly recorded multiple exposures of the band to bring their every movement—bathed in hallucinogens, no doubt—to life. "It was a tedious and complex process to keep the frame synchronized," Frankel writes. "After exposing one frame, I had to first rotate a ring around the shutter button and simultaneously press a button on the bottom of the camera while rewinding the film with a hand crank. The shutter button could be cranked back no more than one revolution to keep the frame in registration." But Frankel wouldn't be finished just yet: "I then turned the shutter ring back to its original position, released the button on the bottom of the camera, and advanced the film back to its former position so the shutter would be again cocked but the film would be ready for the next image place on the same frame."

Frankel's working relationship with the Airplane would reach its fever pitch during his August 1969 sojourn to Woodstock. He attended the famed festival at the band's express request, and Jefferson Airplane's standout set, which showcased such time-eclipsing numbers as "Somebody to Love" and "White Rabbit," would demonstrate not merely the potential but the sheer mettle of his evolving kinetic photographs. For Frankel, the whole experience proved to be a revelation. He was mesmerized by his good fortune at being present at one of rock history's most momentous occasions. "All of twenty years old, dazed and dazzled by the events that led up to my charmed position that afternoon now swimming in my head."

Frankel's knack for replicating a band's stage energy in his photographs would become his hallmark, making for a pictorial representation of the sound, flash, and gusto of psychedelic rock. By the time he took up his familiar position in front of the Fillmore East stage at Pink Floyd's September 1970 performance, Frankel's technique was in full vogue, having advanced well beyond his efforts back at Woodstock. For the photographer, the results would be nothing short of "the most multiple layers and exposures I had ever employed." With Pink Floyd, Frankel recognized that viewers often "get lost trying to isolate and focus on all the embedded components of these three-dimensional-like images, produced by the sounds and movements of the band members." But in the photographer's estimation, there was simply no more exhilarating way of recording the actual experience, "which stunned my eyes and inspired me to represent what I was seeing in this dynamic fashion."

The fruits of Frankel's efforts that evening enabled him to create a dramatic, eight-frame extravaganza, as always in camera with no postshow alterations. He produced a staggering composite image that captured the band in full psychedelic swirl as the group unleashed a vintage setlist that included the likes of "Astronomy Domine," "Set the Controls for the Heart of the Sun," "A

Saucerful of Secrets," and the showstopping "Atom Heart Mother." Frankel's brilliantly arrayed photograph constitutes one of the most evocative Pink Floyd artifacts in existence, especially when it comes to the concert performances that would define them for the ages.

With equal doses of energy and artistry, Frankel's kinetic photographs account for a key innovation in terms of the ways we memorialize the concert experiences, particularly during rock's psychedelic era. In such instances, Frankel revealed a perceptiveness well beyond his tender years, a yearning for experimentation that helped define both a period and a genre that stands among the richest in popular music's storied history.

ACKNOWLEDGMENTS

As I embrace my seventy-fifth year and look back on my life, I see that I have done so many diverse things. But the most memorable experiences are from my photography work in the late '60s in the company of the great Jefferson Airplane. That relationship was central to my evolution as an artist and to my odyssey. The story of how this relationship came to be and my life after is one for anyone with ambitions and dreams in life.

Essential to this story are my wonderfully loving parents, Nate and Lil. They bestowed on me an aura of eternal light and hope that has even allowed me to keep safe and complete this book during the raging storm of COVID-19. They nurtured, encouraged, and fed my creativity so that I may be able to achieve success in a bitter, challenging world that gave no quarter. *Try hard, don't quit, and just do the best you can in every endeavor.* I have held those words tightly through all the challenges and victories over the years. This philosophy has aided me in staying strong through many difficult times, when success seemed fleeting or unsustainable.

Acknowledging everyone who has aided me, inspired me, or championed my cause and extended friendship and camaraderie is impossible, but there are some people who are so important they need to be singled out and praised for their support. They all know the personal stories that are associated with me, and I am grateful to each and every one. I apologize if I have left anyone out.

First and foremost there is the late Daniel FX Sweeney, my brother, mentor, and until his untimely demise in 2015 lifetime artistic coconspirator. "Sween" was one of the most talented artists I've ever known and will forever be an inspiration to me all the days of my life.

Joe Rubin has accompanied me on my life journey almost since day one. He is an amazingly talented and far too modest musician, and we have lived through each other's triumphs and tragedies since we both waited at a bus stop in our hometown of Interlaken, New Jersey (me in fourth grade, him in second).

Charlie Winders, my seventh-grade teacher, was one of the first besides my mom and dad to encourage me and build my confidence at a critical time in my life.

The late Arthur Scott, over forty years of friendship, never ceased his "animated" encouragement for my quest to publish a book of my work. Though he will not be here to see it, I know he will be smiling down in glowing appreciation of seeing this volume finally come to life.

Bill Reynolds, whom I met when we were both around eighteen, has been a tireless champion of my photography from the start.

The one of a kind "brother from another mother" Michael Green is responsible in a direct way for this book that you're holding in your hands. He has been my partner in both legal and hilariously "questionable" activities for over a half a century.

I have known Robert Groden for nearly half a century and he has been with me through the best and the worst of times as an inspiration and source of support through them all. A tip of the hat as well, to Robert's wonderful wife Janet and to his amazing son and my only godson, Michael Groden.

Joe Crownover, whom you will learn more about later, has been my all-time gallery champion and happens to be the greatest salesperson I have ever encountered.

In early 2017 I began to see and "like" the posts of a young lady on Facebook, mostly concerning classic movies and their stars. We "friended" each other after a few weeks. Following a totally chance meeting at a local grocery store, the deal was sealed. Through ensuing conversations, trips, shared experiences, and meeting two of each other's several beloved cats, Meesha and Mira, my relationship with Ms. Kathleen Leatherwood blossomed. The peace, security, and serenity Kathleen has brought lights the way for a brilliant future as we meld our lives as well as those of my three cats, Mira, Maxwell, and Madeline, and her one cat, Molly.

The late Eugene Munger, my first Flagstaff friend and prolific author, coached, coerced, and encouraged me to write my story for years, and continues to be an inspiration in my life.

Jim and Nancy DeBlois, whom I also have known since I moved to Flagstaff, have helped me through so many times both good and bad, and their generosity and kindness to me have known no bounds.

Darren Rudy, whom you will meet in the text, is my newest friend and artistic collaborator.

Gregory Schwartz helped pave the way for my exhibit in Monmouth University in 2019, which led me to meeting Ken Womack, who arranged my Monmouth exhibition and graciously extended the opportunity at Penn State University Press for this book.

I thank all my dog and cat and other animal spirits for the inspiration and comfort they provided me over my lifetime. There are well over thirty, and I wish I had the space to enumerate them all. My lifelong journey with my spiritual animals began in the 1950s with my first cat, Puff (of all original names!) and then fully blossomed in 1969 with the arrival of my first dog, Merb, a floppy-eared Shepherd Husky mix who brought overflowing happiness into my life for the thirteen years he was by my side. Cats Rupert and Mira represent the others well, with over thirty-four years between them. In addition, after moving to Flagstaff in 2002, I was bestowed with a companion of twelve years, Satchel, my beloved mixed-breed Pitbull, whom I met and adopted on the outskirts of a Native American reservation. He along with all my other animal spirits live deep in my heart and inspire me every day.

I am grateful to the members of Jefferson Airplane, both alive and gone far too young, without whose early encouragement (you'll soon read the whole story) none of you would be reading the present volume and seeing my work. And thanks especially to Jorma Kaukonen and Jack Casady for laying the hands of fate on me and choosing an image of mine for the cover of their first Hot Tuna record over fifty years ago.

Huge kudos to the amazing Sally Mann Romano for all her massive amount of help on so many occasions.

I also thank Jon Chambers, who has become the leading collector of my rock and roll work.

I must extend a very special thanks to my editor at Penn State University Press, Ryan Peterson, who, along with copyeditor Nicholas Taylor, has had the inexhaustible patience and knowledge to help make my words more coherent and logical. In addition, the work of Regina Starace, Brian Beer, and Cate Fricke has been immeasurable in the, design, layout, and marketing of my work.

Others that are not acknowledged in the book but have had an impact on my life are listed below in no particular order. Some are still with us, others have passed on, but I am confident they all know their contributions and my deep appreciation: "Uncle" Harry Walters, "Uncle" Phil and "Aunt" Min Rudolf, Murray and Phyllis Fisher, Don Rudolf, John Barry, Fred Bates, Lorene Porter, Vincent DiMattio, Fred Toback, Sandi Long Parker, Mary Ellen Reulbach, John and Terri Leatherwood, Joyce Kneisel, Matthew Sutphen, Frank "Skip" Hildebrand, Bill Frantz, Jim "Thud" Hores, Karen Plunkett-Powell, Colleen Tucker, Gia Sicola-Crownover, Susan Lidz Heckler, Lois Parcells, Molly Munger, Lou Gotz, Jeff Tamarkin, Douglas Holcomb, Mary Lang Mindas, Randy Ellis, Mike Stern, Pamela Solomon, Eli Friedman, Charles Platt, Ken Stunkel, Guy Oakes Wendy Eisimont Fornatale, Mike Fornatale, Tom Bernard Karen and Scott Miller, Marlise Gross, Brad Rossi, Brian Pigott, and Alan and Rick Esner, Beth Mason, and Danielle Furci, members of my "newfound birth family."

I am extremely lucky to have had these people in my life. In the ensuing pages, alongside many never-before-published photographs, I will tell my story.

Feelin' good
this mornin' now I
feel like I wanna
rock a while.

—**Goree Carter**, "Rock Awhile," April 1949

Introduction

Rock and Roll and Photography

My own birth and fortuitous adoption, itself a fascinating and compelling story, coincided with what many scholars contend was the birth of rock and roll itself: a recording committed crudely to vinyl in April 1949. Goree Carter's "Rock Awhile" came to life in a small recording studio in Houston and was released on the Freedom label. The very first chords use the exact guitar style of Chuck Berry's now-familiar riffs, which would not come into existence for another six years. "Rock Awhile" has been deemed by some music scholars to be more worthy of the moniker "first rock and roll record" than the more often cited "Rocket 88" released in 1951. So it may have been inevitable—and even predestined—that my later life was to have some connection to this brand-new sound.

Music was always a part of my childhood. My parents had a modest yet extremely eclectic record collection, and so I was surrounded by classical, jazz, and swing music from the beginning, starting with 1940s 78 rpm records. However, when I received my first transistor radio, life was never the same. The transistor was a green Zenith box the size of a large iPhone but about two inches thick; it was as liberating then as any personal communication device of today. No longer were my listening choices monitored. I wasn't told what I could and could not listen to. Though I was only able to receive AM signals, these were enough to fill my head with the sounds that would shape American life for years on end.

Each night I would lie in my bed with the covers over my head, listening to what was called at the time "devil music." At one point I acquired a rudimentary one-ear headphone that prevented my parents from hearing any of the sounds at all.

At first, I listened to mostly jazz. Al "Jazzbo" Collins and Martin Block's *Make Believe Ballroom* began the journey, but things really took off when I heard the disc jockeys Alan Freed, Jocko, and eventually the great and much underrated Murray the K. Murray was behind the important and regrettably short-lived "music quake" of "free form," which forever changed FM radio. I'd listen well into the night. Jocko played many more of what were called "race records," so I could hear the original versions of songs that after proper homogenization made the "hit parade" by white artists. Later, in 1959, when Jocko went head-to-head with Murray the K, I continued to listen to them both after Alan Freed left under the dark scandal of "payola," in which record execs paid DJs to play their records.

Radio opened a whole world for me—not just music but strange stories, mysteries, and entertainment. Long John Nebel's late night shows included eccentric guests talking about flying saucers, otherworldly abductions, and the hollow earth, while on WOR Jean Shepherd recounted hilarious stories about life and culture in America.

My father's best friend, Barney Niessen, who had had a modest career as a songwriter, opened in the 1950s the Niessen Music Center in downtown Asbury Park, virtually directly across the street from Dad's office. Almost every week Dad would bring home to me a 45 rpm single that Barney suggested to him. The first was "Oh-Oh, I'm Falling in Love Again" by Jimmie Rodgers on Roulette Records. Not the most rockin' of jams, but it did light the fuse. The only problem was, at the time, I had only a tiny "Mickey Mouse" record player, which had no problem playing my childhood nursery rhyme records at 33 rpm and 78 rpm. The Rodgers platter was 45 rpm, which the player also could accommodate; but owing to the large hole in the center of the record, as all 45s had back then, I was out of luck. I had no adapter to fit in the hole allowing the record to be played. As always, necessity is the mother of invention (pre–Frank Zappa, of course), and so I fashioned a 45 adapter out of Silly Putty and experimented till I got the disc centered enough to play without a warble or a wobble. I played 45s like this for many months until I received, on one birthday, an upgraded, portable record player that indeed had a spindle and could play both single 45s and a pile of them, which they used to call "stacks of wax."

Constantly listening to the radio, my interests turned to pure rock in the form of early Chuck Berry, Bo Diddley, Elvis Presley, Buddy Holly, and the Everly Brothers. Little by little, I would encourage Dad to fine-tune Barney's suggestions. And when I had the good fortune to go down with Dad and pick out my own 45s and see the store myself, it was there—among the Baldwin grand pianos and other musical instruments, reams of sheet music, and home appliances—that I found my "wall of wonder." Before my eyes, on specially designed shelves, were the "Top 100" singles from *Billboard* magazine's weekly charts of popular songs. I was like a kid in a candy store. I always examined all the labels on the shelves, paying particular attention to the lower-rung numbers in search of new artists to feed my now growing obsession with music.

My selections tended to be more hard-core rock than Barney would pick out. I would tell Barney through Dad, or in person, about new releases I had heard on the radio and wondered if any of them had shown up yet on the "wall of wax." On one occasion, I heard a new Bobby Darin single called "Dream Lover" and so I asked for it by name. Barney told me there was no such release in his catalog. Though I was still young and unsure of my musical knowledge, I replied, respectfully, "You must've somehow missed it." Lo and behold, a week later "Dream Lover" showed up on the wall, to Barney's amazement and I think some embarrassment.

Eventually I found stations from Buffalo, New York (WKBW), Chicago (WCFL and WLS), and even later "Wolfman" Jack at XERB from Mexico, who all played many local and national songs that didn't show up on New York radio. I soon realized that for some reason late at night I could tune in to radio stations far from my New Jersey home. I found out that during nighttime hours AM signals can travel over hundreds of miles by reflection from the ionosphere, a phenomenon called "skywave" propagation. Many local AM stations back then would go off the air overnight and by way of their powerful transmitters WKBW, WCFL, WLS, XERB, and others would take the place of the off-air stations on the same frequencies.

In the wake of the British Invasion, many of the faraway stations played new music from the Beatles, the Rolling Stones, and other English bands, including some tracks that the New York stations weren't playing at the time. It was a mystery as to where these new songs came from. I discovered that there were always other tracks on British record releases that did not show up on their US equivalents. This was attributed to the British buying public, who demanded longer albums because they were still suffering from postwar rationing up through the mid-1960s and had little money. British artists would have a 45 rpm single released and sell huge numbers of copies. But when the time came to release a full-length album, there was resistance by the public if it contained that same single, which fans had already bought. The British wanted all different tracks for their hard-earned money. American audiences, who were more affluent, were driven more by the hit singles, and they were more likely to buy an artist's album if it contained a few songs they already knew. Thus, US records normally had eleven or twelve tracks at the most, whereas the British ones had fourteen tracks, some of which naturally did not make it to the American release. I found out these differences in the British and American versions when I visited London with my parents in 1964 and purchased the *Beatles for Sale* LP and others, which, once back home, I compared with the American releases.

The stations I listened to would play these "unreleased" songs, and often I felt I was hearing them from another dimension. It was like I was a member of a secret club. My friends didn't know of the songs or believe me that they were on the radio. Later compilations of these songs combined with other more known tracks would finally be released in the United States. One such compilation was the notorious Beatles album that had the shocking and notorious "butcher cover"—

showing the band, dressed in white coats, covered with decapitated baby dolls and slabs of raw meat—which originally, and for a short time, graced the cover of their *Yesterday and Today* album. There are contradictory stories of why they did it, most prominently that the idea originated with their photographer, Robert Whitaker, as either a political statement against the Vietnam War or one to "dirty up" the Boys' squeaky-clean image. I vividly remember the controversy before the album was pulled and rereleased after DJs reacted with horror and disbelief at the Fab Four's choice of image.

Sometime later, my dad and I built a shortwave radio, which had the effect of expanding my world even more. I was now able to tune into stations from around the world. I listened to what was later called "world music," and I also enjoyed the incomprehensible blasts and weird sounds that emanated from tuning between the stations, some of which I later found out were part of the communication platform of Morse code. Listening to this and other codes being transmitted to unknown places made me feel like a spy monitoring nefarious messages. These truly bizarre sounds, in addition to the experimental jazz of Miles Davis (whom I photographed in the 1960s), John Coltrane, and Sun Ra, opened my ears and prepared me for what would become a love of dissonant twentieth-century music from Igor Stravinsky, Charles Ives, Béla Bartók, and Olivier Messiaen to the lesser known Carl Ruggles as well as the bold experimental work of Edgard Varèse and his self-described spiritual disciple Frank Zappa. Thus, I was more than ready for the soon-to-arrive "progressive rock" of bands like Procol Harum, whom I believed to be the unheralded creator of the genre, and subsequently Soft Machine, King Crimson, Van der Graaf Generator, and the French band Magma, who developed their own genre of "zuehl music" in which they sang in their own language called "Kobaïan," created by their leader and drummer, Christian Vander. This "sonic evolution" for me, paired with my love of art, contributed heavily to my photographic explorations to portray music and the musicians in a unique, dynamic fashion.

From the transistor radio, head covered and listening through a single low-fi earphone, to more full-range stereo headphones and at times stereo speakers, the music was always with me. Eventually I would find my voice, my craft, slowly and surely, through my photography, and I never dreamed that it would intersect with my love of music.

Though I was brought under the spell of music at a young age, my parents introduced me to all art forms. My mom was a voracious reader and had a large library, which, in turn, gave me a love for reading. It was from books that my artistic imagination first formed.

Perhaps the most influential discovery I made as a young boy was a strange book called *Weegee's Creative Camera* by an equally strange photographer named

Arthur Fellig, a.k.a. Weegee, as he was popularly known. Weegee was a groundbreaking crime photographer in New York City, famous for getting the drop on his competitors. He would carry around a complete dark room in the trunk of his car, allowing him to process and print his photographs on the fly and therefore be the first to submit them to the early editions of the New York newspapers. Weegee dabbled in highly outrageous and original images shot through mirrors and objects that would distort and bend his subjects, creating wild portraits of celebrities he photographed. In this book—and this was the key part—he shared his techniques. This, along with the work of Marcel Duchamp and the "Futurism" and "Rayonism" art movements, set my young, impressionable, and excited mind aflame with inspiration for how I may be able to employ these influences and innovate on them in my own photography.

Comic books and the artists and writers who created them influenced my work significantly. I discovered comics at a local soda fountain and newsstand named Danny's in Asbury Park. There I discovered *Superman* #113, which consisted of a three-part episodic story about Superman on Krypton. From that I followed all the DC and soon Marvel books, and as the art progressed so did my thinking on how images could be created and delivered. In particular, the amazingly innovative work of Jack Kirby who is considered the "King of Comics" blew me away, because of the technology, machines, spaceships, and intergalactic landscapes he came up with, combined with his altering of the panel structure of the comic page, transforming it into more of a 3D experience with dazzling special effects. These techniques were injected directly into my developing brain from repeated readings.

My reading of Kirby led me to one of the most experimental comic artists of all time, Jim Steranko, whose work stirred my thoughts on what I wanted to do with my photography. Steranko used a lot of special effects and collages, often opening up and expanding the common eight-panel-to-a-page format. His pages used radically different constructions and were accompanied by words and sound effects that blew through the outside of the frame. Steranko took it one step further when, in 1968's *Strange Tales* #167, he created a battle tableau that stretched to four pages—one needed two copies of the issue to see the full impact. Steranko also used interference patterns and Ben Day overlay effects to the max, all of which drove me, as a young boy, to think of what I could do by combining these kinds of effects in art, film, or photography. I met Jim in 1971 and we planned to collaborate on a film project that never materialized, but he was instrumental in helping market the first-ever Marvel superhero holograms I created in 1979.

Other early influences on my young imagination were silent films and *Metropolis* in particular, directed by the German cinematic master Fritz Lang. For years, I knew of it via magazines I consumed as a kid, namely *Famous Monsters of Filmland* and *Spacemen*. I longed to see the actual film, but it was so hard to find other than the 8mm condensations that just would not satisfy. So, when I saw in the *New York Times* a listing for a screening of what was then a complete print at a YMCA in New York, I begged my parents to permit me to go up to the city unchaperoned. Indulging my passion as they most often did, they allowed me to go. At the age of fourteen, I boarded the bus in Asbury Park and made the hour-and-a-half trip to the Big Apple. I found my way uptown to the 92nd Street YMCA, and I came to a small room housing a 16mm projector. There was a slight delay because the person in charge of threading and running the projector obviously had no clue what they were doing, and so I had to volunteer to help get the show running. I knew the technology well due to my experience in school as a member of the crew tasked with setting up projectors for showing educational films. I threaded up the device and got it running, to the delight of the small crowd; yet we quickly discovered that the print, incomplete and repaired in many places, was totally silent. Missing was any of the original orchestral music that accompanied the film in Germany or even a simple piano or organ which often played at many silent movie screenings. The only soundtrack was that of the pots, pans, and dishes clanking rather loudly from the adjacent kitchen. Seeing *Metropolis* in motion was nonetheless a revelation. It was Lang's use of montage that first gave me ideas of using multiple images in still photographs.

But for many years my artistic experiments were confined to my imagination, because my first camera was a small, brown box camera from Kodak known as a "Brownie." It had a fixed lens and there was no way to change any setting but it was mine, and I worked with it as best as I could knowing its limitations. I was proud of the camera, and I took scores of pictures of my parents, their friends, my sweet first cat, and my surroundings.

Things changed radically when I went with my father to a convention in Atlantic City in 1959. I was all of ten years old, and with camera in hand I eagerly took pictures of people and structures along the famous boardwalk. I found myself fascinated with what was then the premier attraction on the boardwalk's Steel Pier amusement park: a diving horse, ridden by a daring female bathing beauty, leaping into a pool around fifty feet below. Looking back now with a more enlightened perspective, the act was horrendous animal abuse. But as a kid, not knowing any better, I was startled by the spectacle and attempted to snap a picture during the brief time that the horse and rider were in midair. When I received the developed pictures from my day in Atlantic City, one stood out. To the amazement of my parents and many of their friends, I had indeed captured the horse and rider at the exact midpoint in their daring dive. Of course, in truth, the shot was easier than anyone knew, owing to the high-speed fixed shutter on my simple device. All I had to do was press the shutter at the right time. However, the praise and adulation boosted my growing confidence and cast the die for my future photographic exploits. I started to feel as if I had perhaps found my artistic medium.

I was looking for a way to improve my camerawork but was hamstrung by the Brownie. I began to pursue a more sophisticated camera and found one almost in my backyard. Jack Perlmutter, my parents' neighbor, was a semiretired New York businessman with a lot of free time on his hands. He was large and imposing but always gentle and kind, and he had a 1940s Rolleiflex Twin Lens Reflex camera in mint condition, which he showed me when he found out about my budding interest in photography. Seeing and holding this very professional camera was a revelation.

The camera, housed in a strong leather case, was well built and sturdy with a sharp German-made lens. To my amazement, Jack said he would let me borrow it if I was very careful and took good care of it. I eagerly agreed to his more-than-generous terms and used the camera on a regular basis, always fastidiously making sure to return it promptly. During the times I had the "Rollei" in my hands, I taught myself how to use the various settings and, perhaps even more important, how to photograph fireworks and night scenes. Because the Rollei had only manual controls and no light meter, I used it to learn exposure techniques and how to alter a finished image using both the f-stop and shutter controls. This experience of not having the ability to meter light laid the groundwork for my non-reliance on automatic controls and metering to achieve my imaging goals.

After some years, Jack passed away from a heart attack, unexpectedly and certainly prematurely. I was devastated. He had been so patient with me and had helped my evolution as an artist and photographer in such an outsized way. His wife, Hindel, a very gracious woman, gave me the camera after he passed, stating, "I know Jack would want you to have it because you will take such good care of it." I still have and use the camera to this day.

During the summer before I entered eighth grade, I got my first job as a locker boy at the Monte Carlo pool in Asbury Park for a whopping seventy-five cents an hour plus tips. After a summer of this, I spent each succeeding summer working jobs at various establishments and food concessions along the storied Asbury Park Boardwalk. I made slightly more at each job and was able to put away some money so that I could buy increasingly sophisticated cameras. I graduated from my Brownie to a 35mm Yashica "rangefinder" camera, which was certainly a step up. Though I was amazed at what you could do with just a fixed-focus lens, it was the rangefinder focus and 35mm film format that gave me new tools with which to expand my skill set.

Later, again with my savings and a little help from my parents, I obtained a Nikkorex F, which was a more affordable version of the Nikon F, but it was an advanced SLR, allowing me to change lenses. With that device, I learned a lot about the workings of a higher-end camera, beyond the fixed-lens restrictions of the Rollei and the Yashica. In 1964–65 I took the camera to New York's World's Fair, where I practiced with its advanced features, which would contribute to my later work.

After many stints at menial jobs on the Asbury Park Boardwalk, I secured employment at a local record store, Harmony House, which fed my now rabid record-buying habit but at a discount—and thankfully not to the detriment of my camera dreams. In late 1968 through the middle of 1969, I was fortunate to be allowed to present on a local radio station, WRLB in Long Branch, examples from my eclectic record collection. I played a lot of songs that were not readily available and were quite possibly heard for the first time in the entire metro New York region. My all-too-brief appearances on the radio were well received, as I learned from many phone calls I took while the records were spinning. Finally, after getting a job deep in the bowels of the photo processing darkroom at Stickler and Morse, a camera store in Asbury Park, I was able to save up enough money to buy at an employee discount the camera of my dreams: a Nikon F. I felt I had arrived.

It was at Convention Hall in Asbury Park where I witnessed my first rock and roll shows. Barney Niessen would often get from the promoter Moe Septee free tickets to shows at the Hall. Often, because Barney didn't want them, he would give them to my dad who would take me or, when I got older, let me go alone. In 1963 Joan Baez played the Hall, and I was there. Her set was powerful, including a combination of traditional tunes and more socially conscious songs, some penned by an up-and-coming singer-songwriter named Bob Dylan. Toward the end of her show, Joan introduced Dylan, who joined her in a stirring rendition of "We Shall Overcome." After the song, the crowd erupted in cheers, no doubt in response to the power of the music in the face of the growing civil rights movement of the early '60s.

Once the show was over, because the security at Conventional Hall was reasonably lax at that time, I used my seat pass to inveigle myself into the nether realms of the venue. After poking around, I found a door that led out to an exterior walkway that surrounded three-quarters of the building and overlooked the Atlantic Ocean. As I stuck my head out the door, I noticed someone alone, leaning against the protective railing and staring out at the ocean as if in deep thought. I was startled to see it was Dylan himself, and I slowly approached him, ever respectful of his space.

I didn't want to disturb him. I had heard many of his songs on WBAI, a politically radical station in New York City, and so I knew of him quite well. When he discovered my presence he turned and smiled, and then pointed to the vast sea before us. He told me how calming the ocean was, and how great it was to be so close to it since there was nothing like it in Minnesota. I was taken aback at how young he seemed and how graciously he accepted my intrusion. Halting, I told him what an honor it was to meet him and that I found his music and the ideas behind it inspiring and hopeful. His response was not just a thank-you, but a question that to this day still shocks me. He asked in all sincerity, "Do you really think the crowd liked me?" I responded without hesitation and with the most gravitas that a fourteen-year-old could muster, "Are you kidding, they sure did, and I'll bet that there's much more to come."

He smiled and said, “I sure hope so.” I answered, “I think you can bank on it!” We talked a bit more about where he came from in Minnesota, and how he was now based in New York and had enough material for many more records. I said I would sure be looking forward to buying them and then respectfully retreated, letting him alone as he continued to look out at the ocean. Unfortunately, I didn’t have my camera with me that day, and so it remains only as a memory. But it’s a powerful one, and it reverberated with me as I continued my own struggle for artistic confidence throughout the years.

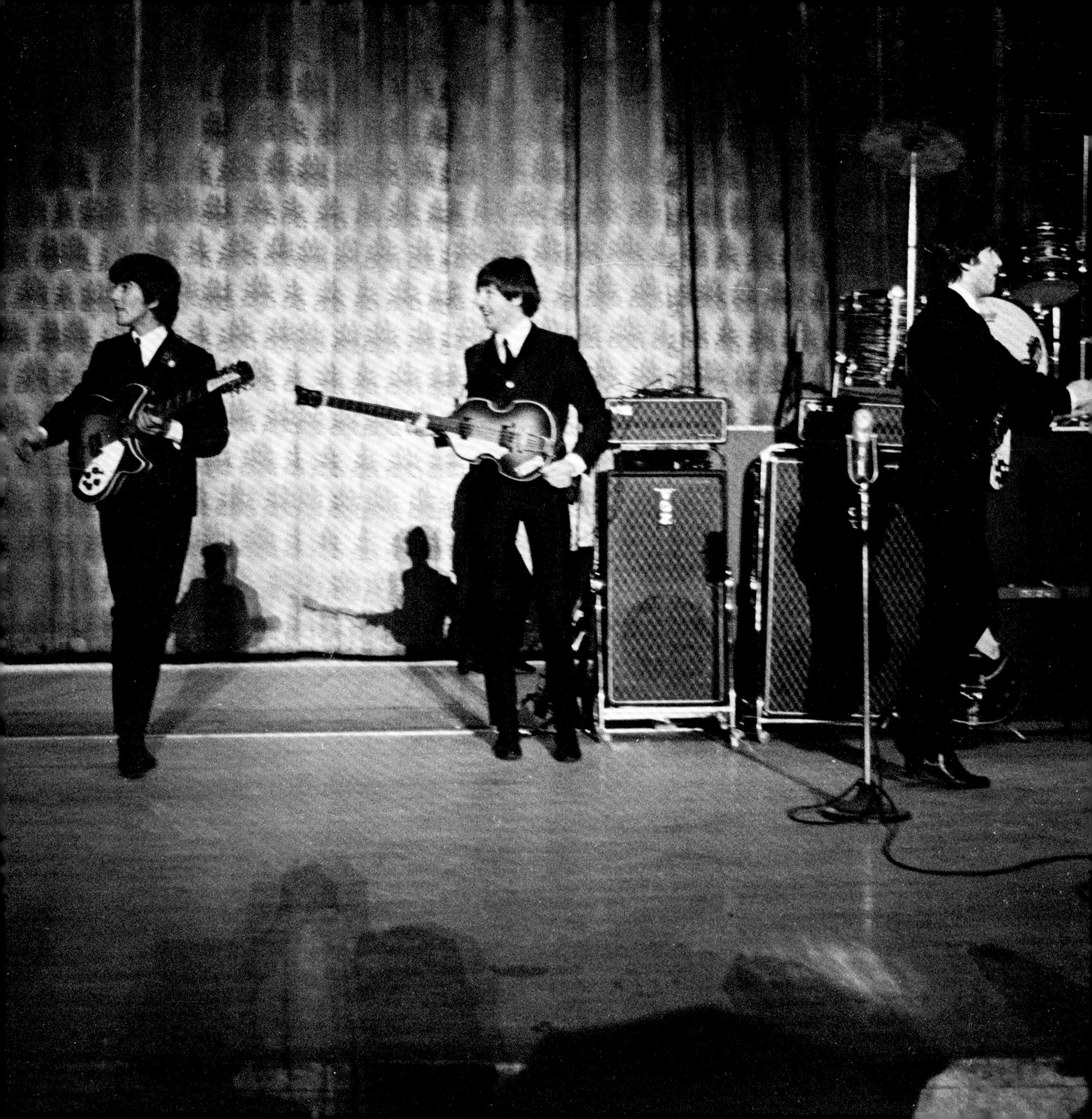

1

The Beatles in Philadelphia

In February 1964, John, Paul, George, and Ringo appeared on *The Ed Sullivan Show*, which reignited the rock and roll fuse in America like no one could have anticipated. Dad, Mom, and I watched, entranced, along with seventy-three million others, as Beatlemania took hold, and we went on to witness the subsequent appearances on *Sullivan* and other shows. I, of course, bought every record as soon as they reached Barney Niessen's, and he was startled at the increase of business as equally rabid fans flooded his store, buying out each new Beatles release. I even attended the first night's screening of *A Hard Day's Night* in August. But it wasn't enough! My dream was to experience the Fab Four live.

On September 2, 1964, I woke up beyond excited because—through Barney Niessen and Moe Septee—we had secured three tickets to the Beatles concert in Philadelphia that afternoon. I checked with Mom and Dad, and we were on schedule to leave and get to Philadelphia in plenty of time. I then checked my film. Unfortunately, I had a limited amount. I had only one roll of Kodachrome II color slide film and a couple rolls of much higher speed Tri-X black-and-white film, which I grabbed because I had no idea what kind of lighting I would encounter and I wanted to cover all contingencies. It was, as usual, a hot day in New Jersey with high humidity. We piled into our car, a Pontiac LeMans, which was good on gas but had no air-conditioning.

Normal capacity for the Philadelphia Convention Hall (which is different from the Asbury Park Convention Hall where I met Dylan) was approximately twelve thousand people. However, it is said that that day there were fifteen thousand Beatle fans crammed into the space manically primed for this historic moment. After we parked and began to walk toward the Hall, we were

The Beatles, Philadelphia, September 1964.

inundated by hundreds of teenage girls and a few boys, approaching the building in a near frenzy.

As we made our way toward the facility, I ran right into an Asbury Park policeman, Joe Montaparo, who covered security at the New Jersey Hall. I knew Joe from all the shows I attended. He always reminded me of a much more serious version of the TV cop "Gunther Toody" played by Joe E. Ross on *Car 54, Where Are You?* (He was indeed more serious, and many years later died "on the job," stabbed by a criminal he tried to apprehend in Asbury Park.)

Joe welcomed me with a big smile. "Mike, good to see a familiar face. This is a total madhouse. What are you doing here? Are you a fan of these longhairs?" I told him, "We got tickets from Moe, and I'm here with my camera and hope I have a good enough seat to take some pictures of the band." Joe responded, "Well, I may be able to do you one better. How would you like to get into the press conference with your boyfriends?" I was stunned. I stopped dead in my tracks, not expecting this turn of events or even having the chance to let my good fortune sink in before I responded, "Are you kidding me? I would give my right arm to do that."

"Follow me," Joe said. I moved quickly, attempting to explain this turn of events to my parents, whom I was now about to leave to fend for themselves among the screaming mob encircling all four of us.

Joe let me through a side door and into a big room that was filled with reporters, photographers, and local DJs. I waited patiently, the youngest member of this press pool by far. After about twenty minutes a chaotic firestorm of activity broke out as a door opened and in strode the focus of the gathering, John, Paul, George, and Ringo, in the flesh. They were laughing and jostling one another, their handlers, PR people, Moe Septee himself, and the DJ Hy Lit from WIBG (or "Wibbage," as it was popularly known). This whirlwind finally settled around the table where the Boys were to hold court, in the face of this crushing dynamo of reporters, photographers, and various interlopers like myself.

The room was filled with adults, certainly not screaming teenagers, but the air was electric, and people clapped and hollered for them. It took a good five minutes to settle the crowd. After being awarded some kind of ceremonial plaque, the Beatles began to take questions from this adoring mélange of humanity, answering in their usual cheeky manner and taking none of this adulation too seriously.

In the excitement of the moment, I loaded my camera up with my sole roll of color slide film, thinking this was an opportunity that warranted color, though later I came to regret my choice. I fired away and used my whole roll and some black-and-white for the duration of the press conference, which lasted only twenty minutes or so. As the crowd filed out just before showtime, I merged with the reporters and other photographers, not imagining where we were headed. I found out rather quickly, and to my utter shock and awe, that our destination was the press section in front of the stage after a crushing journey down a long hallway. I realized that I only had black-and-white film left but I thought nothing of it since I expected my only coup to be photographing the press conference. In retrospect, I wish I had had the presence of mind to use the color film for the concert, since there are so few pictures in color of the band on stage from the first tour. But as they say, hindsight is 20/20.

After I got my bearings among all these professional photographers, I photographed singer-songwriter Jackie DeShannon, who opened the show, but saved most of my film for the Beatles. The experience was a total blur, since as soon as the Beatles hit the stage there occurred an explosion of teenage girls screaming so loud you could hardly hear any of the music. I took in the spectacle, letting the music wash over me as I fired away. I was flabbergasted at my amazingly good fortune to be front and center, even able to see the sweat fly off the Boys as they banged out their set in a frenetic fury. Many decades later I came to find out that *Rolling Stone* rated the show the eighth greatest Beatle concert of all time. And to think, there I was only a few feet away from my idols witnessing history. I was not being paid like the other photographers, but there I was on the front lines with them, at the age of fifteen. This filled me with confidence and gave me direction for my work and my art in ways I didn't understand at the time.

I later found, after reuniting with my poor parents, that during the show they were overcome by fans climbing over top of them, like a crazed and unrelenting insect invasion from a 1950s monster movie. My parents withstood as best they could the teenage onslaught and stayed firmly planted in their seats, enjoying the spectacle while catching fleeting bursts of music. As we made our way home, we compared our very differing experiences in more detail. I don't know whose was more was exciting, to be honest—my witnessing the press conference and the concert from such a privileged position, or their near life-and-death struggle to stay upright in their seats.

That next year, in fact, I had the opportunity to see and photograph the Beatles again, this time on their home turf. Dad, Mom, and I were in London over the holidays, on a family trip precipitated by my mom's first bout with, and recovery from, cancer. We were staying at the Regent on Oxford Street, and on the afternoon of Saturday, January 2, 1965, mere days before our departure for home, I detected a palpable buzz in the lobby. I went over to the concierge to investigate and found that the Beatles were in the middle of a several-week holiday engagement at the 3,500-seat Hammersmith Odeon. And there were plenty of tickets to go around. Shocked, I asked the concierge politely to please hold three tickets for me. I hightailed it back to our room, where my unsuspecting parents were resting, plotting our final moves in London, and with breathless exigency I informed them of the incredible turn of events. Being the always-amazing parents they were, Nate and Lil agreed to go to the show, even, I must say, with some guarded excitement, expressing the hope that it would be a little less frenetic than the one in Philadelphia. I raced down with the ticket fees, only a few US dollars, and our day was now set. After a late afternoon bite to eat, with my camera in tow, we trekked to the nearest bus station, boarded our conveyance, and arrived close to the theater with ample time to get our bearings and find our seats. To everyone's dismay, we were in the upper balcony, which precluded any chance of my taking good pictures; but I took it in stride, since we *were* seeing the Beatles again! I did take some pictures from afar, later enlarging some through a microscope—they didn't turn out as I would have liked.

But what was most interesting about that show, I thought, was that I could hear all the music and vocals, even being so far away. That is, during the performance all the teenage girls were sitting in their seats like they were in school. Sure, there were screams like in the United States, but no one leapt out of their seats, in a riotous mob—even when, before their set, the Beatles would tease the audience by running quickly across the stage in crazy costumes. This behavior by the Boys would certainly have blown the roof off arenas in America, so it was startling to see the subdued reaction in their homeland.

The contrast for me between the London and Philly shows was marked. The former was incredible, to be sure, but the audience was tame, reserved even, perhaps suppressing the sensibilities of true rock and roll and what it could be. And while I was in the balcony, witnessing from afar, I wanted to be part of the action.

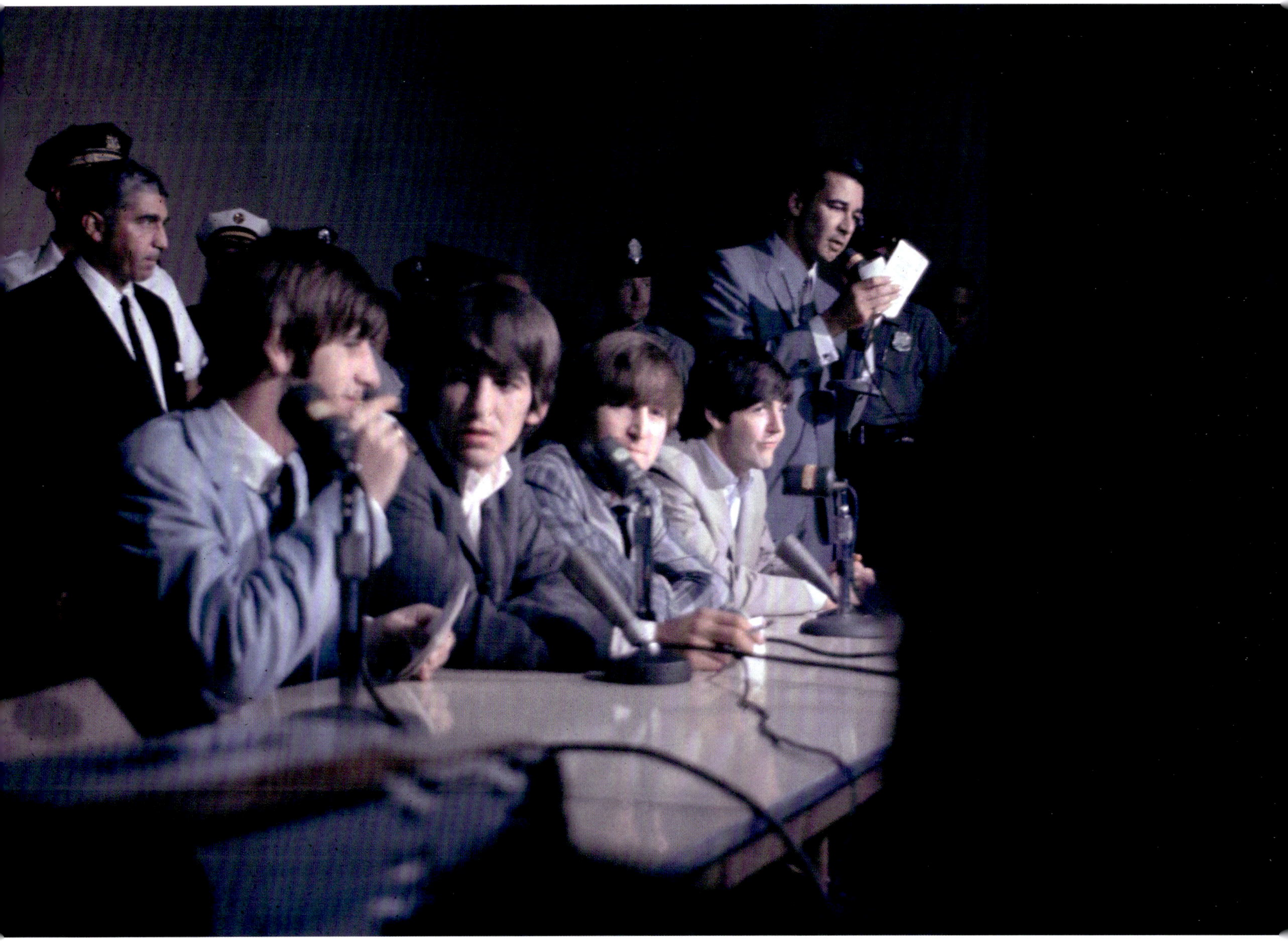

The Beatles, Philadelphia, September 1964.

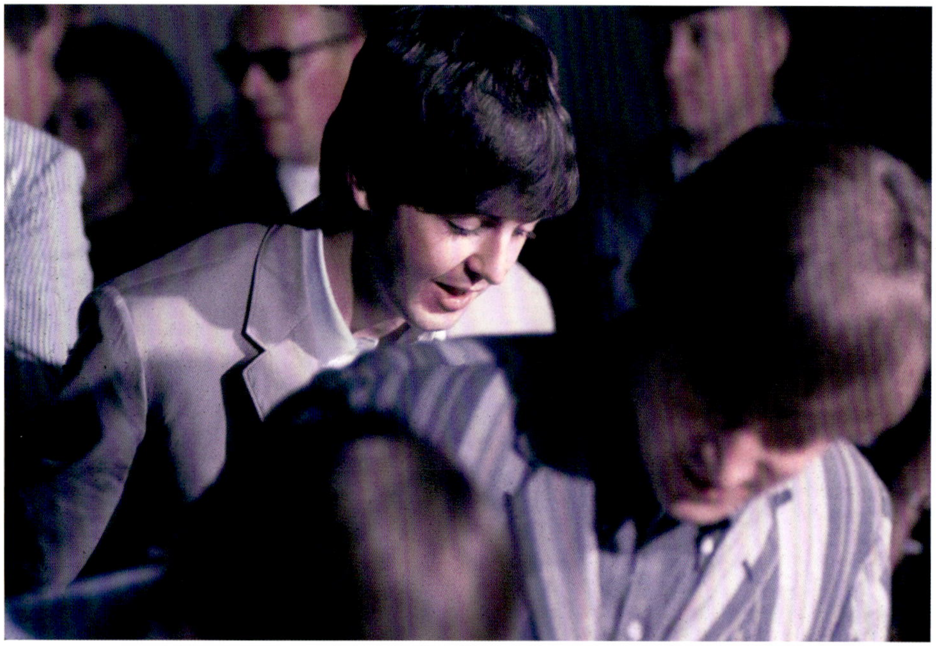

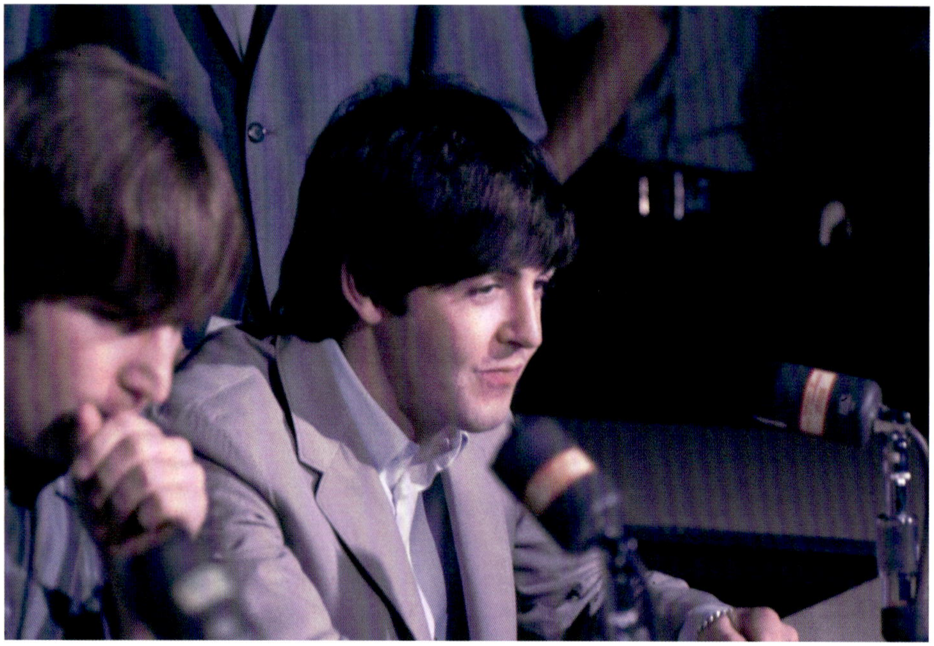

Top: Paul McCartney and John Lennon, Philadelphia, September 1964. *Bottom*: Paul McCartney, Philadelphia, September 1964. *Opposite*: The Beatles press, Philadelphia, September 1964.

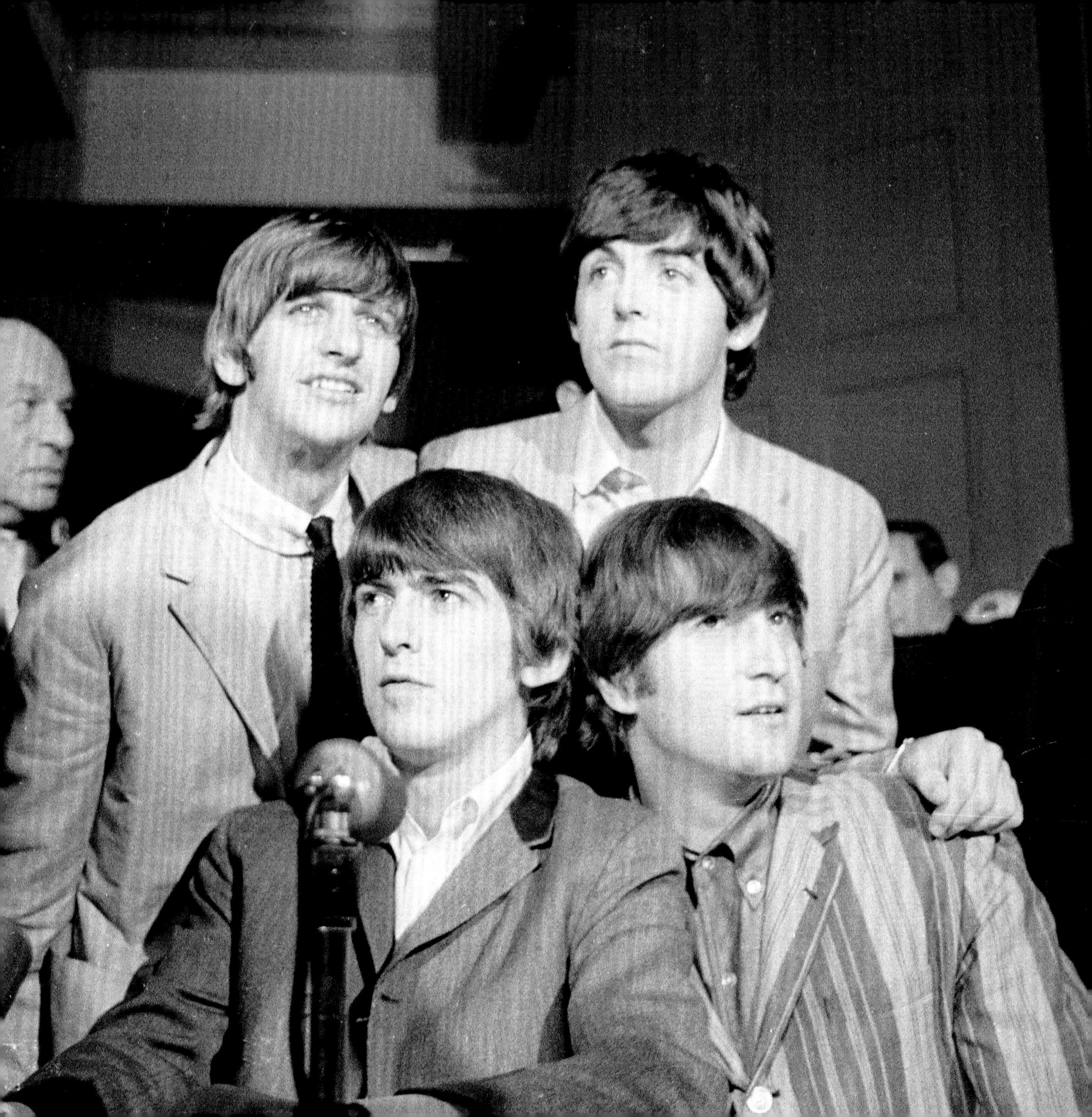

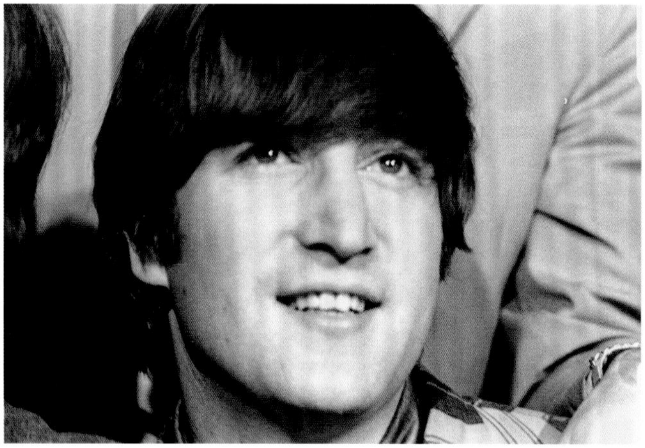

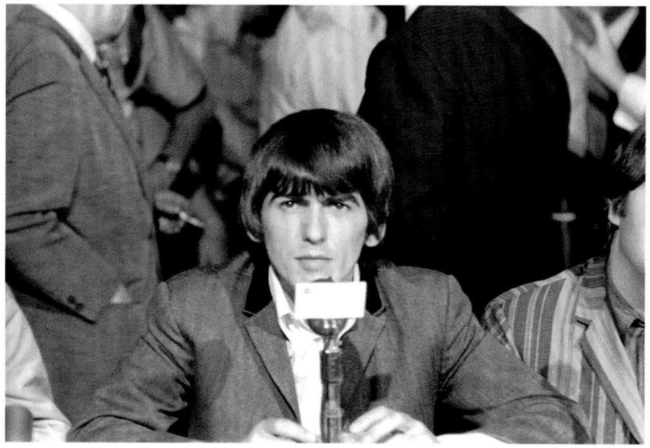

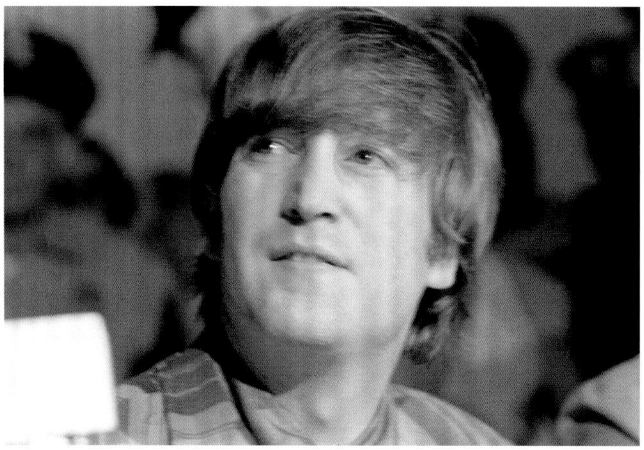

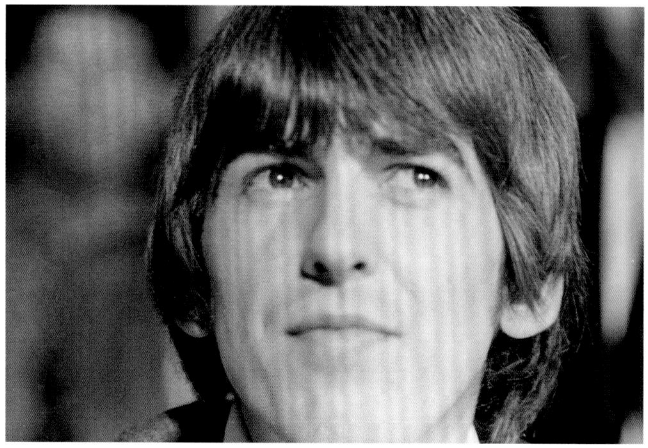

Top left & bottom: John Lennon, Philadelphia, September 1964. *Top right & bottom:* George Harrison, Philadelphia, September 1964. *Opposite*: Beatles press, Philadelphia, September 1964. *Overleaf*: The Beatles, Philadelphia, September 1964.

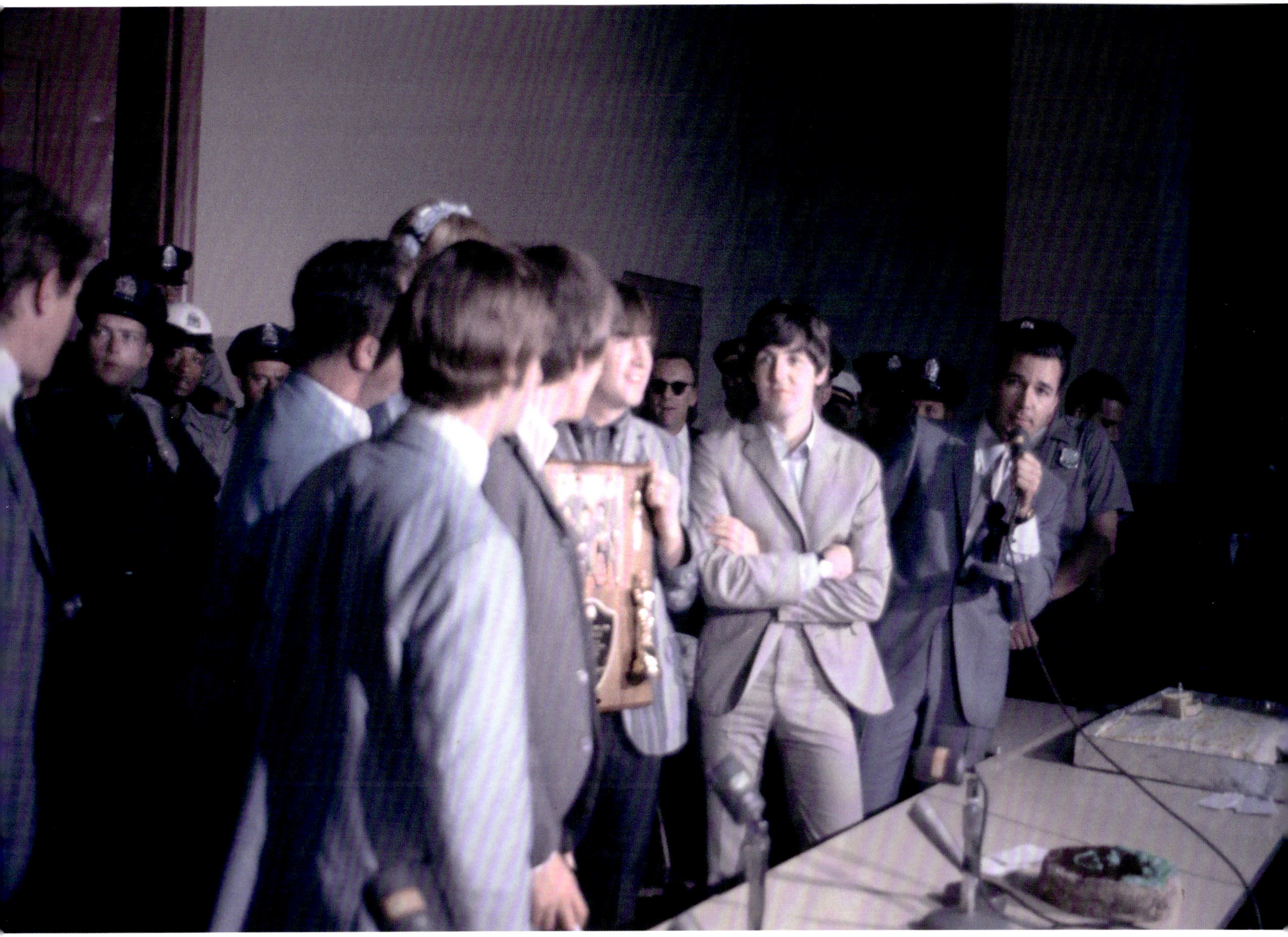

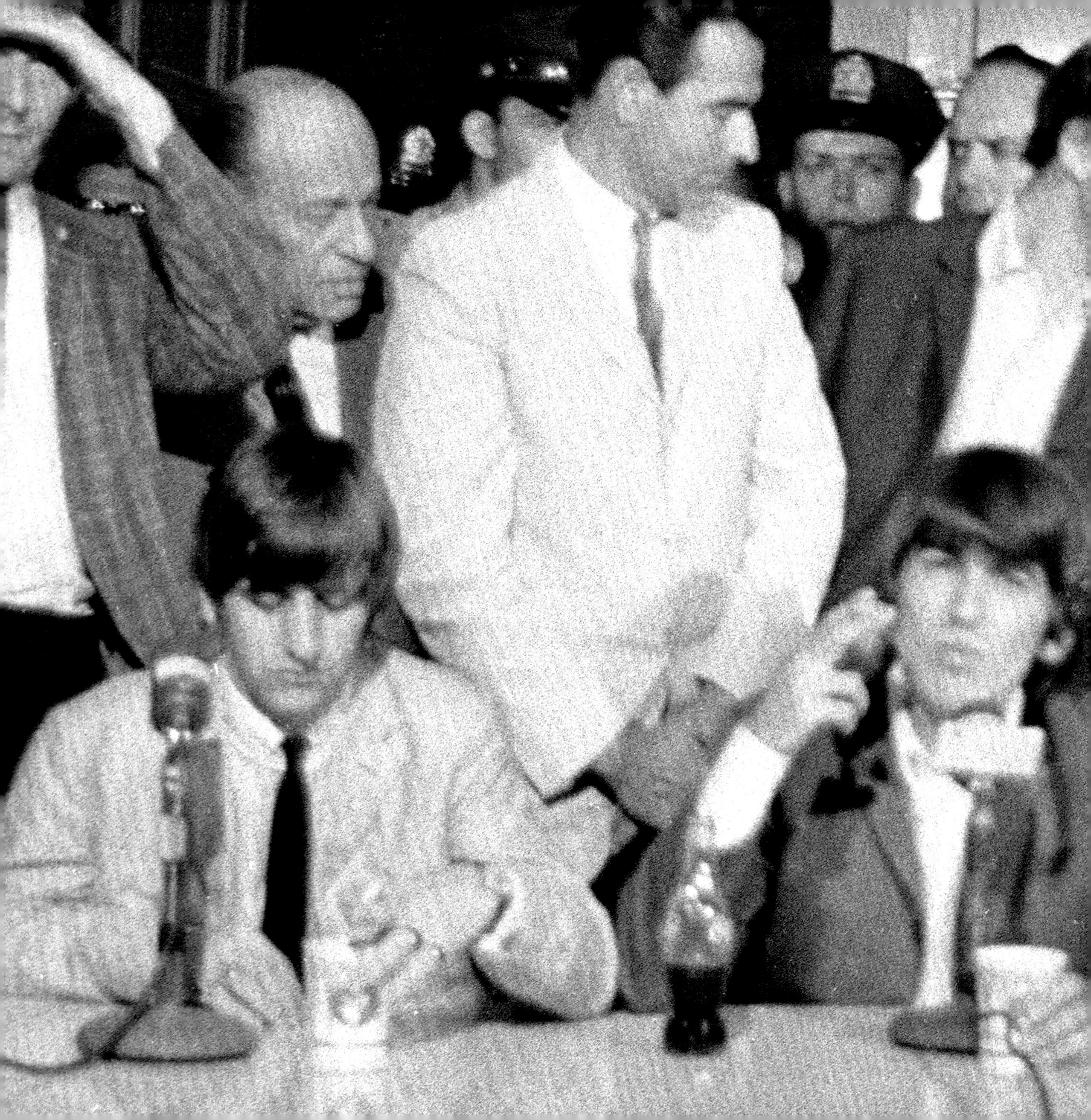

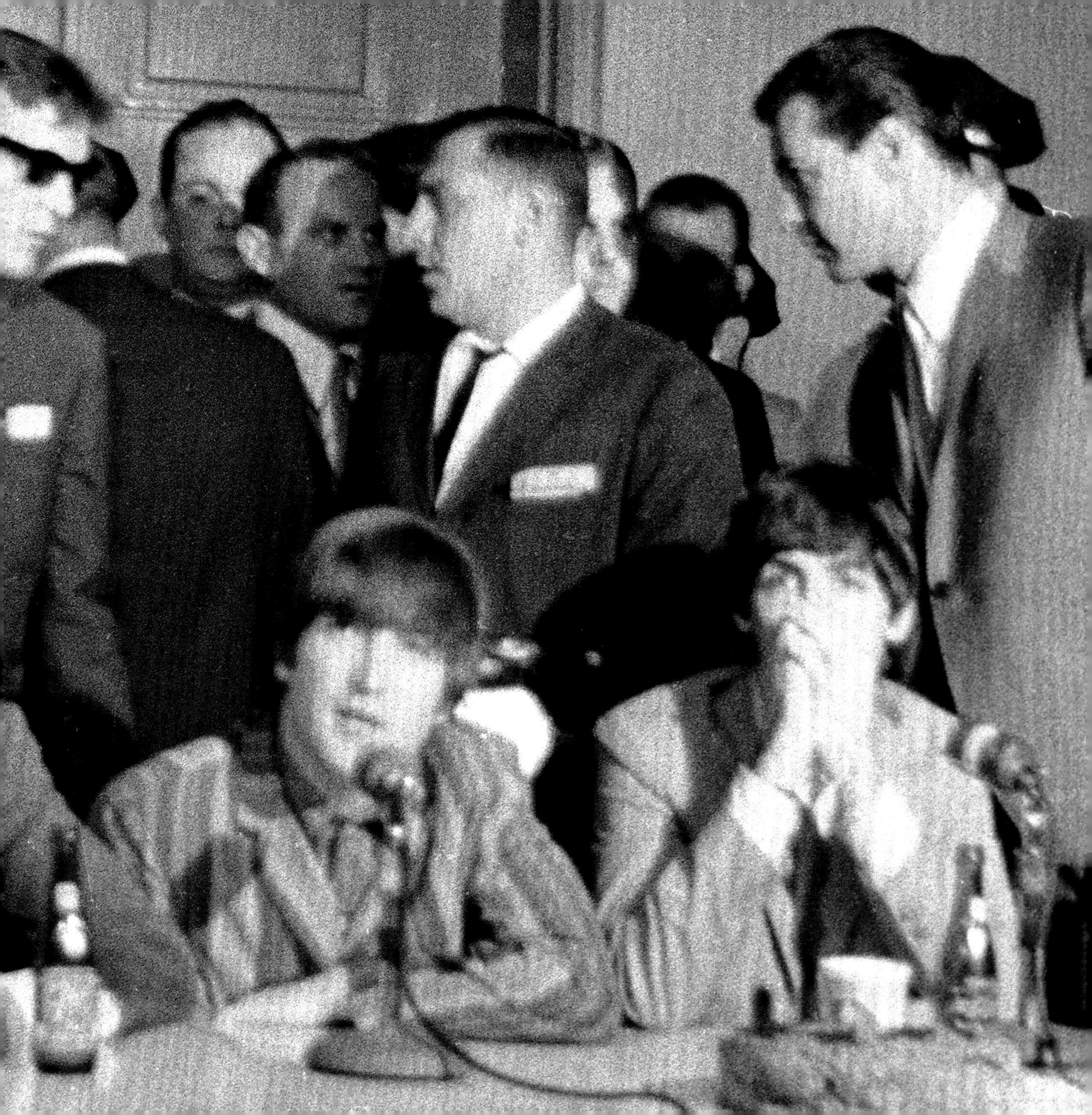

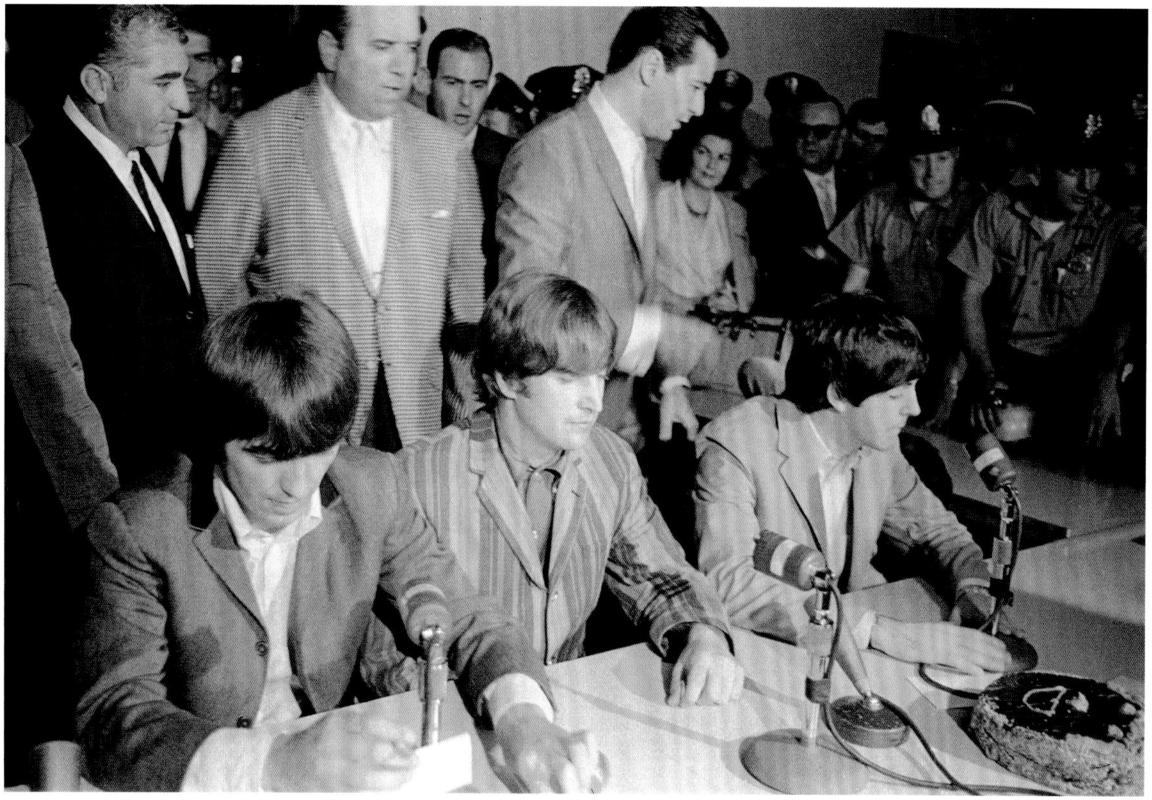

Above & opposite: The Beatles, Philadelphia, September 1964.

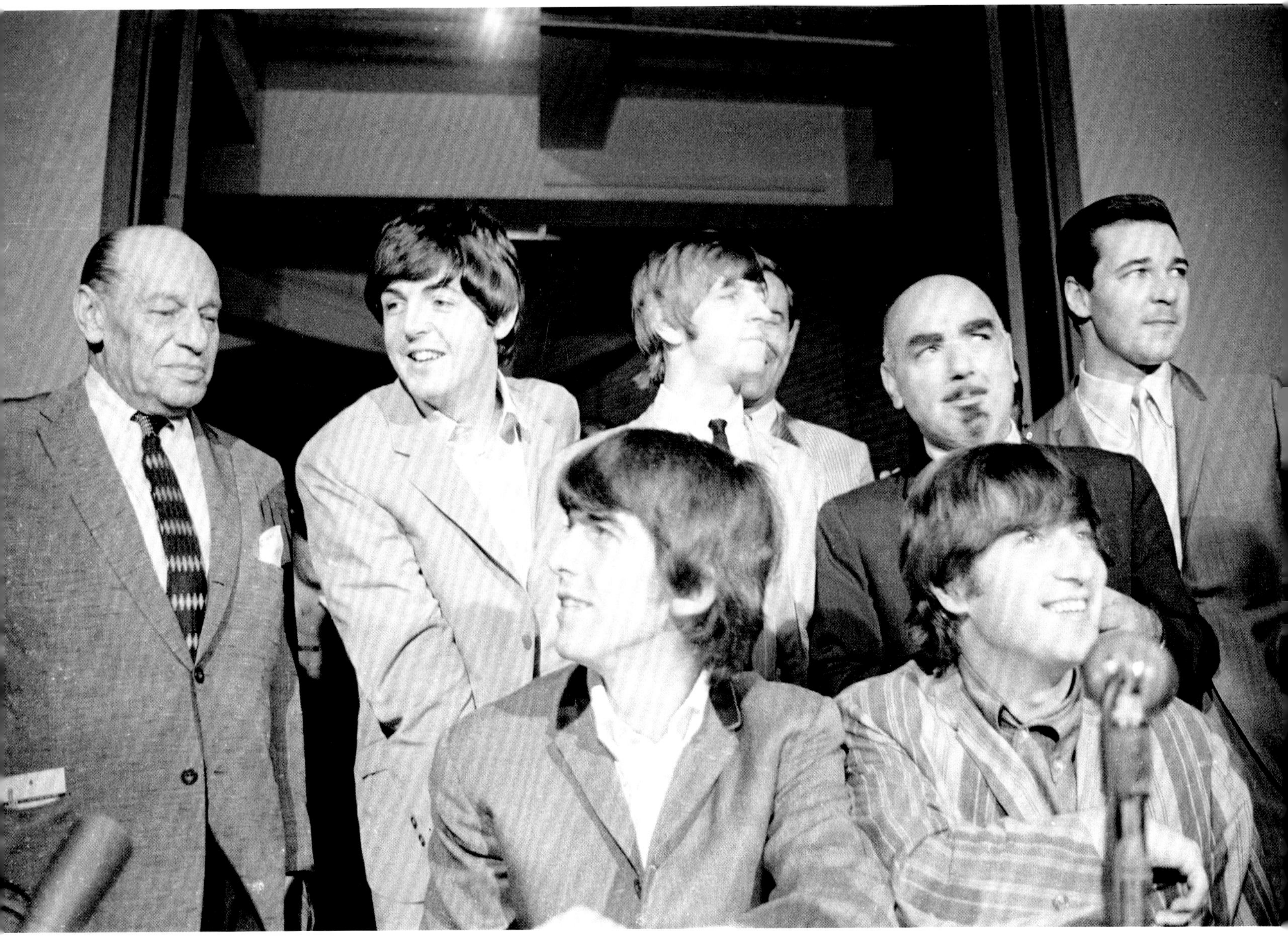

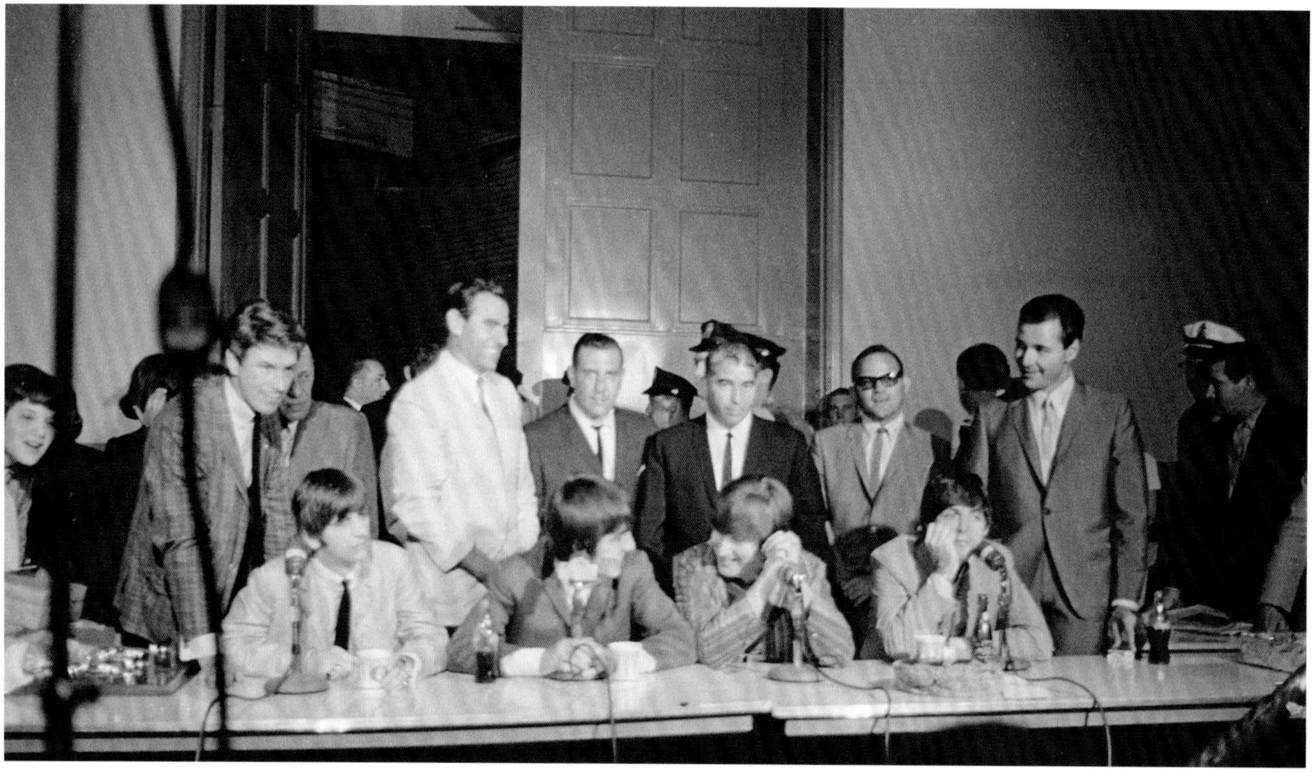

The Beatles, Philadelphia, September 1964.

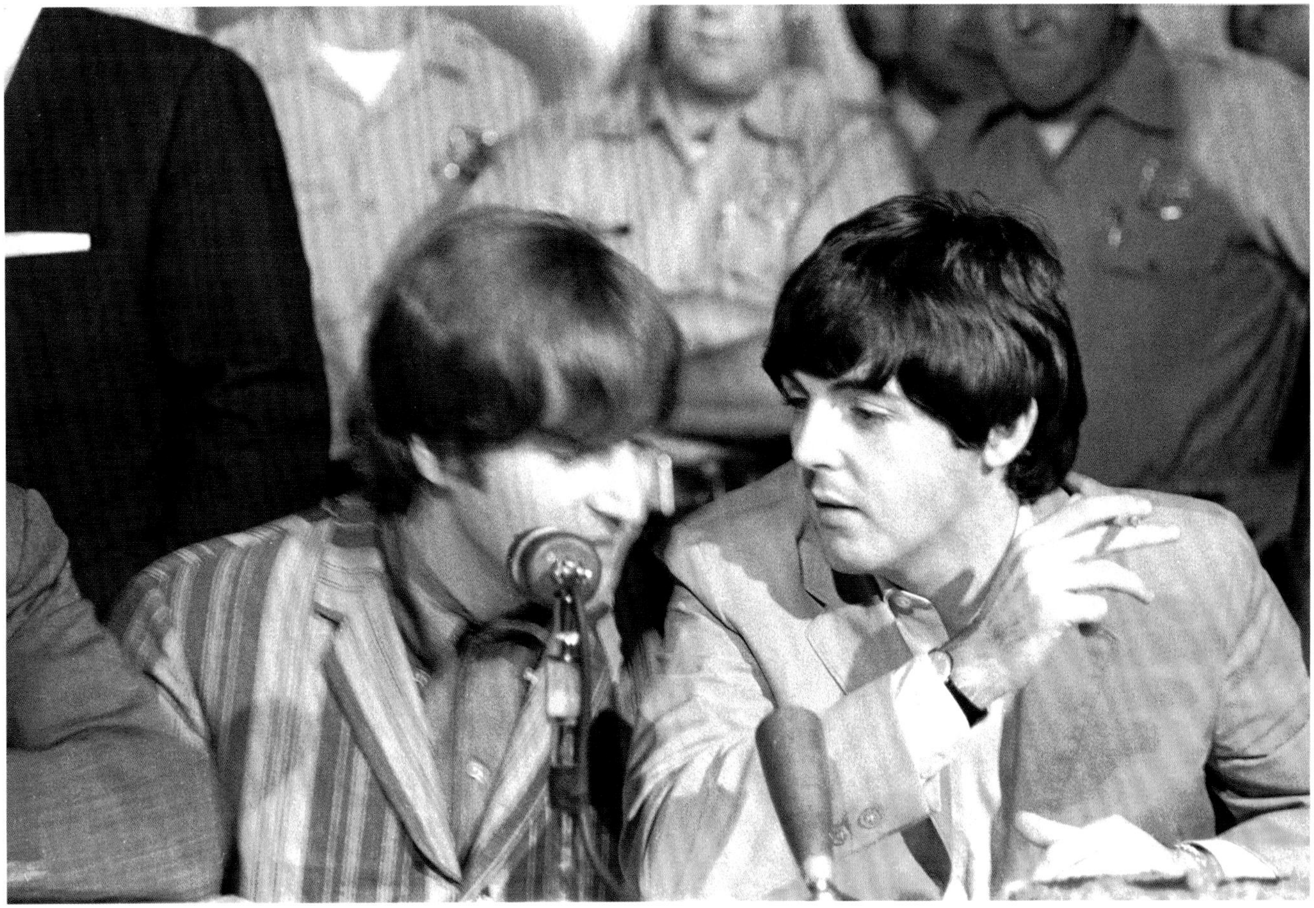

John Lennon and Paul McCartney, Philadelphia, September 1964.

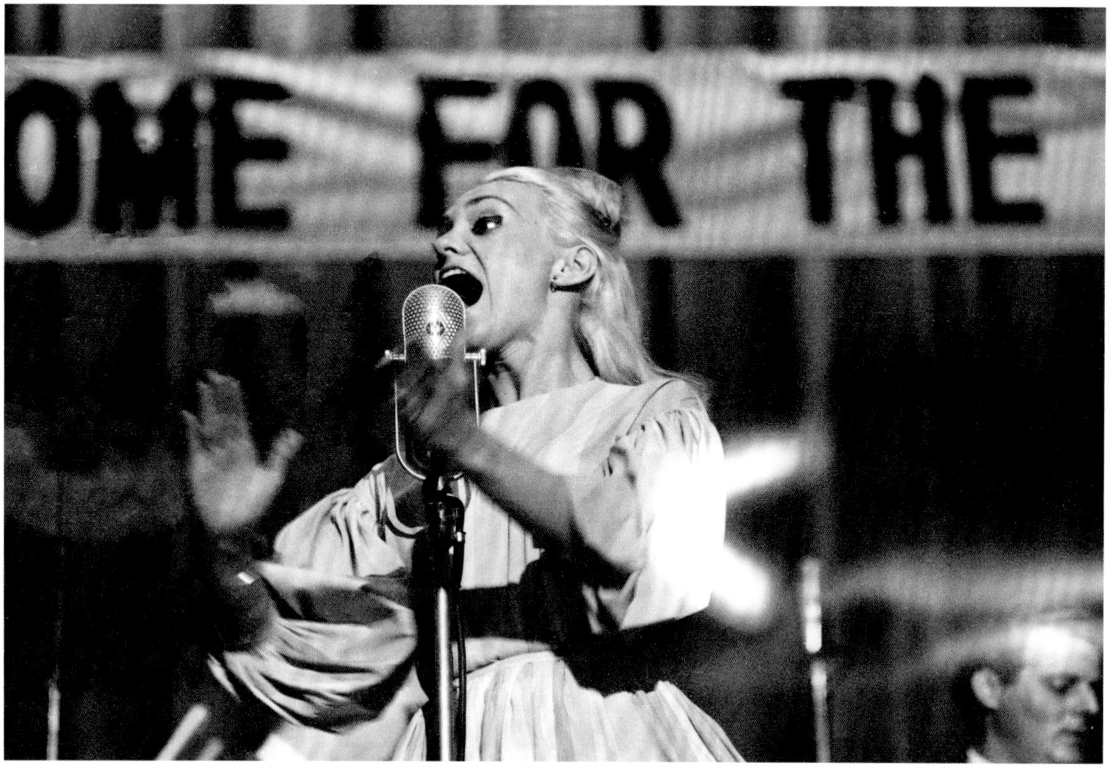

Jackie DeShannon, Philadelphia, September 1964.

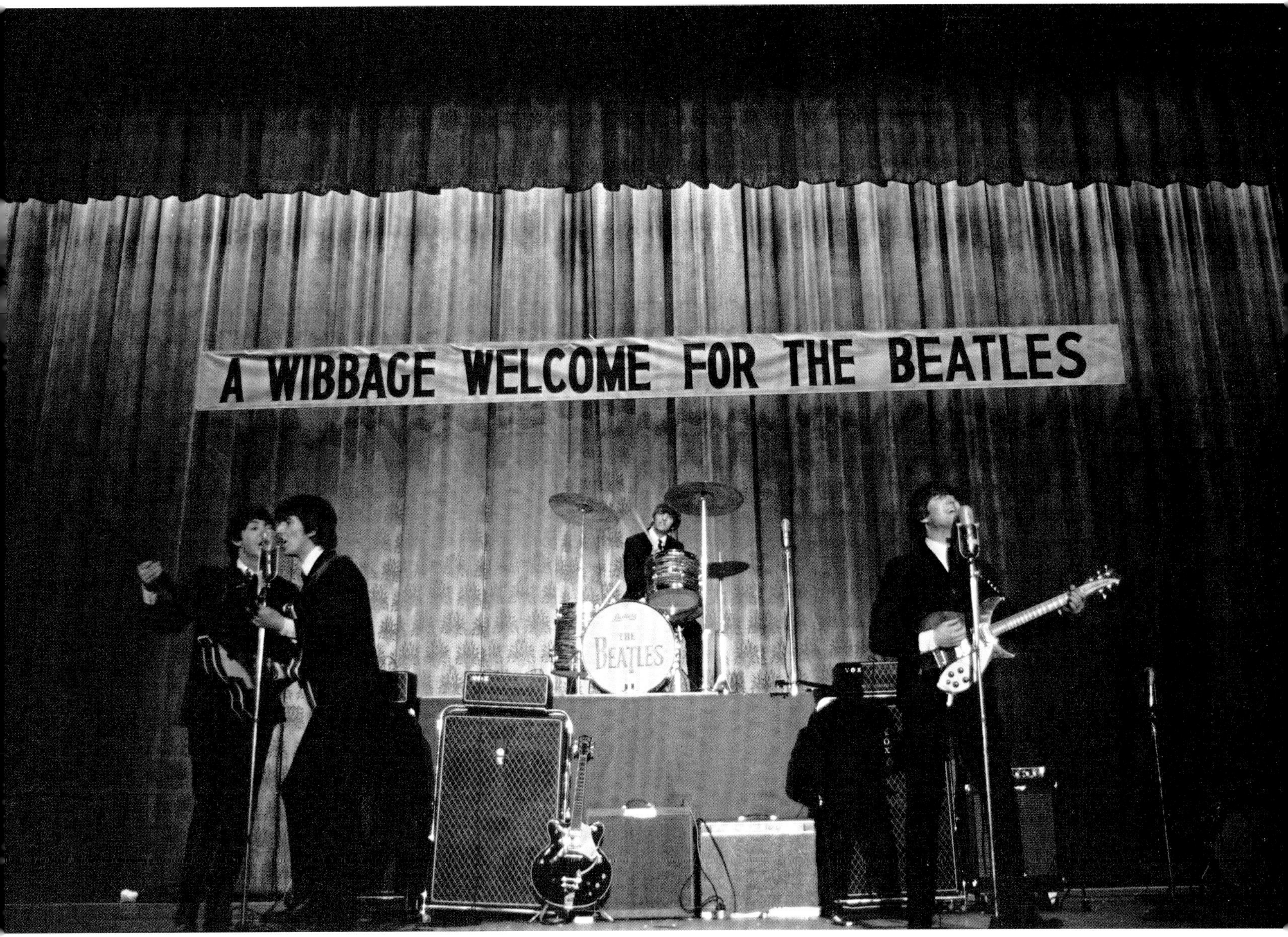

The Beatles, Philadelphia, September 1964.

As soon as the Beatles hit the stage there occurred an explosion of teenage girls screaming so loud you could hardly hear any of the music. I took in the spectacle, letting the music wash over me as I fired away.

The Beatles, Philadelphia, September 1964.

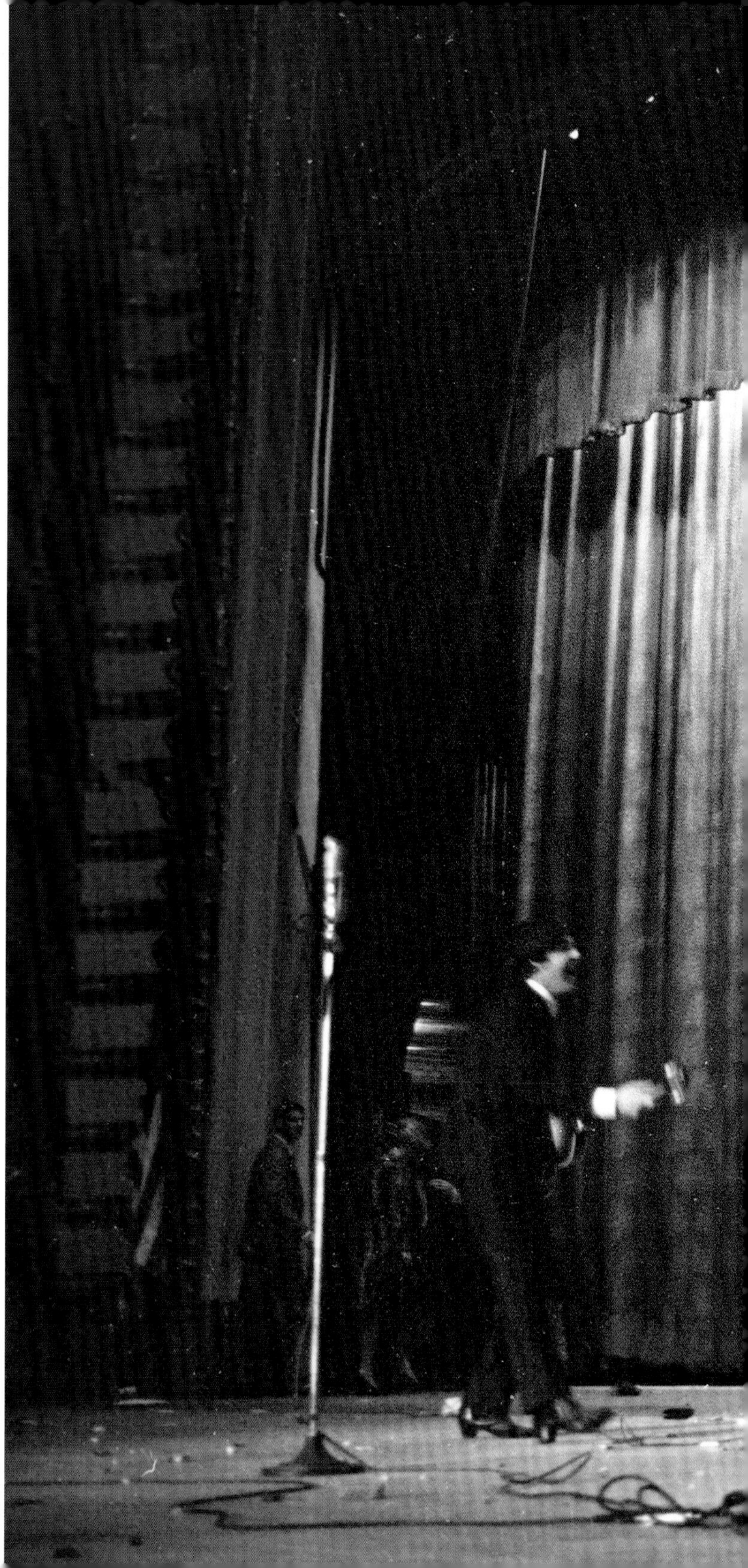

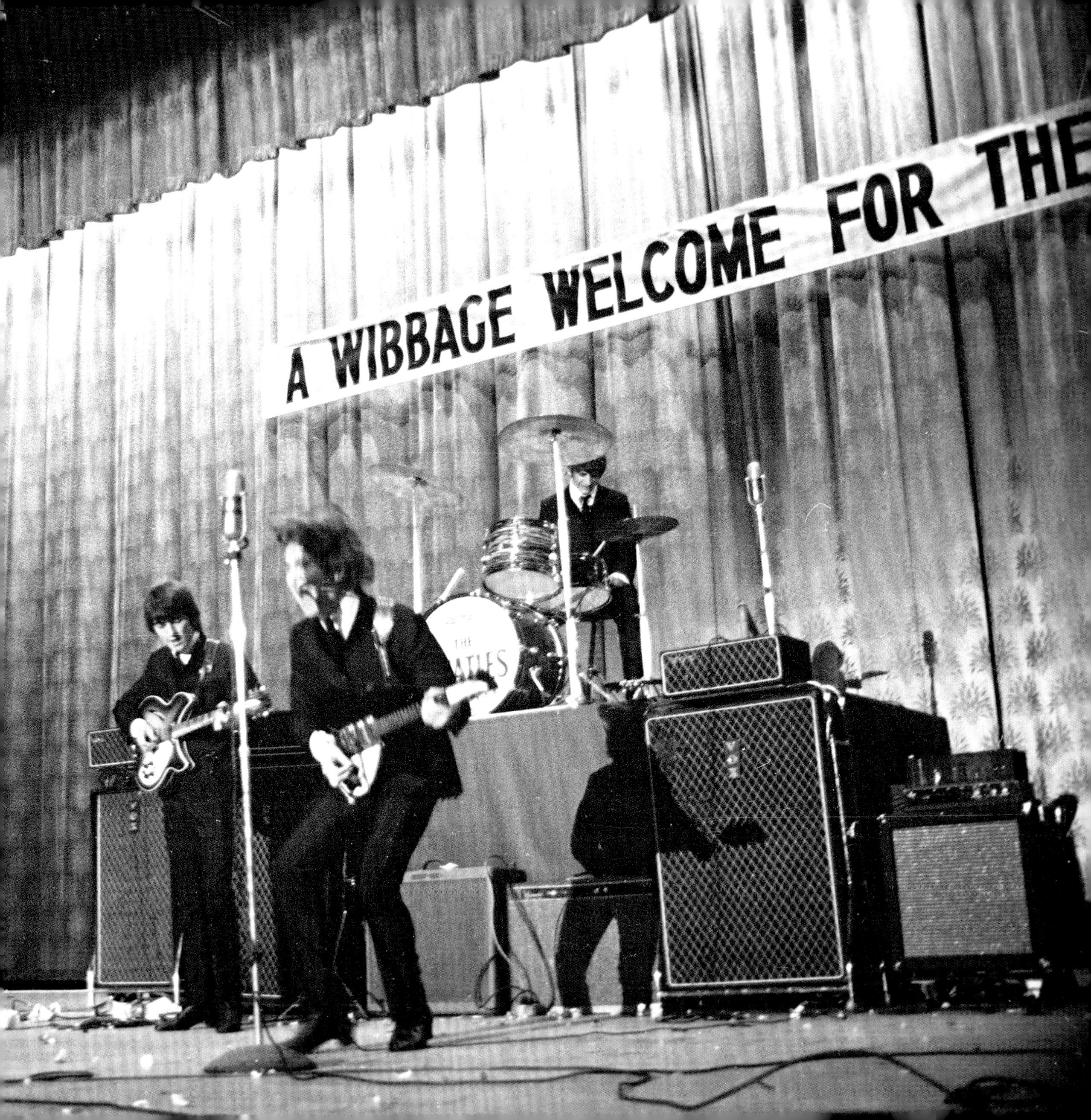
A WIBBAGE WELCOME FOR THE

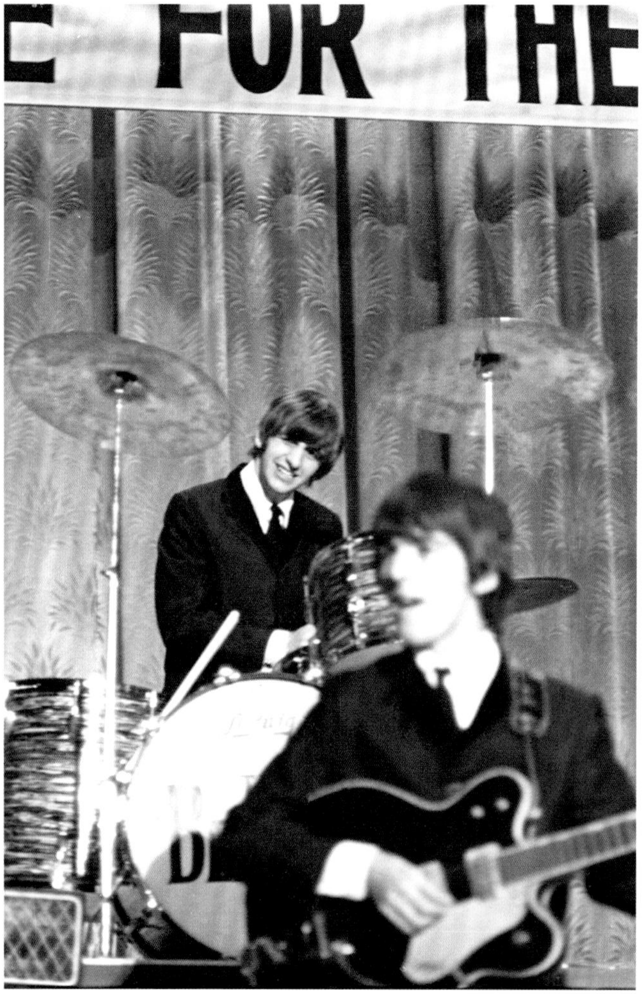

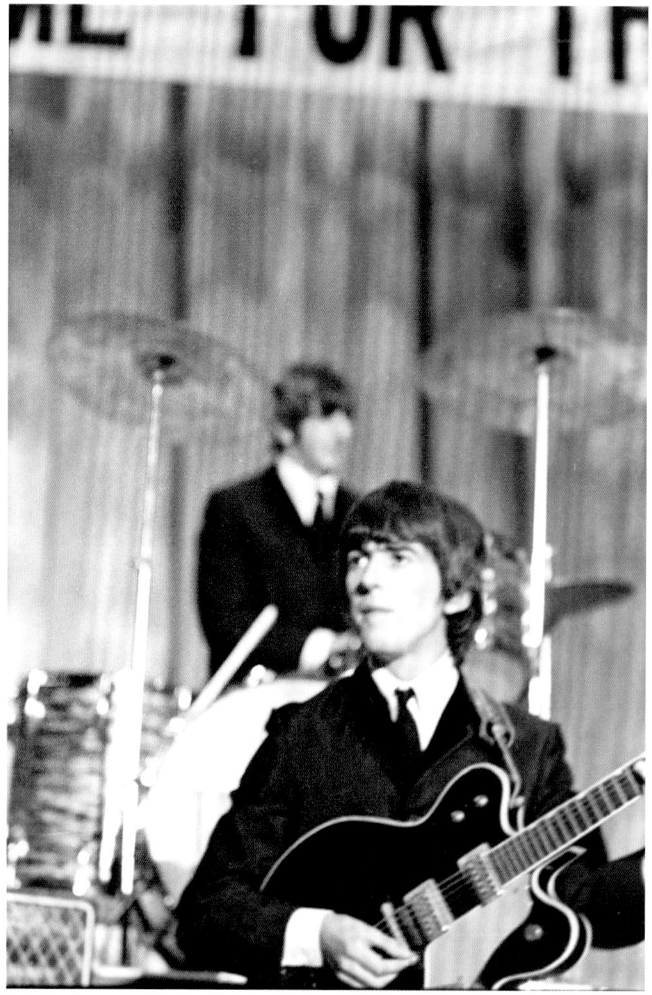

Above, left and right: George Harrison and Ringo Starr, Philadelphia, September 1964.

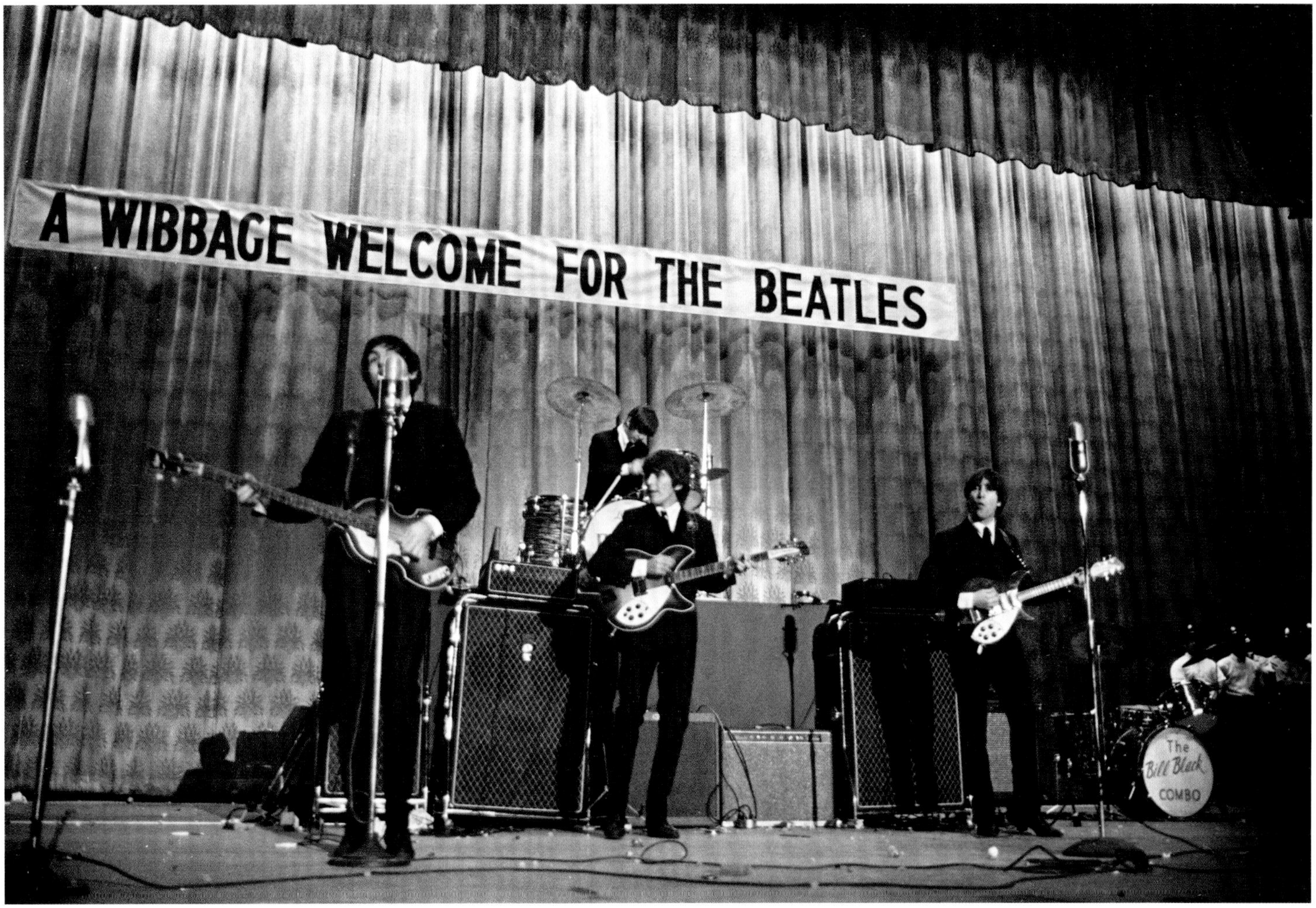

The Beatles, Philadelphia, September 1964.

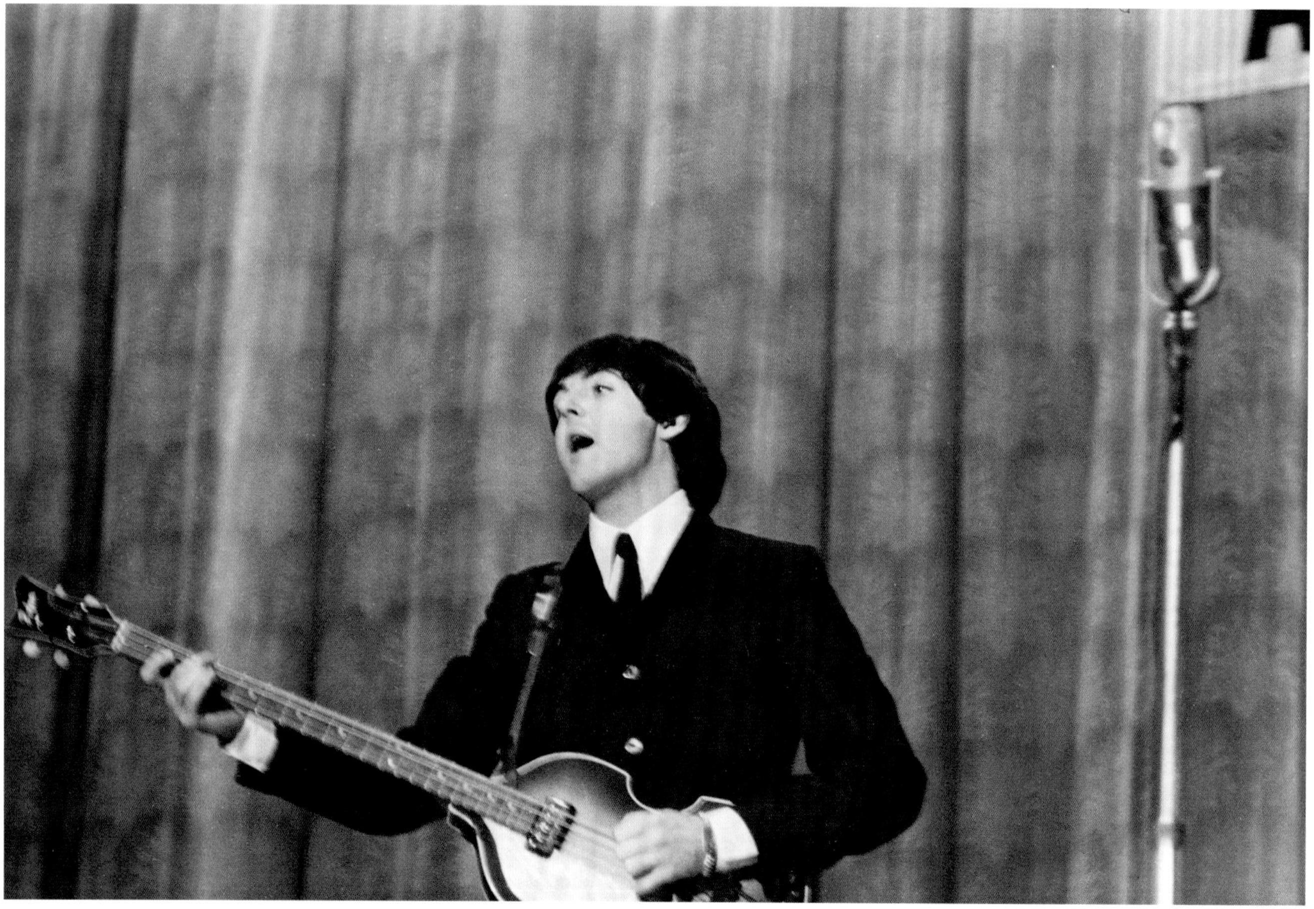

Paul McCartney, Philadelphia, September 1964.

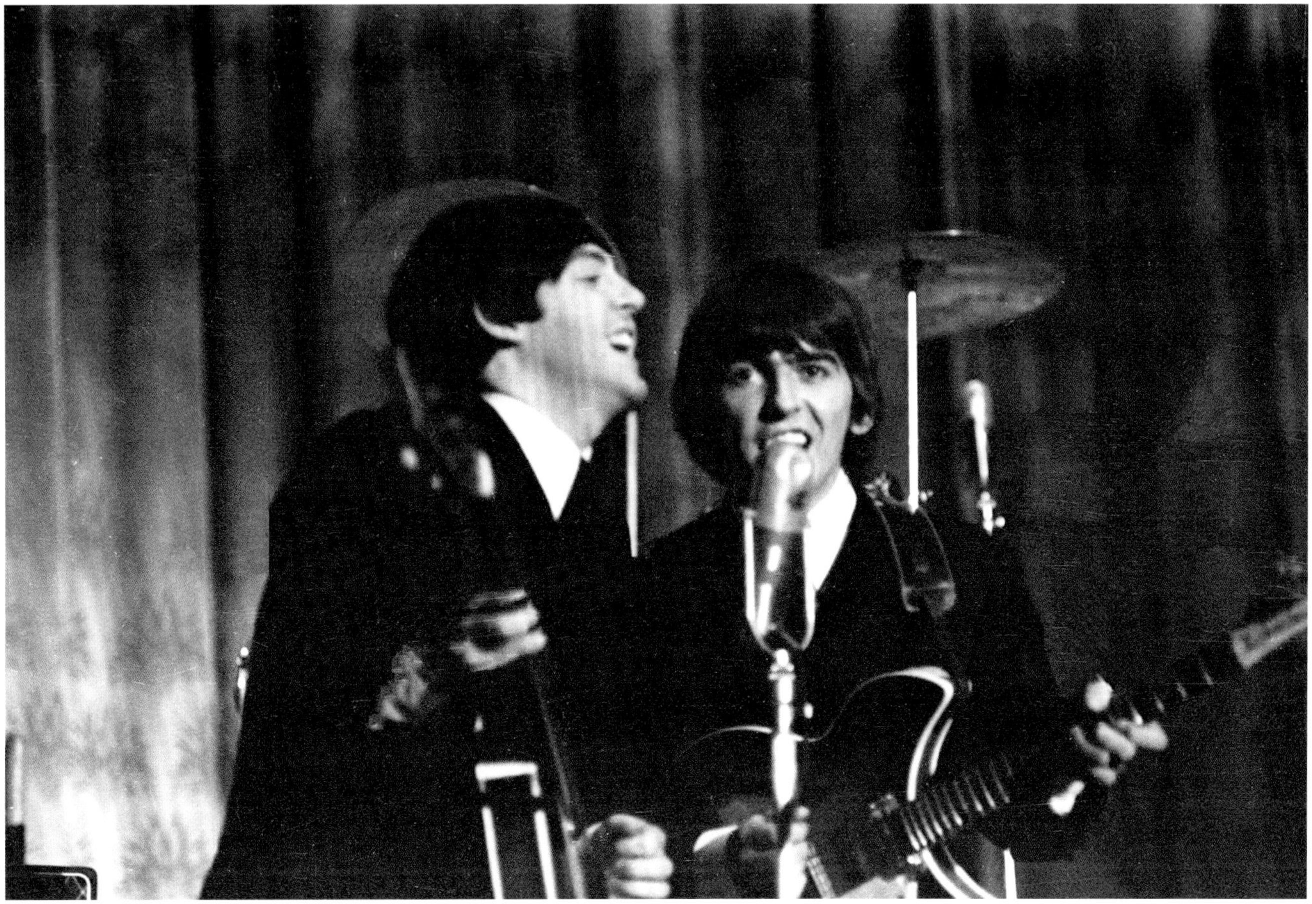

Paul McCartney and George Harrison, Philadelphia, September 1964.

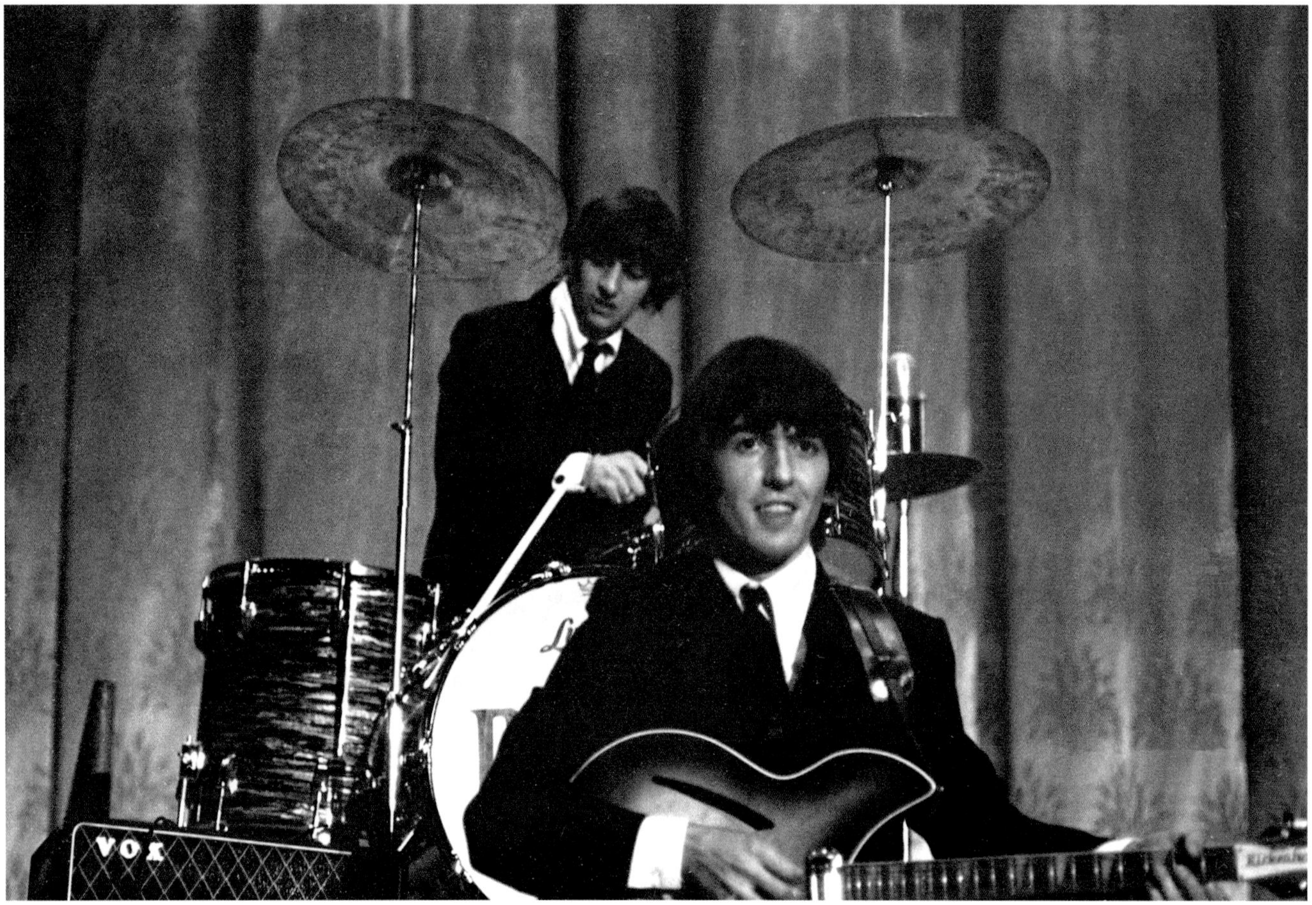

George Harrison and Ringo Starr, Philadelphia, September 1964.

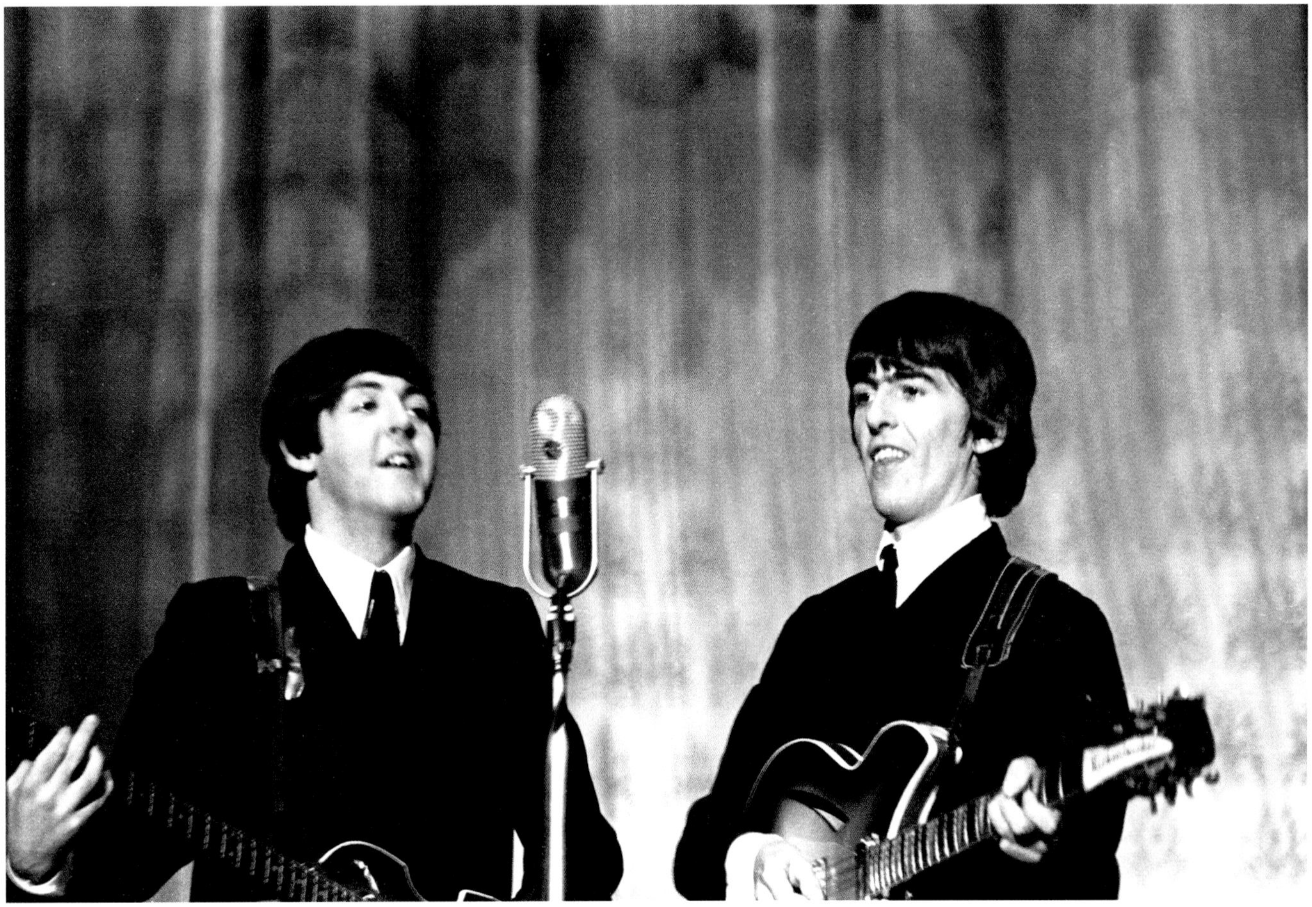

Paul McCartney and George Harrison, Philadelphia, September 1964.

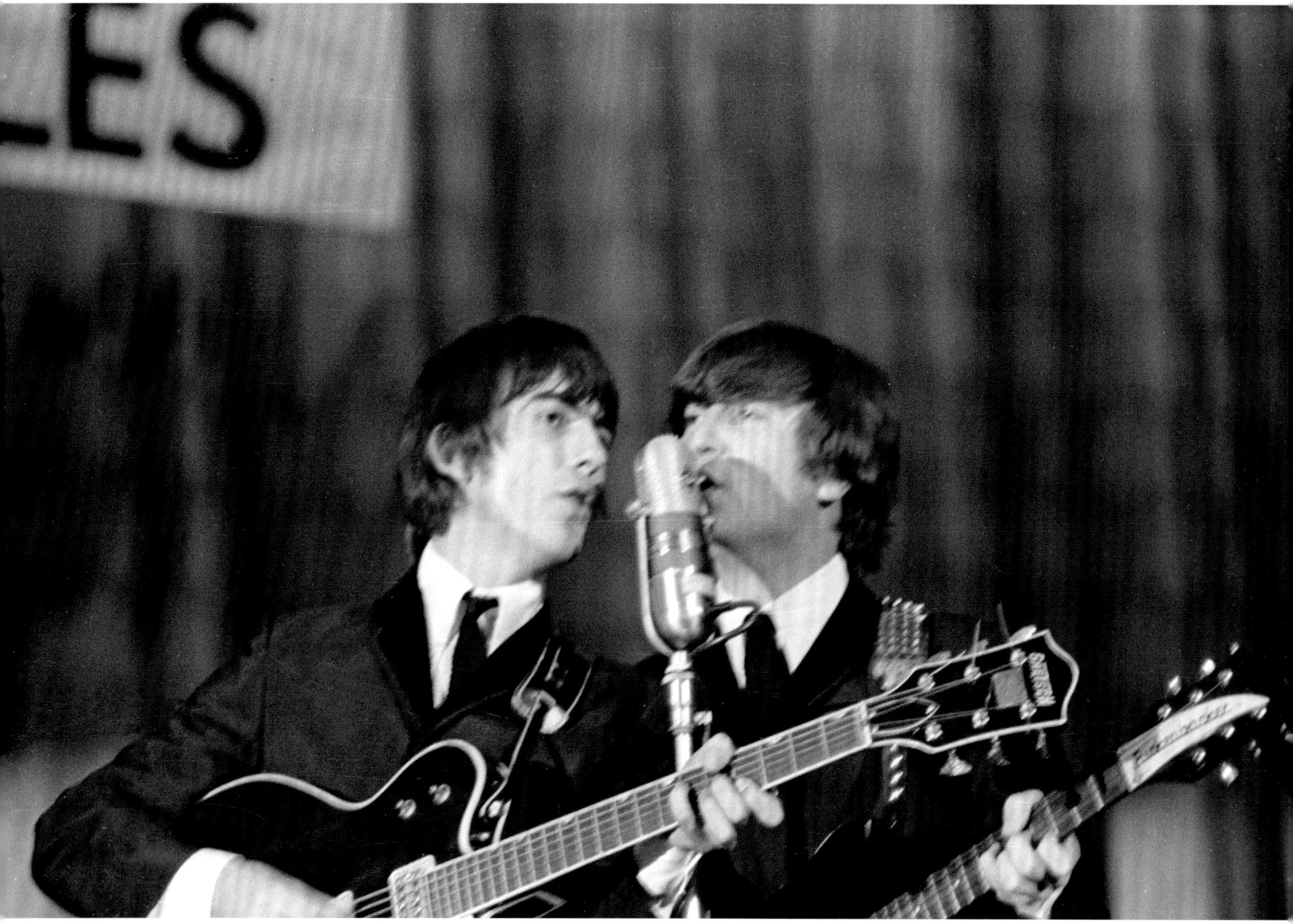

George Harrison and John Lennon, Philadelphia, September 1964.

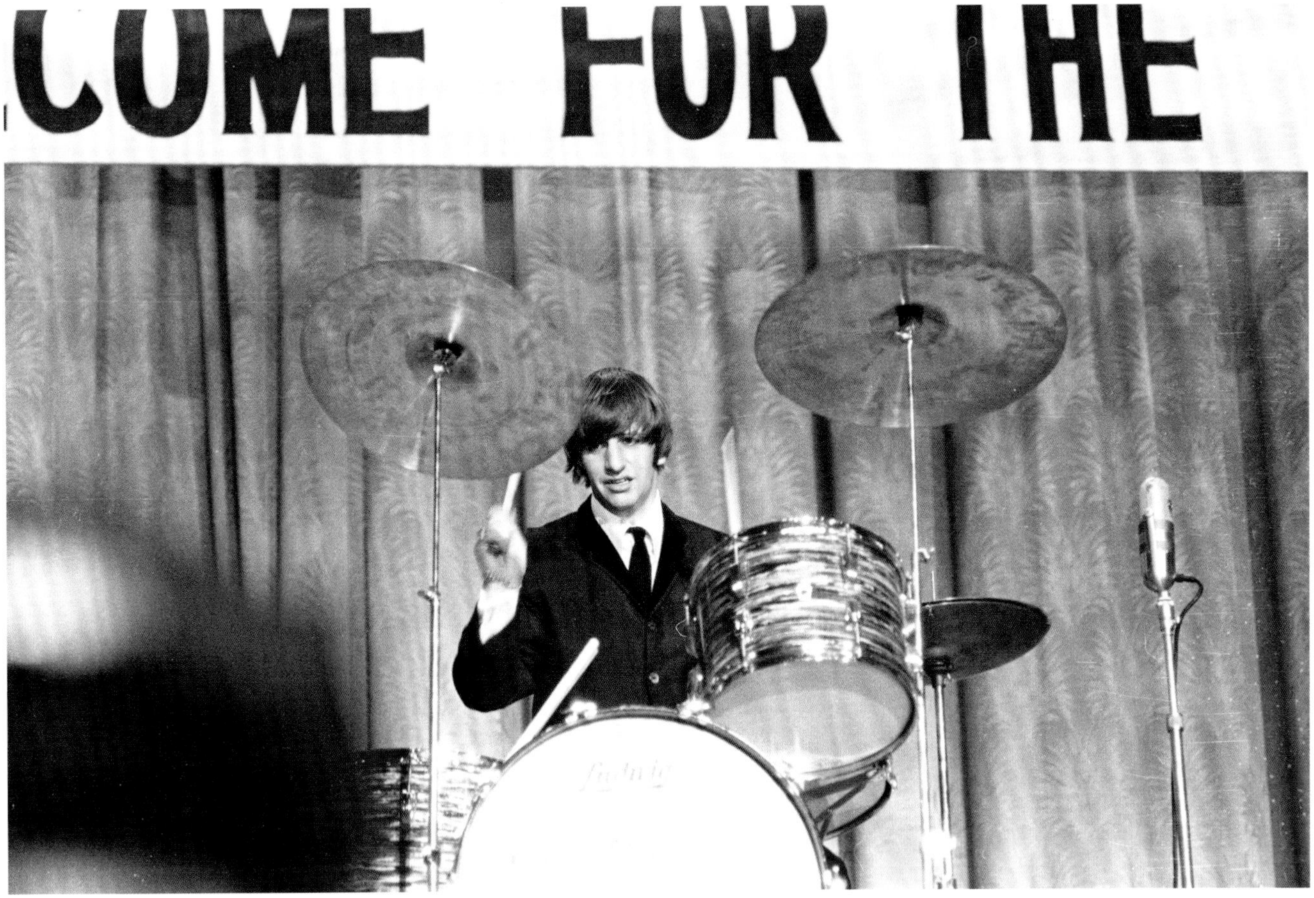

Ringo Starr, Philadelphia, September 1964.

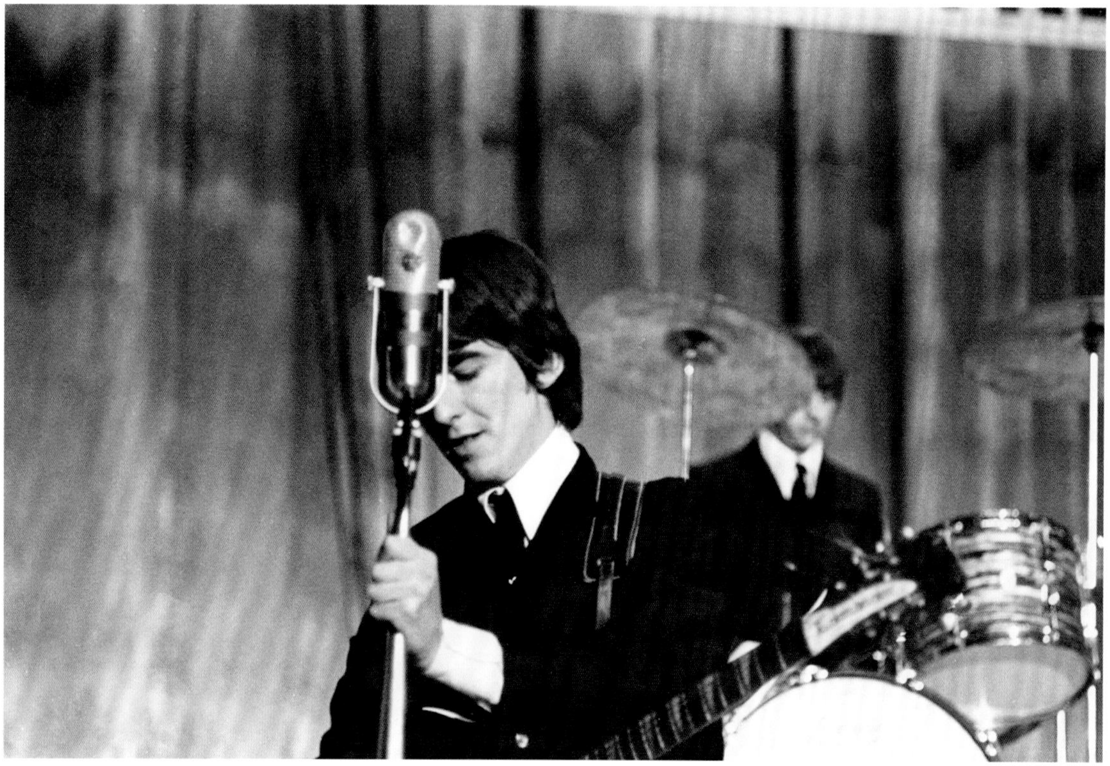

George Harrison and Ringo Starr, Philadelphia, September 1964.

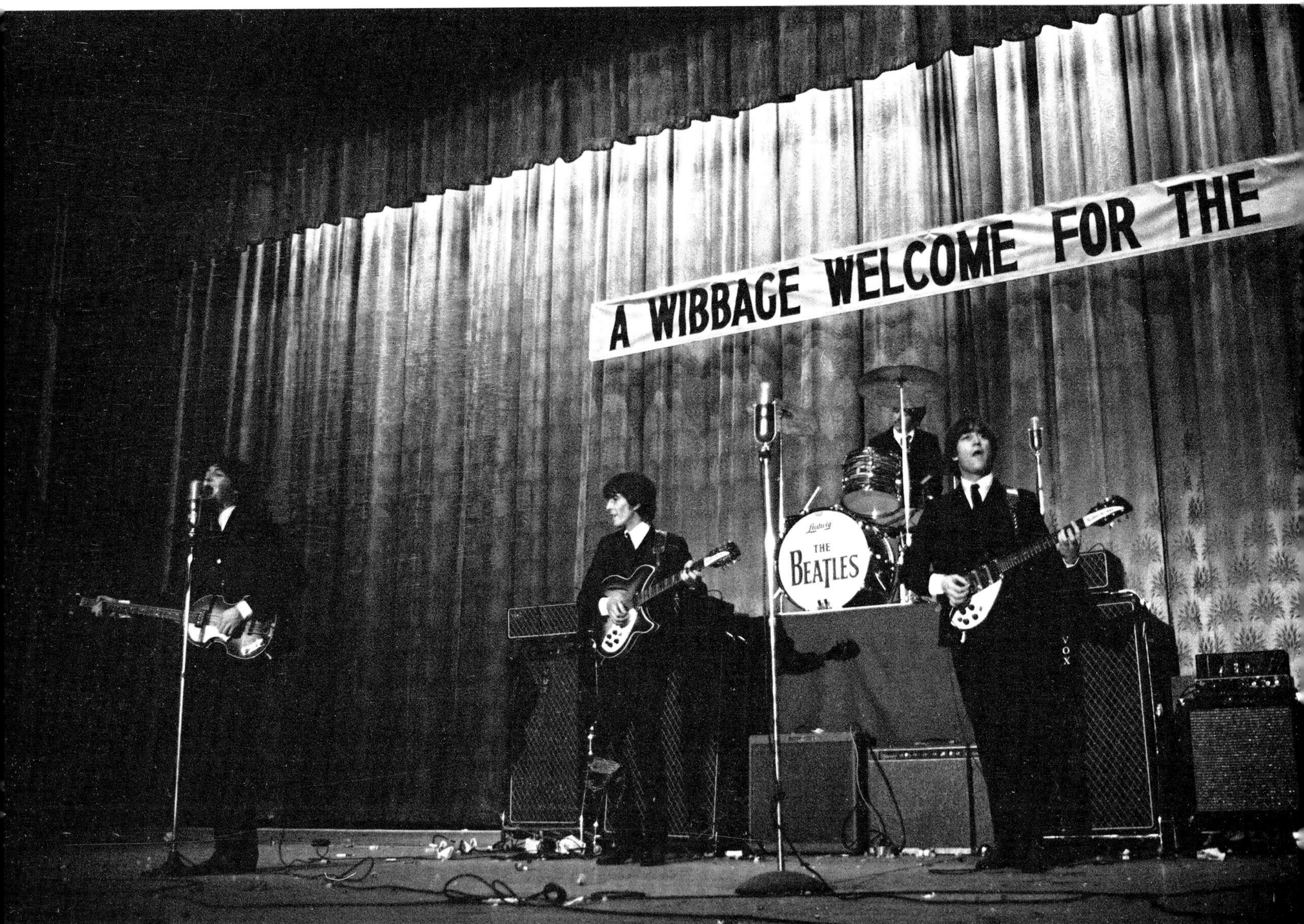

The Beatles, Philadelphia, September 1964.

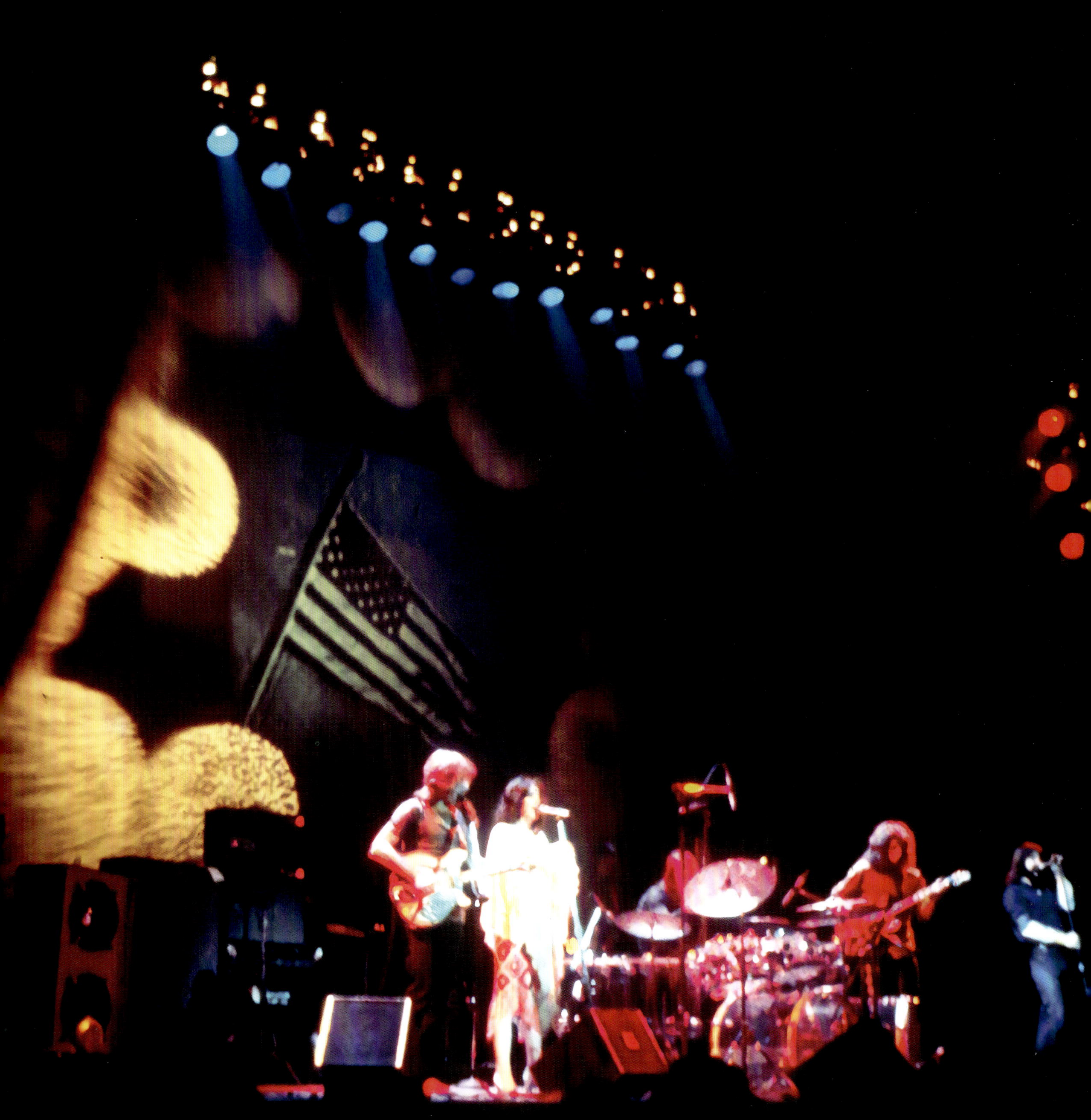

2

The Landing of Jefferson Airplane

In late 1965 I visited San Francisco. While I was there I happened to notice posters throughout the city promoting a band I had never heard of, Jefferson Airplane. Intrigued by the name, I wondered about their sound. Once I returned home, I haunted my favorite music stores, looking for records by my newfound idée fixe. My inquiries were for naught, and even met with laughter and derision at such a band name, as unusual names were still in their infancy. Undaunted, I continued to search for the band's recordings and soon secured the Airplane's second single release, "Come Up the Years." (The first had limited release due to censorship of its B side.) I was hooked. The lilting lament of the ballad and fresh sound of vocal harmony and guitars convinced me most assuredly that Jefferson Airplane was to be my next favorite band. Then, in the summer of 1966, the LP *Jefferson Airplane Takes Off* came out. I snapped it up right away and was enthralled. The music truly was heavily influenced by, and a direct extension of, the work of another of my favorite bands, the Byrds. The Airplane implemented a similar Rickenbacker twelve-string rhythm guitar, which thoroughly complemented their strong lead guitar and bass. They featured three-part harmony like the Byrds, too, but with the twist of one of the singers being female: Signe Toly Anderson in the beginning, and later of course, the legendary Grace Slick. The music on the first record was strongly folk rock with a tinge of blues, but under that veneer was an undercurrent of something more powerful and potentially explosive.

In 1967, the Airplane's second album, *Surrealistic Pillow*, was released, which included two singles that made the Top 10 on all the music charts. "White Rabbit," a psychedelicized version of Lewis Carroll's *Alice's Adventures in Wonderland*, became their most popular and enduring song. So, when it was announced

Jefferson Airplane, Fillmore East, New York, May 1970.

that they would play at the Asbury Park Convention Hall, during their 1967 summer national tour, I hatched a plot. I secured front-row tickets and brought my camera and lenses along to the concert to take some photographs, albeit under the usual less-than-optimum lighting conditions. This setup at the Hall would ever thwart my attempt to achieve a kind of visualization of the music, which even from my early days I had always longed to do.

By then, I knew the layout of the Hall like the back of my hand, so it was easy for me to get backstage after the Airplane had completed their performance. I met the band members, recounting the story of how I came to discover them two years earlier and had followed their ascent to the top of the US music charts. They could not have been more open and down to earth. The band members were still dealing with newfound fame and were slowly becoming comfortable with their role as rock stars. These were early days in the music media, and the crushing attention to celebrities by paparazzi and fanatical followers were still in their infancy, precipitated by the public reaction to the Beatles and their English mates. Marty Balin, Grace Slick, Paul Kantner, Jorma Kaukonen, and Jack Casady all took interest in me and were excited to see that I had a camera, asking if I had photographed them that evening. I replied, "You bet I did," and Grace and Paul, most impressed, asked if they could see the results the next time they came to play. I replied that they sure could and I would see them as soon as they returned to the area. During the concert, early in the set, I had also tossed up to the drummer, Spencer Dryden, a black cowboy hat, which I had brought with me because I knew he often wore one. Smilingly he donned the hat for the remained of the concert and thanked me for the loan. As he tried to return the chapeau, I told him to keep it and he was more than happy to oblige. I left with stars in my eyes, astounded at how welcoming and kind they all were to this kid who came out of nowhere. This was to be a major turning point in my life, and I vowed to not let this opportunity slip through my still inexperienced hands.

After this encounter with the band, I made sure I connected with them on subsequent tours, always showing off my latest images. My photographic experiments would become more audacious, just as the trajectory of the band's music took the same path.

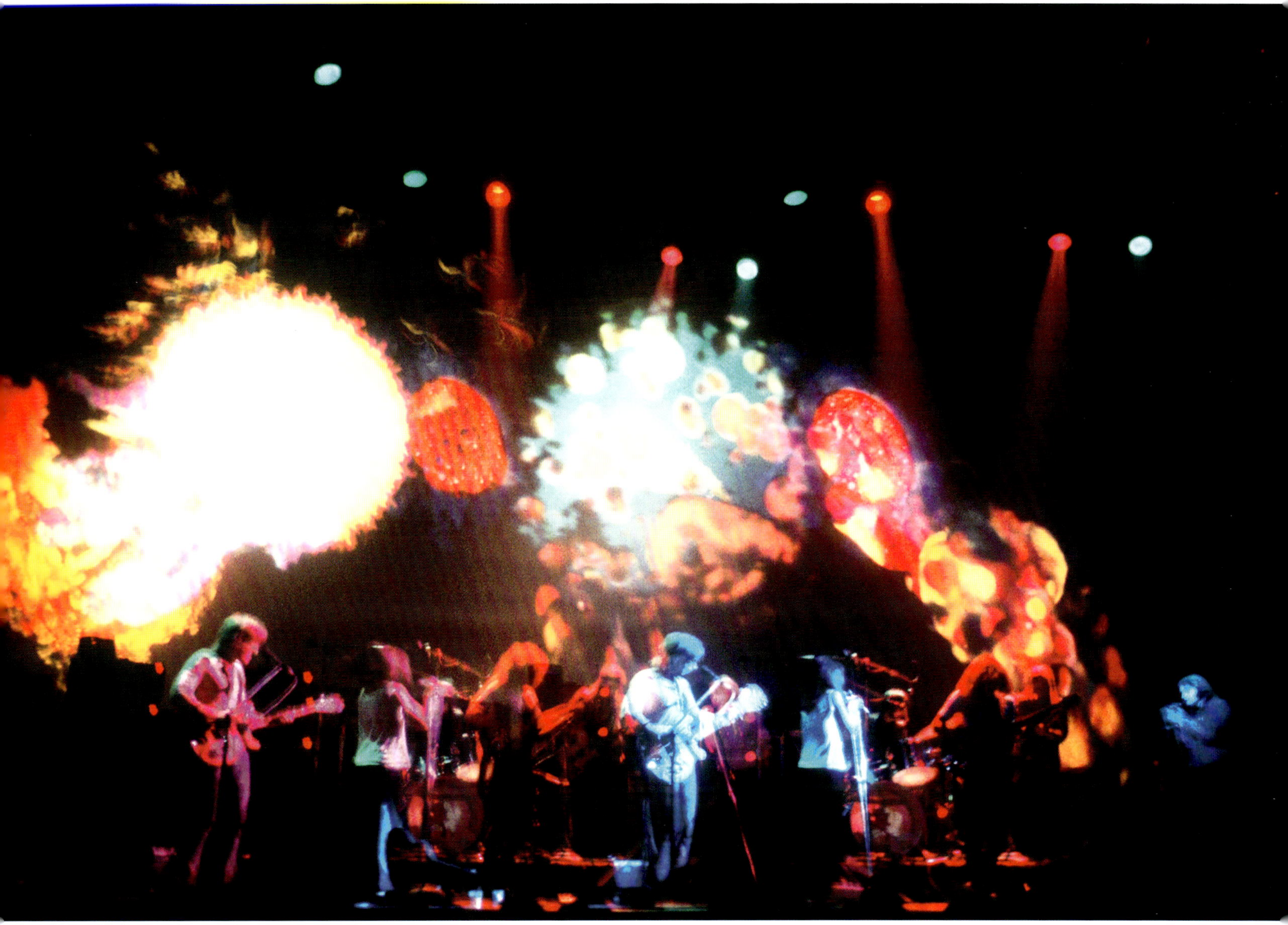

Jefferson Airplane, Fillmore East, New York, November 1969.

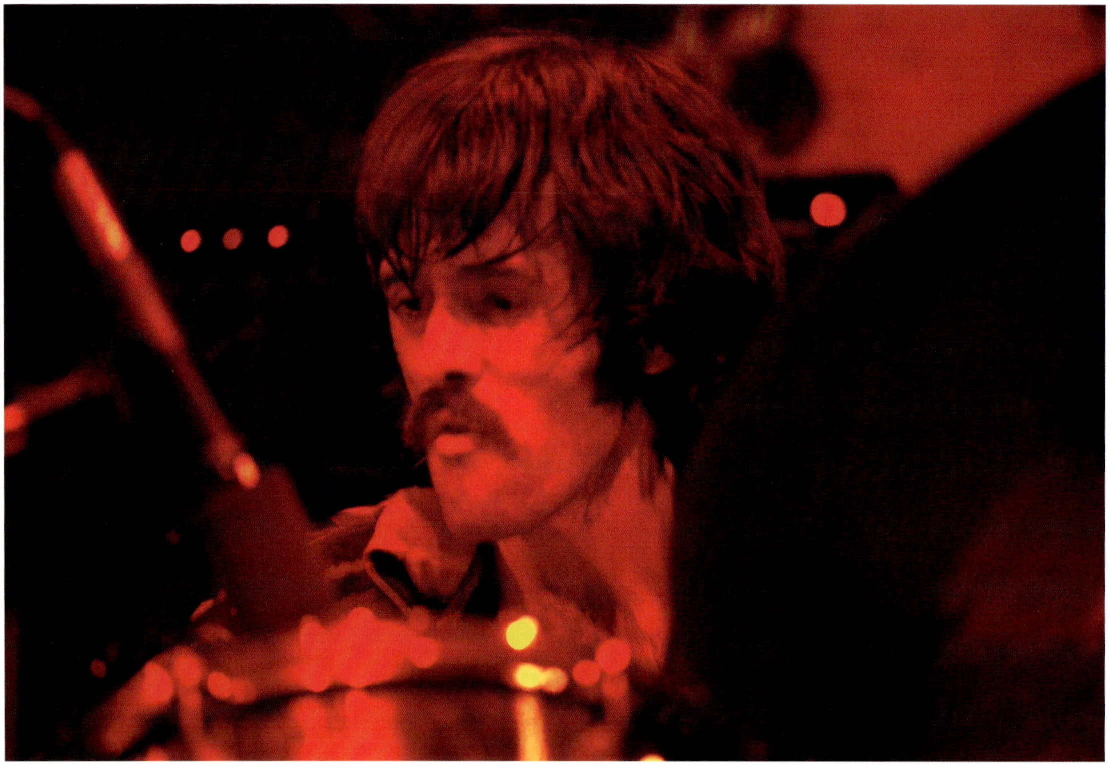

Spencer Dryden of Jefferson Airplane, Fillmore East, New York, August 1969. *Opposite*: Paul Kantner and Grace Slick of Jefferson Airplane, Fillmore East, New York, July 1968.

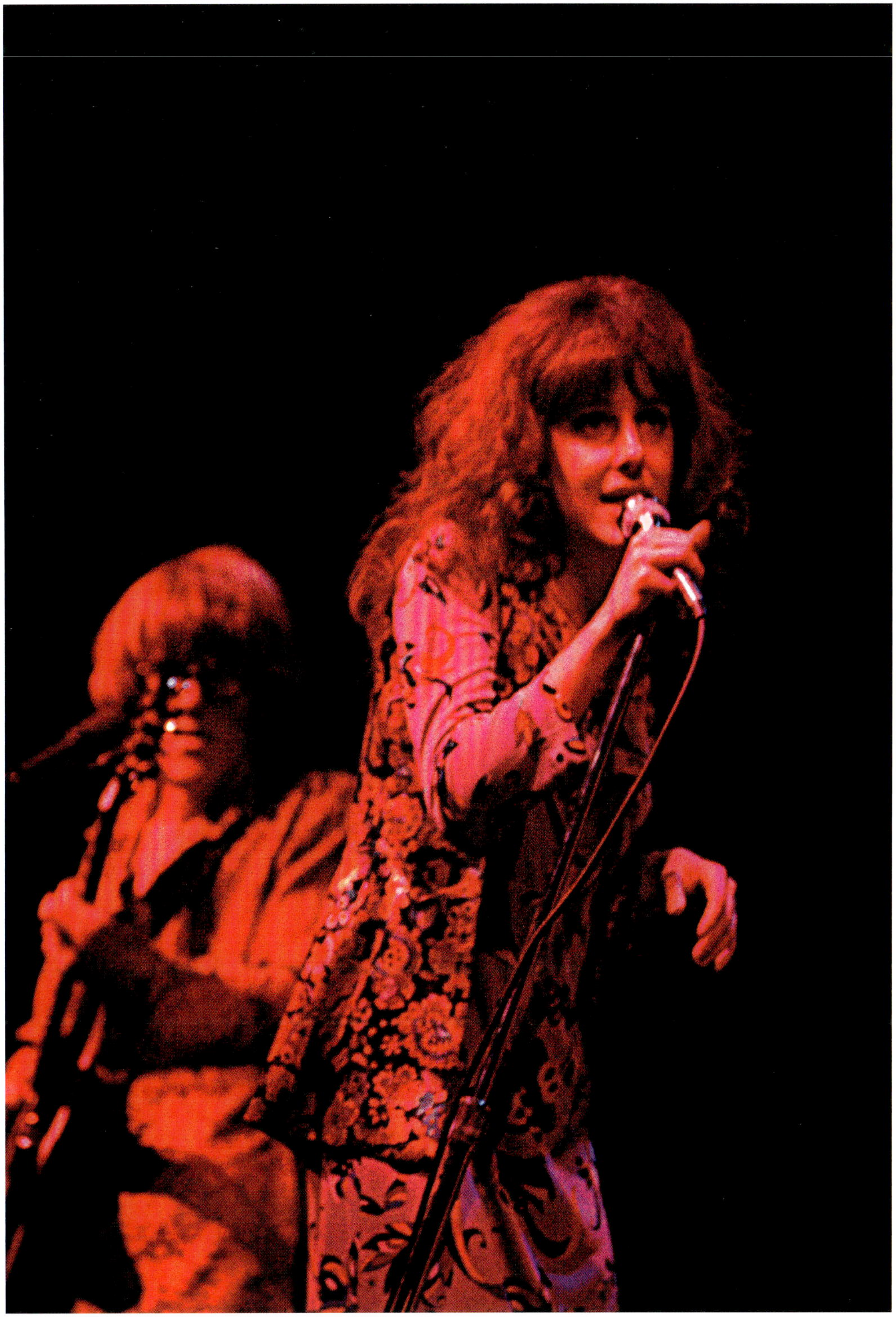

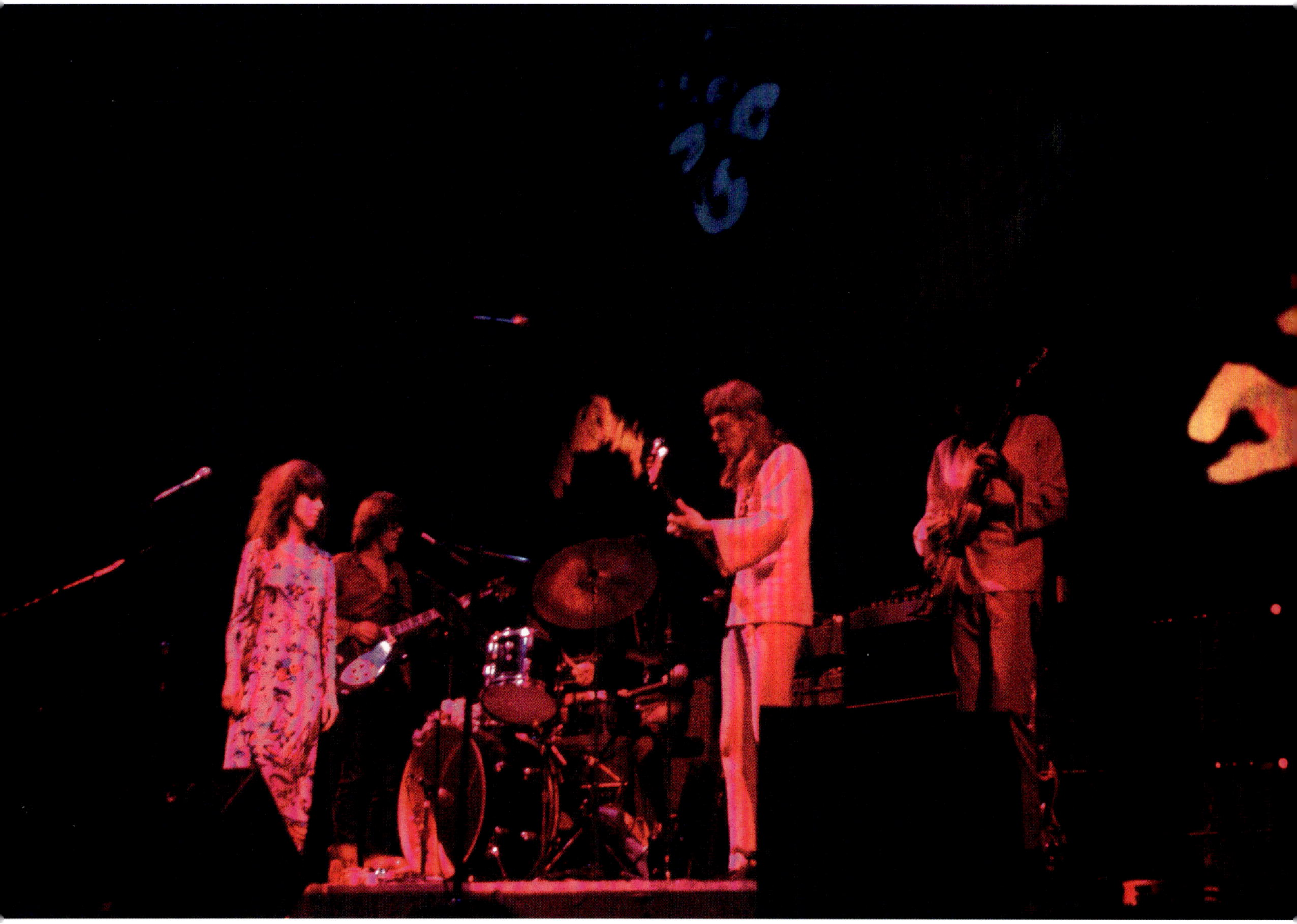

Grace Slick, Paul Kantner, Jack Casady, and Jorma Kaukonen of Jefferson Airplane Fillmore East, New York, July 1968.

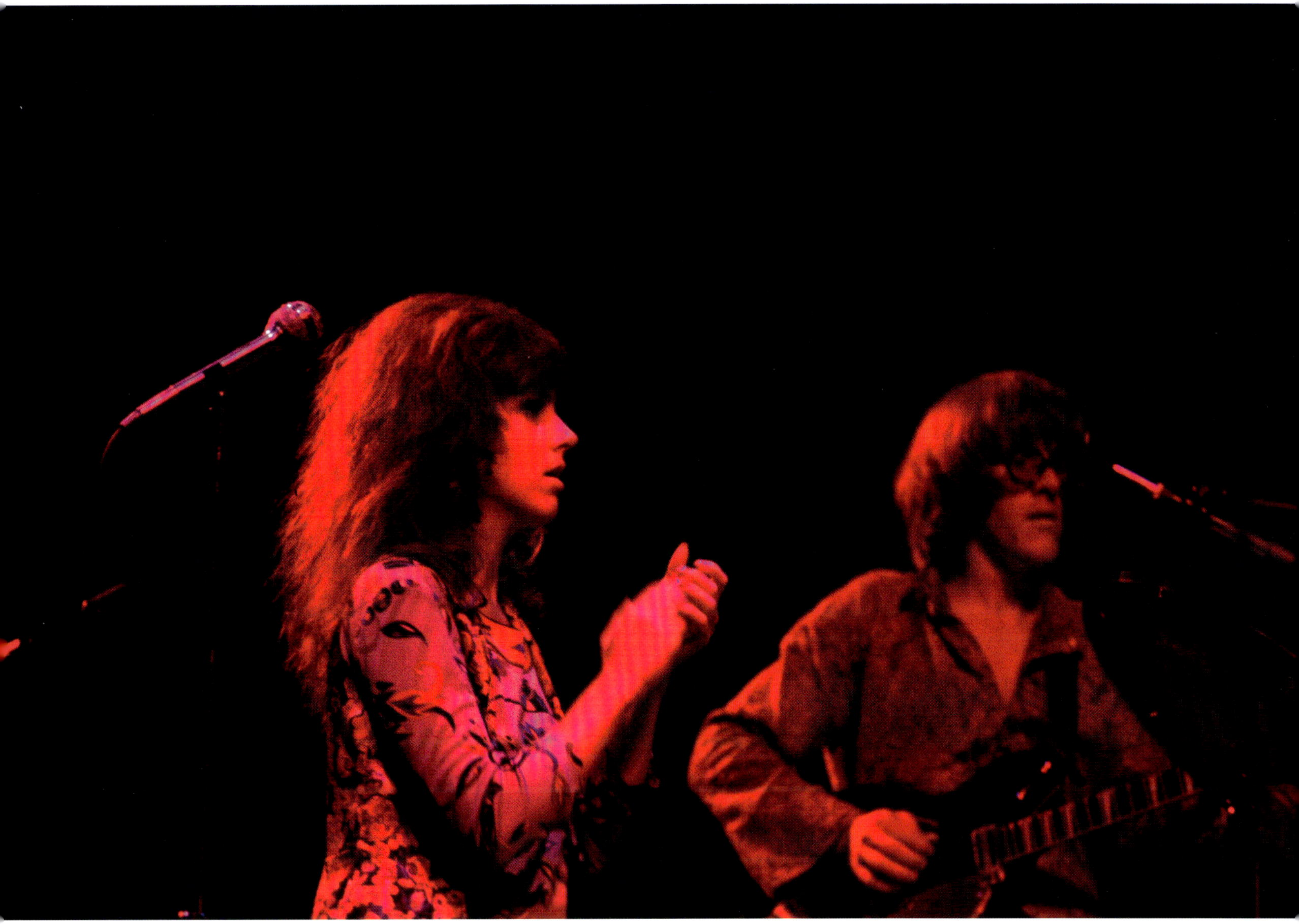

Grace Slick and Paul Kantner of Jefferson Airplane, Fillmore East, New York, July 1968.

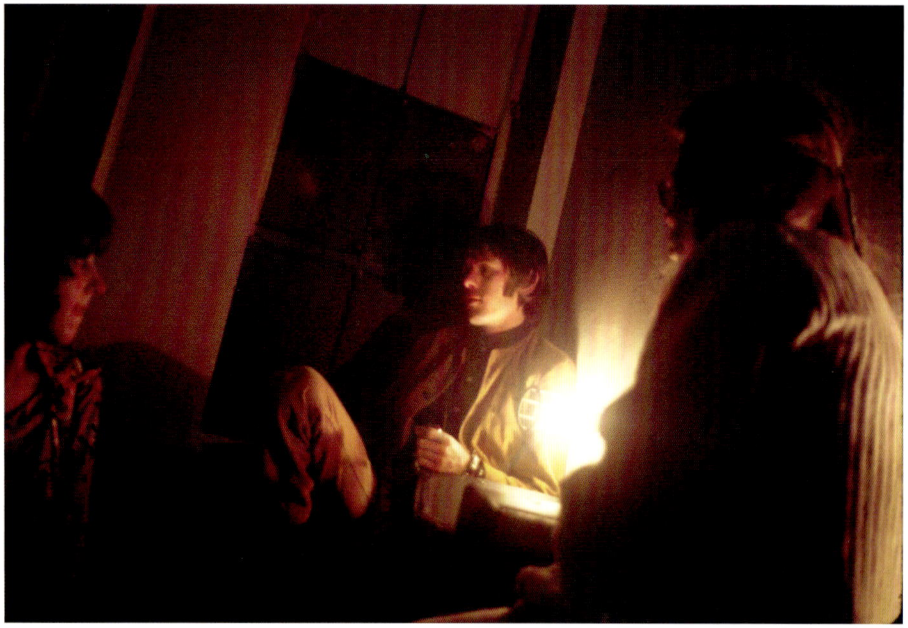

Grace Slick, Spencer Dryden, and Jack Casady of Jefferson Airplane, backstage, Fillmore East, New York, July 1968.

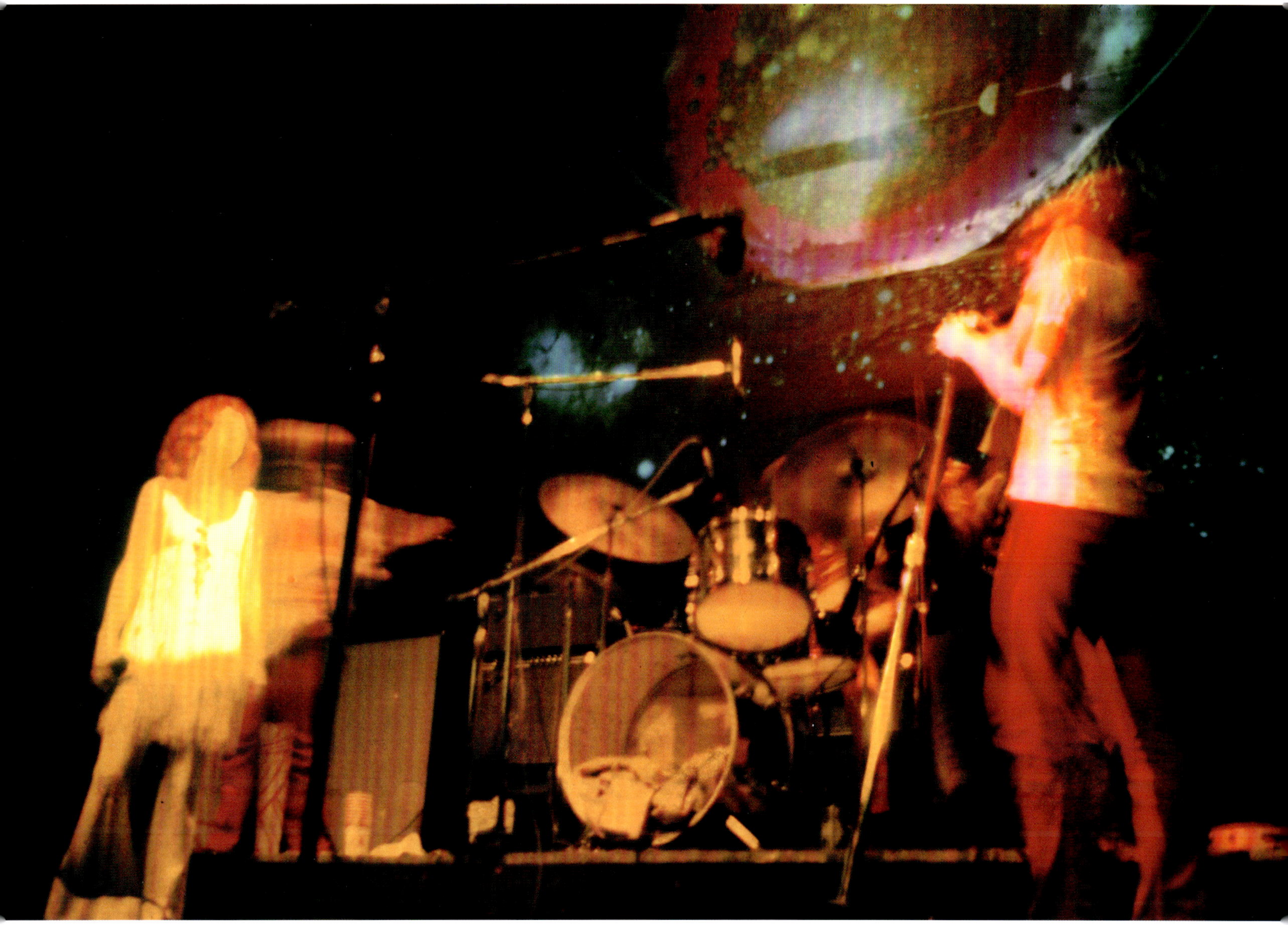

Grace Slick, Paul Kantner, and Marty Balin of Jefferson Airplane, infrared image, Fillmore East, New York, August 1969.

Overleaf: (left) Jorma Kaukonen and Jack Casady of Jefferson Airplane, Fillmore East, New York, November 1970; (right) Jorma Kaukonen, Jefferson Airplane, Fillmore East, New York, May 1970.

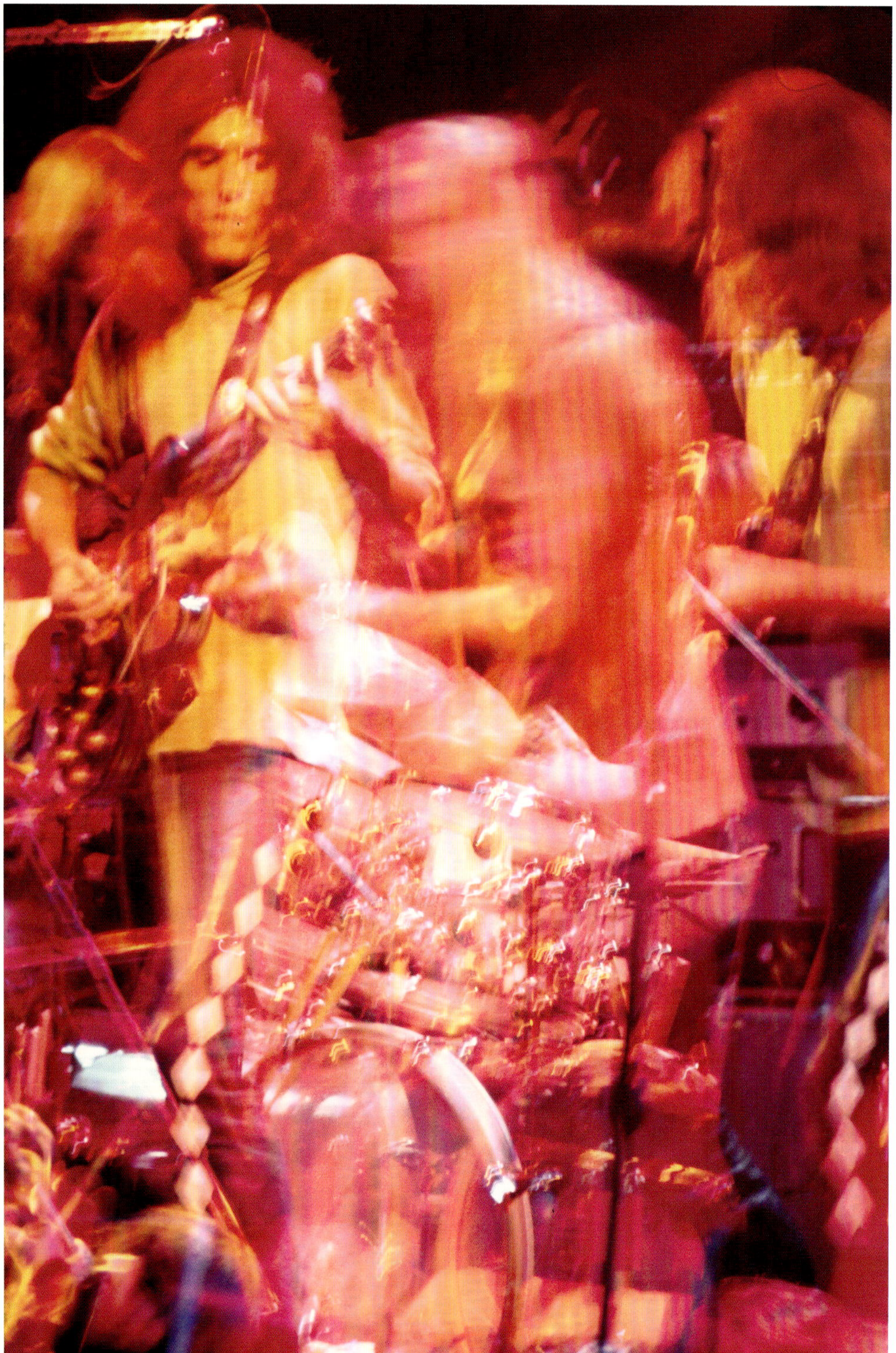

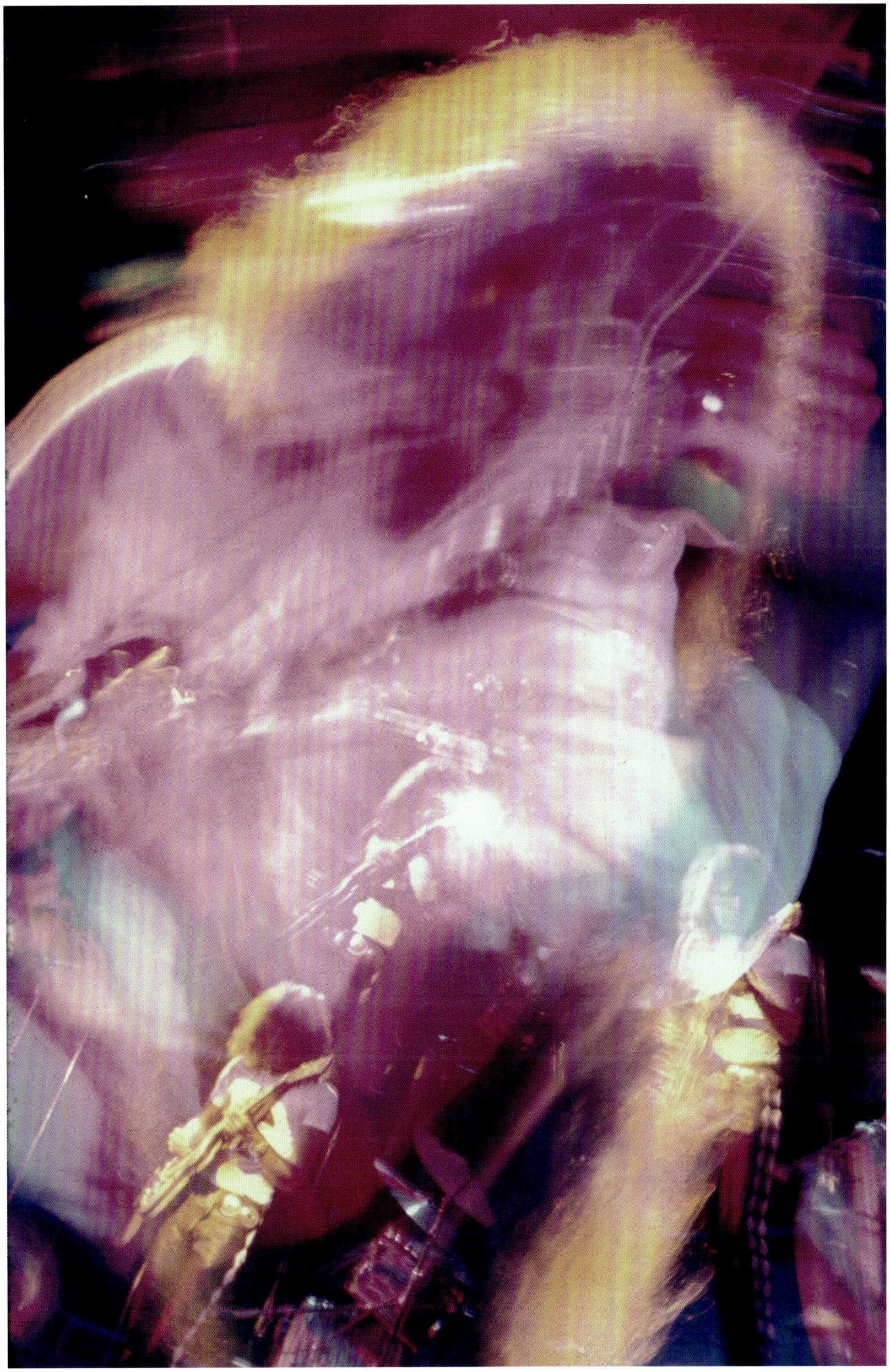

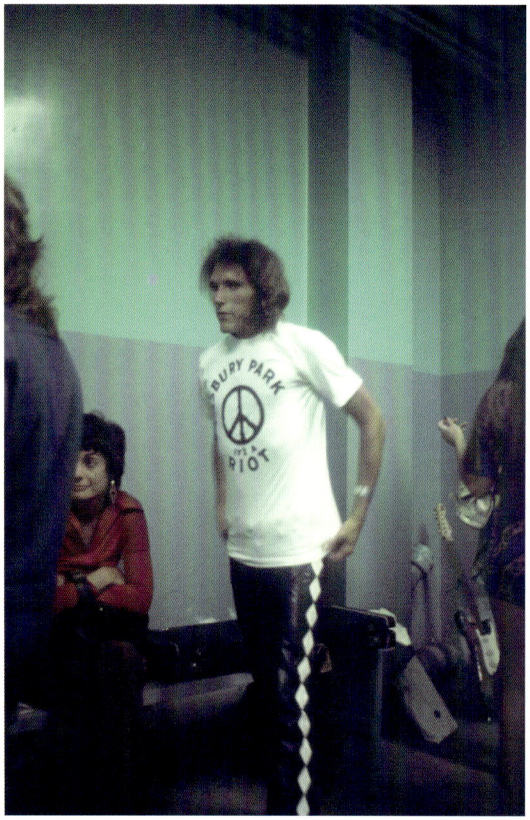

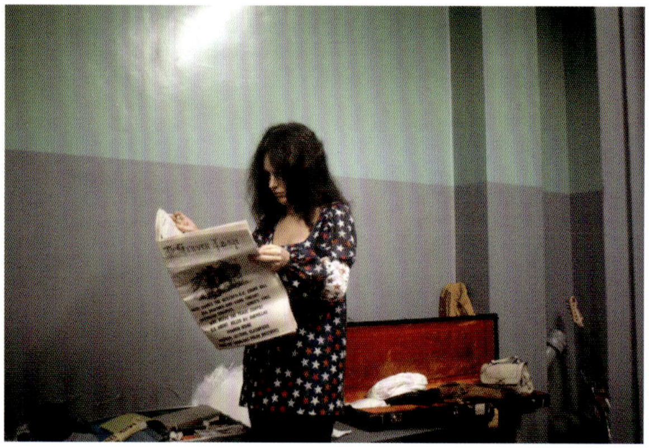

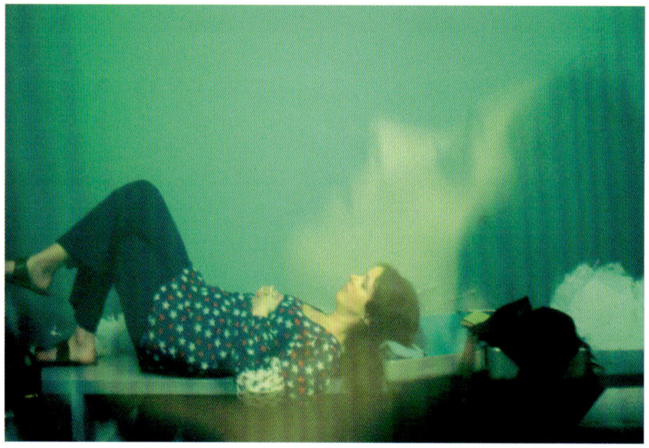

Jefferson Airplane backstage, Convention Hall, Asbury Park, August 1970.

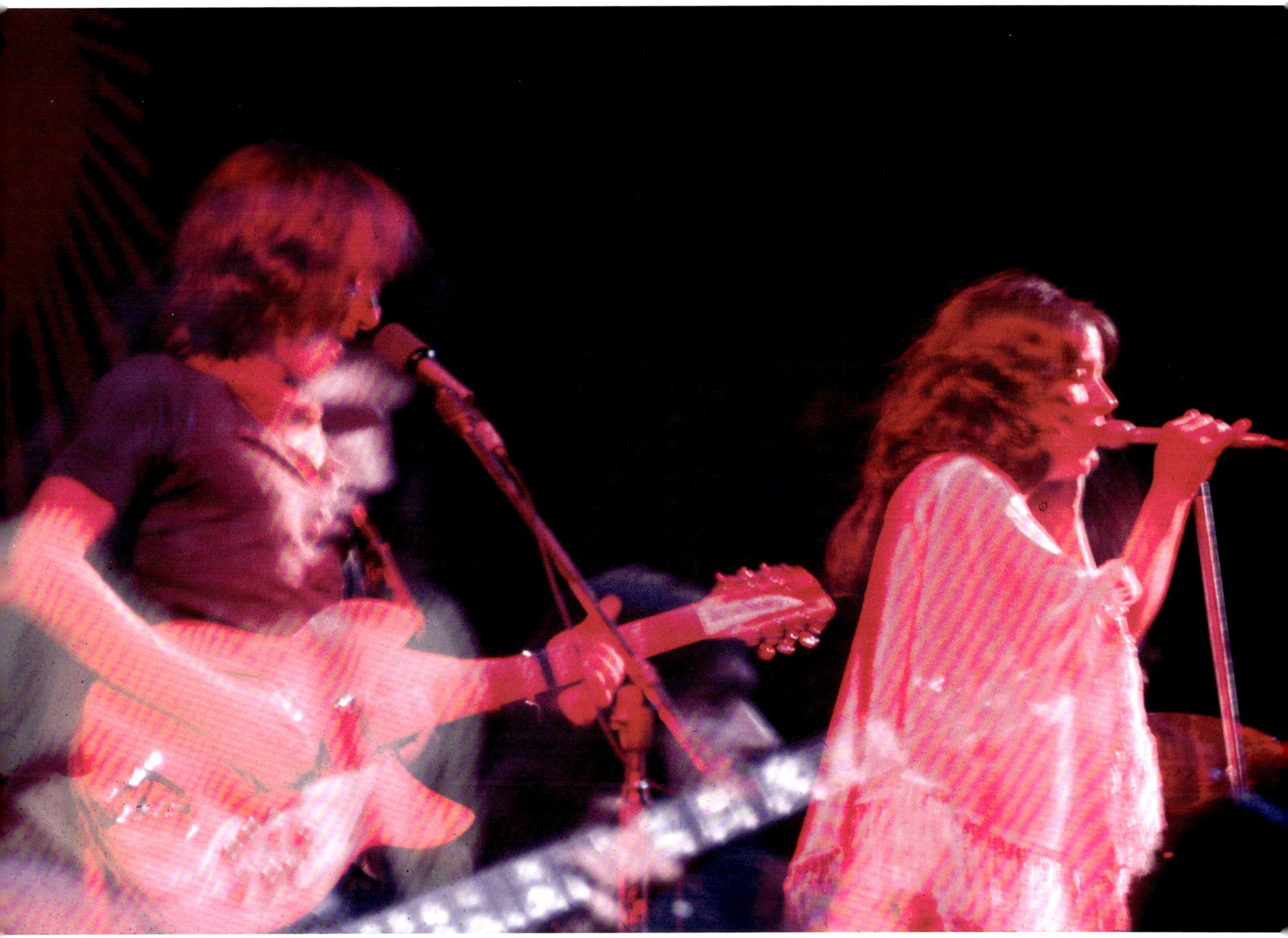

Paul Kantner, Jorma Kaukonen, and Grace Slick of Jefferson Airplane, Fillmore East, New York, November 1970.

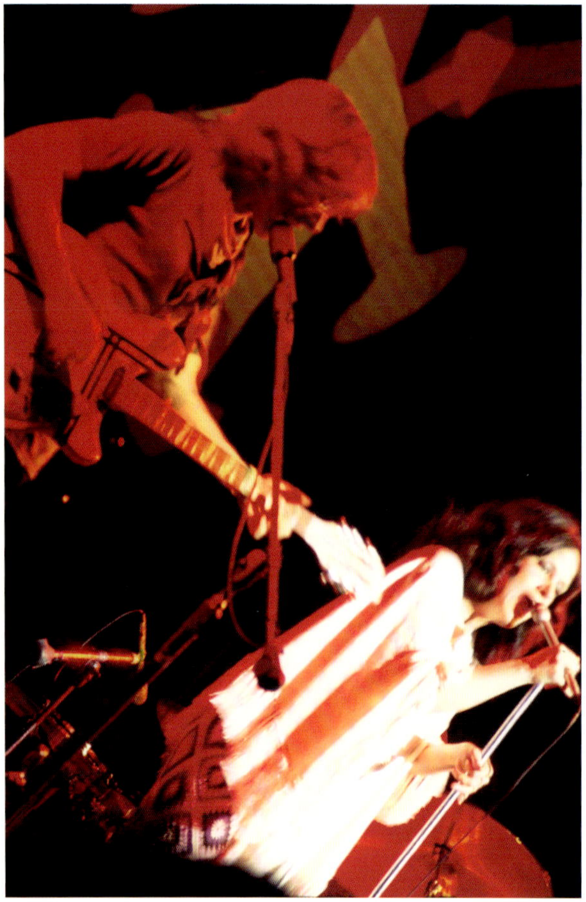

Paul Kantner and Grace Slick of Jefferson Airplane, Fillmore East, New York, November 1970. *Opposite*: Jefferson Airplane, Atlantic City Pop Festival, August 1969.

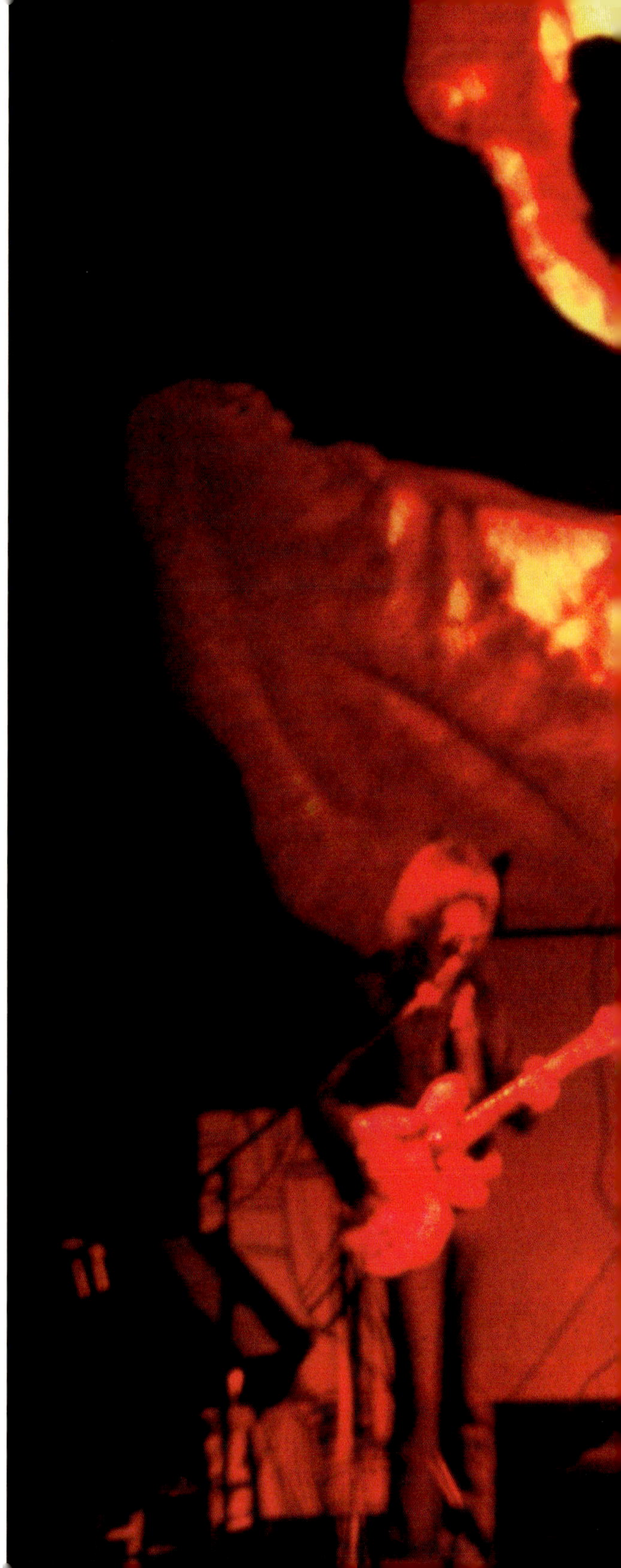

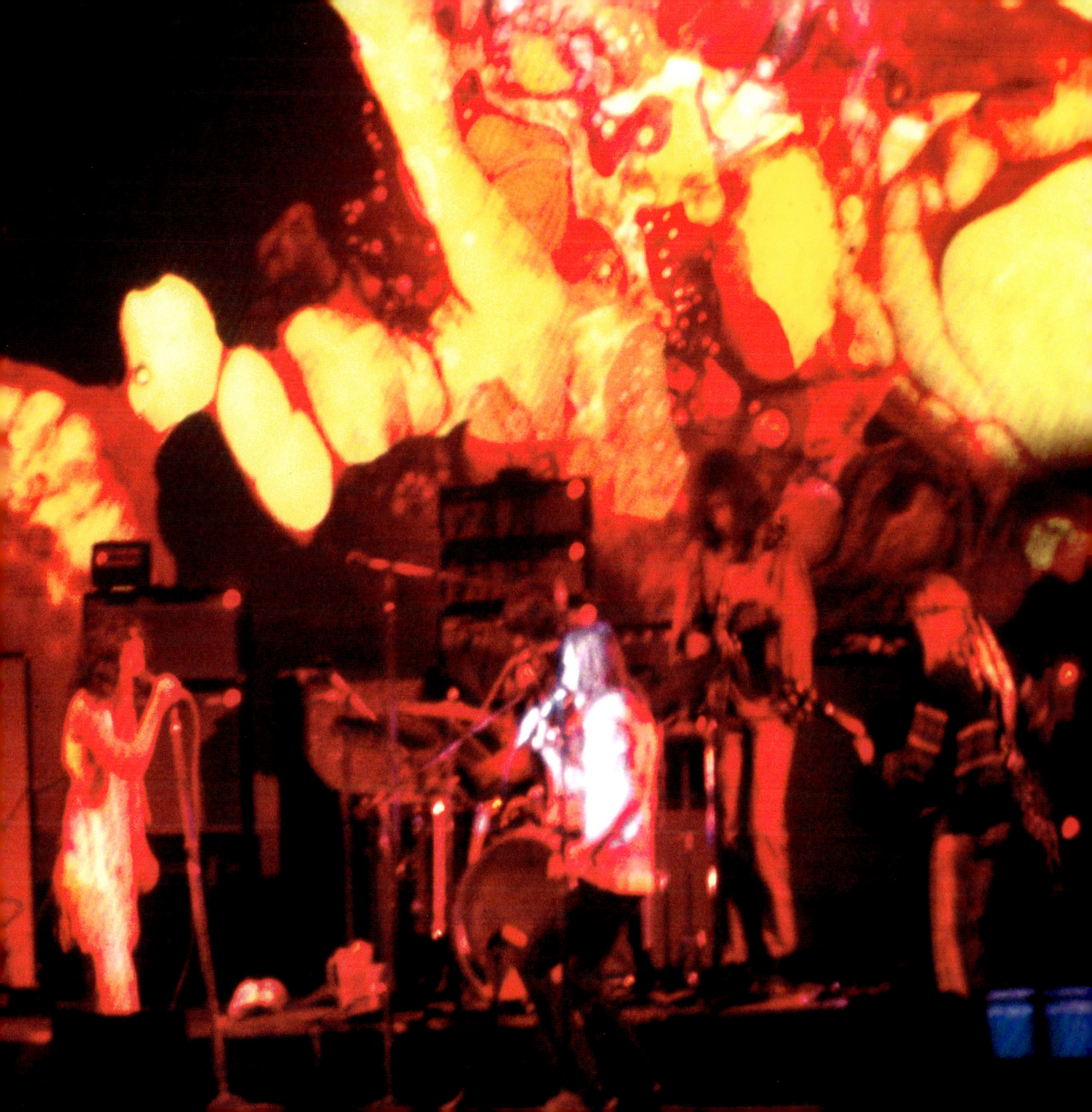

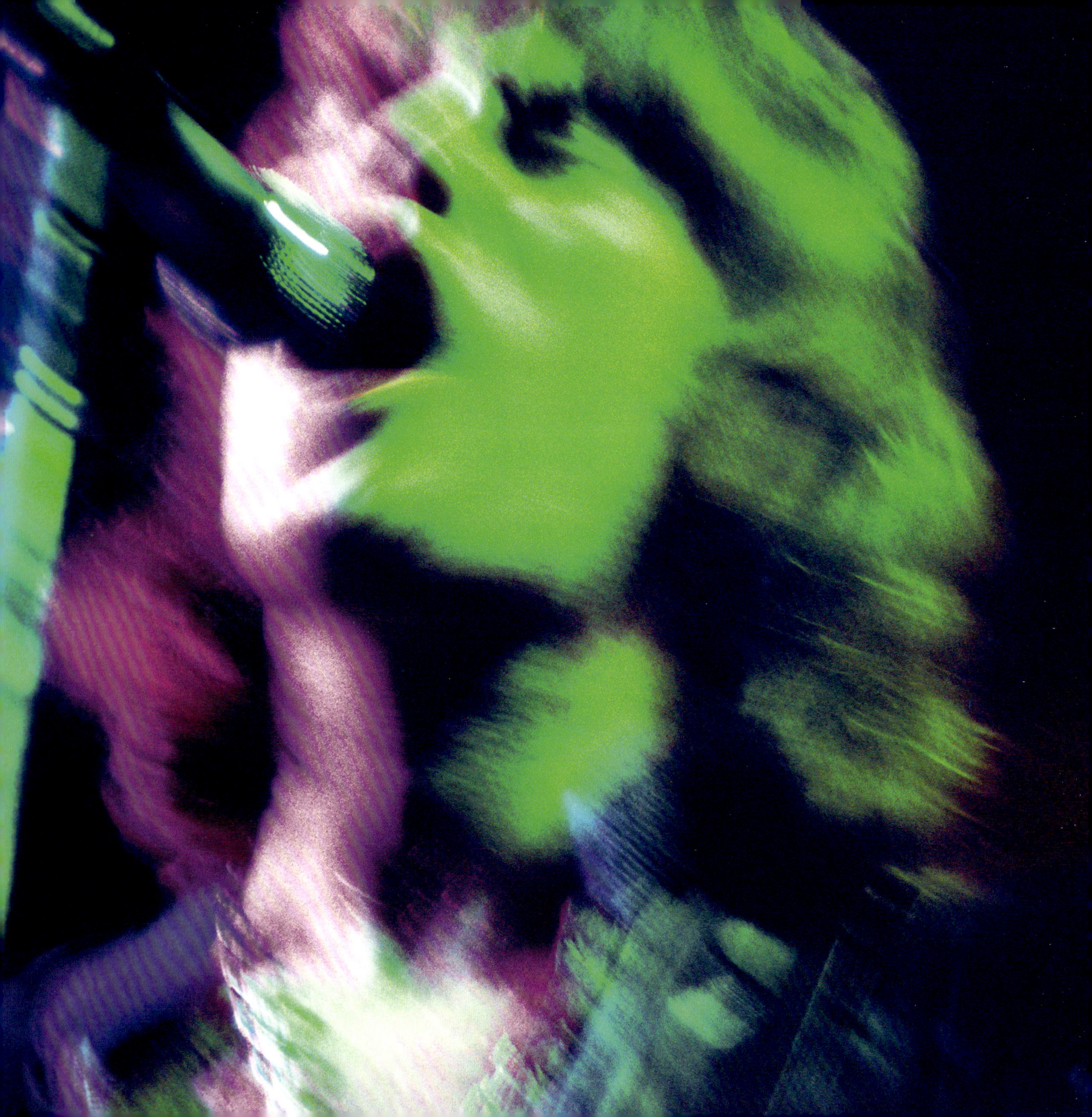

3

My Experiences at the Fillmore East

It was a foregone conclusion that I would go to college, mainly because my mother always said, "Get an education and no matter what else you do, you can always fall back on that." I chose to study at Monmouth College (now Monmouth University), after a disastrous experience at the University of Maryland. Mom also always told me that all things happen for a reason, and that year I found her words to be true. It turned out to be fortuitous that I remained in New Jersey, near New York City.

In early 1968, shortly after I began my studies at Monmouth, it was announced that the San Francisco concert promoter Bill Graham was to open a new venue, the Fillmore East, in New York. The light bulb in my head went on. I began to think about the upcoming concerts at the Fillmore and whether the lighting would be more amenable to executing some of my photographic experiments in a proper venue.

It was mostly at the Fillmore East, with its freewheeling yet highly efficient presentations of the best music of the time, that I began my journey as a witness and small participant in music history. I would attend countless concerts and, over time, gained nearly unlimited access to the shows, having become a "friend of the family" through my growing association with Jefferson Airplane and the kind employees' interest in my photography work.

The Fillmore East was near perfection as a concert venue and laboratory for my experiments in color, light, exposure, and motion. The weekly parade of artists and bands astounded and inspired me. During each show I felt the power of what I had only experienced before on record, and my senses of sight and sound were overwhelmed as the music flowed over me. This irresistible force was to meet the sometimes-immovable object of my camera. Up to that point, my experiments were only

Alvin Lee, Ten Years After, Fillmore East, New York, April 1969.

plans, visions in my head, but at the Fillmore they came alive in my hands. I produced not only representational portraits, just to show that I could accomplish them, but finally I carried out my motion and multiple-exposure techniques, which I firmly believed illustrated the dynamic power of the aural experience I was witnessing and attempting to capture through my unique style. I saw billowing blasts of color from the amplifiers and the sound system merge and intertwine in a synesthetic assault. I felt akin to one of my other idols, Nikola Tesla, as I captured and interpreted the bolts of pure creative electrical energy in the tight and constricted space of the 35mm image in my camera.

It was at the Fillmore East that I spent many Thanksgiving weekends with the Airplane. There were many dinners and animated conversations with them at the famed Chelsea Hotel, where they stayed when in New York.

I witnessed and photographed many other major events at the Fillmore East, including in May 1969 the Who's rock opera *Tommy*, which was its first concert presentation in New York. The show was postponed by a day owing to a fire next door. But when the Who did play, they astounded the audience. In my photographs of the show I tried to capture the unbridled energy produced by the band, as the story of Pete Townshend's work blazingly unspooled like a film before my eyes.

Even more important, I was there when Led Zeppelin played their first New York dates at the end of January 1969. I had already known of the band, having been a huge Yardbirds fan. (Led Zeppelin of course evolved from that legendary group and may not have been as big had they not changed their name from their original moniker, the New Yardbirds.) I had purchased their first record on its day of release, playing it on my short-lived, post-midnight stint on a local radio station. I was ready for history. The band came on and blew the ears off the mostly unsuspecting crowd. The powerful blend of blues and rock was delivered with devastating effect. Jimmy Page's searing, masterful guitar (even if he was beaten to the punch in bowing his guitar like a violin by Eddie Pickett of the then little-known band the Creation), Robert Plant's screaming vocals, the equally heavy drumming of John Bonham, and the deep driving bass of John Paul Jones were jaw-dropping. The audience remained stunned, pinned to their seats, and uncharacteristically silent after their staggering set. The headliner, Iron Butterfly, still riding high from their psychedelic symphony "In-A-Gadda-Da-Vida," then took the stage. But their music received modest applause—so modest in fact that after only a few songs, they announced that they couldn't compete with what was just heard and walked off the stage.

Another British band, the Move (later to evolve into the Electric Light Orchestra), a favorite of mine, was originally scheduled to play that night as the third band on the bill but sadly they canceled. It is surely controversial to write this, but I thought then that the Move, had they played, would have topped the show with the power of their songs and unrelentingly heavy sound. They may have made their career that night, even overshadowing Led Zep, instead of being relegated to their position as one of the most underrated bands of all time.

In September 1969, Crosby, Stills, Nash, and Young made their much-anticipated Fillmore East debut, just a month after their appearance at Woodstock. I had heard their first record and, along with the sellout crowd, was expecting an amazing blend of voices when Crosby, Stills, and Nash opened the show with an acoustic, nearly a cappella version of "Suite: Judy Blue Eyes." No one was disappointed. I can still remember the first time they broke into the chorus, holding the end notes for what seemed like a full minute. The crowd exploded, and each time they repeated the burst of harmony chills went up and down my spine. This was something new, breathtaking, and historic. The three continued to wow the audience with more acoustic songs. And then, when Neil Young came out, the group produced an electric set that was as powerful as any I had witnessed at the venue. I was dumbfounded and produced portraits of each member, some hopefully representing the intensity of these epic performances. The sonic fusion of these incredible talents on stage surely created a "supergroup," which was the popular descriptive term used at the time. The show is still one of my most vivid memories, one that has not dimmed a single iota in over fifty years.

I was already a huge Pink Floyd fan as well, and an intense, psychedelically drenched concert in September 1970 led me to produce some of my most complex photographs in terms of layers and exposures. Viewers of these get lost trying to isolate and focus on all the embedded components of these 3D-like images, produced by the sounds and movements of the band members, which stunned my eyes and inspired me to represent what I was seeing in this dynamic fashion.

Another memorable concert was the Grateful Dead in February 1970. The Dead played as strongly as I could remember, and the images seemed to run through my camera as if guided by an external force, interwoven with the nonstop music that went on for hours. This culminated early in the morning of the next day with an extended version of the song "Dark Star" in which the band was supplemented by the surprise appearance of the Allman Brothers Band's Duane Allman and Fleetwood Mac's Peter Green and Mick Fleetwood. Witnessing this mega jam was an experience almost too intense, leaving me drained of energy as I staggered home in the predawn hours.

There were so many other musical milestones I witnessed at the Fillmore East, too many to recount here. But it was a venue that made my work explode with exuberance and originality. The space and the lighting were exactly what I needed to capture the music as I had wanted to for so long. Many times as I photographed I would have to take a break and just let the pure joy of the music wash over me. I found that by doing this I came back even stronger with more ideas of how to utilize my equipment to its fullest potential, producing the many images that orchestrated my ideas on film. It was truly a sad day in 1971 when Bill Graham decided to close the Fillmore and move on. But what he achieved is remarkable: the greatest rock and roll venue in New York history.

Overleaf: Grateful Dead, Fillmore East, New York, February 1969.

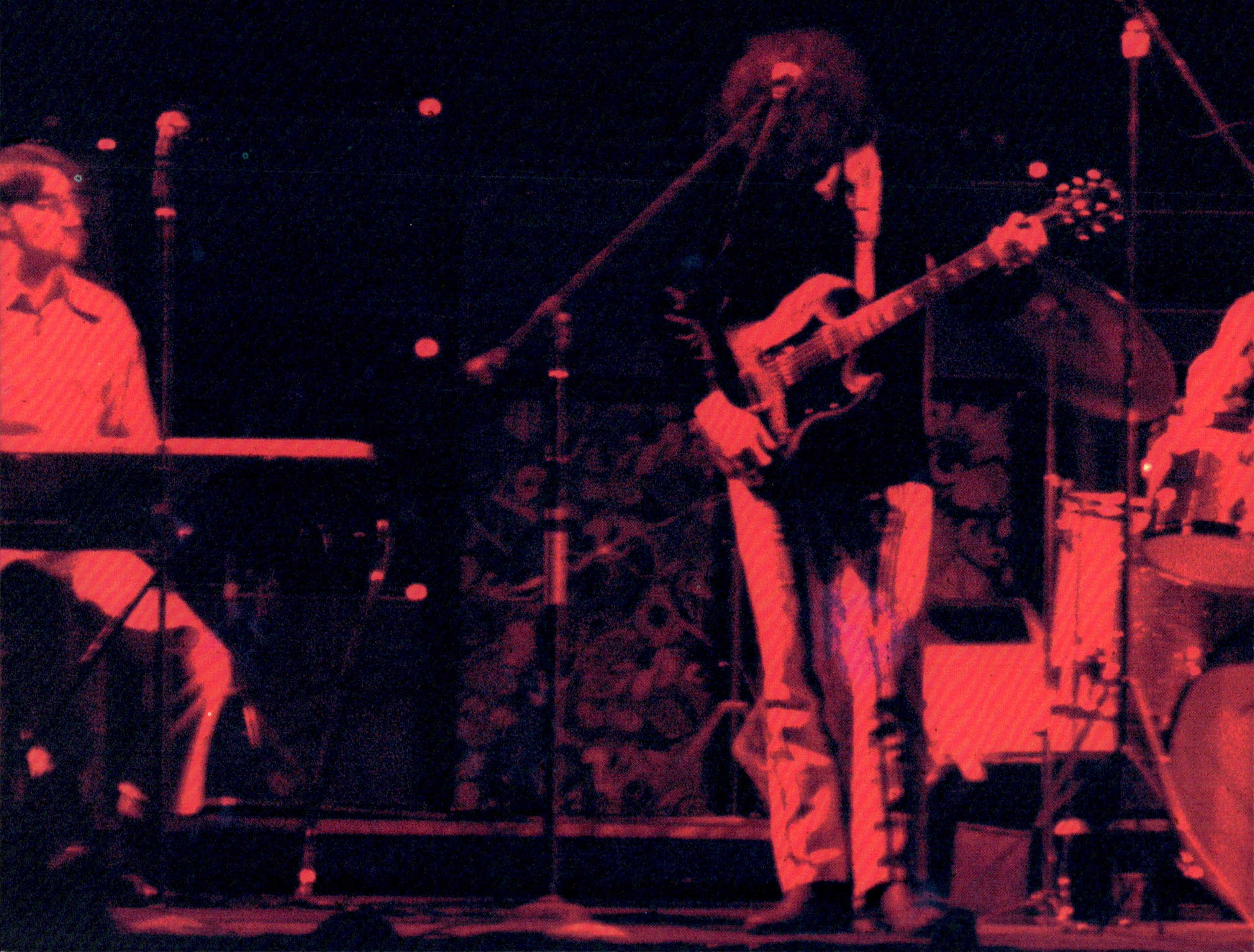

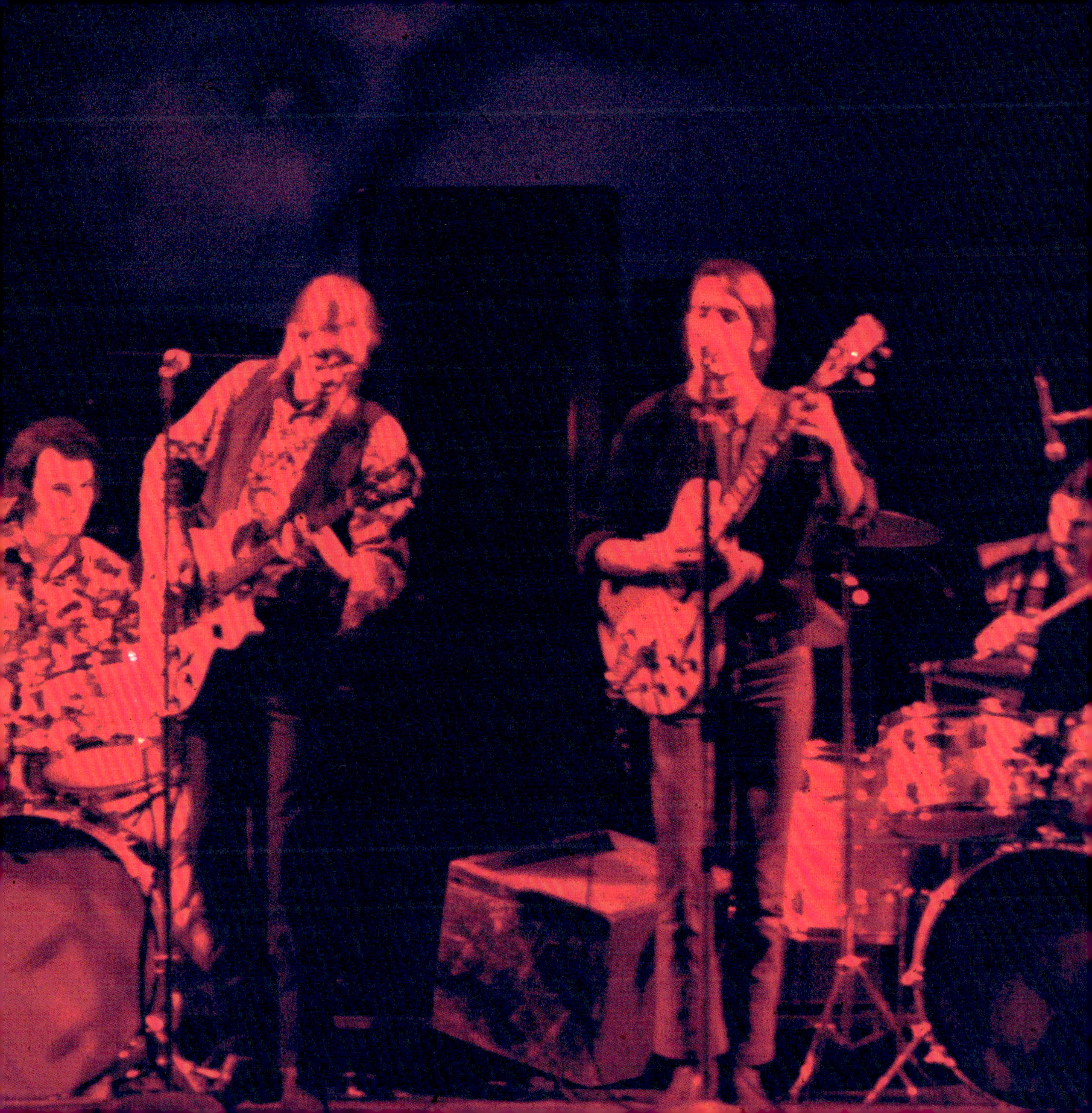

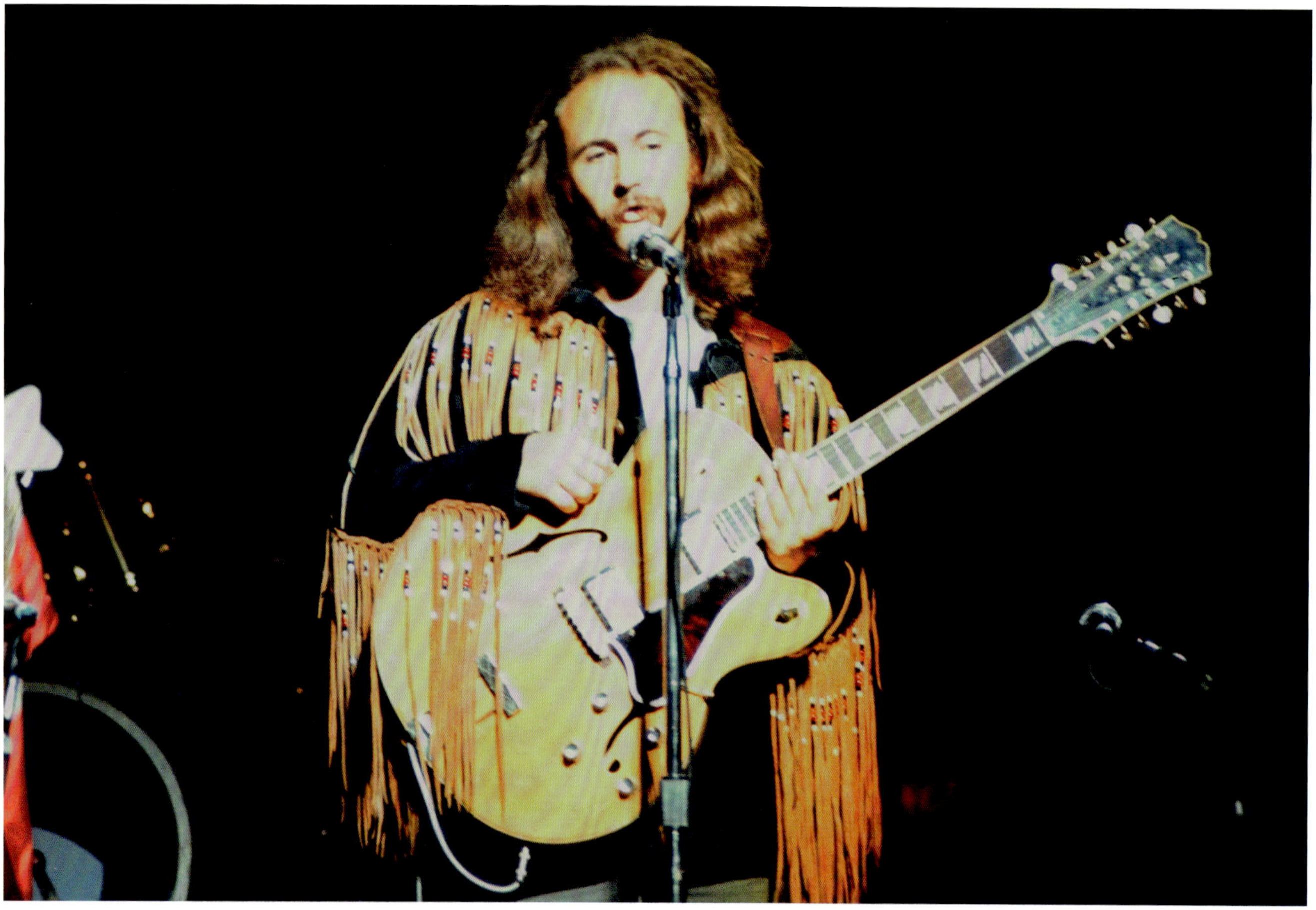

David Crosby of Crosby, Stills, Nash, and Young, Fillmore East, New York, September 1969.

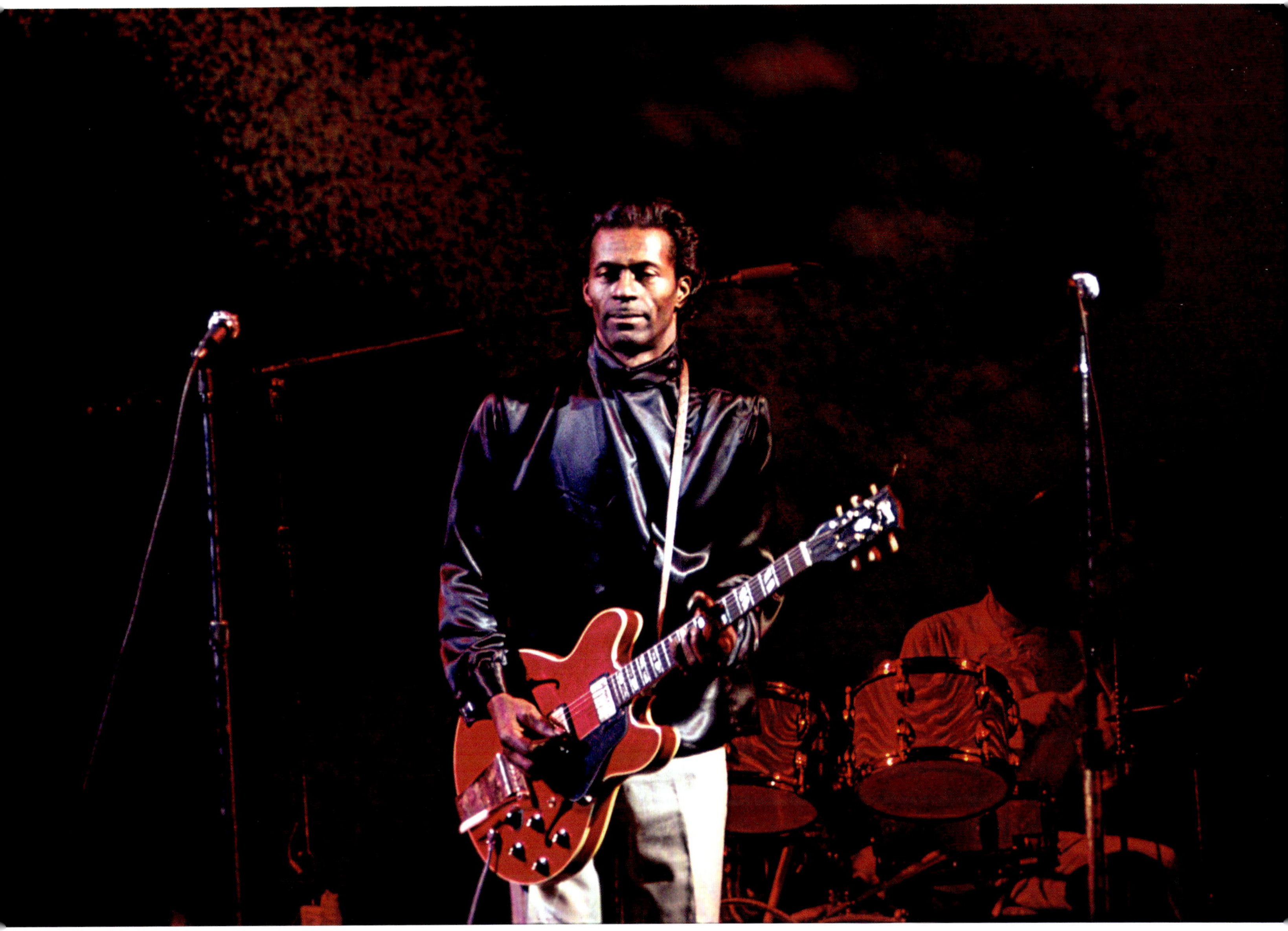

Chuck Berry, Fillmore East, New York, February 1969.

The Fillmore East was near perfection as a concert venue and laboratory for my experiments in color, light, exposure, and motion. . . . My senses of sight and sound were overwhelmed as the music flowed over me.

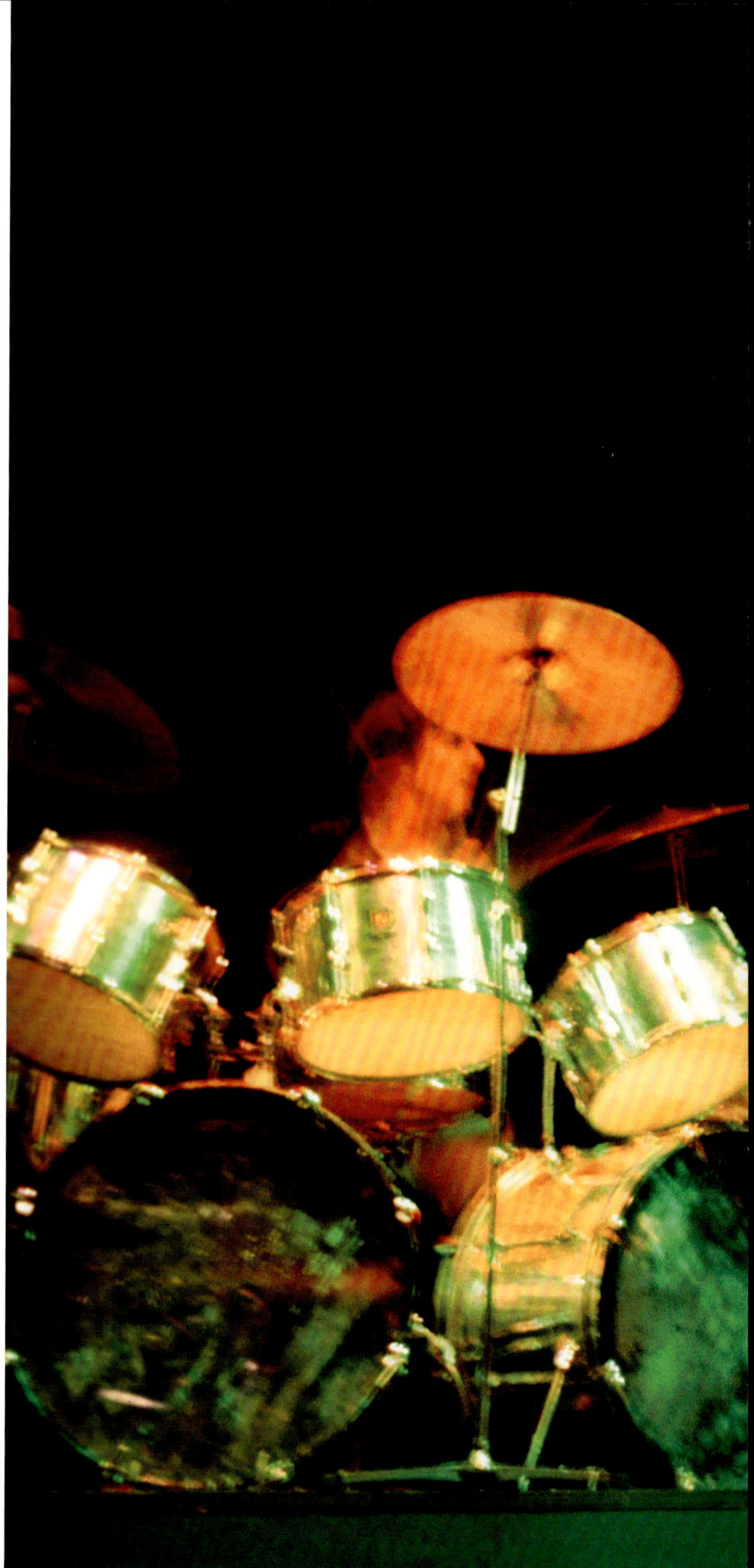

Keith Moon (left) and Pete Townshend (right) of the Who, Fillmore East, New York, May 1969.

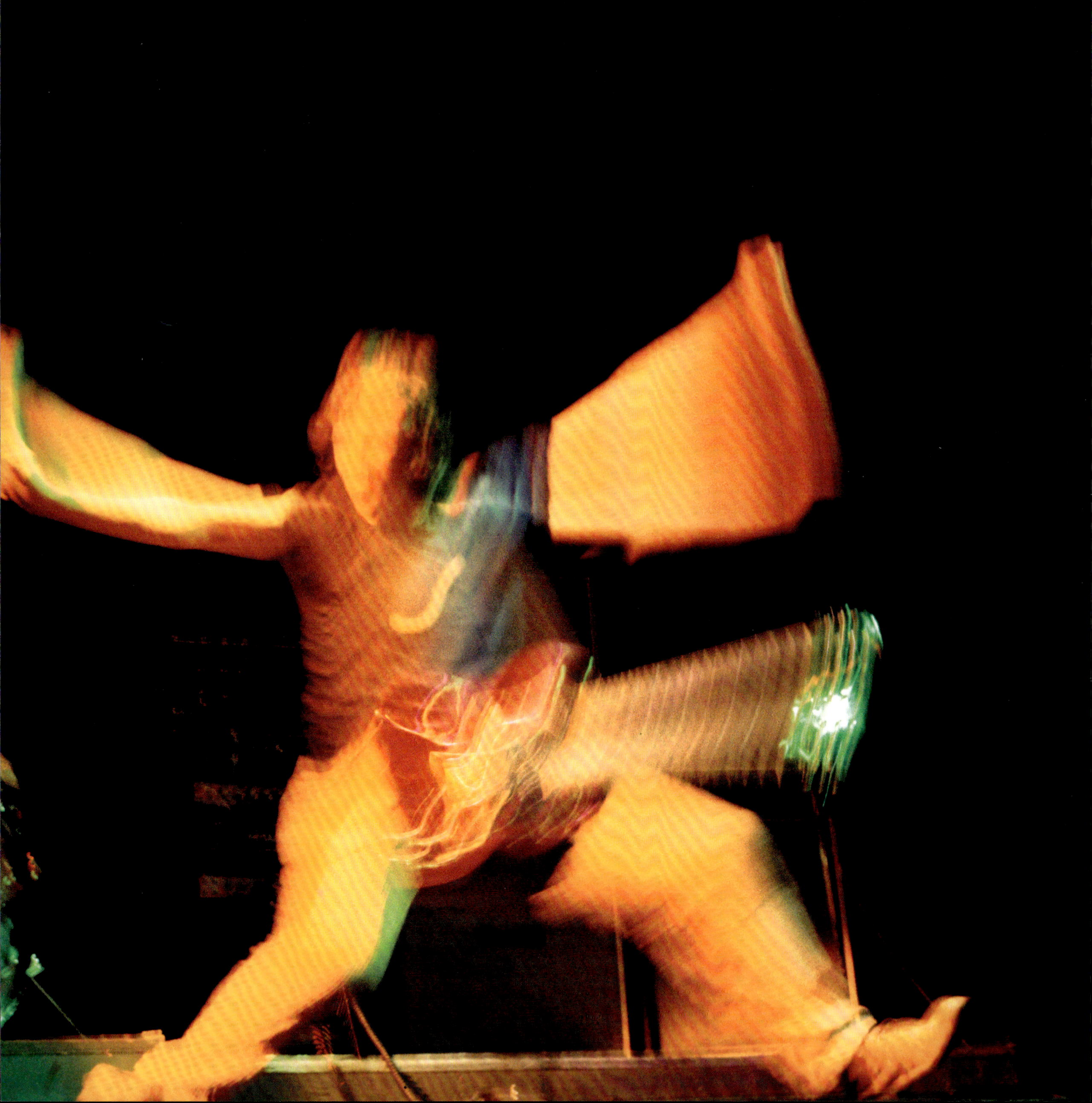

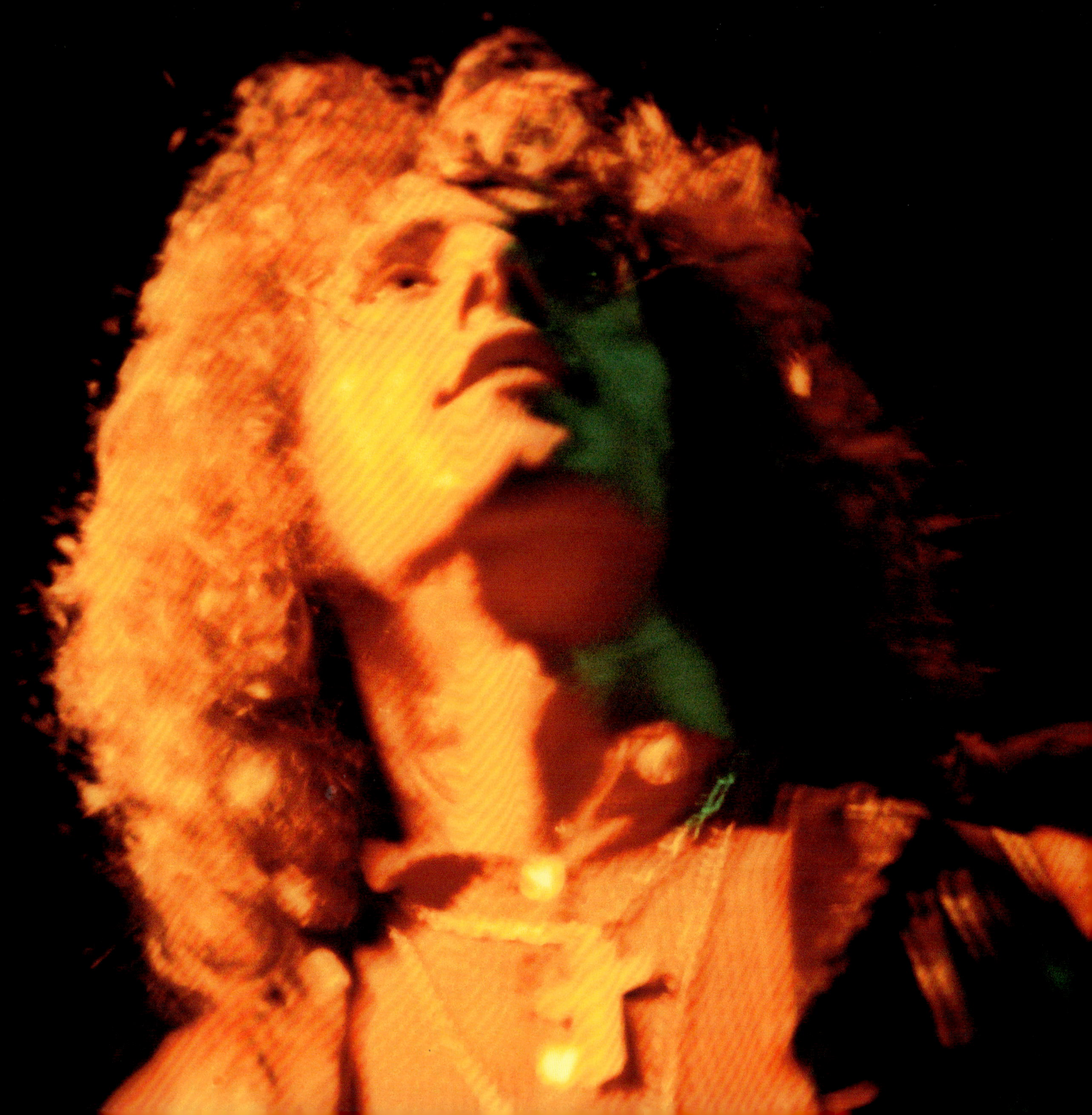

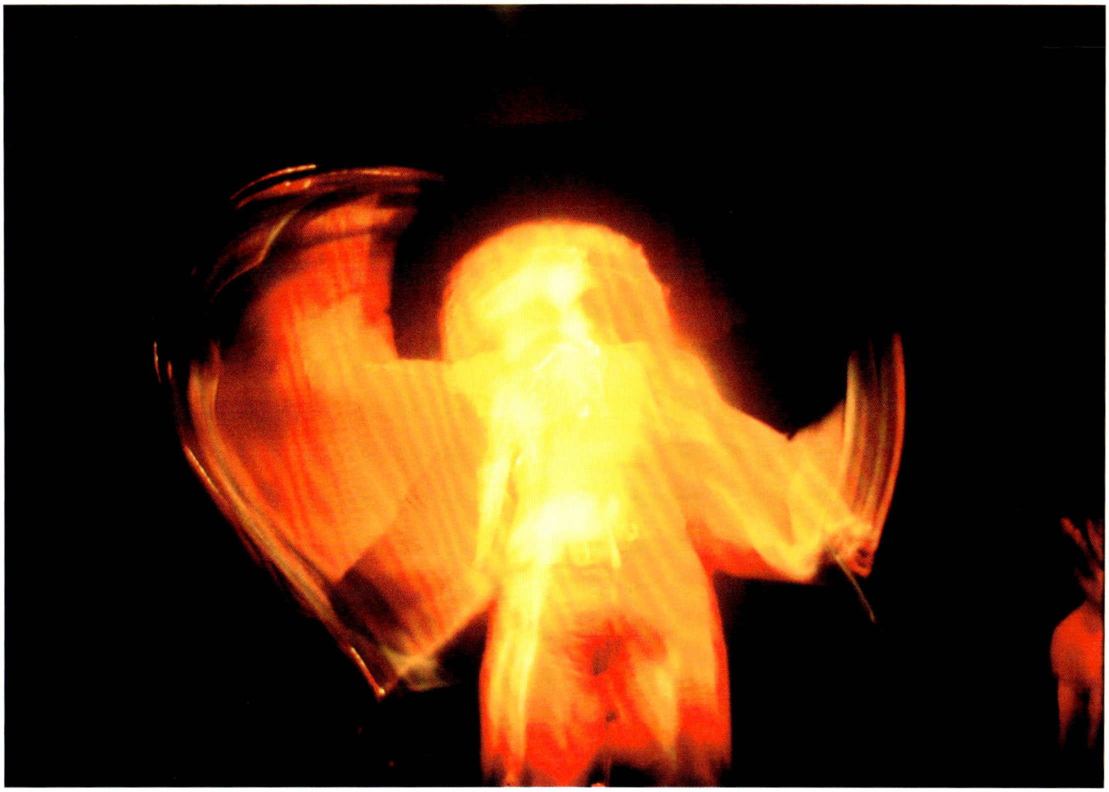

Roger Daltrey of the Who, infrared image, Fillmore East, New York, May 1969. *Opposite*: Roger Daltrey of the Who, Fillmore East, New York, May 1969.

Overleft: (left) Jack Casady of Jefferson Airplane, Fillmore East, New York, July 1970; (right) Alvin Lee of Ten Years After, Fillmore East, New York, April 1969.

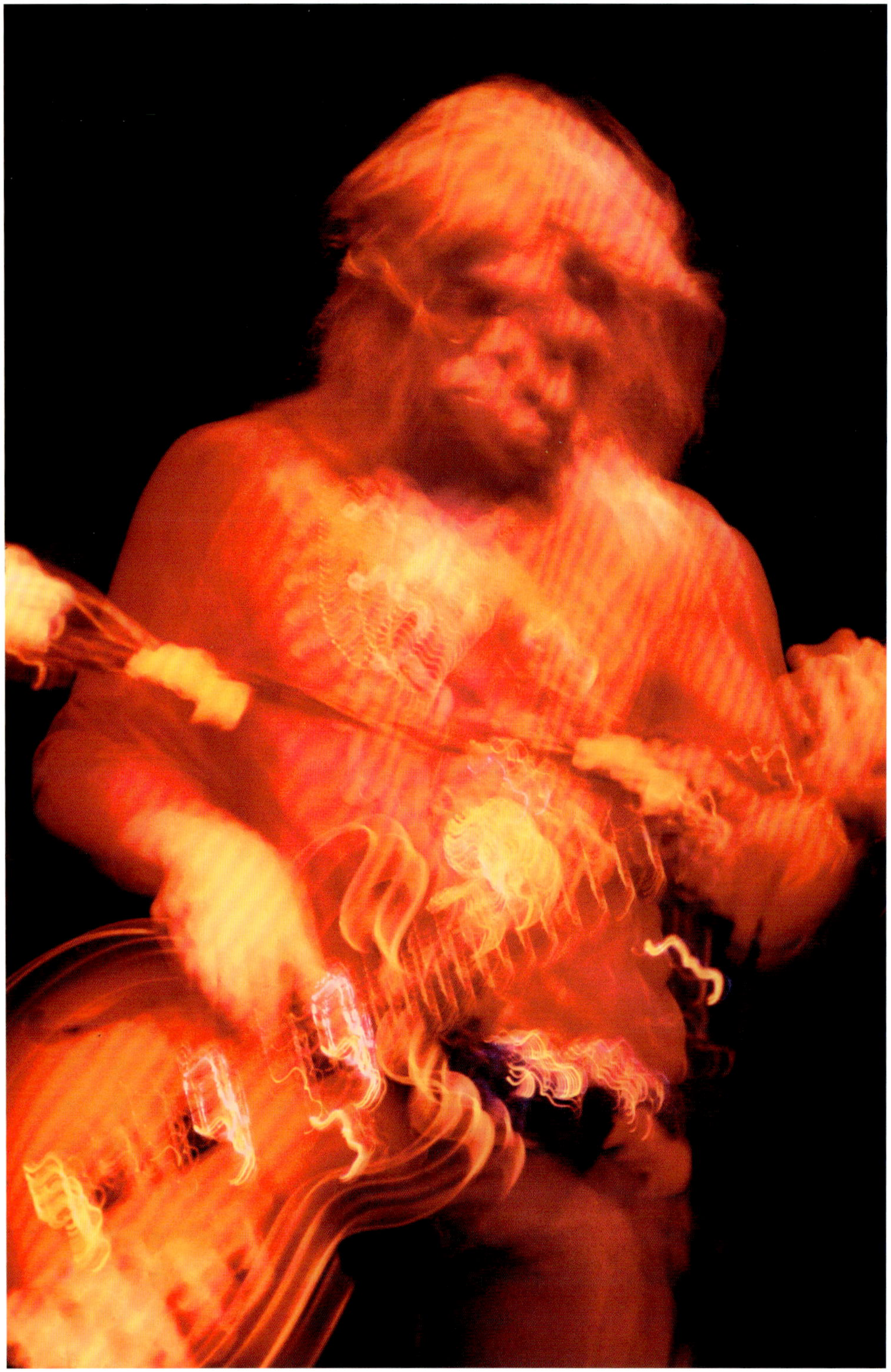

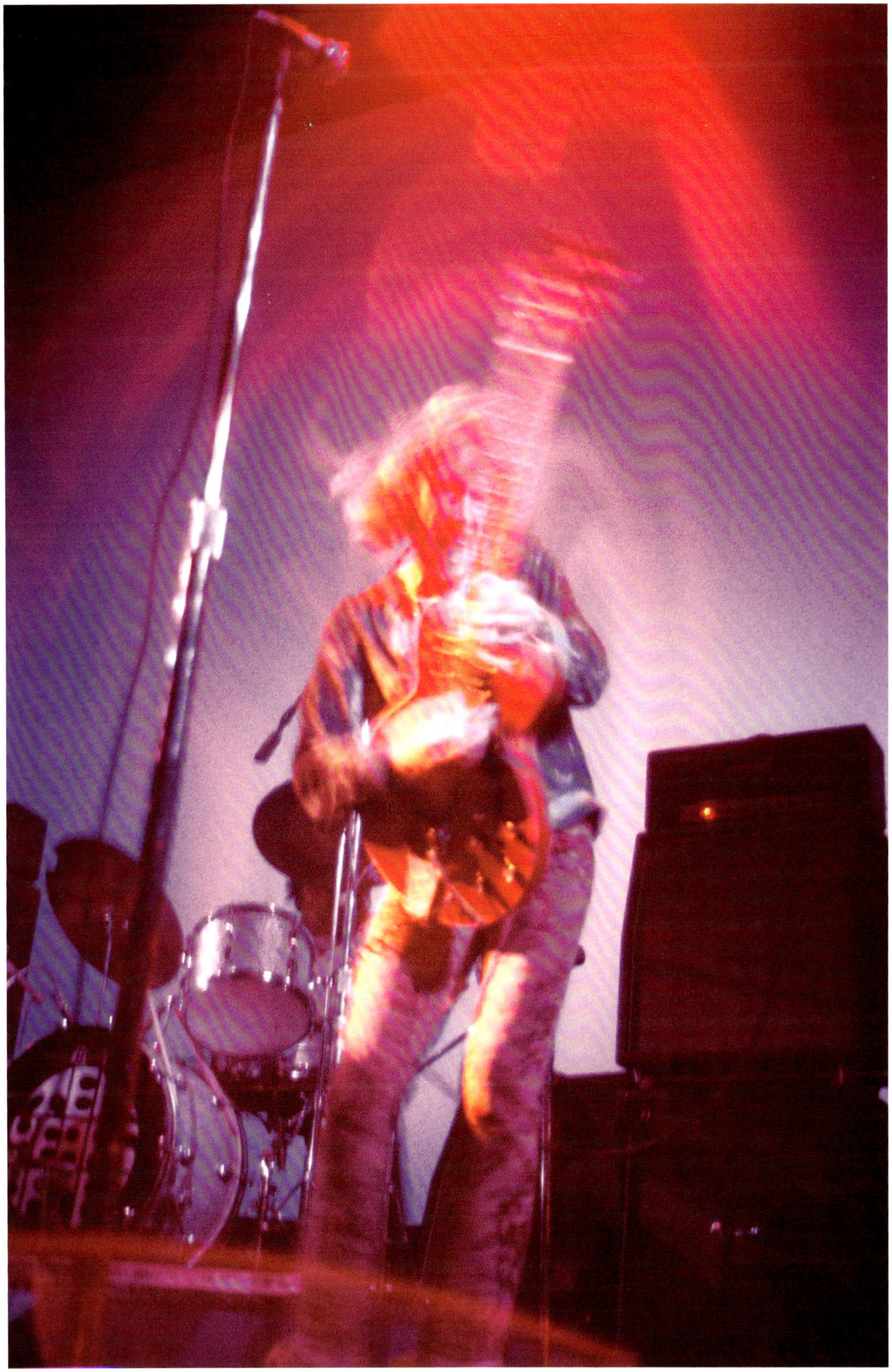

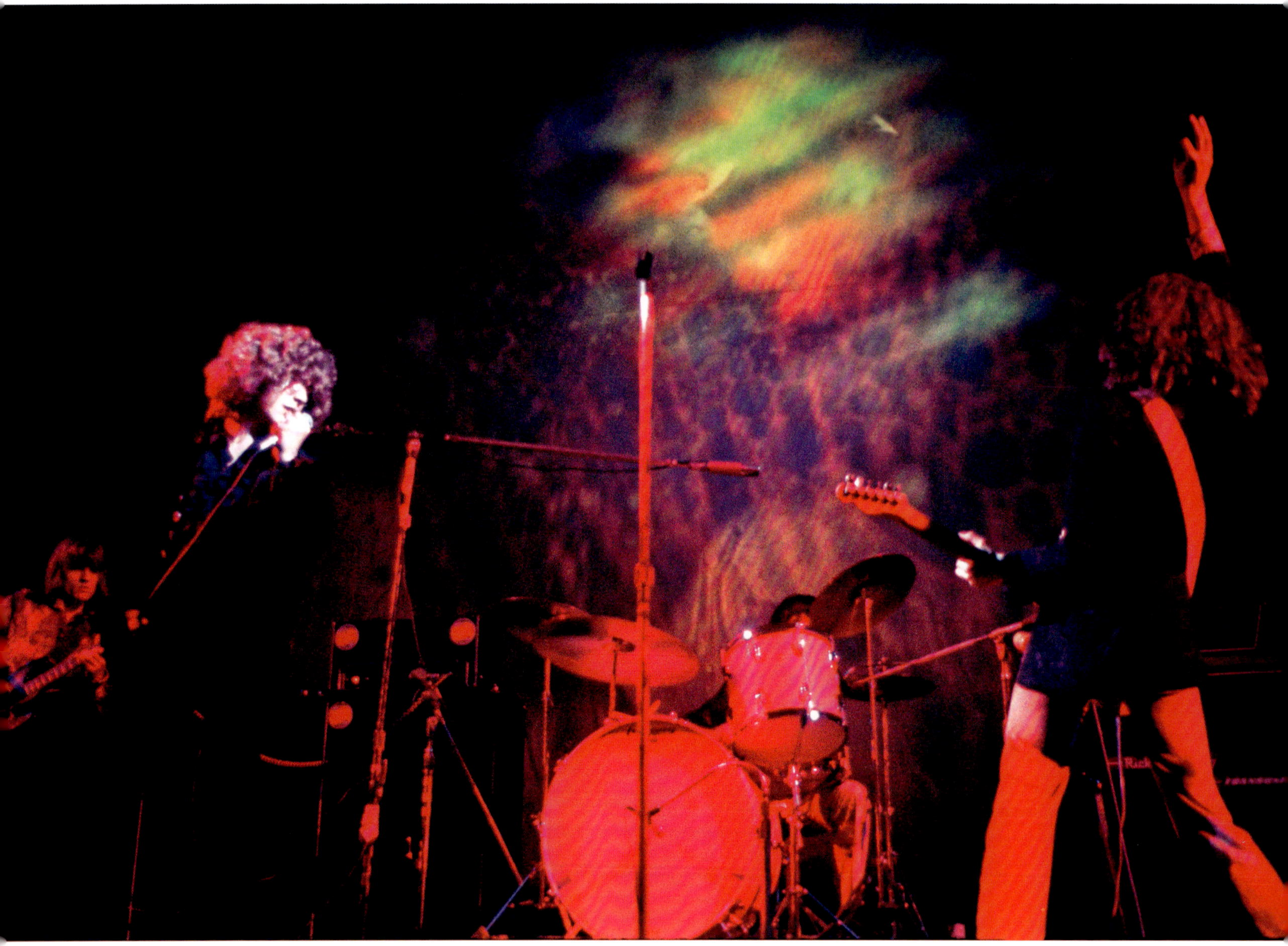

John Paul Jones (left), Robert Plant (center), and Jimmy Page (right) of Led Zeppelin, Fillmore East, New York, January 1969. *Opposite*: Robert Plant of Led Zeppelin, Fillmore East, New York, January 1969.

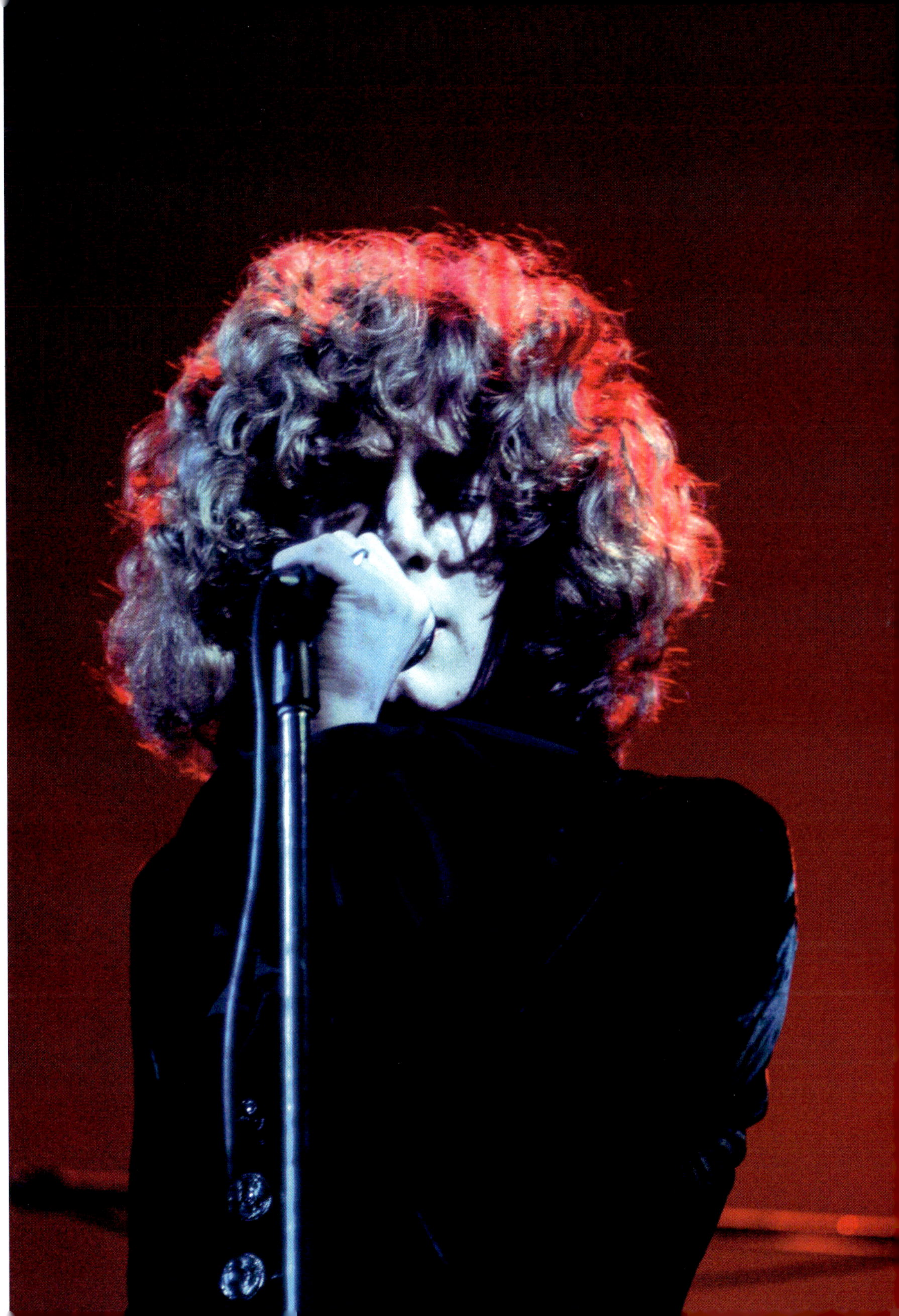

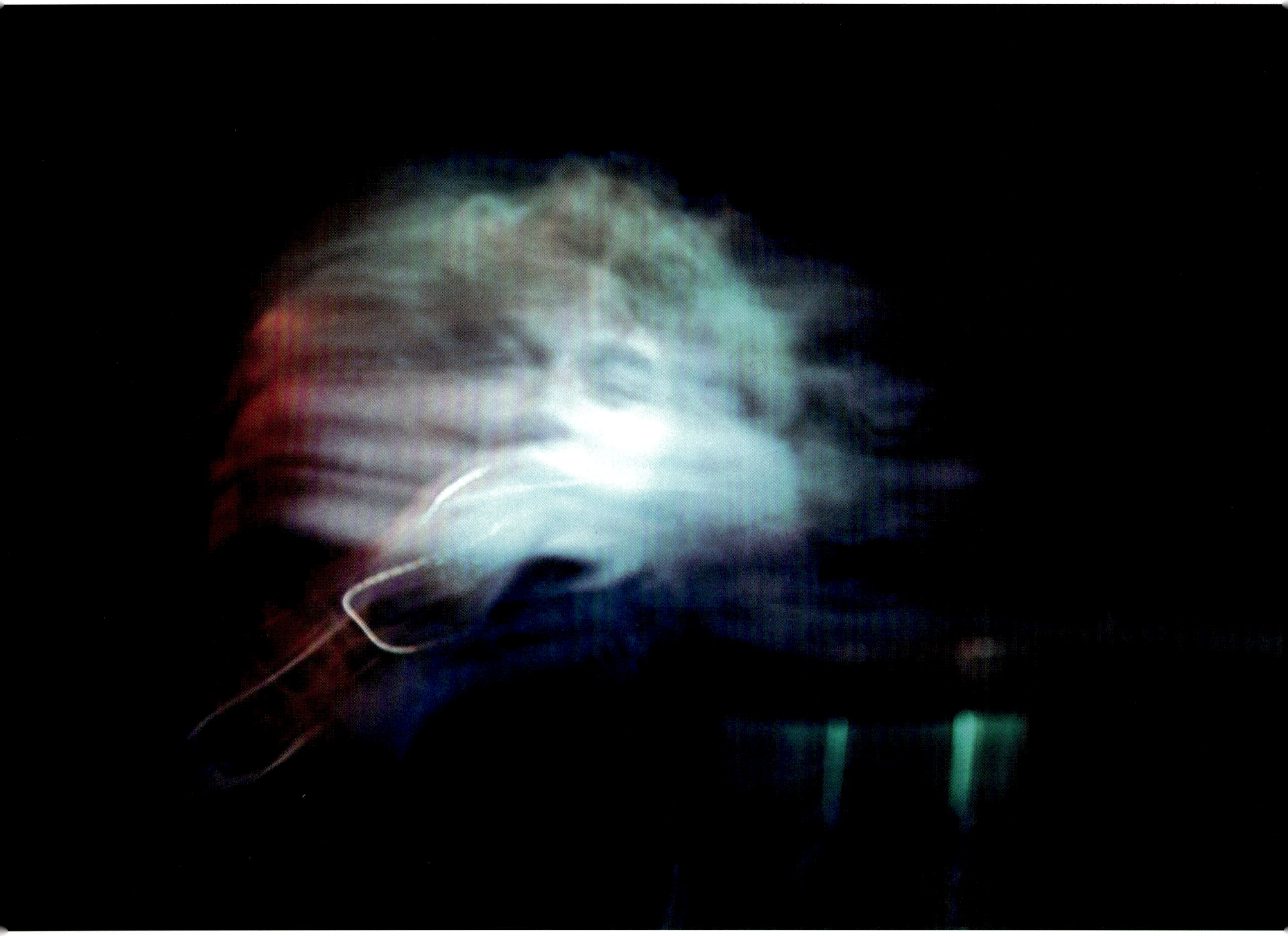

Robert Plant of Led Zeppelin, Fillmore East, New York, January 1969.

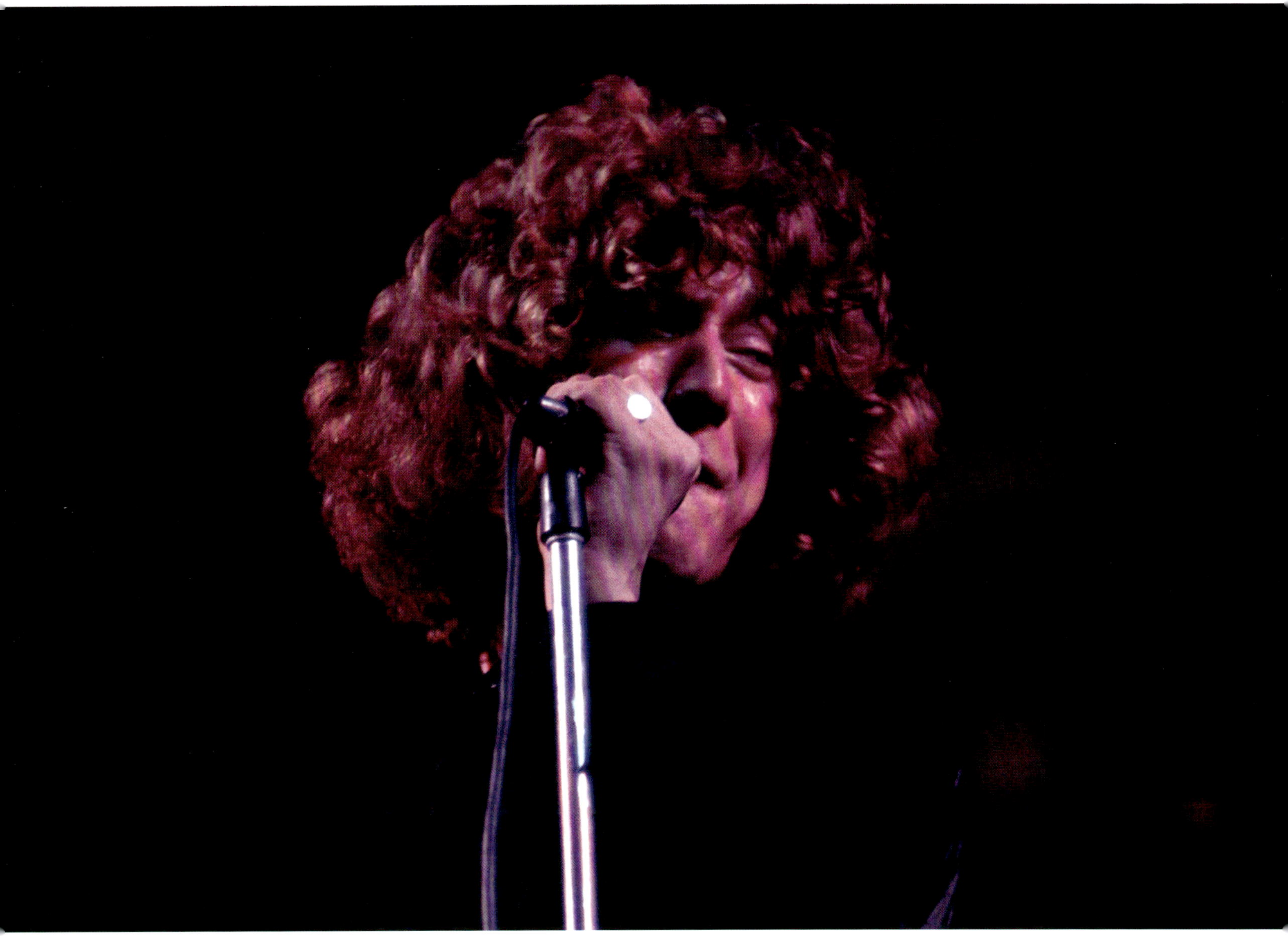

Robert Plant of Led Zeppelin, Fillmore East, New York, January 1969.

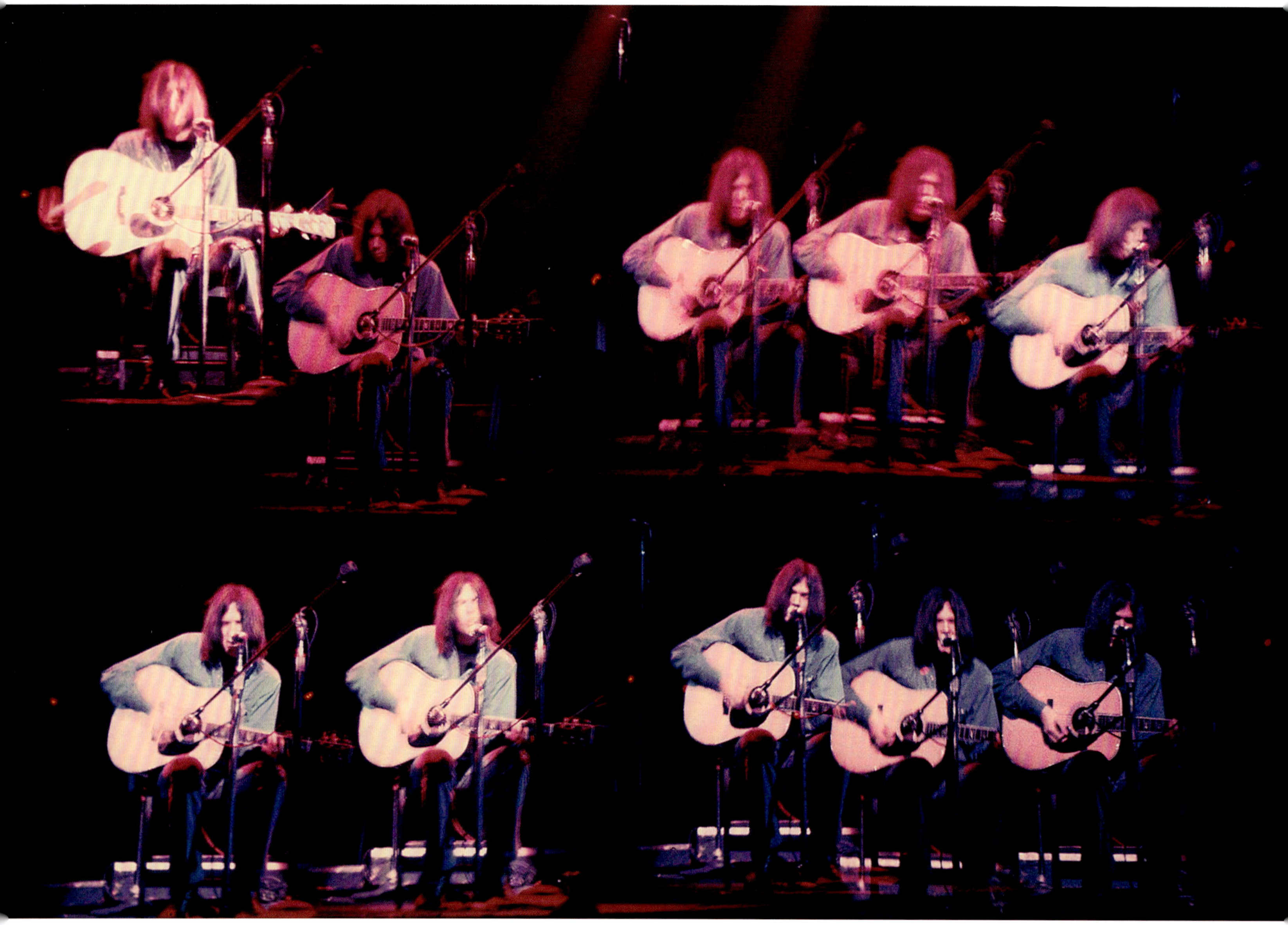

Neil Young, Fillmore East, New York, March 1970.

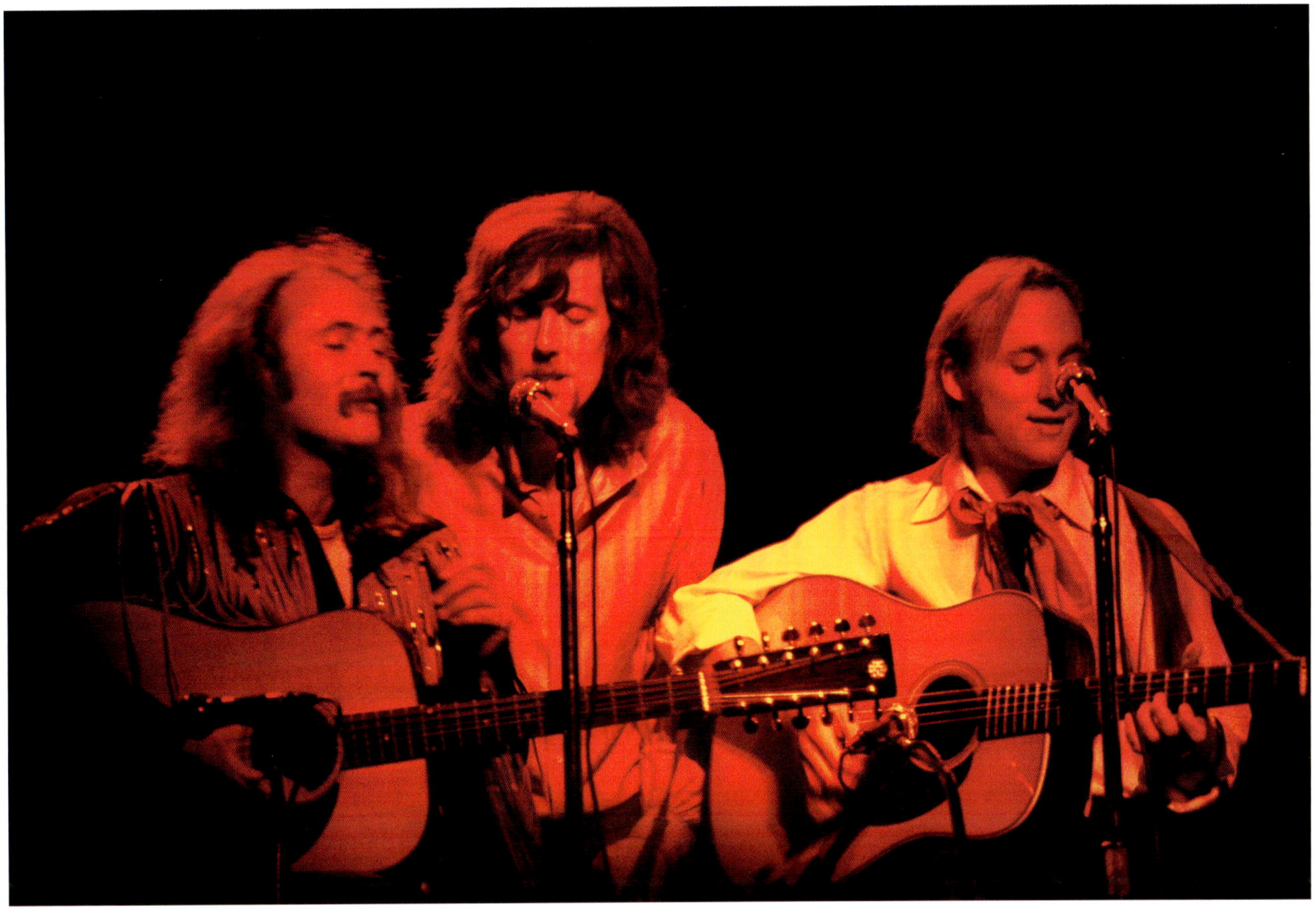

David Crosby, Graham Nash, and Stephen Stills, Fillmore East,
New York, September 1969.

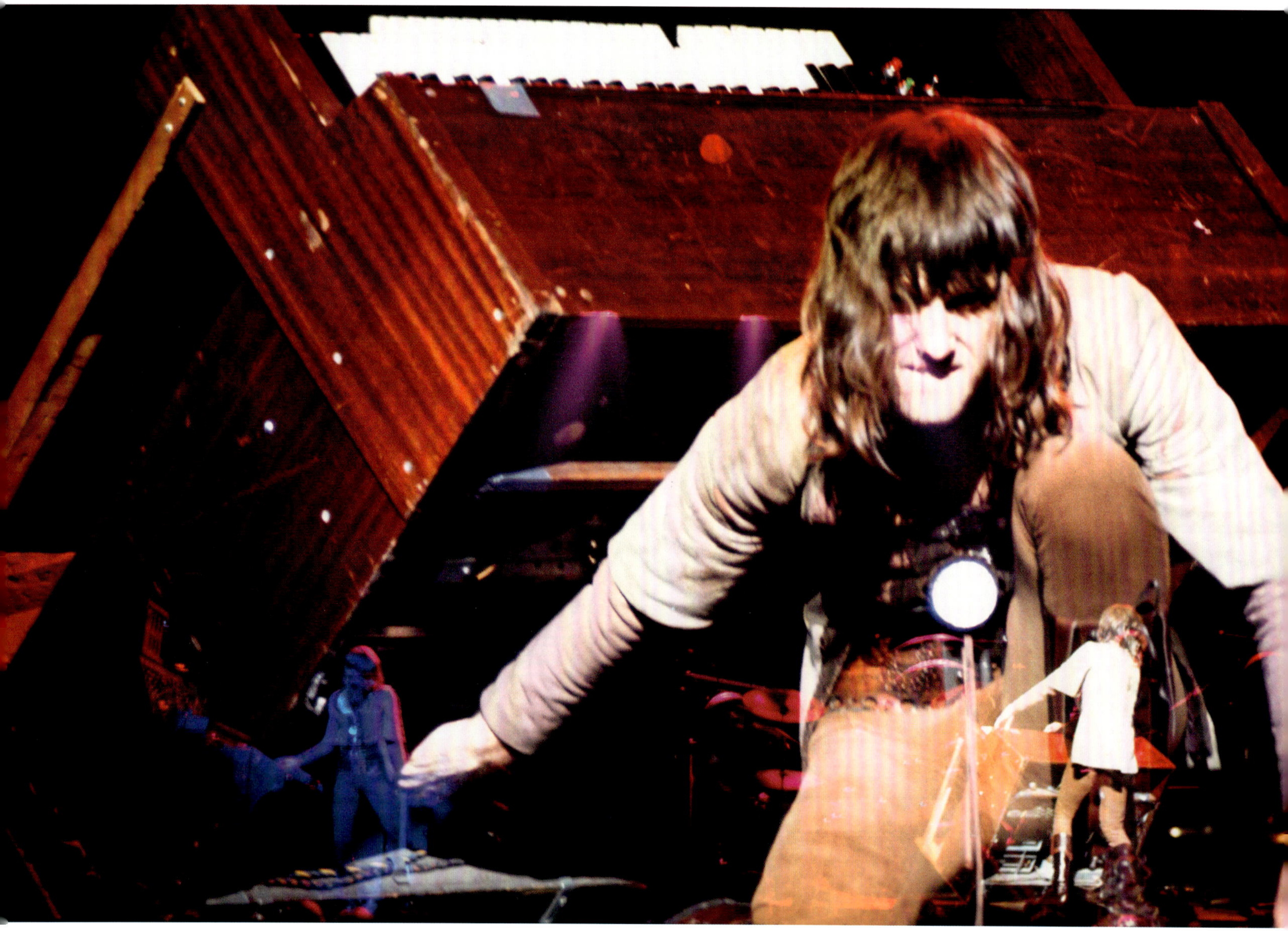

Keith Emerson of Emerson, Lake & Palmer, Fillmore East, New York, May 1971.

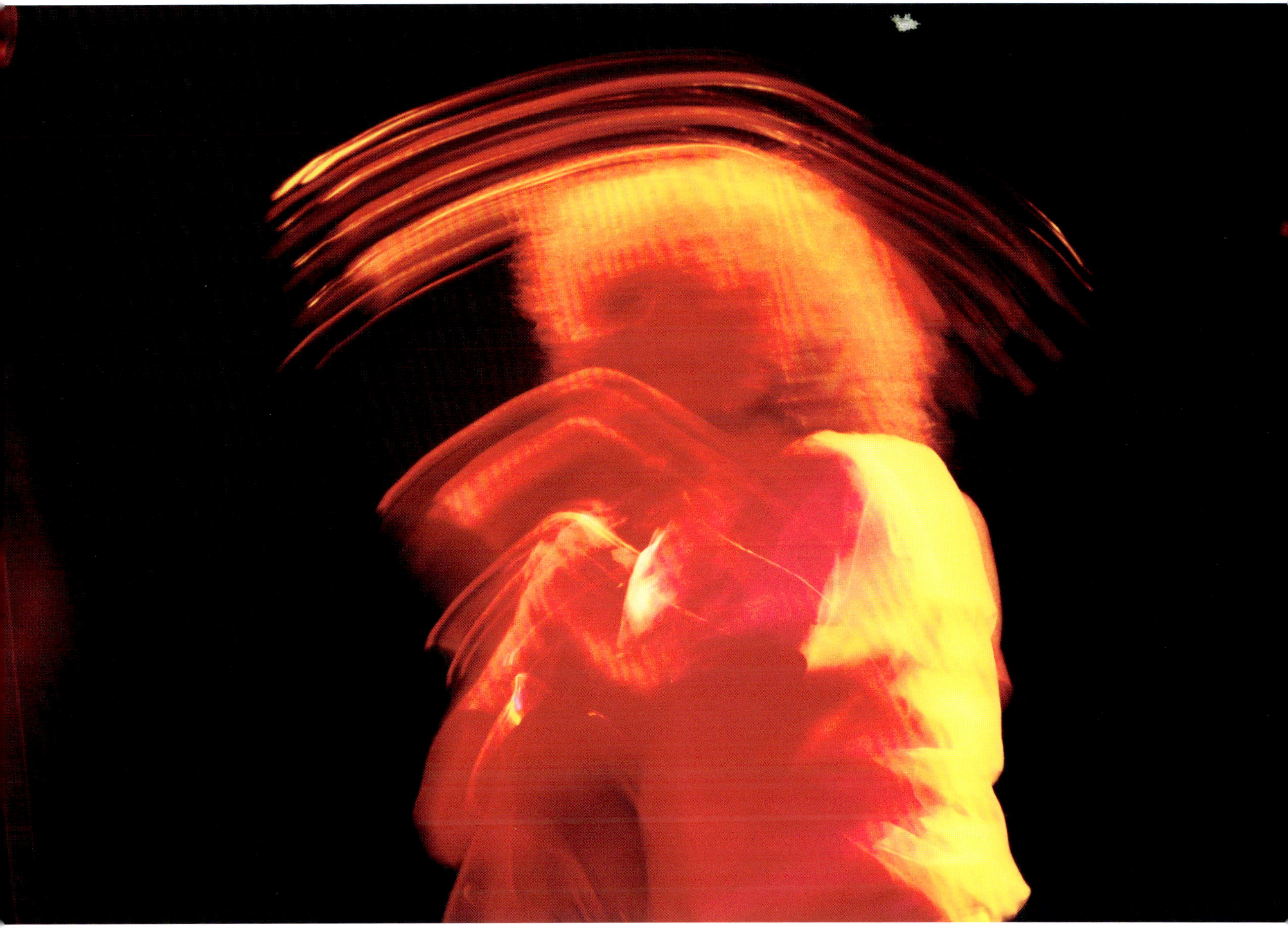

Barry Melton of Country Joe and the Fish, Fillmore East, New York, September 1969.

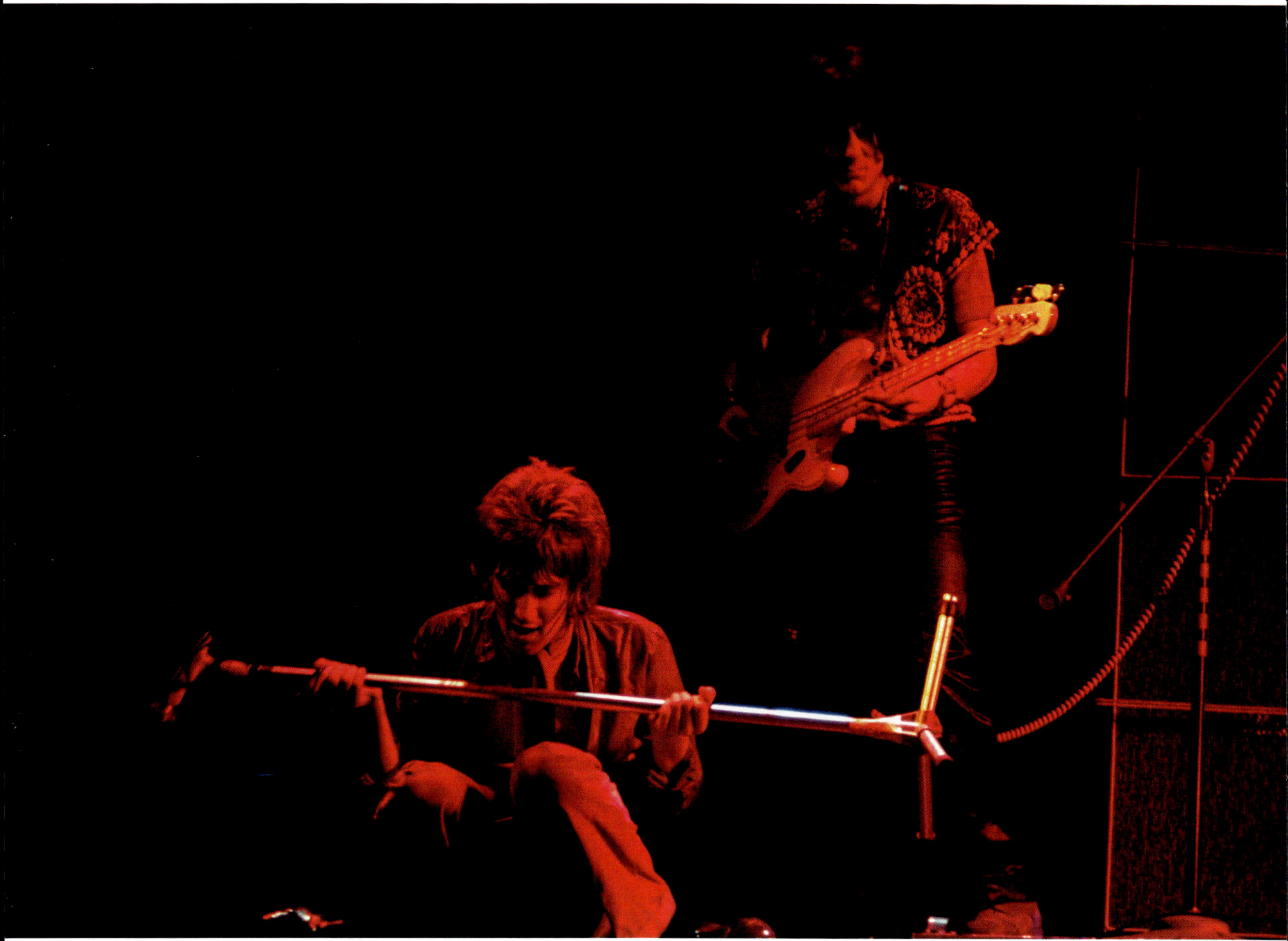

Rod Stewart (left) and Ron Wood (right) of The Jeff Beck Group, Fillmore East, New York, October 1969.

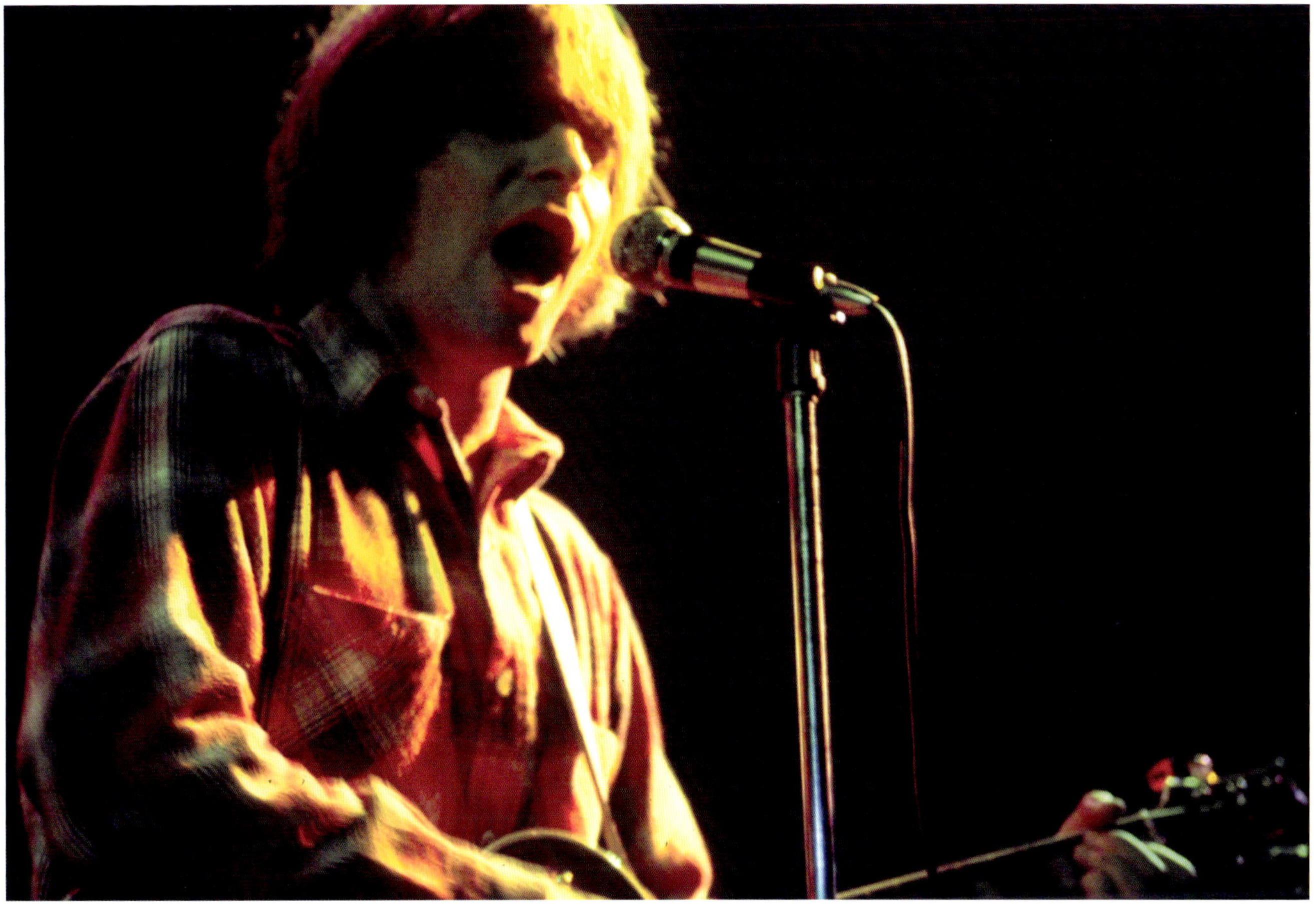

John Fogerty of Credence Clearwater Revival, Fillmore East, New York, March 1969.

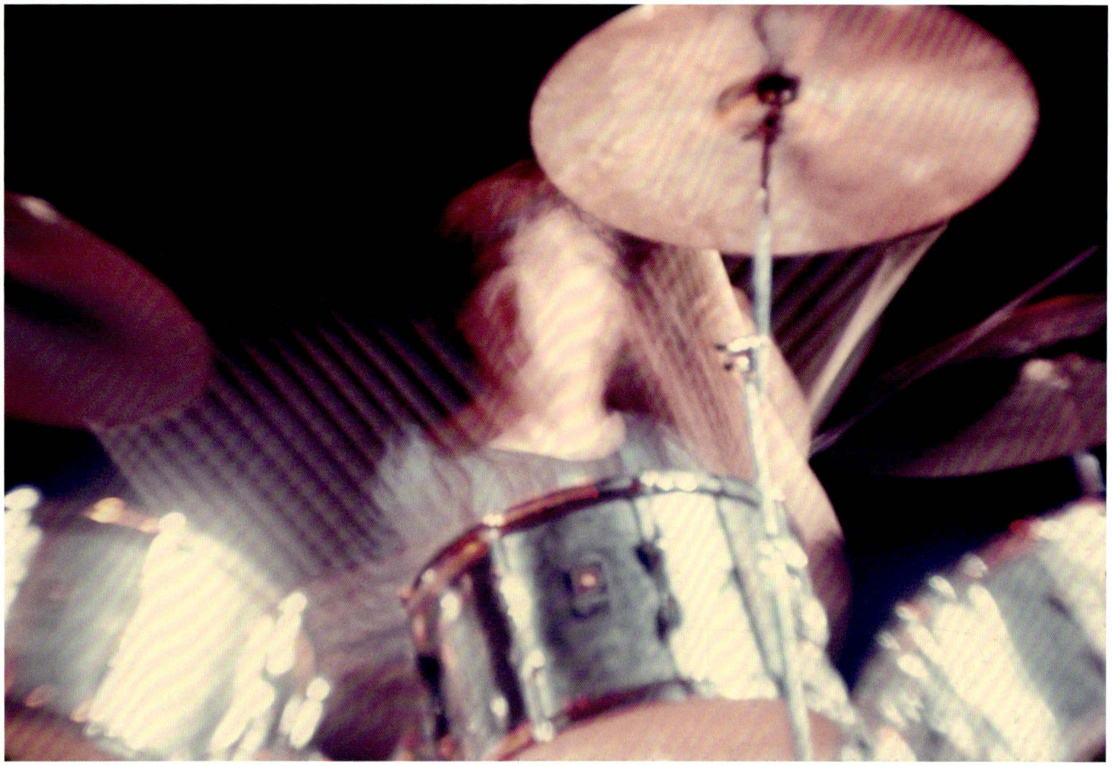

Keith Moon of the Who, Fillmore East, New York, May 1969.

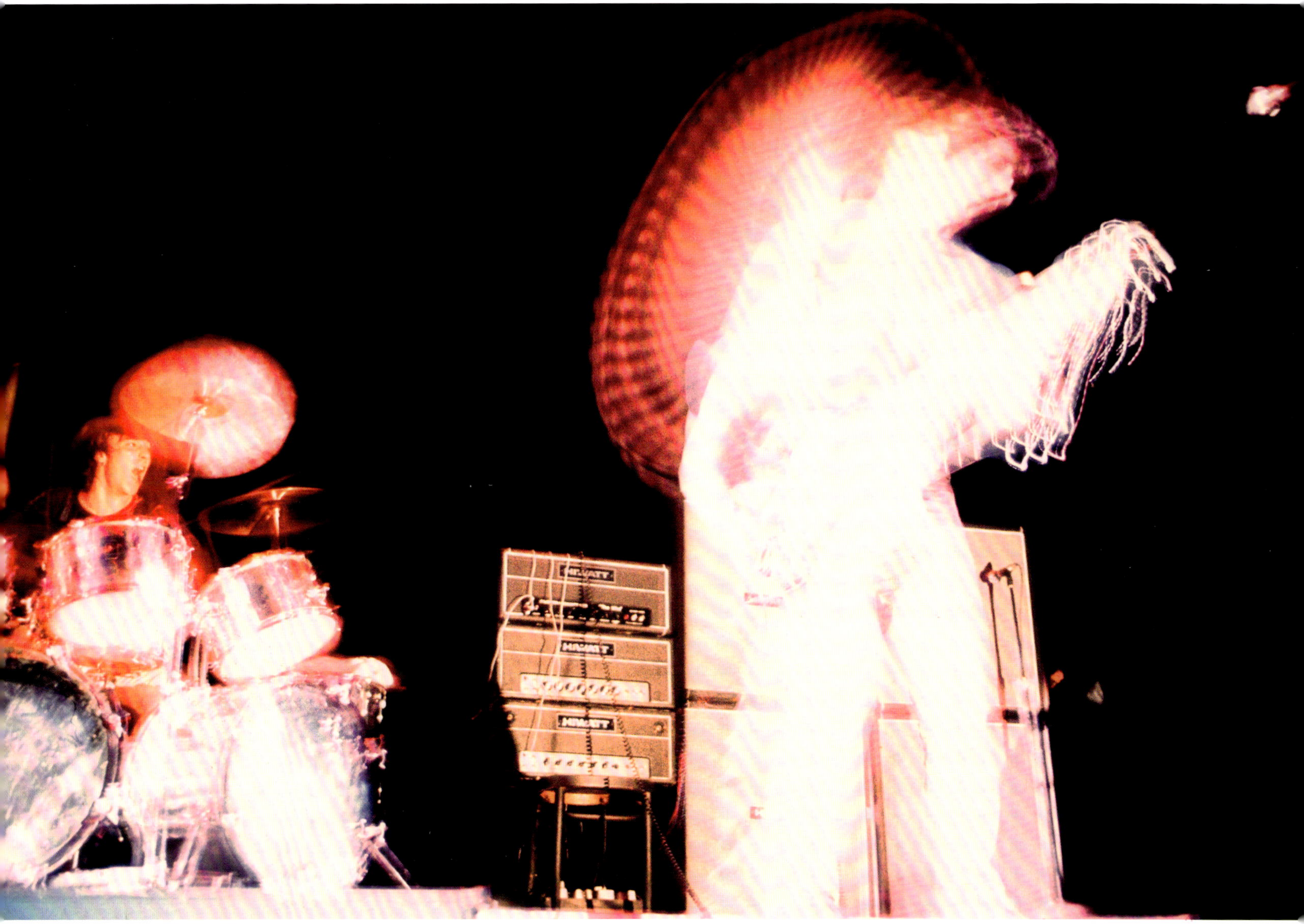

Keith Moon and Pete Townsend of the Who, Fillmore East, New York, May 1969.

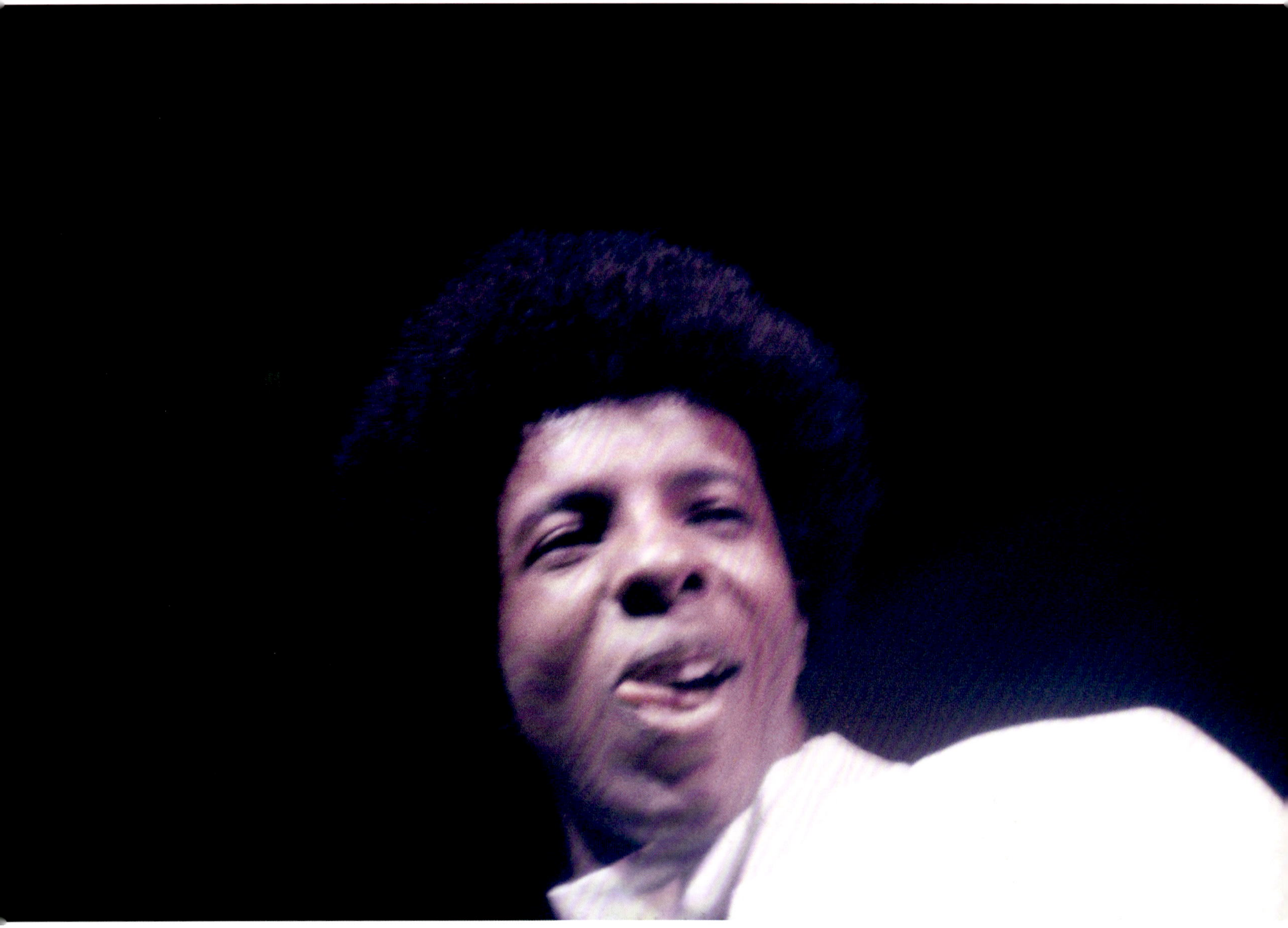

Sylvester "Sly" Stone, Fillmore East, New York, May 1968.

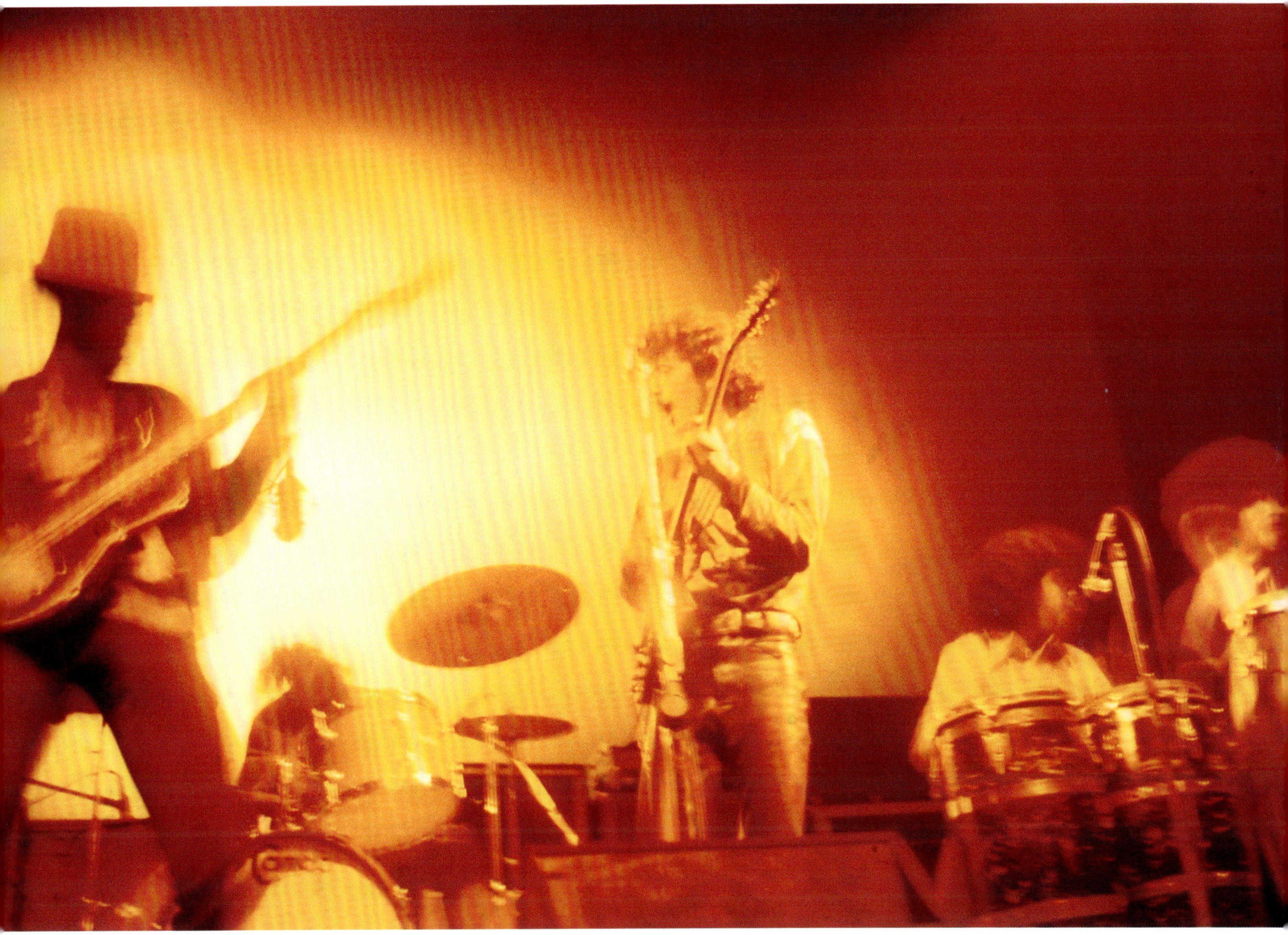

David Brown, Michael Shrieve, Carlos Santana, Jose Areas, and Michael Carabello of Santana, Fillmore East, New York, November 1969.

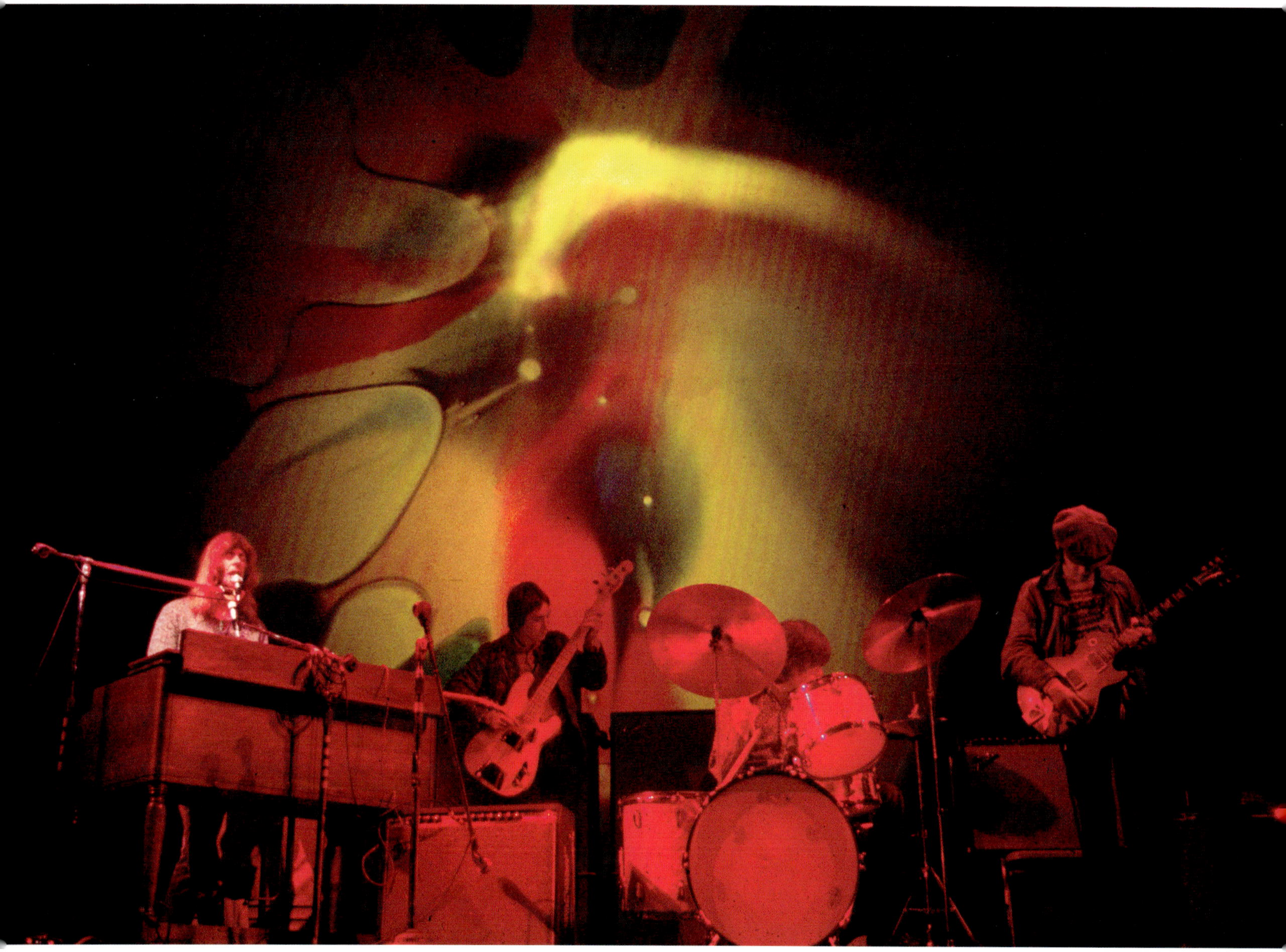

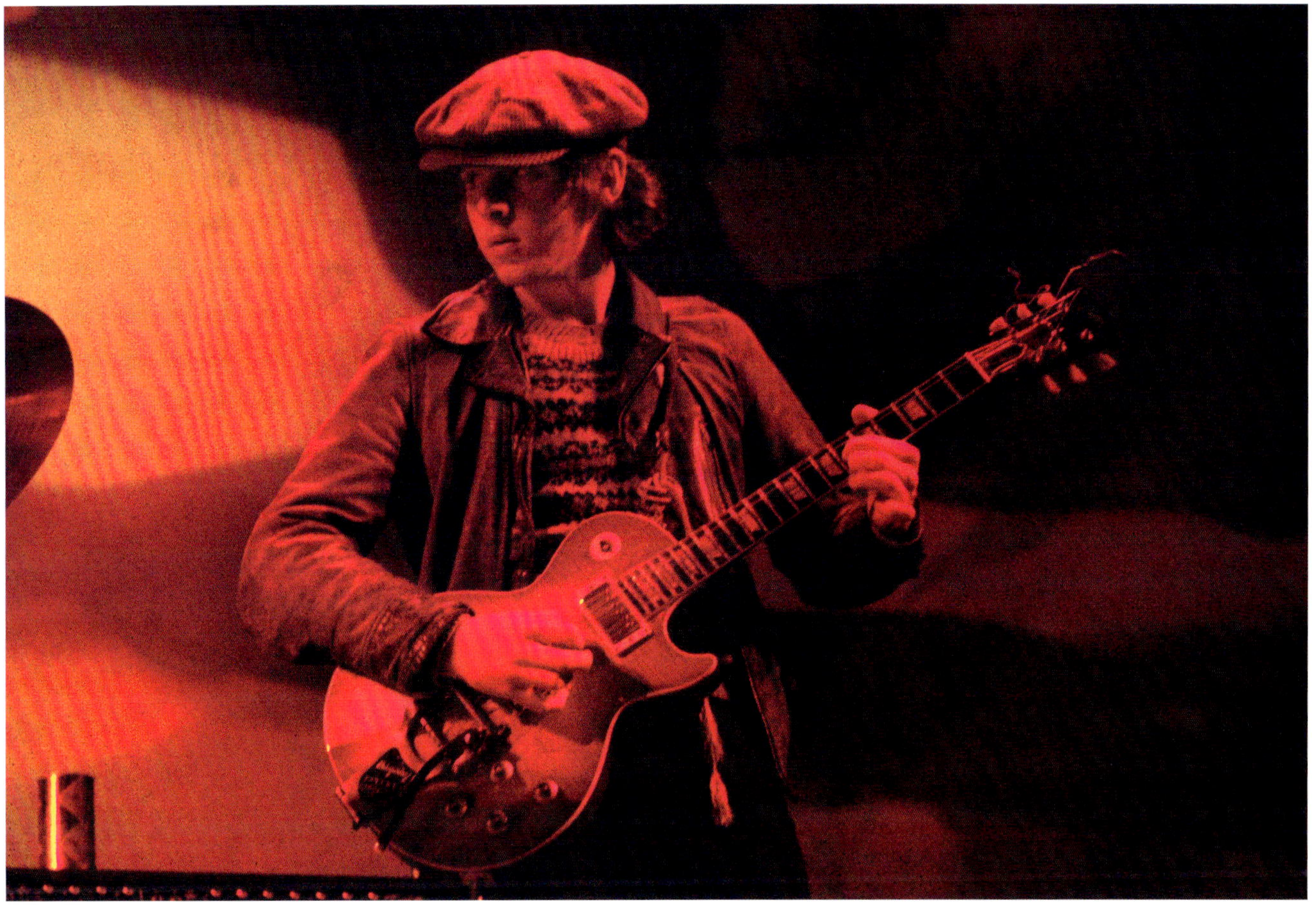

Opposite: John Mayall, Steve Thompson, and Mick Taylor with John Mayall's Bluesbreakers, Fillmore East, New York, October 1969. *Above:* Mick Taylor with John Mayall's Bluesbreakers, Fillmore East, New York, October 1969.

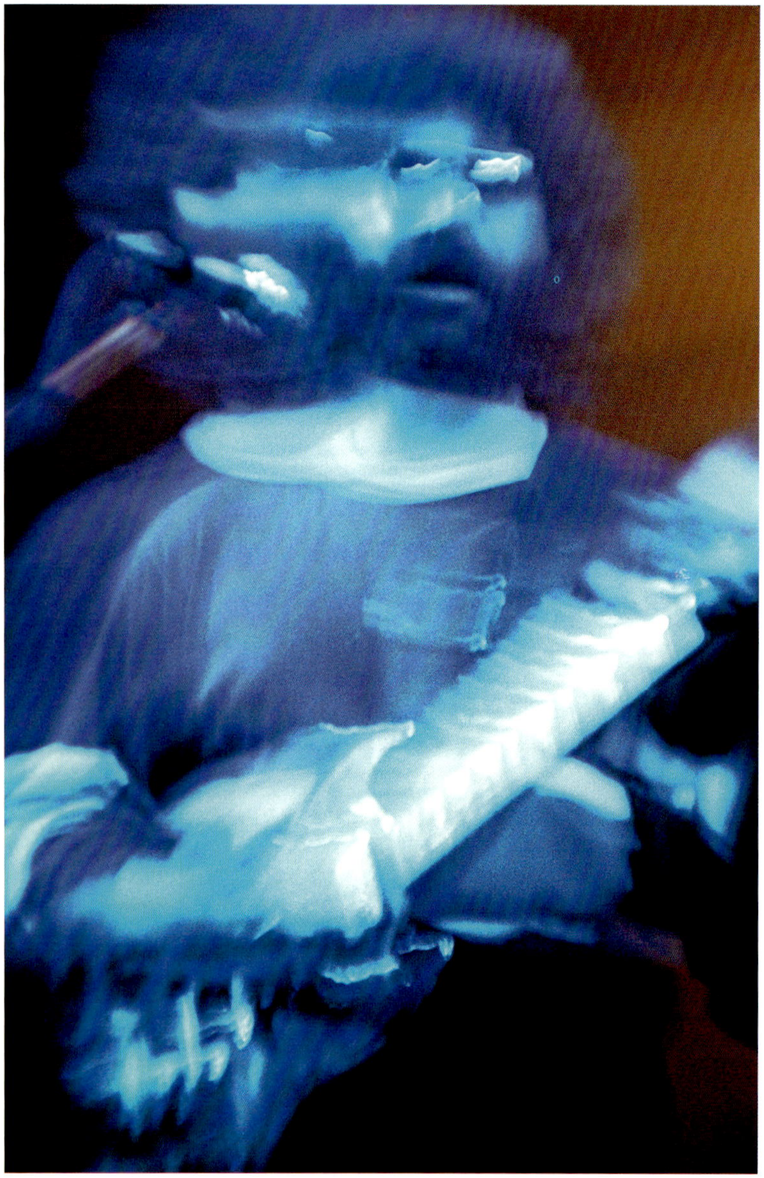

Jerry Garcia of the Grateful Dead, Fillmore East, New York, June 1969.

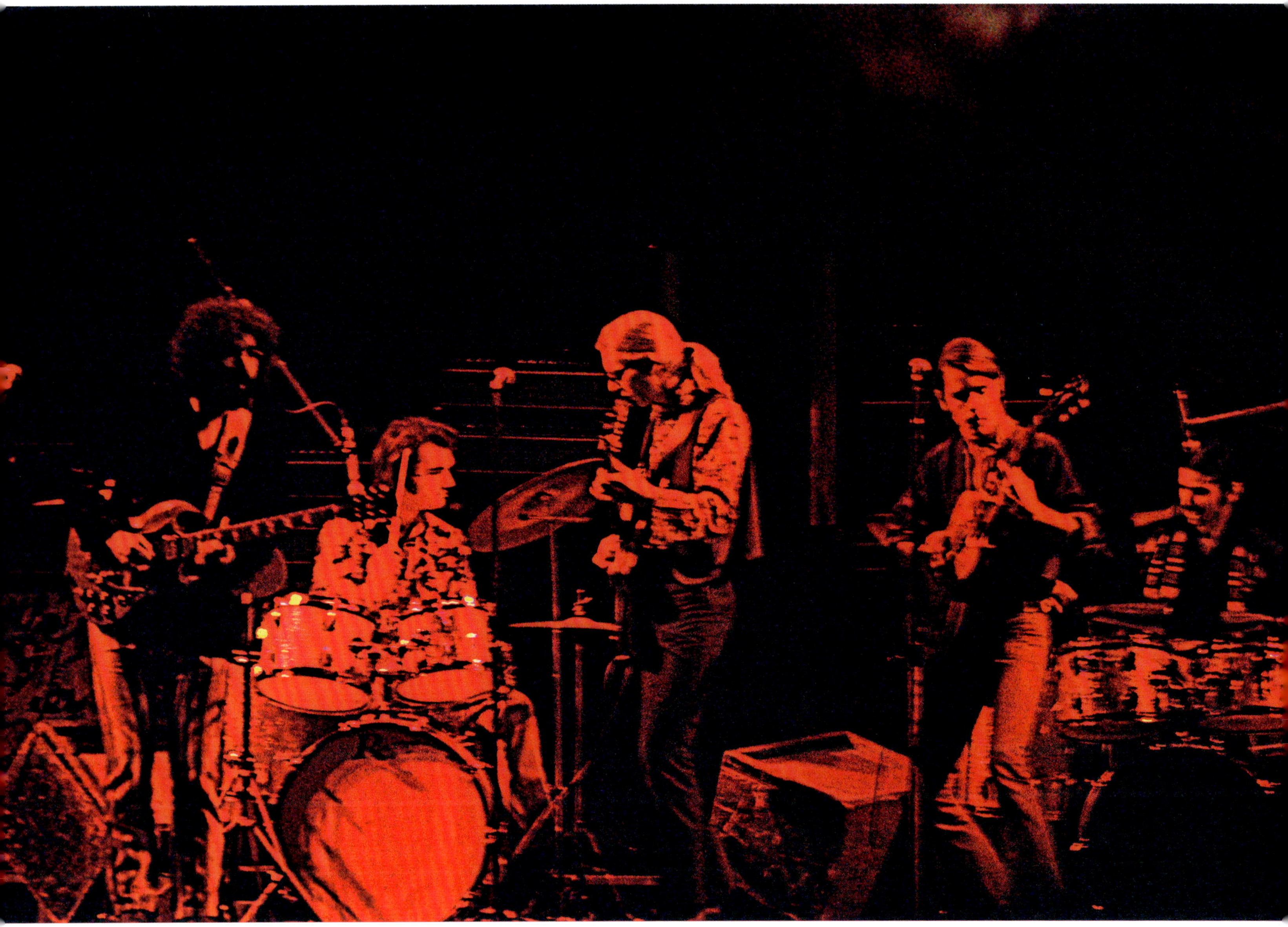

Grateful Dead, Fillmore East, New York, February 1969.

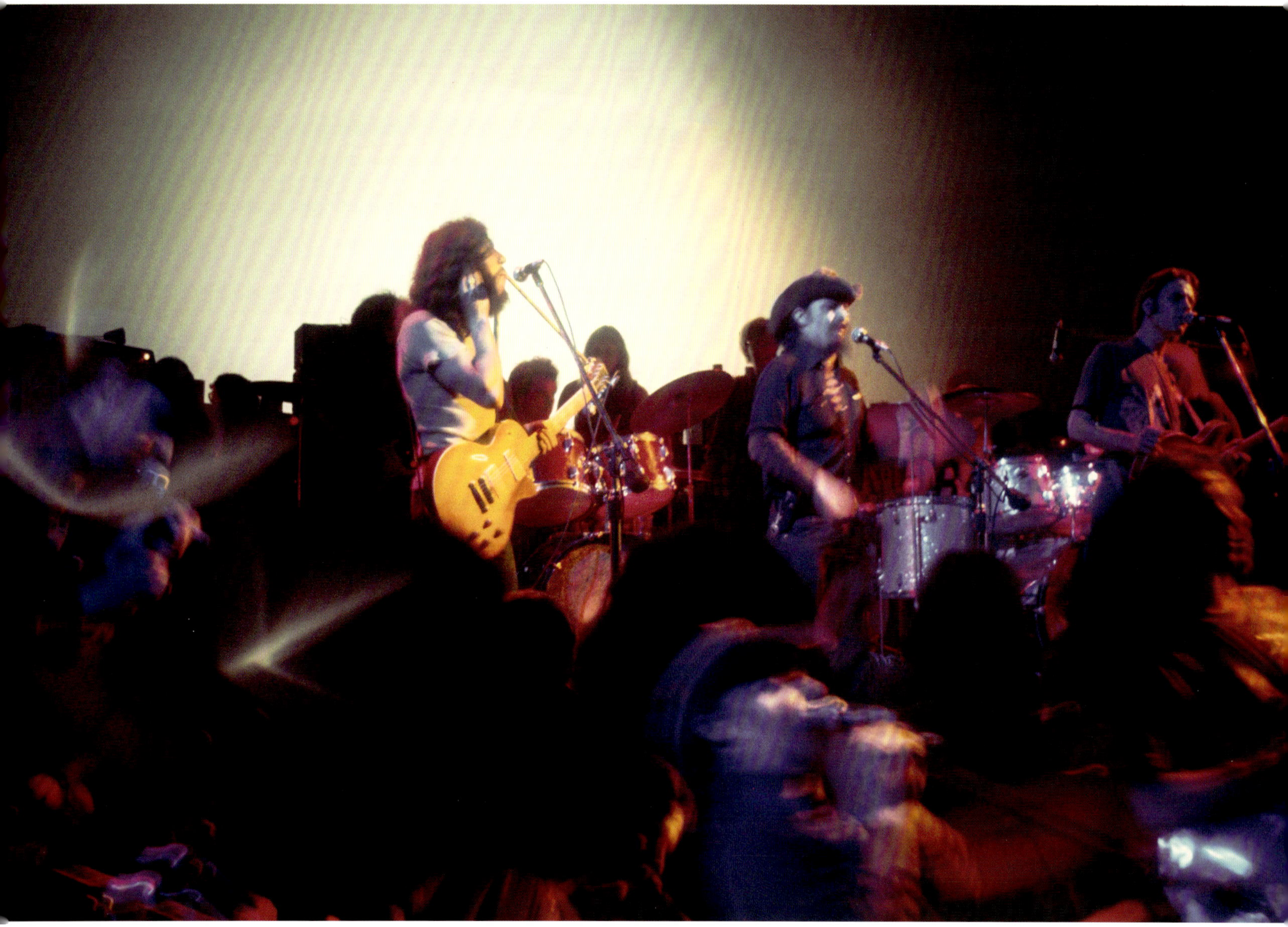

“Dark Star” jam, the Grateful Dead with Peter Green of Fleetwood Mac, Fillmore East, New York, February 1970.

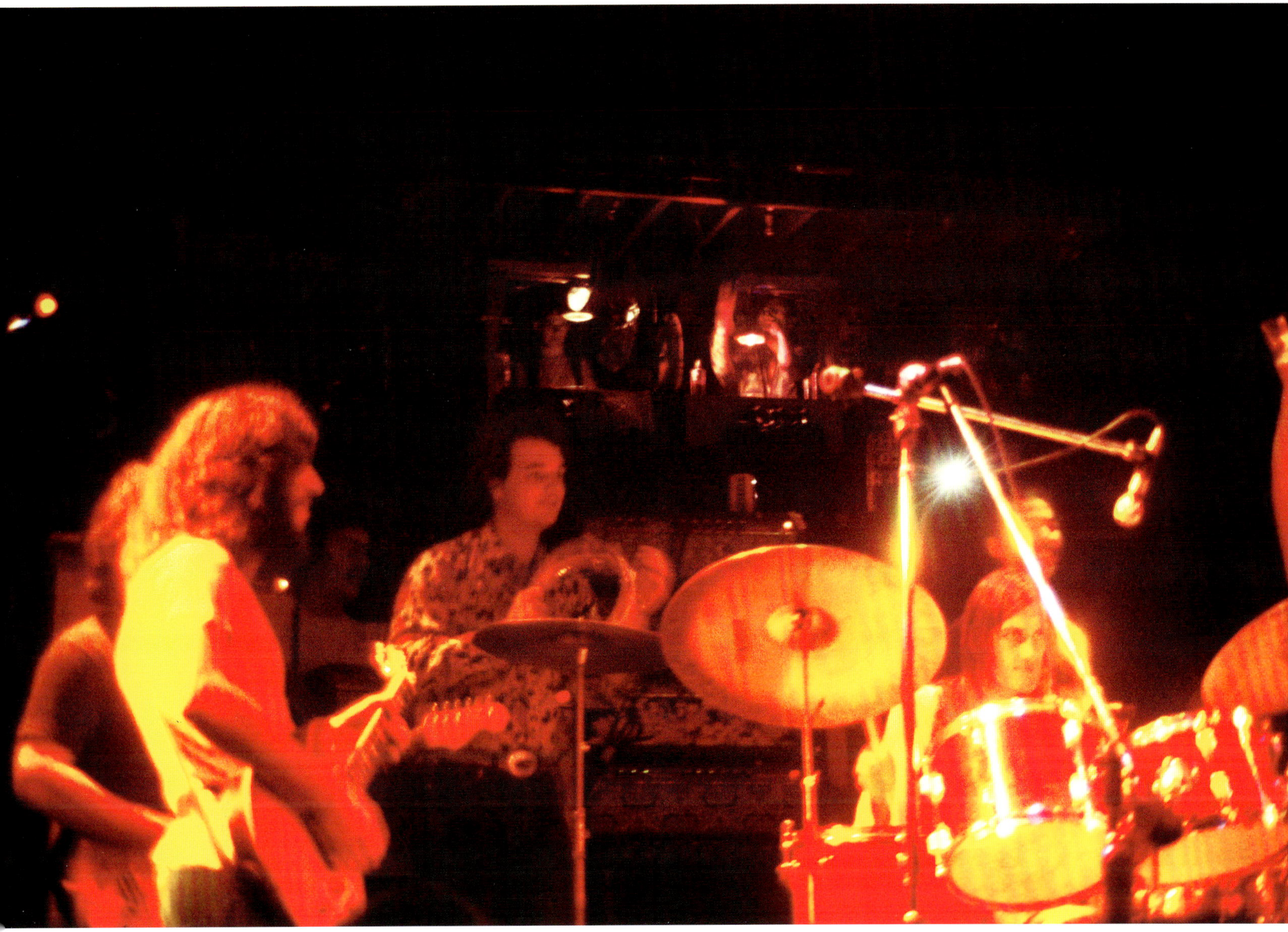

"Dark Star" jam, the Grateful Dead with Peter Green and Mick Fleetwood of Fleetwood Mac, Fillmore East, New York, February 1970.

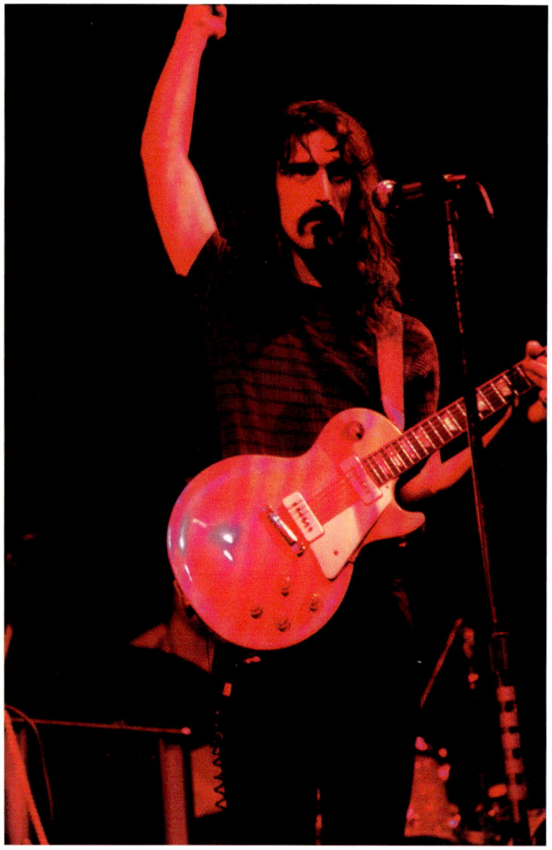

Frank Zappa, Fillmore East, New York, February 1969. *Opposite*: Frank Zappa and the Mothers of Invention, Fillmore East, New York, February 1969.

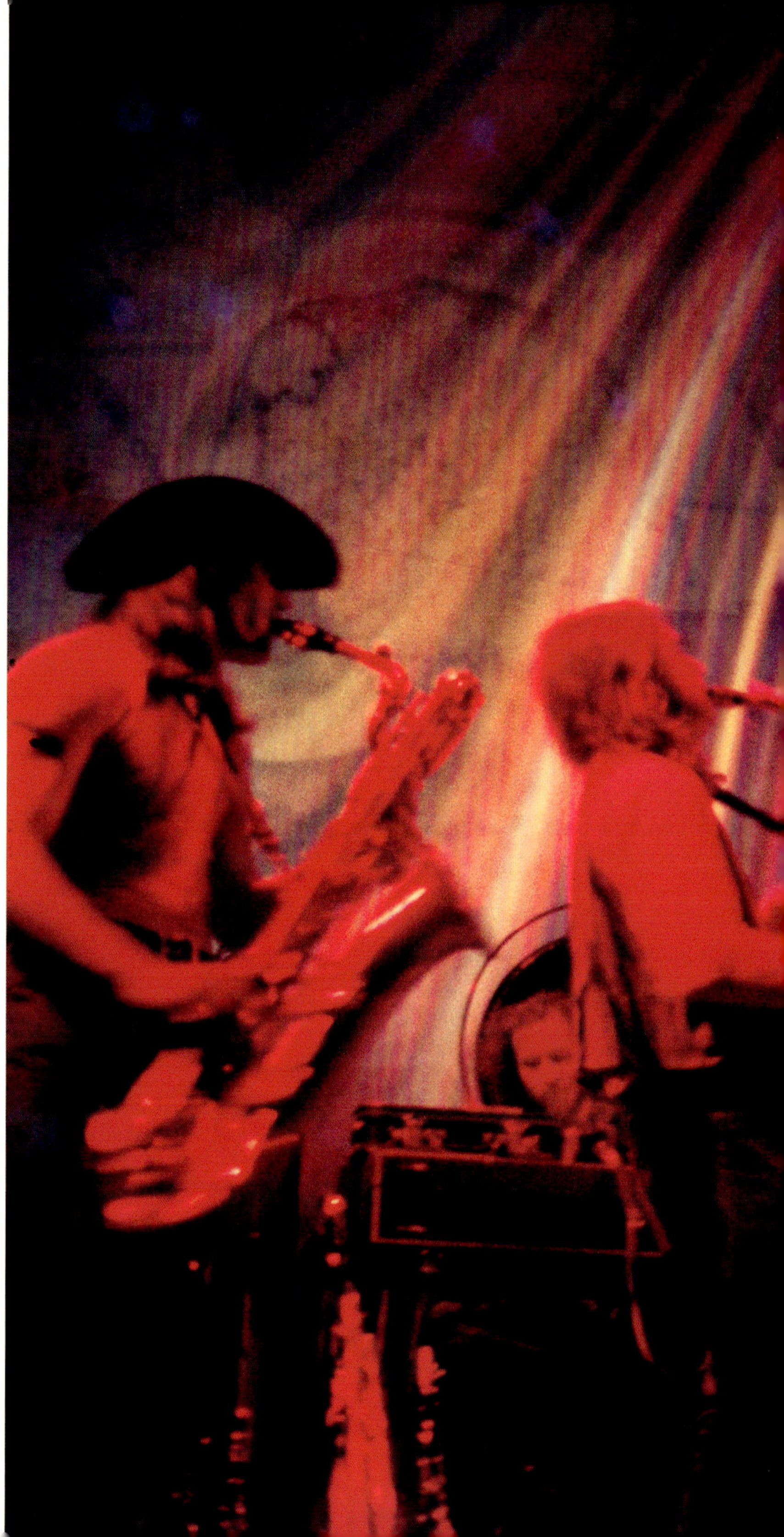

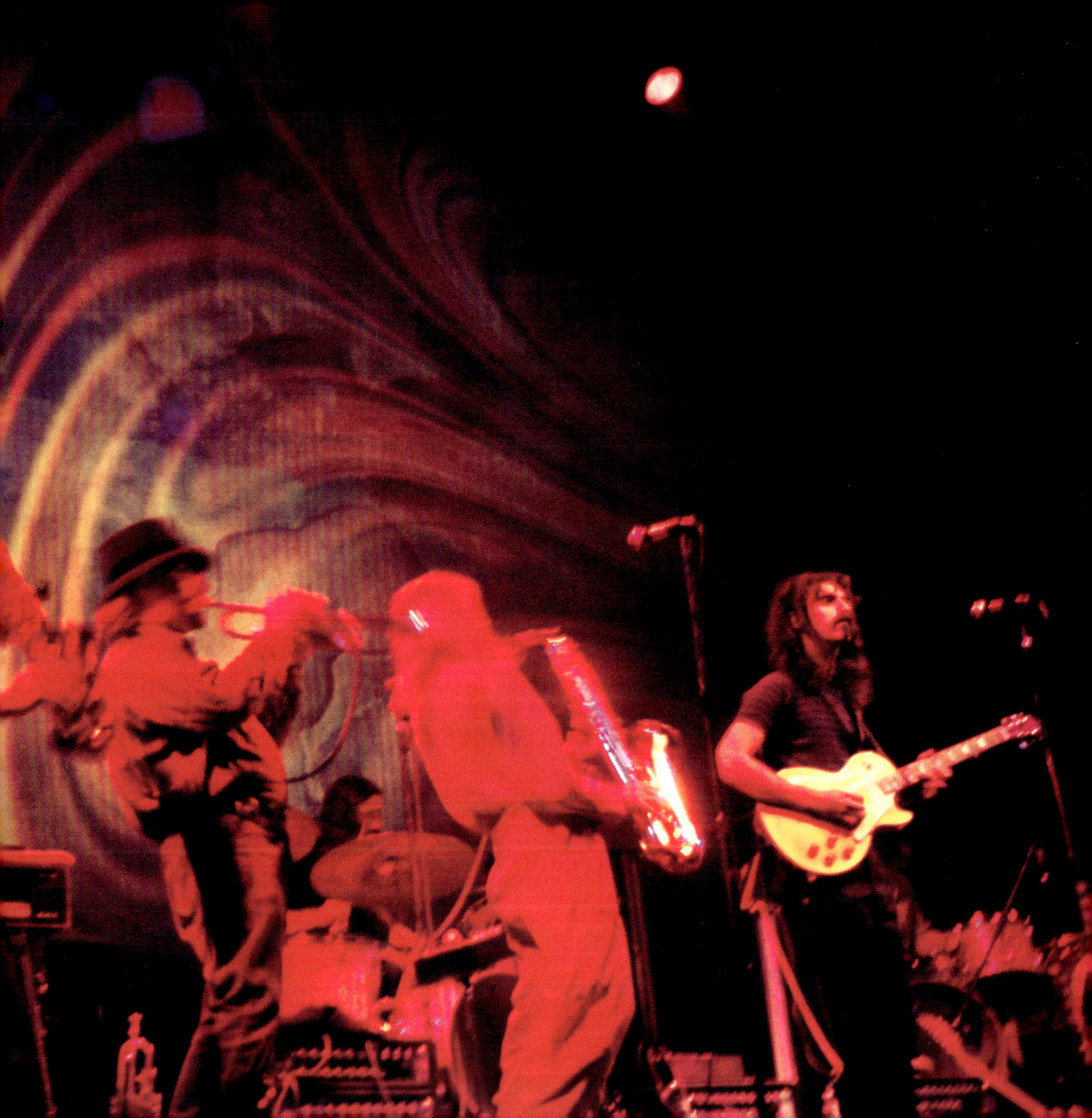

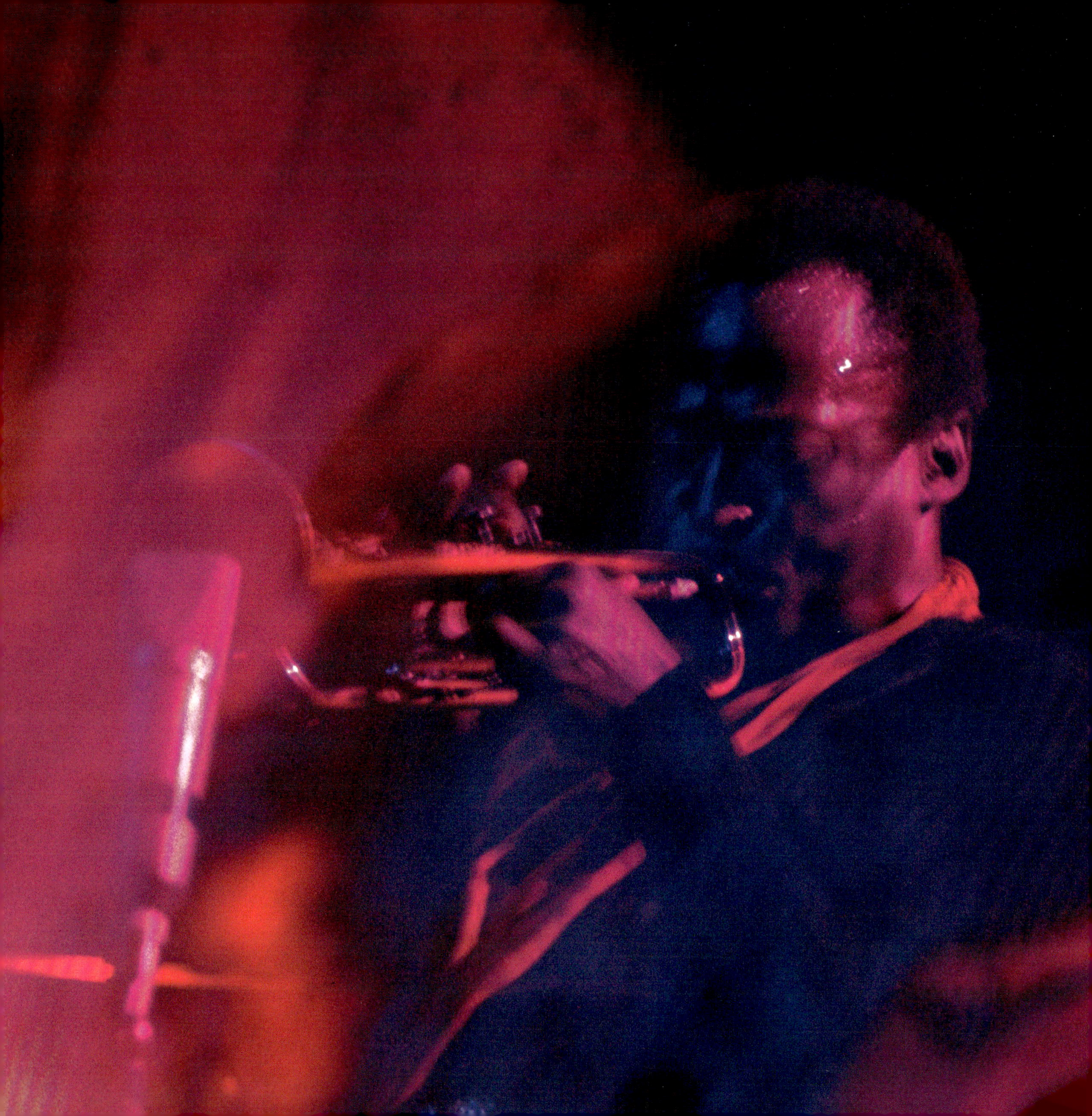

4

Developing an In-Camera Style

By 1968, because of my growing relationship with the Airplane and my work at the Fillmore East, I was confident and experienced enough to try new experiments in my photography, some of which I had been thinking about for some time.

The lighting at the Fillmore was very bright, with the primary colors combining on the stage, bathing the artists in constantly changing hues. And behind the artists was an ever-changing background light show. This offered me a vast palette of colors to experiment with, using the technology at hand, which was basic compared to today's Photoshop-driven photography. I was determined to never use a flash, because I knew it would startle the performers. I wished to be as unobtrusive and stealthy as possible. In addition, flash, even then, would certainly not be allowed by the management of any major venue. But more important for my photography, flash would blast all color out of an image, ruining my plans. My representational portraits were easy to produce. It was my more ambitious and experimental images that represented what I wanted to convey with my work, which would no doubt challenge my audience just as the work of other artists had challenged me. I wanted to bring together, with my own vision, techniques and ideas that I had spent so many hours studying to create a new form and style.

One of the important influences on my work was Alexander Scriabin's *Prometheus: The Poem of Fire* (1910), a symphonic work that included in the orchestra a "color organ," which functioned like a keyboard but projected light rather than sound when played. This fascinating "instrument" connected in my mind with the idea of synesthesia, something I had heard about but didn't fully understand. Synesthesia is a neurological condition wherein one experiences sensation in one sense in response to stimulus in another. In other

Miles Davis, Fillmore East, New York, March 1970.

words, it was a condition that allowed one to "see" sound and "hear" colors. All this fascinated me and led me to develop my own ideas about how to portray my subjects so one could "hear" the colors and "see" the sound in my images of music. It was when I first heard (in an admittedly altered state of mind) the Beatles LP *Revolver*, though—as well as virtually any music by the Airplane, their San Francisco counterparts, and the British progressive bands such as Procol Harum, Soft Machine, and King Crimson—that I had a similar experience of seeing their music in colors, flowing out of the speakers, and at that point I truly began to understand synesthesia.

Using the vivid colors of theatrical lights that could be saturated through exposure, in conjunction with the movement of rock and roll artists performing, as well as multiple angles and sizing to portray the music's dynamism and intensity, I began to create my own style. I wanted my images to match, enhance, and expand the act of viewing bands through traditional "representational" imagery, and so I tried to present the aural encounter with music in a new and fresh way, for anyone, by just "seeing" my images or by "experiencing" my images while accompanied by the artists' music. I set out to capture the intensity of the sound, which at times would propel one to a higher state of consciousness, with or without the assistance of other substances. As the music I listened to became more abstract, my own work became more abstracted as well. I tried to portray visually the long musical jams that both Jefferson Airplane and their sister groups the Grateful Dead and Quicksilver Messenger Service delivered on a regular basis.

The actual mechanics of my techniques evolved once I discovered how I could execute multiple exposures with the Nikon F. It was a tedious and complex process to keep the frame synchronized. After exposing one frame, I had to first rotate a ring around the shutter button and simultaneously press a button on the bottom of the camera while rewinding the film with a hand crank. The shutter button could be cranked back no more than one revolution to keep the frame in registration. I then turned the shutter ring back to its original position, released the button on the bottom of the camera, and advanced the film back to its former position so the shutter would again be cocked but the film would be ready for the next image place on the same frame. This had to be done every time to build the images that I envisioned as I viewed the action, from on and off stage, which allowed for varying viewpoints. I became quite adept at this and could even do it in near total darkness, often with much furious activity surrounding me.

The process took a little bit of time and effort, and I began by trying different exposures without any metering of the images, which was impossible considering the conditions. I had to both rewind the film, previsioning what I wanted to put next on the same frame and either continue using the lens that I used in the first exposure or change it to show an image from different points of view or different angles. I had to do a lot of trial-and-error experimentation with the shutter speed and the f-stop, both of which controlled the light that hit the film. Eventually the components fell into place. I mastered the art of producing the multiple exposures—as many as ten on one piece of film—and having the finished, aggregate image exposed the way I had envisioned it to be. I had to change lenses frequently since there were virtually no high-quality consumer zoom lenses outside of Hollywood. I pretty much had only the choice of fixed focal length lenses in my arsenal, which at the time were a wide-angle 35mm lens and 50mm, 135mm, and 200mm lenses. In addition, many times I masked the lenses off with my hand to allow less light to strike the film, in order not to overexpose the frame and render all the multiple images useless. I exposed numerous frames with a base image and had to memorize what I had done during the concert so that I could rewind the film and "overlay" other images later that day or even a week later, as I did with lasers and other optical devices.

Another factor contributing to the development of my style was the fact that Kodak began to offer what was called "push" processing. This was a film-developing method that allowed the film to be exposed at a much higher speed than it was normally rated. This gave the images a far greater dynamic range and the ability to resolve in far lower light than if the film were exposed at its normal speed. The High Speed Ektachrome slide film that I used was able to be "pushed" to two and a half times the normal speed. This was a visual revelation and, in combination with all the other techniques I developed, gave me the latitude to produce final images that were once only swirling in my head.

As my portfolio increased, my friends and I would gather in an upstairs room at my parents' house. My parents allowed me to transform the space into a listening and viewing room. Because the most affordable way to shoot was with slide film, the only way to really evaluate the worth of the work was to project the photographs on a wall or screen. I used a large white sheet pinned to the back wall of the room. These sessions were key to building my confidence as an artist, mainly because all my friends were brutally honest about my work. Dan Sweeney, my closest friend and one of my mentors, was especially candid but also knowledgeable about art. He had gone to art school for a few semesters and was familiar with how to critique art. "Crits" he called it, sparing no slings and arrows. The room also became a nexus of discussion and thought about many topics both popular and esoteric, a kind of psychedelic Algonquin Round Table. Along with Sweeney, Joe Rubin, Bill Reynolds, and some other guest stars we would figure out solutions to the world's ills and inequities. But mostly we opined on the latest music, art, and literature, much of which was harder to find in that pre-internet age.

During those sessions, my parents looked the other way when we imbibed alcoholic beverages or consumed other substances while viewing my work. It was around this time when I began to use marijuana and found that it enhanced listening to music to such a great degree that I wanted to go back and listen to everything I had in the past with my new ears. Ingesting this forbidden substance allowed me to hear things that, once heard, were never forgotten.

I also followed the evolution of the Beatles, Jefferson Airplane, and so many other bands as they found themselves under the spell of mind-altering drugs. I could detect an effect on their music. There are distinct differences in the sounds of these bands when they are under the influence.

So it was that Jefferson Airplane's second record, *Surrealistic Pillow*, had been influenced by softer substances like marijuana, while *After Bathing at Baxter's*, which was released around the December holidays in 1967, was full-tilt LSD-infused. From the first blast of Jorma's ES-345 Gibson guitar feedback at the beginning of "The Ballad of You and Me and Pooneil" through Grace Slick's highly politicized reimagining of James Joyce's *Ulysses* and culminating with the soaring harmonies on "Won't You Try / Saturday Afternoon," I knew this album was something completely different, outstripping anything they had done before. The record was both an interstellar and innerstellar exploration, including one of Jorma and Jack's earliest solo, Hot Tuna–like experiments, with the nine minutes of "Spare Chaynge," cut down from the full twenty-four-plus-minute, even more cosmic and abstract version, which in recent years has become available on bootleg releases and on YouTube.

I could hear the influences—the infusion—of LSD, which made all music so much more intense, allowing listeners to focus on even the minutest of musical details, and I immediately knew this was to be their masterpiece, despite its lack of commerciality, panning by some misguided critics, and modest sales. Nope, this was a major departure, and a brilliant one at that, even in form, as the record was presented in movements like classical symphonies. It has taken decades for the sentiment to catch up with my first impressions, but *Baxter's* is now seen in the same light I perceived it from the start. It has endured as my favorite record of the rock era. Listening to it, both straight or under the influence, was, and is even now, a holy sacrament, and I feel it is the pinnacle of psychedelic rock music.

As for my own run-ins with LSD, they were few. I first learned about it at the tender age of ten years old when I saw William Castle's 1959 horror film *The Tingler*, in which LSD featured prominently. But it was many years later when I first experimented with it, and these trials were mainly recreational adventures with some of my friends while we listened to music and watched movies with new eyes and ears. Soon after these exploits, though, I was pretty much done with it. So the drug played a fairly small role in shaping or informing my work. Certainly this experience resulted in somewhat heighted perceptions toward visual and sound media, enhancing my ability to create and evaluate what was to become my new art. But in all honesty the impact of LSD on my art falls somewhere on the food chain between the "Cool Ghoul" John Zacherle, visionary Ernie Kovacs's wild video experiments on TV, and the early MAD *Magazine* comic masterpieces of humor and satire. Mainly, the experiences I had only confirmed and expanded the thoughts that I was on the right track with my already formed perspective about how to approach image creation in what I hoped was a unique and original way.

Meanwhile, my work with Jefferson Airplane continued. In the summer of 1969, I attended with the band other outdoor music festivals, one of which I thought would be just another festival on the circuit. It was, however, more historic than anyone could have imagined. The Woodstock Music and Art Fair took place August 15–18, 1969. By that time my work was fully on fire like "hurricanes of color," a term my then girlfriend Carole Bell coined, which I have carried with me for decades.

Overleaf: (left) Alice Cooper, Town Hall, New York, May 1971; (center) Rod Stewart and Ron Wood of the Faces, Fillmore East, New York, February 1971; (right) Eric Clapton of Derek and the Dominoes, Fillmore East, New York, October 1970.

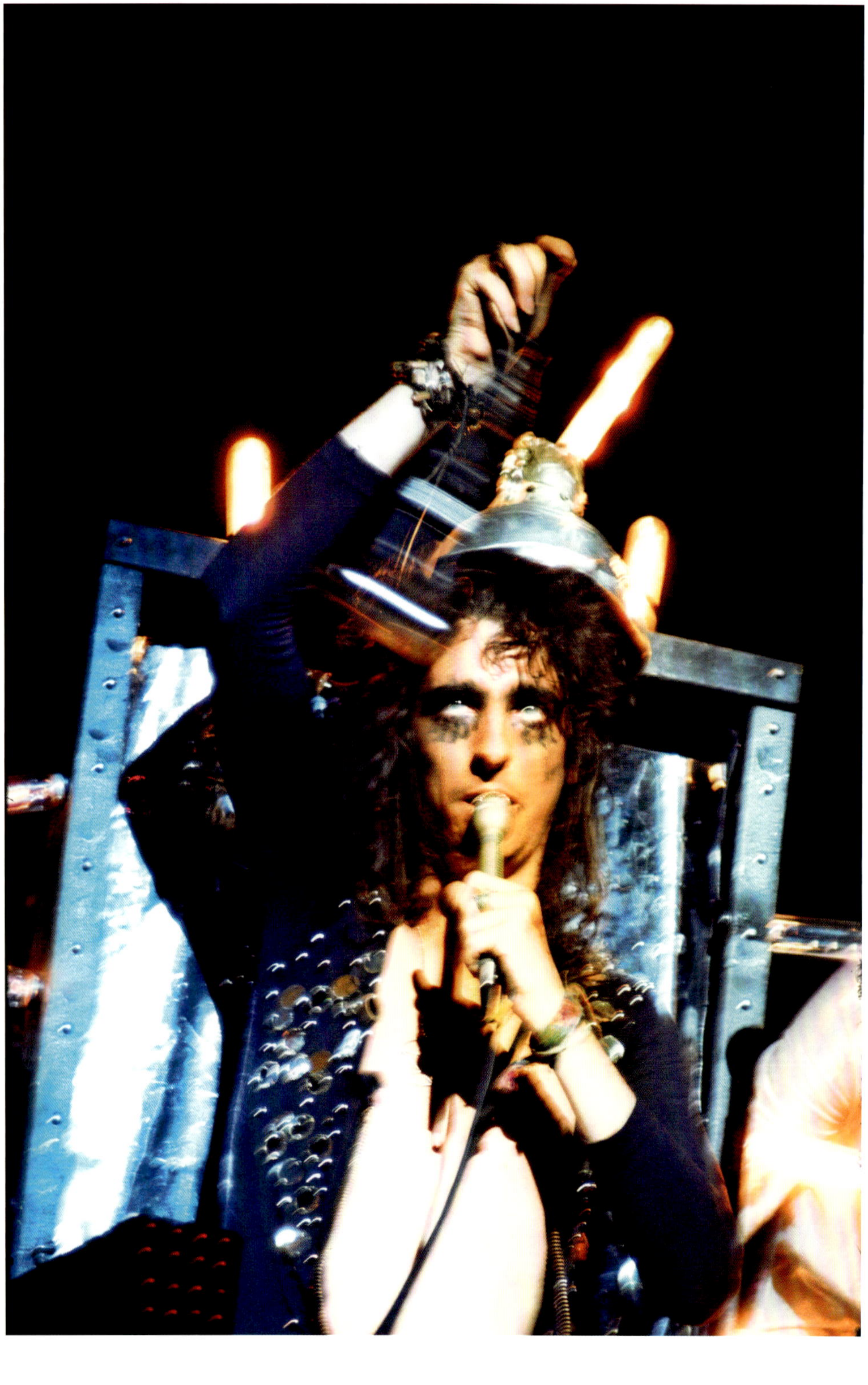

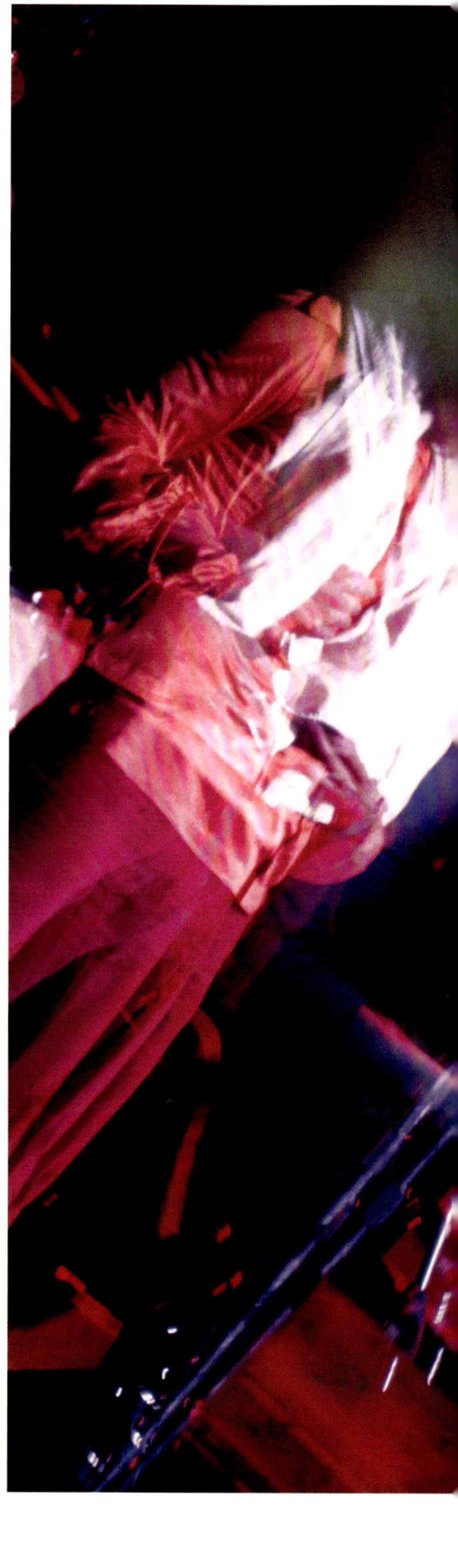

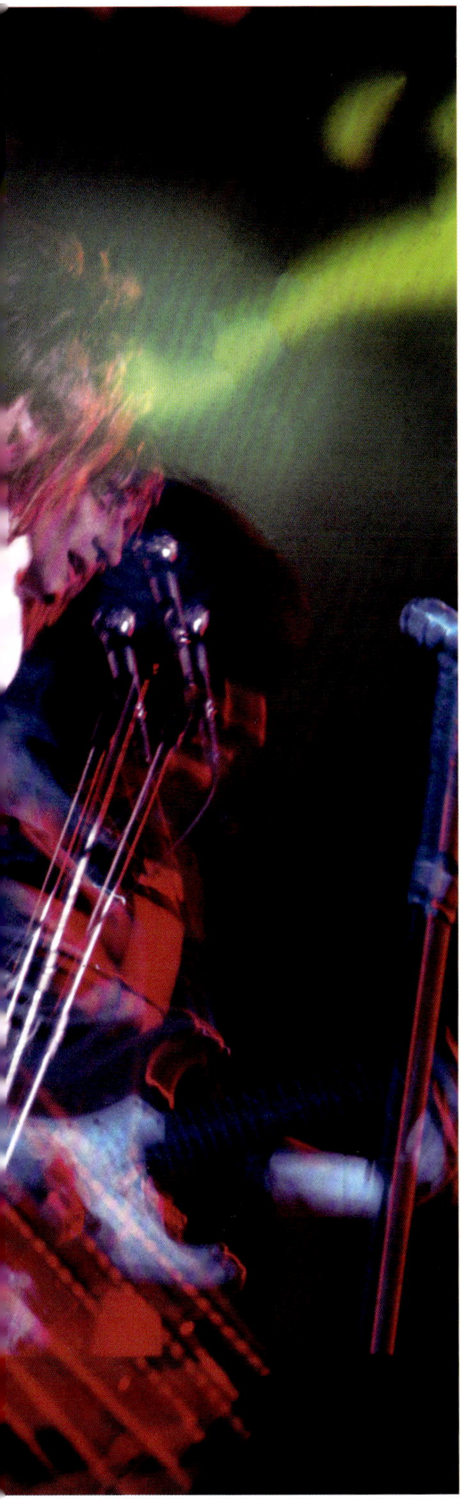

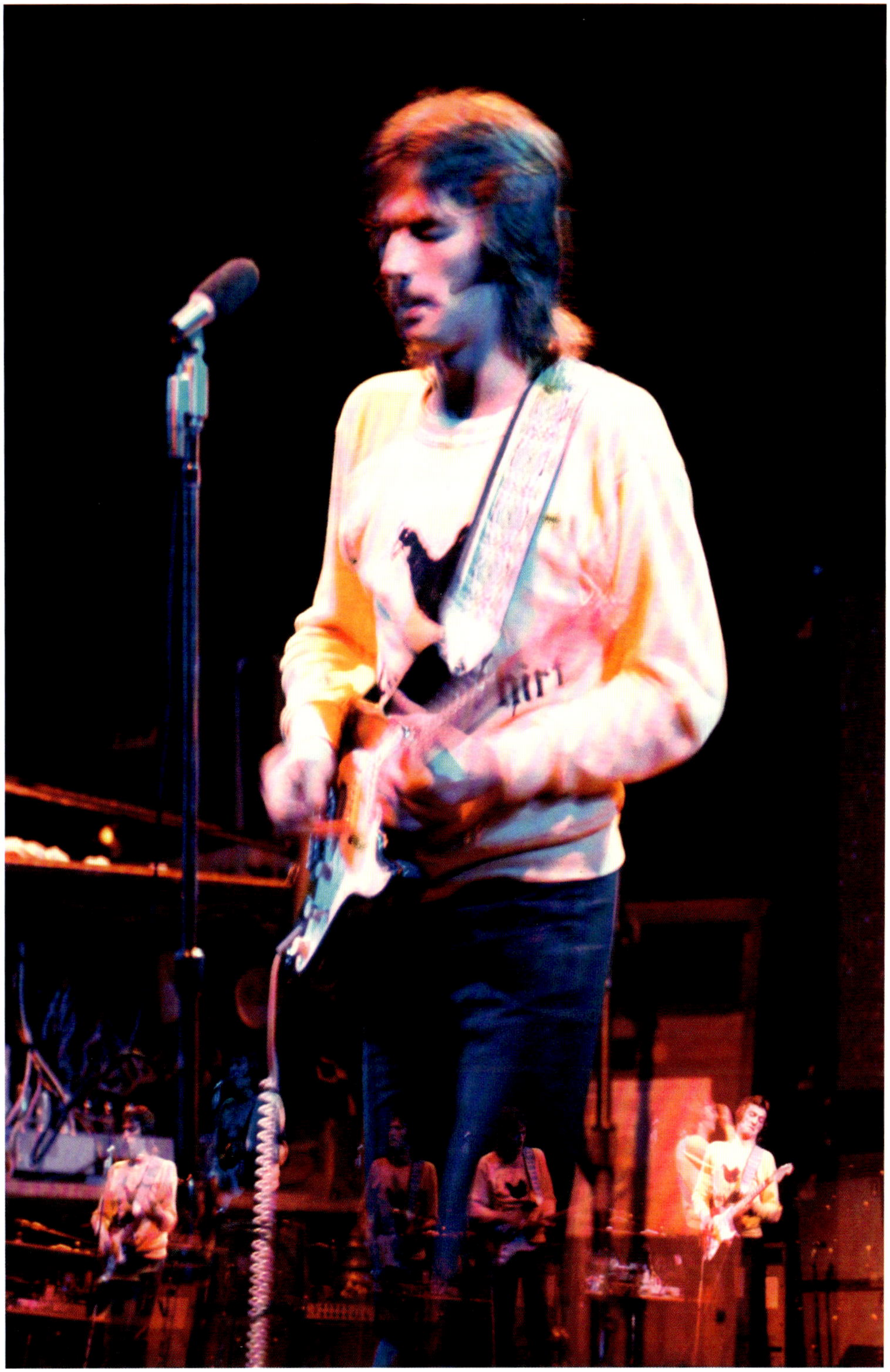

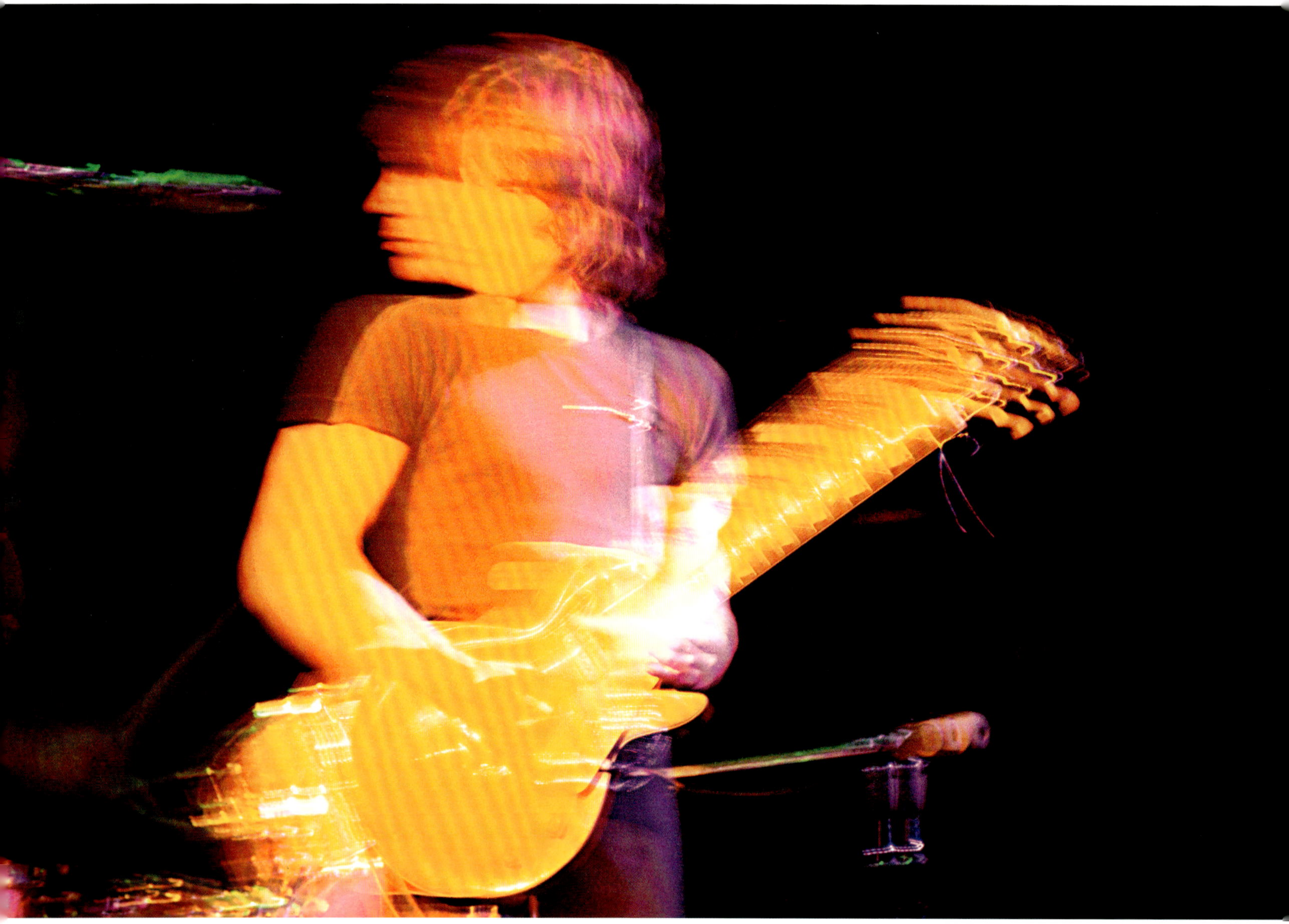

Jeff Beck, Fillmore East, New York, May 1969.

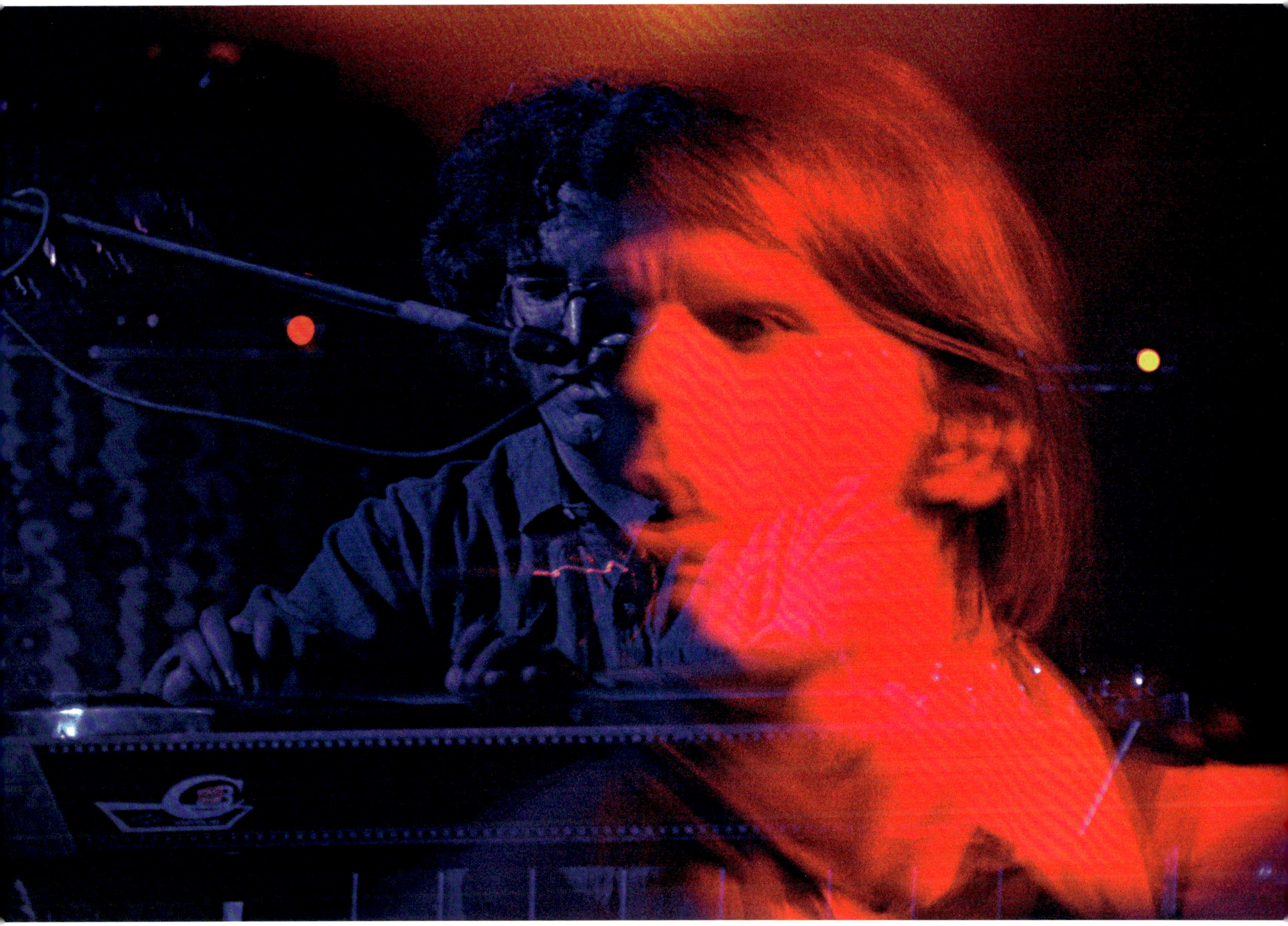

Jerry Garcia (left) and Bob Weir (right) of the Grateful Dead, Fillmore East, New York, February 1970.

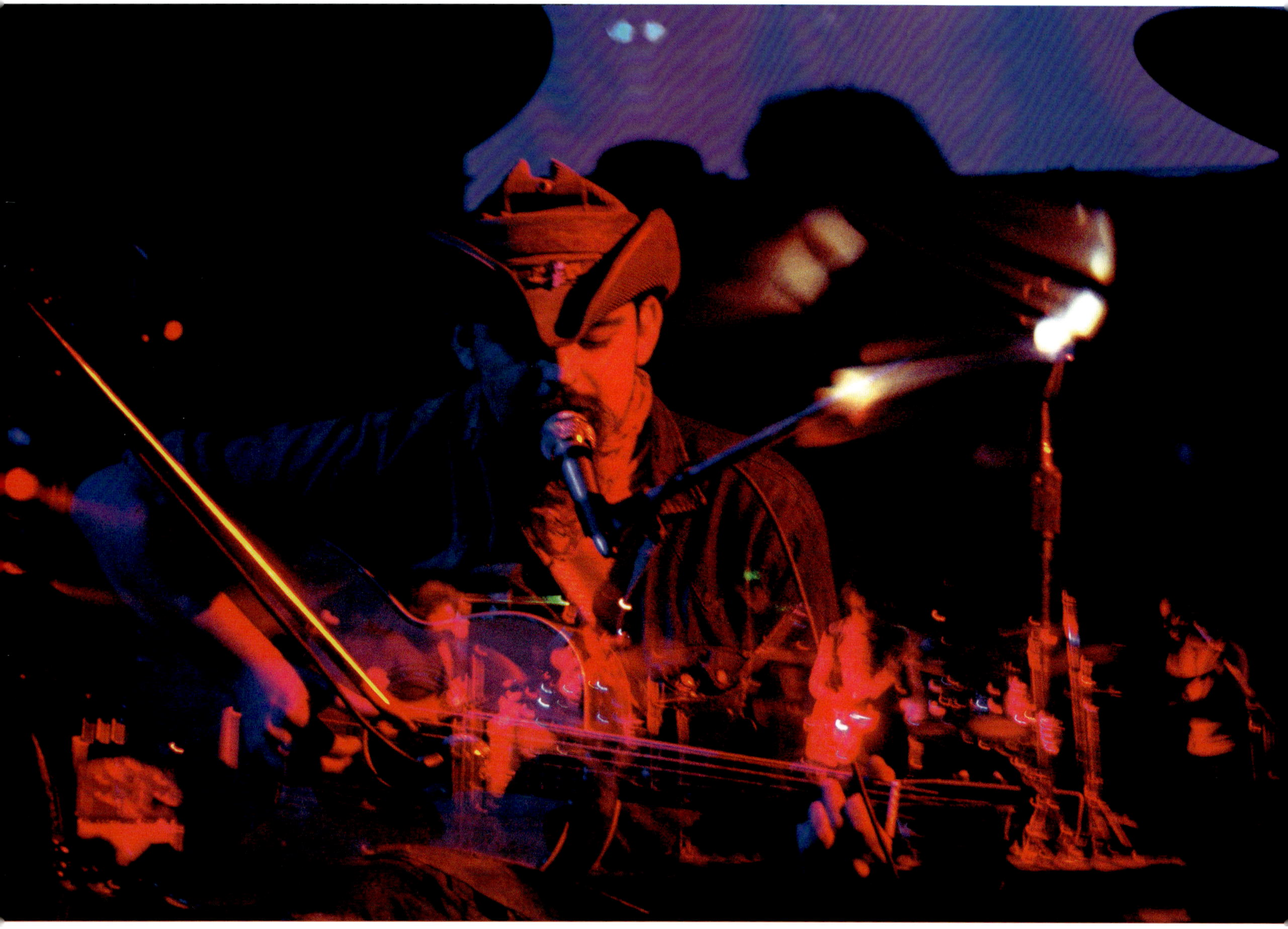

Ron "Pigpen" McKernan of the Grateful Dead, Fillmore East, New York, February 1970. *Opposite*: Jorma Kaukonen of Jefferson Airplane, Fillmore East, New York, November 1970.

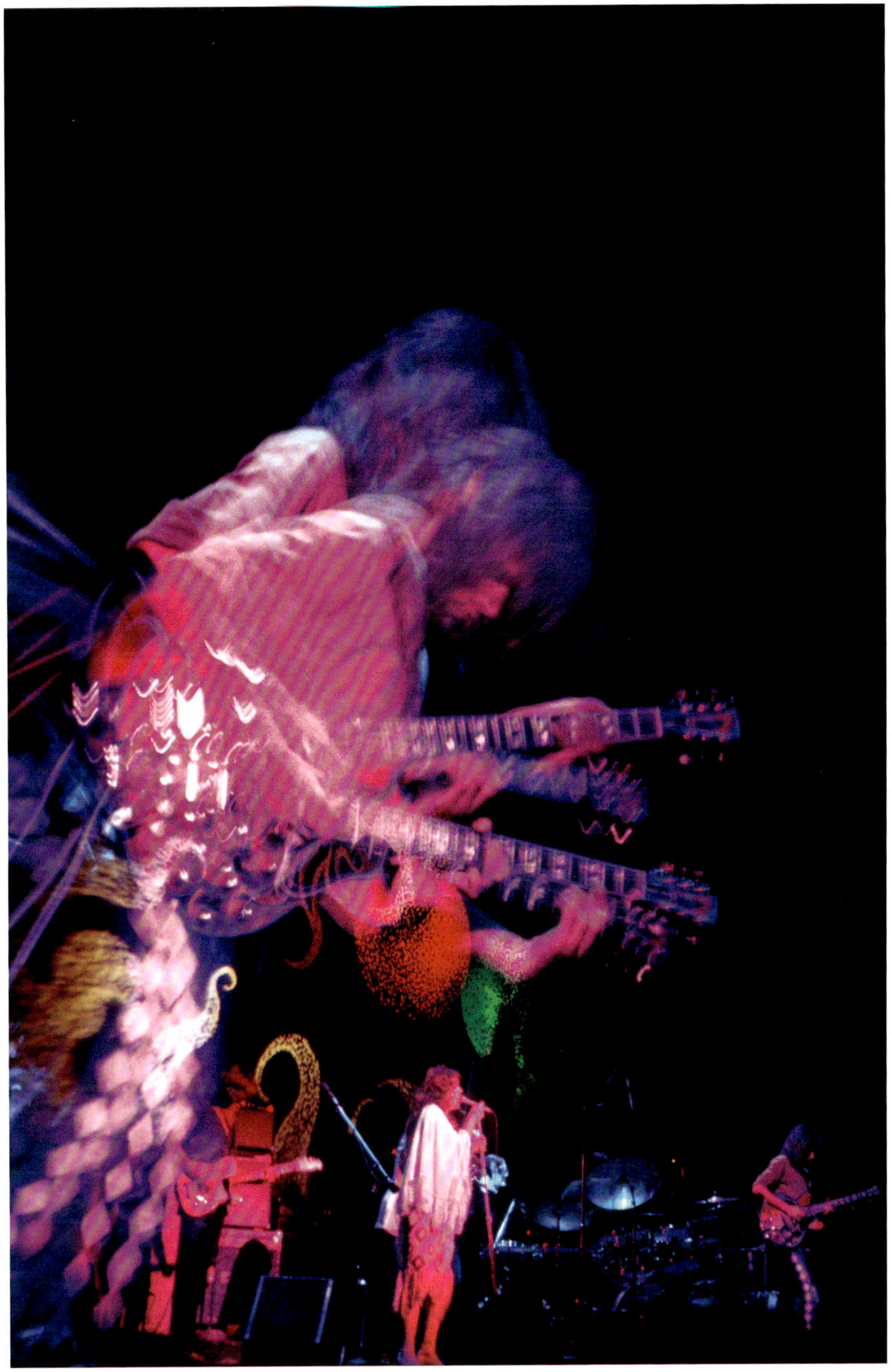

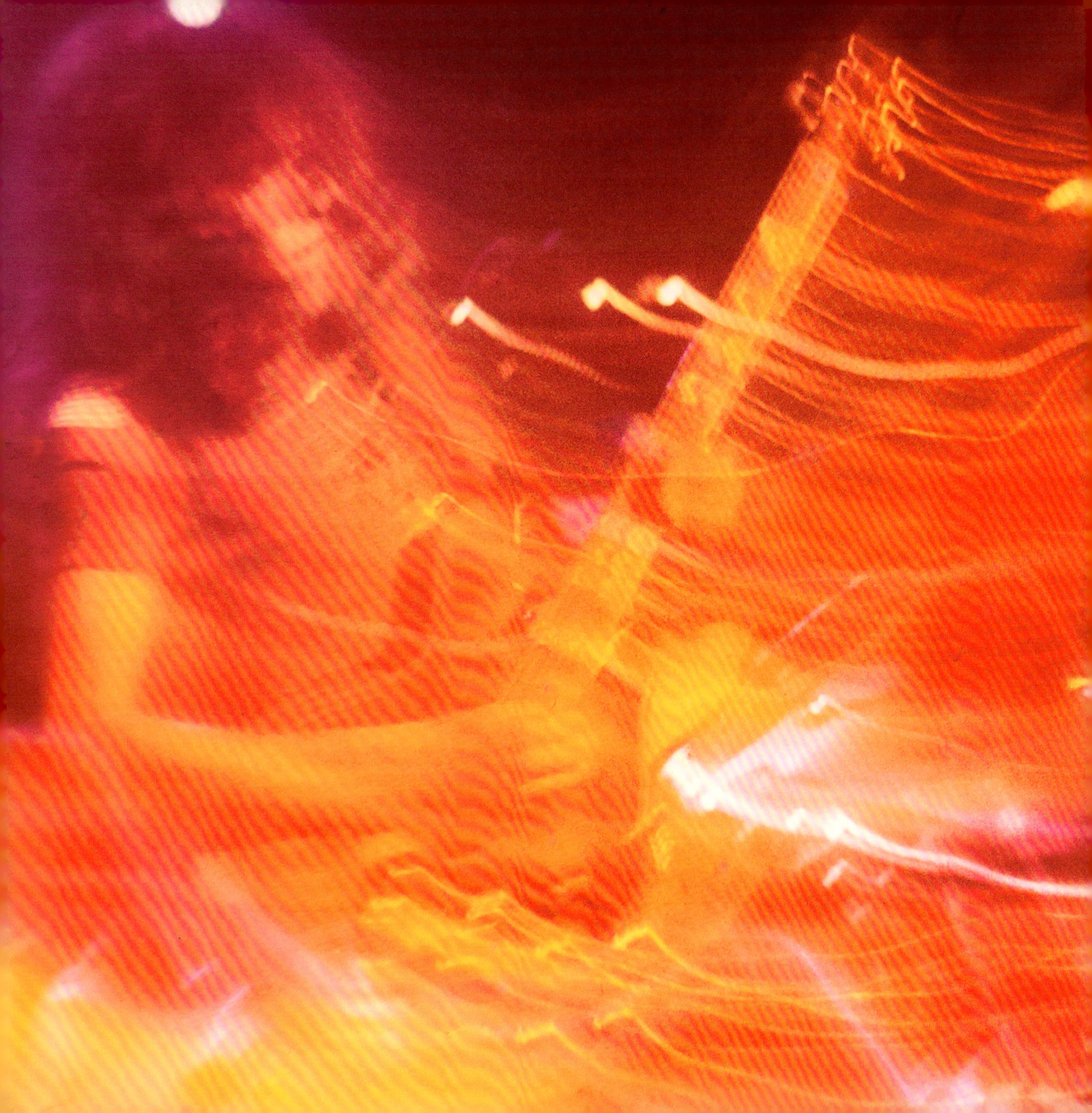

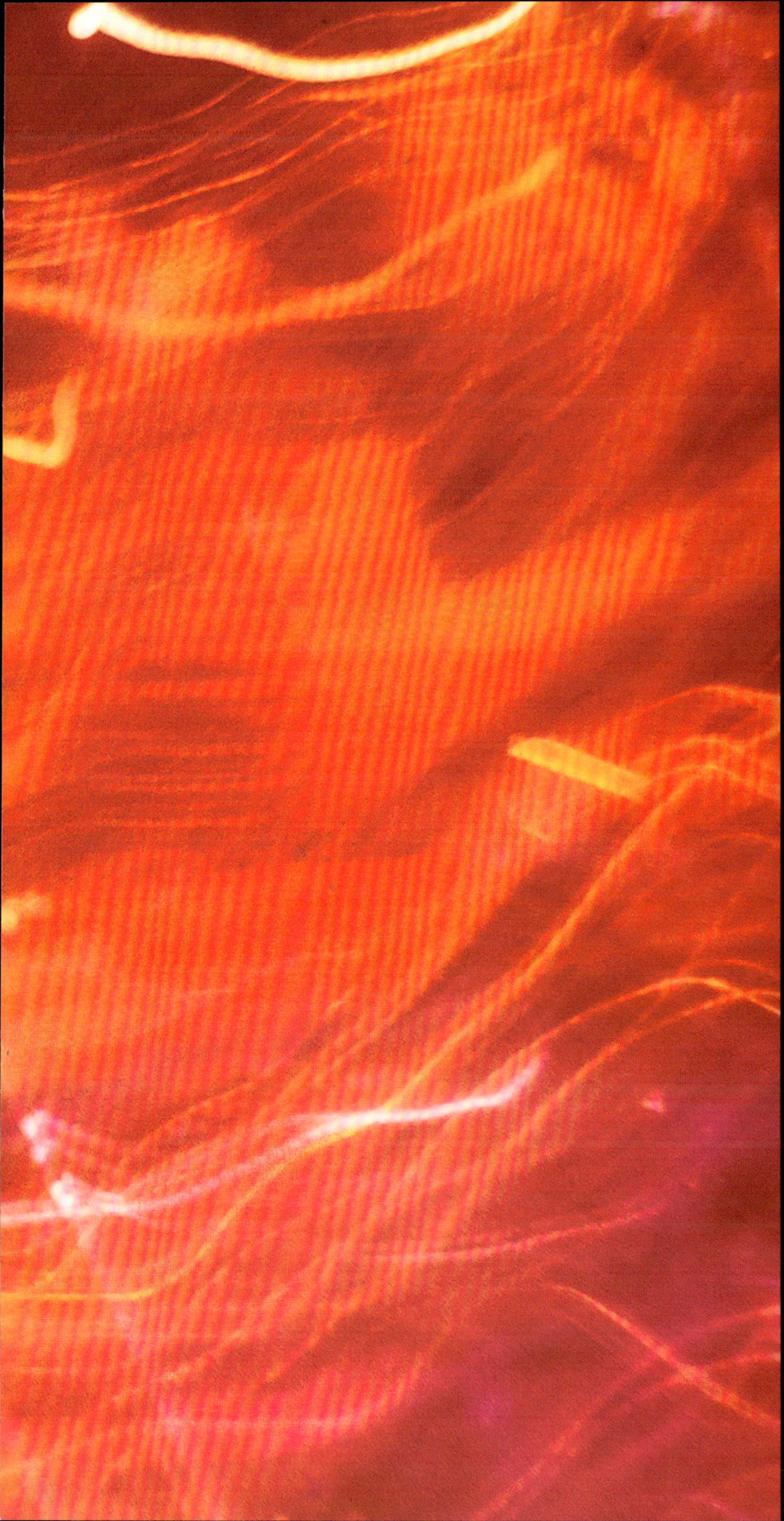

I tried to present the aural encounter with music in a new and fresh way, for anyone, by just "seeing" my images or by "experiencing" my images while accompanied by the artists' music.

Jorma Kaukonen of Jefferson Airplane, Gaelic Park, Ne
August 1971.

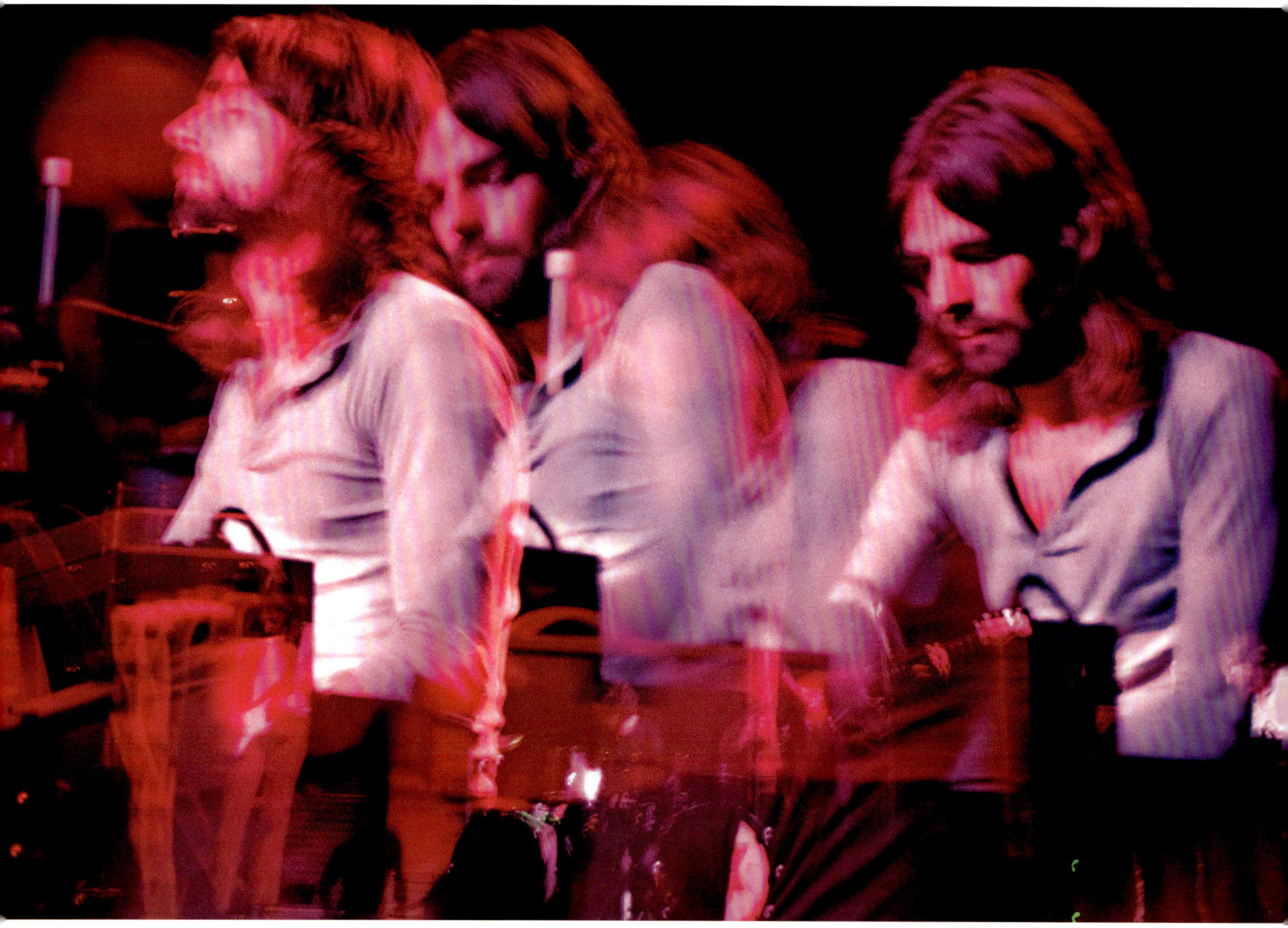

Richard Wright of Pink Floyd, Fillmore East, New York,
September 1970.

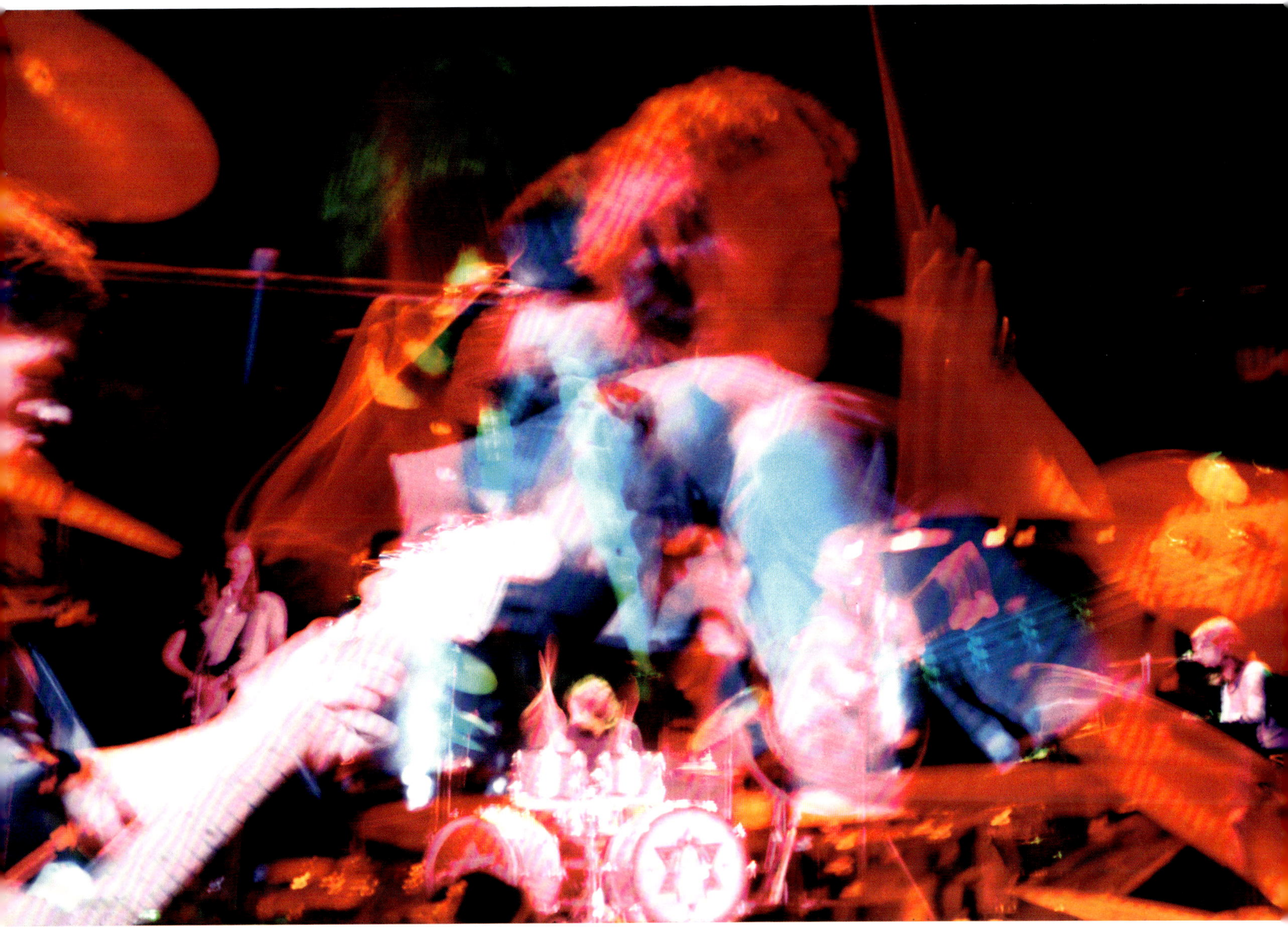

Pink Floyd, Fillmore East, New York, September 1970.

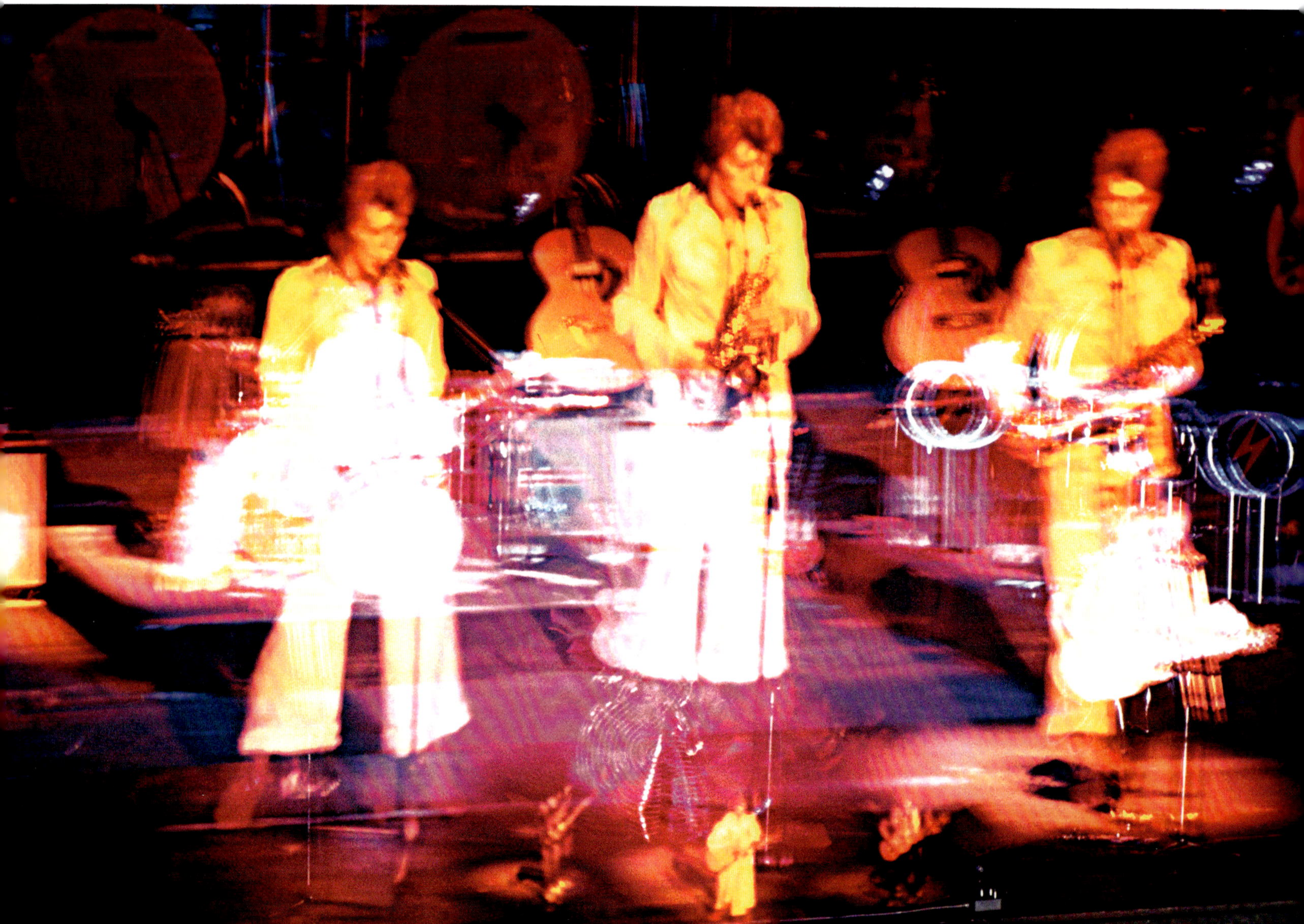

David Bowie, Radio City Music Hall, February 1973.

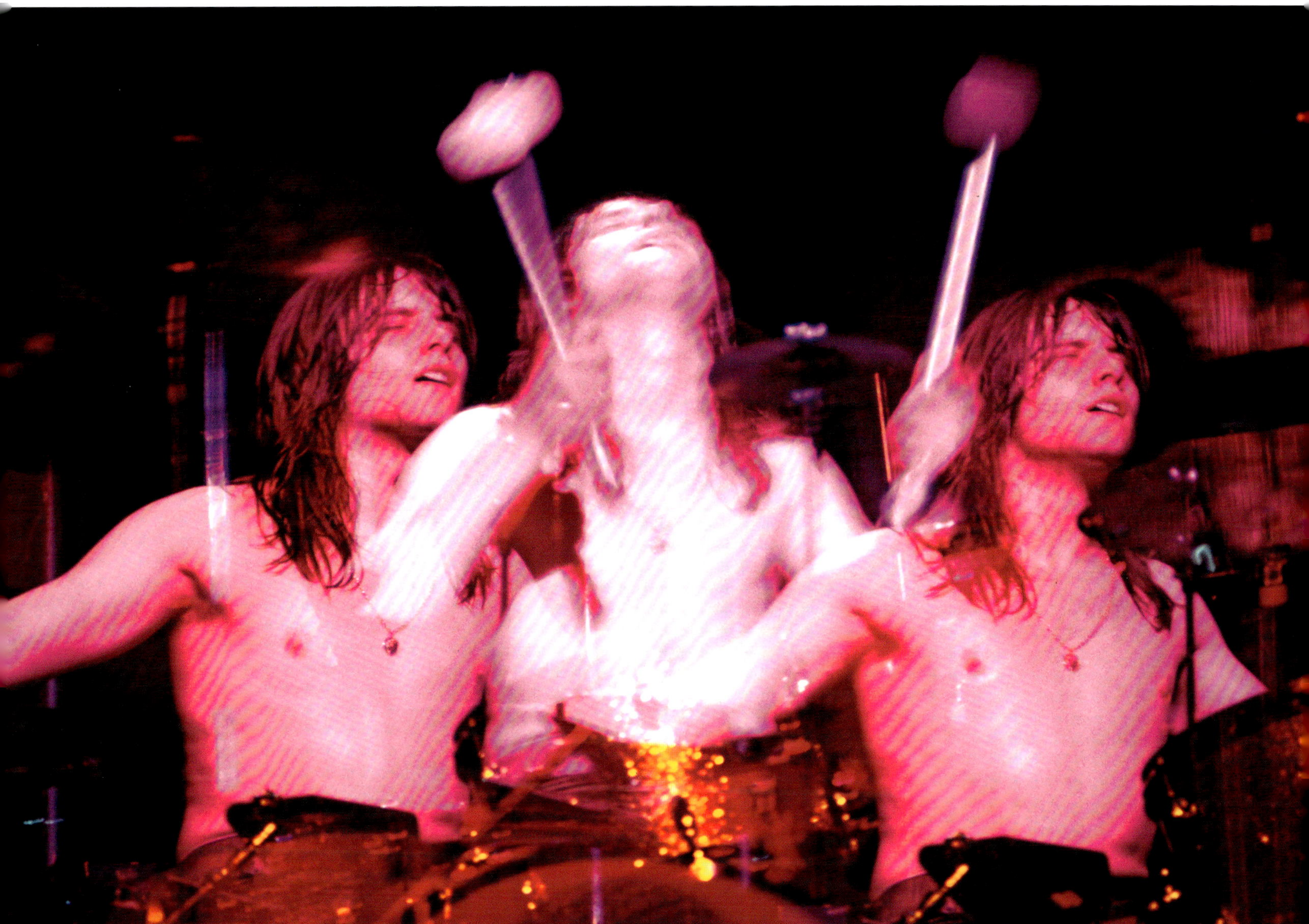

Carl Palmer of Emerson, Lake & Palmer, Fillmore East, New York, May 1971.

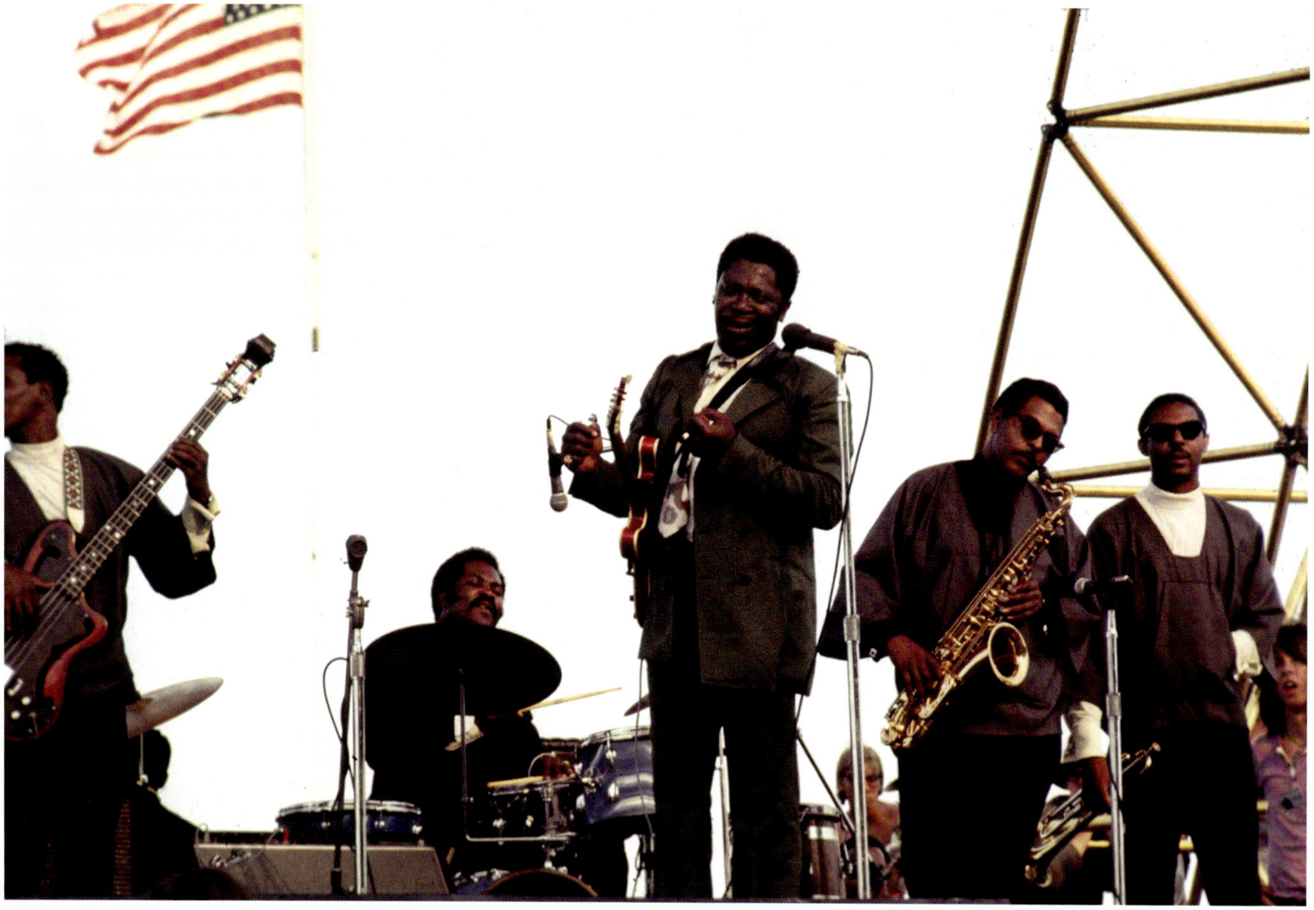

B. B. King, Atlantic City Pop Festival, August 1969.

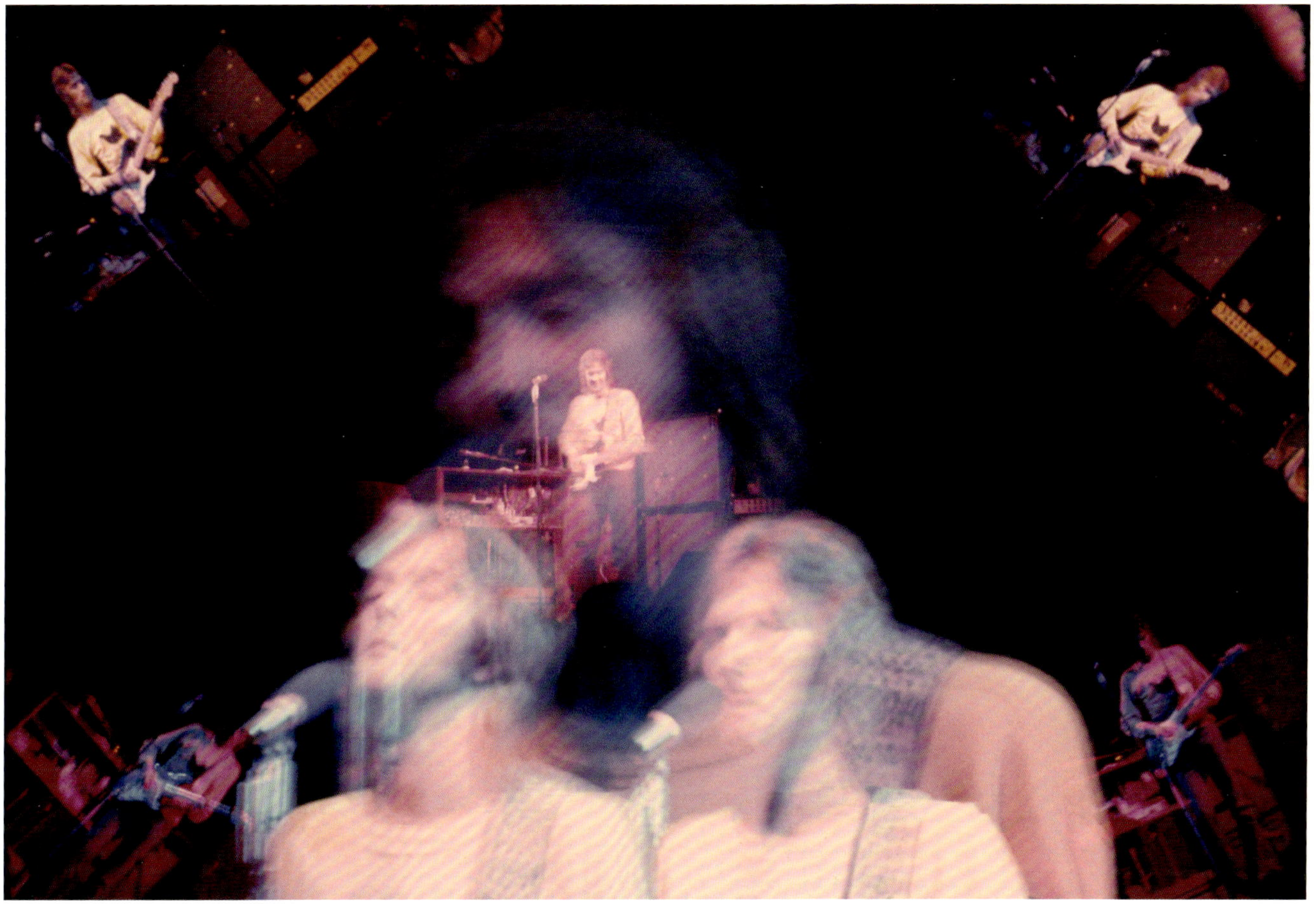

Eric Clapton of Derek and the Dominos, Fillmore East, New York, October 1970.

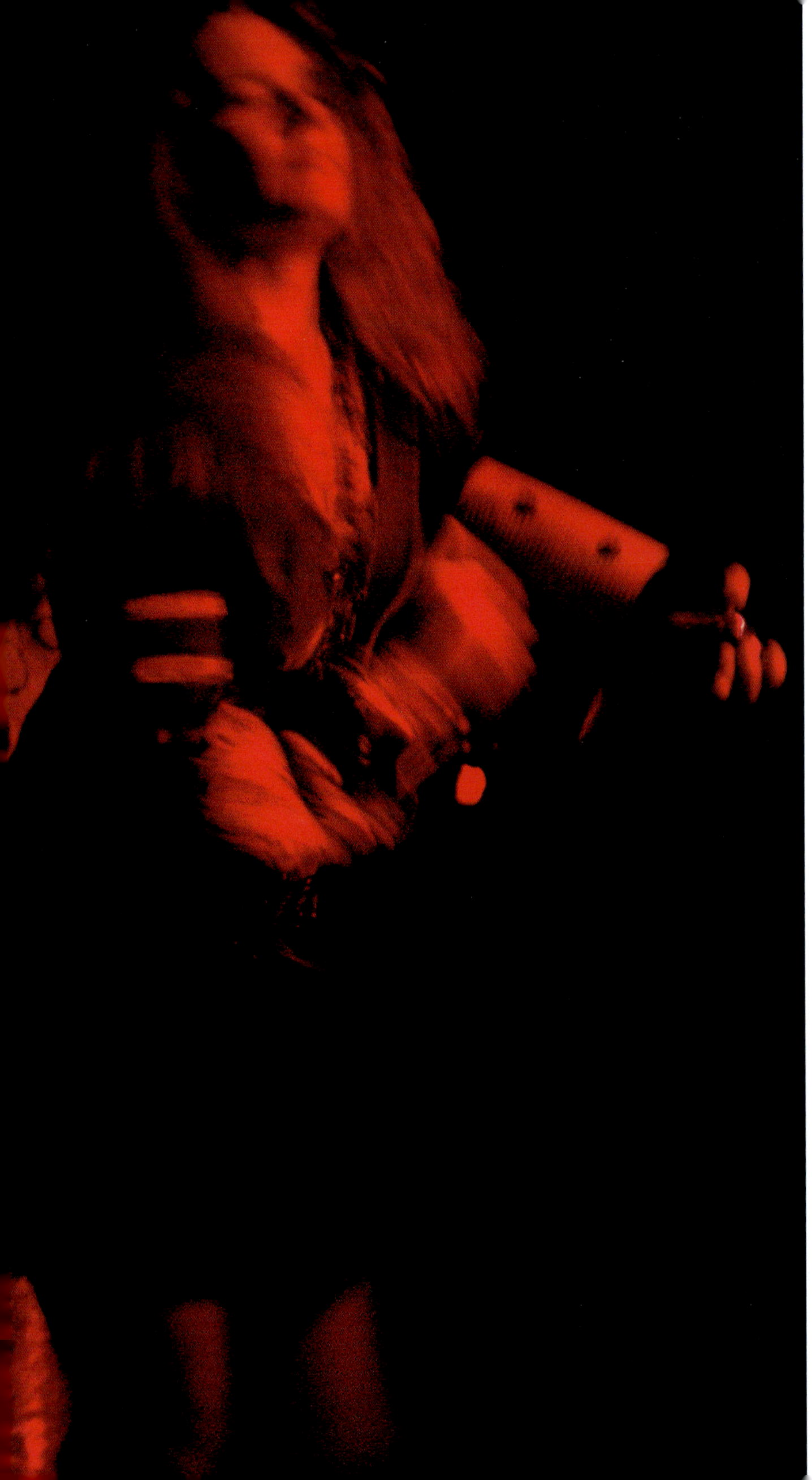

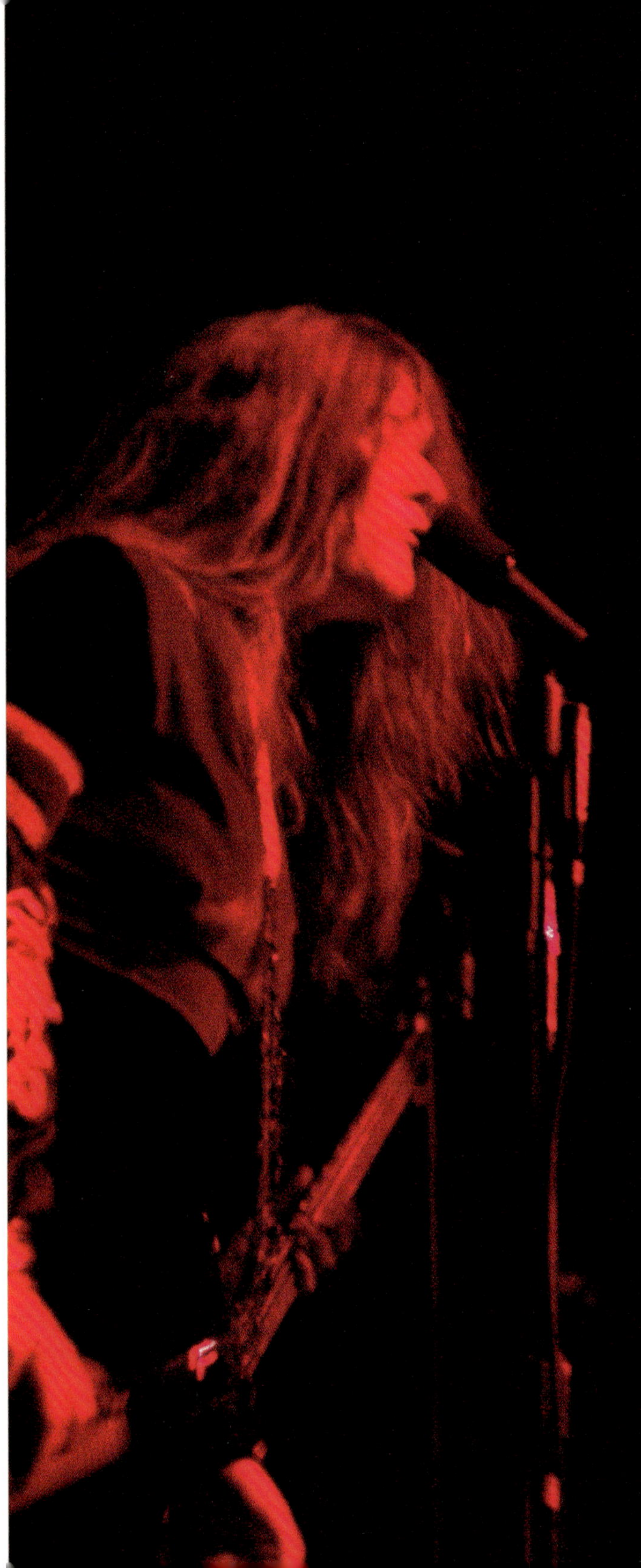

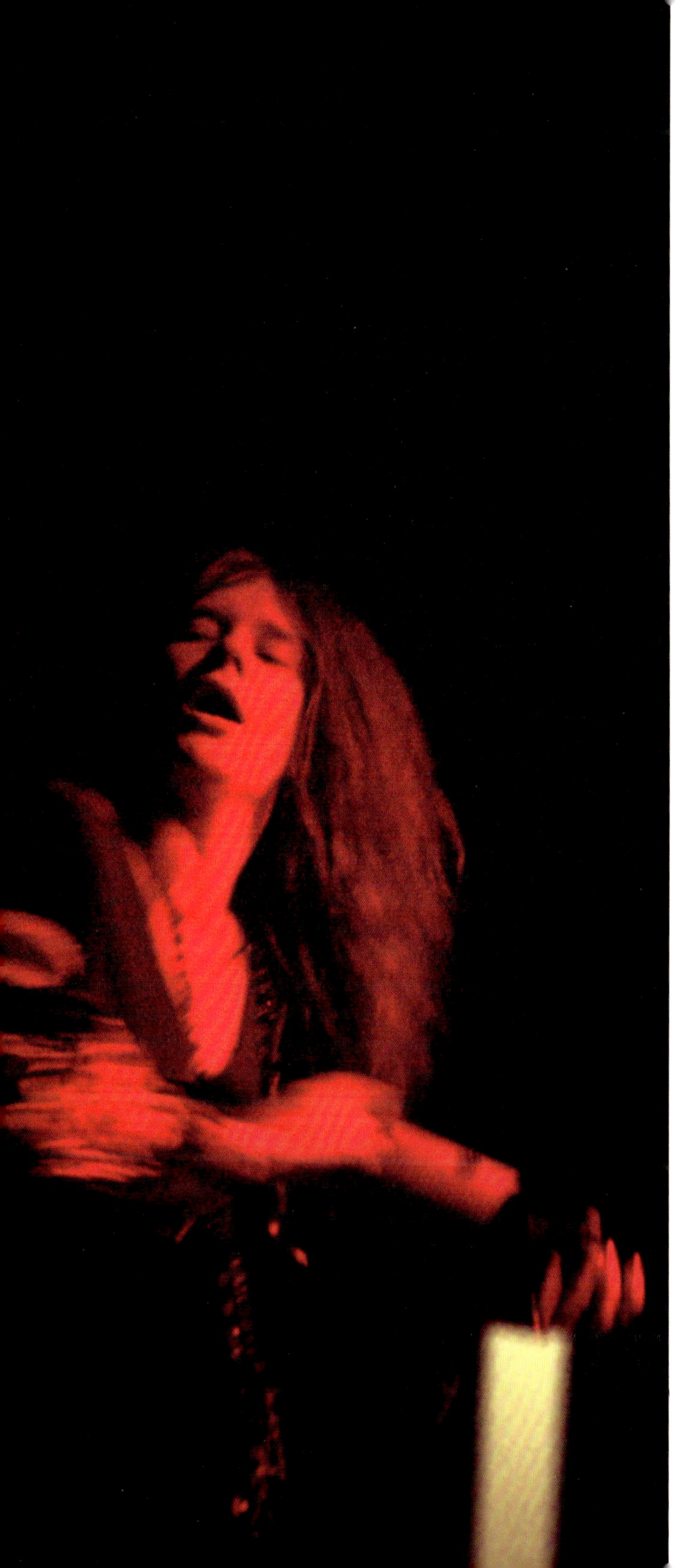

Janis Joplin of Big Brother and the Holding Company, Hunter College, New York, November 1968.

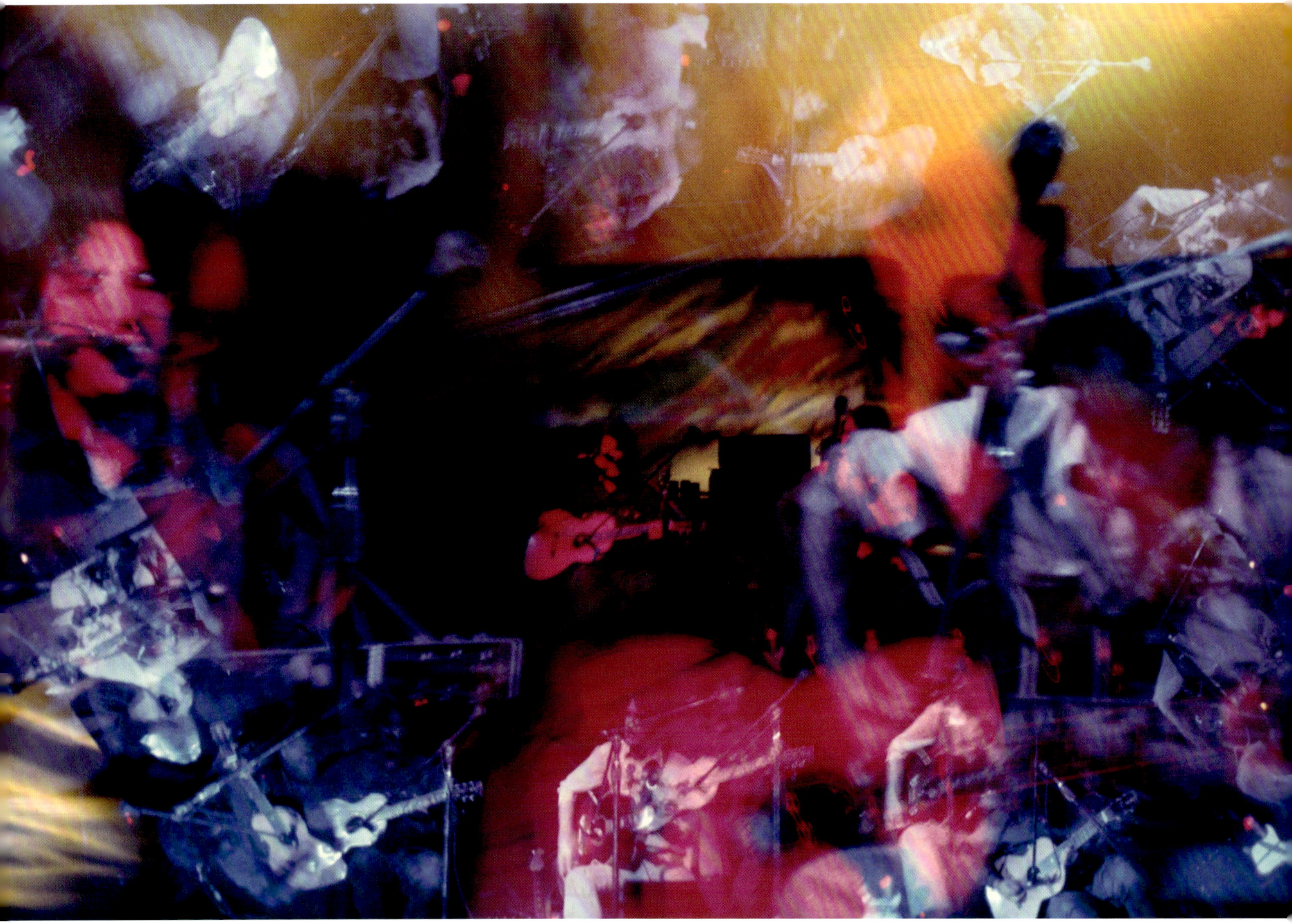

Jerry Garcia and Bob Weir of the Grateful Dead, Fillmore East, New York, May 1970.

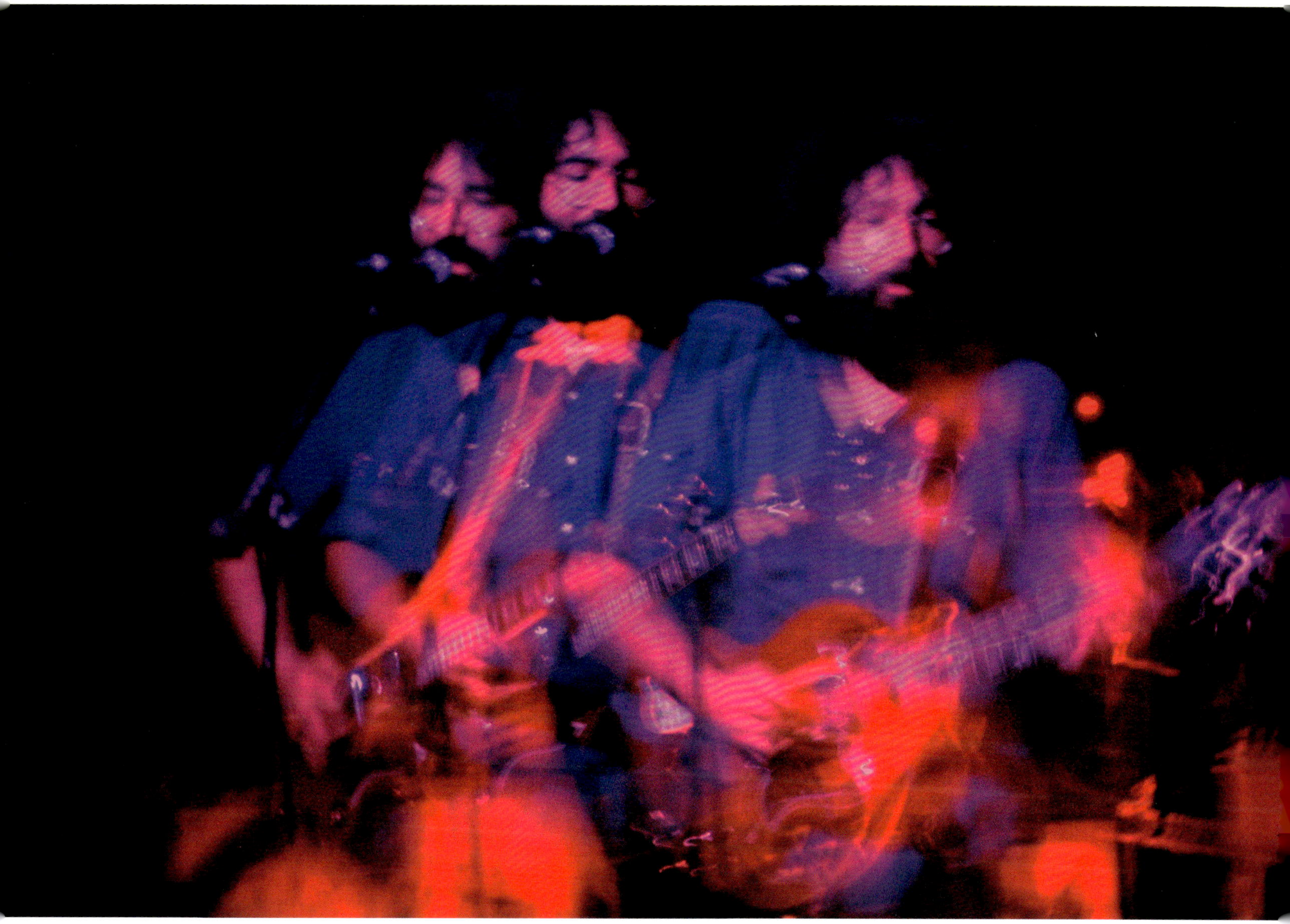

Jerry Garcia of the Grateful Dead, Fillmore East, New York, September 1970.

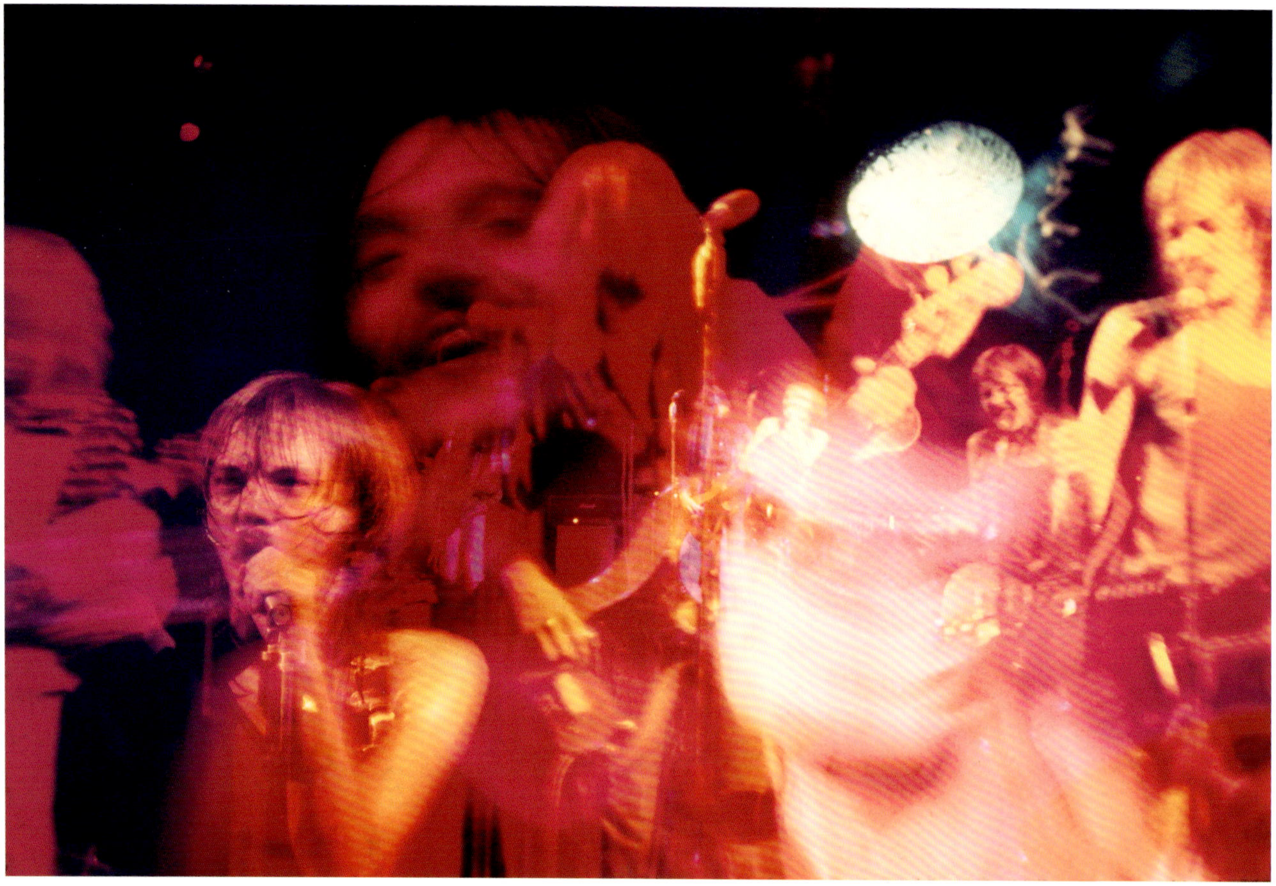

Steve Marriott of Humble Pie, Fillmore East, New York, October 1970. *Opposite*: Jerry Garcia (left) and Bob Weir (right), Fillmore East, New York, May 1970.

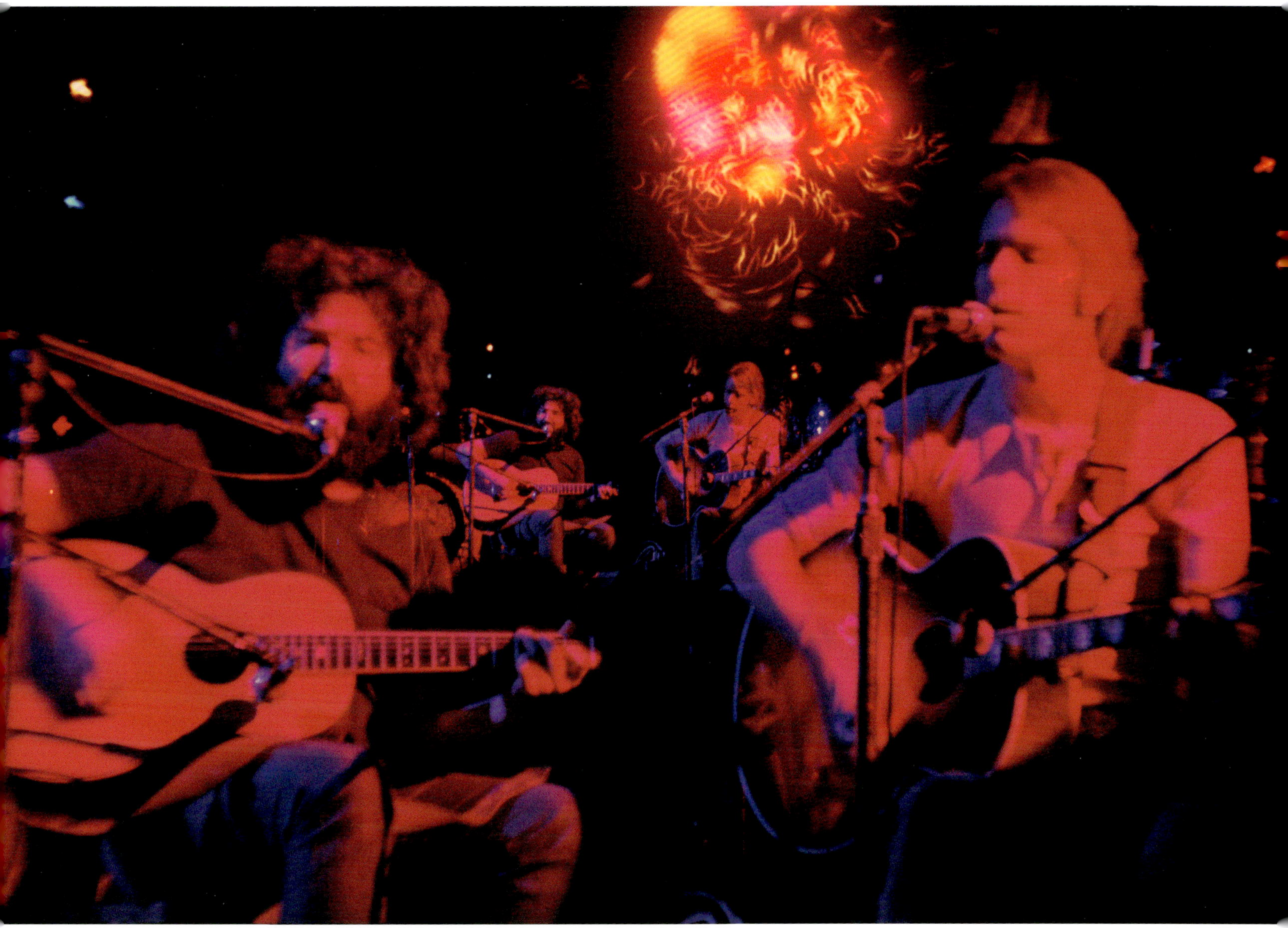

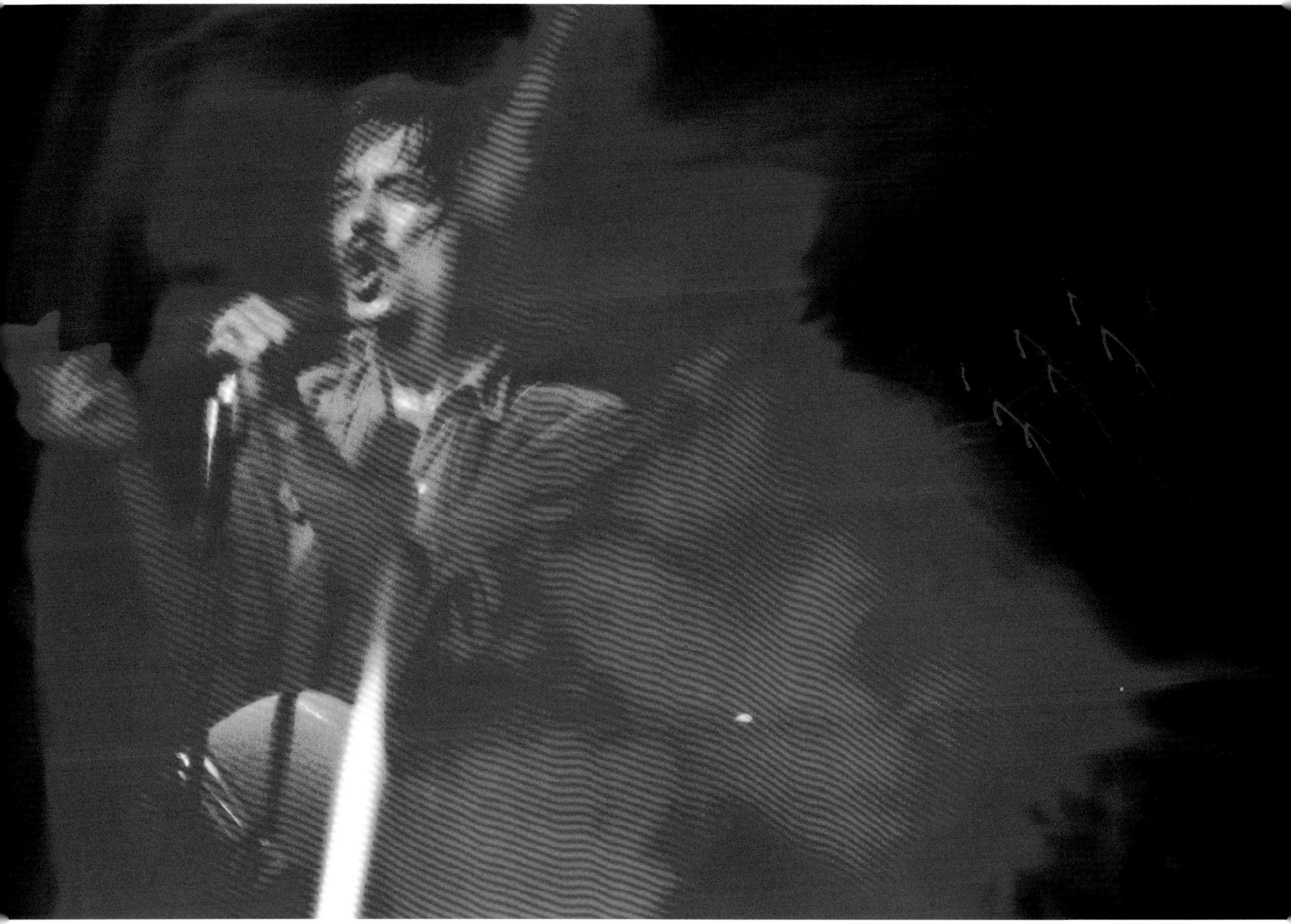

Steve Marriott of Humble Pie, Fillmore East, New York, May 1971. *Opposite*: John Cipollina of Quicksilver Messenger Service, Fillmore East, New York, April 1970.

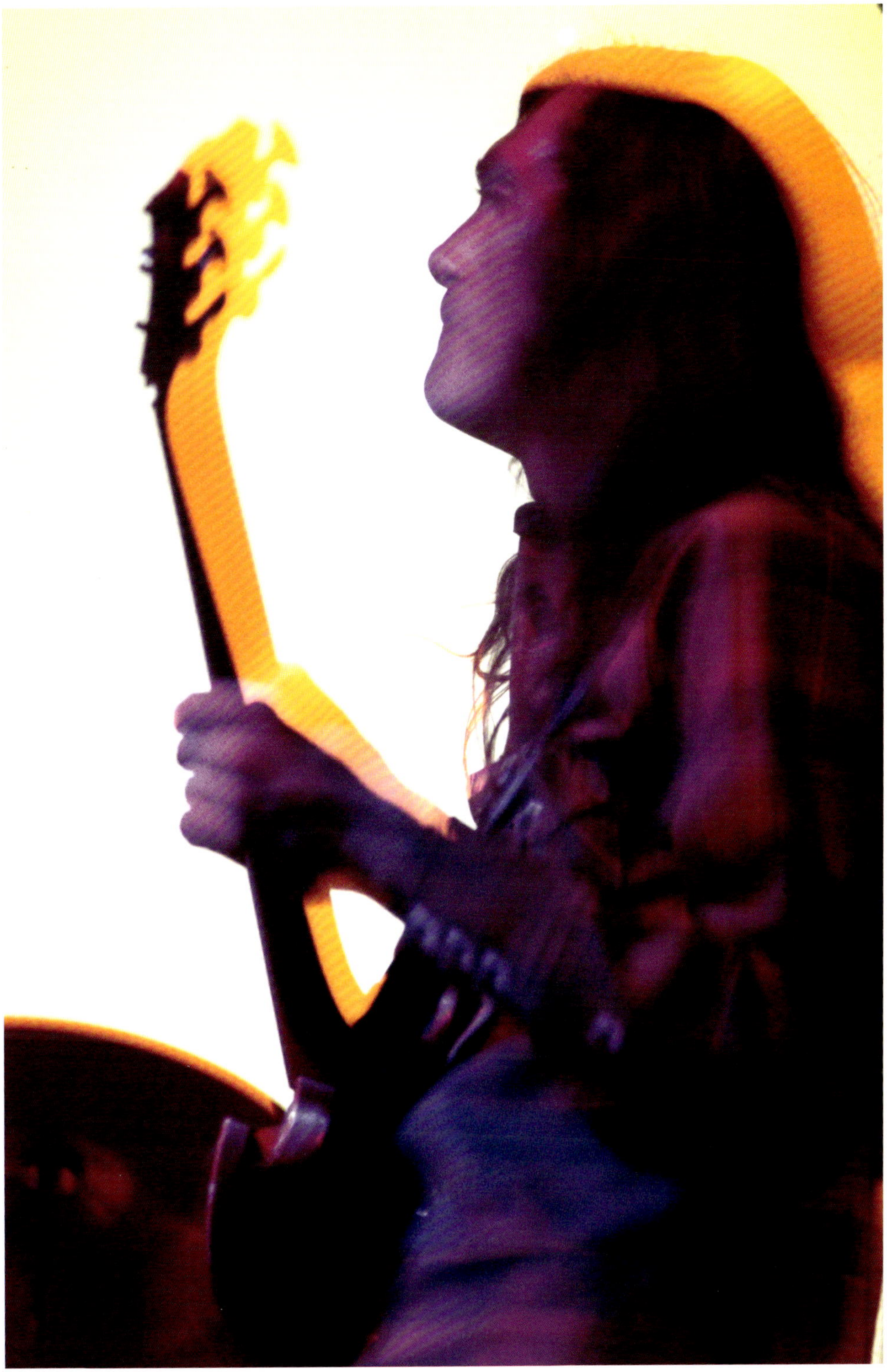

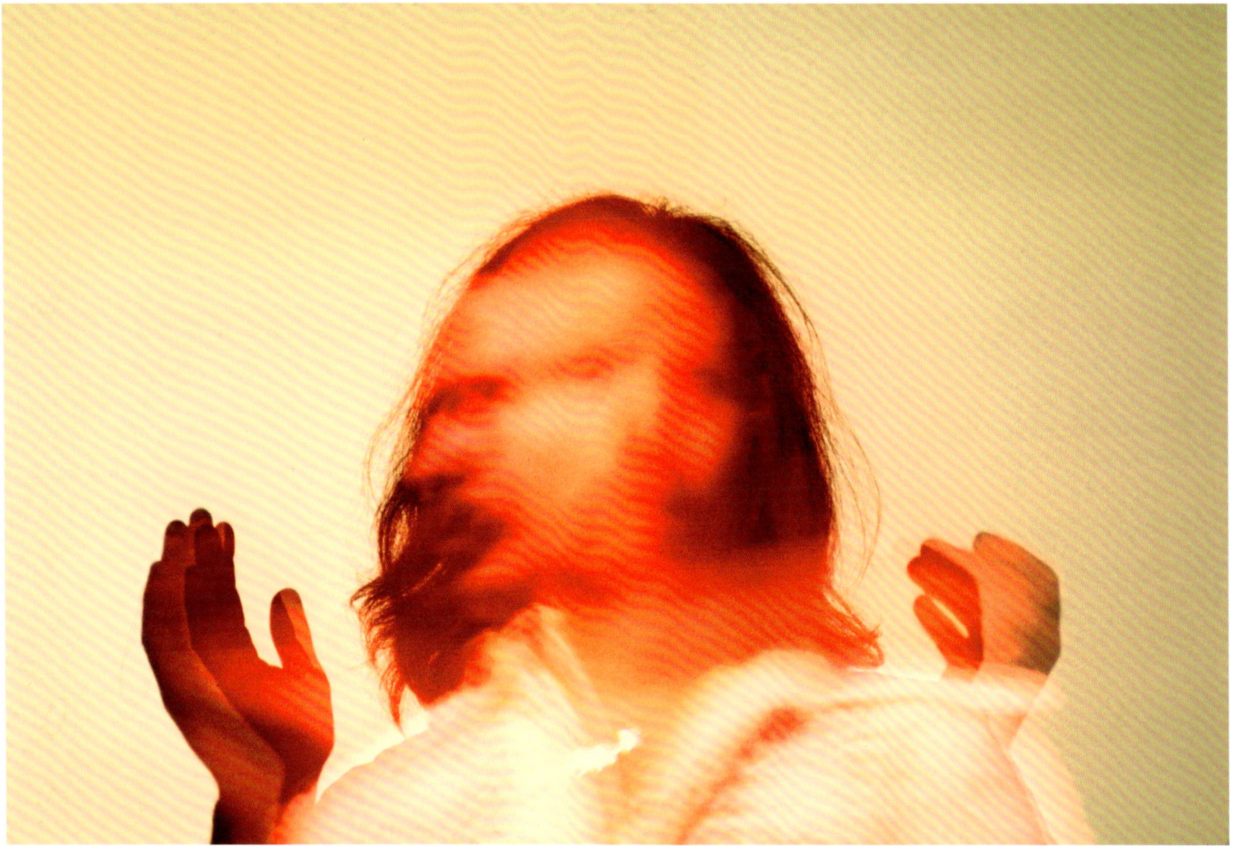

Country Joe McDonald of Country Joe and The Fish, Fillmore East, New York, October 1969.

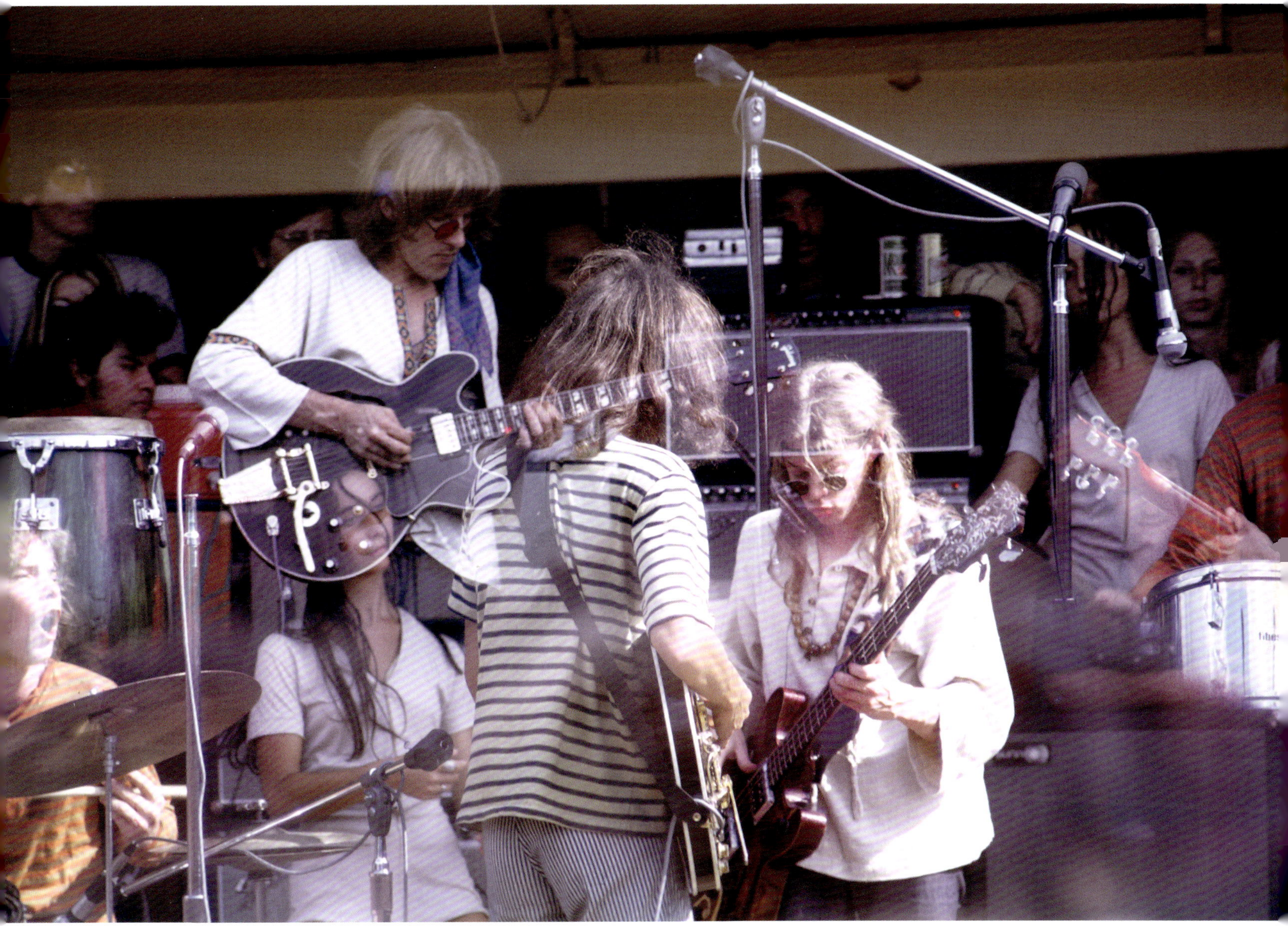

Michael Shrieve and Jose Areas of Santana and Paul Kantner, Jorma Kaukonen, and Jack Casady of Jefferson Airplane, Central Park, New York, August 1969.

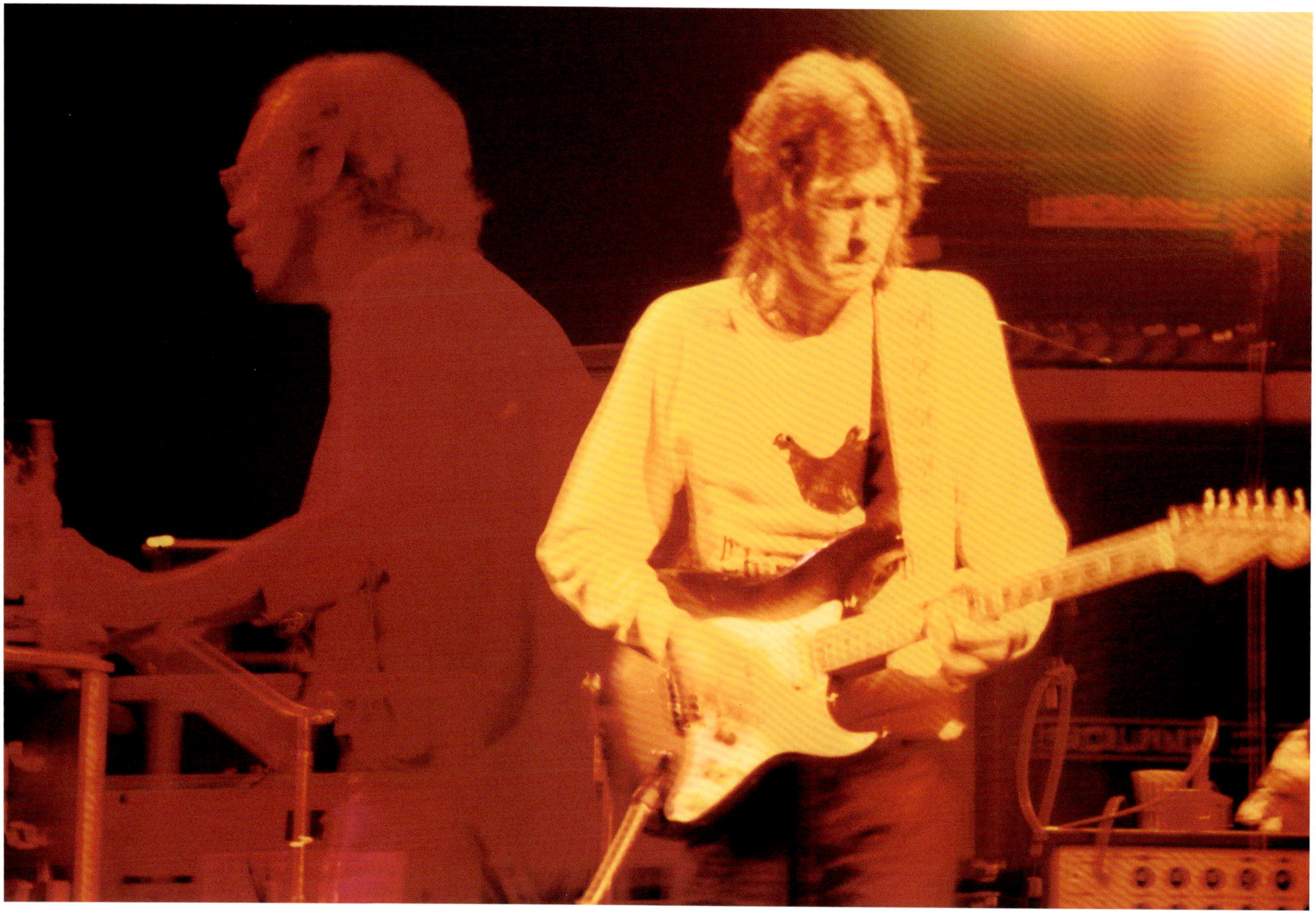

Eric Clapton and Carl Radle, Fillmore East, New York, October 1970.

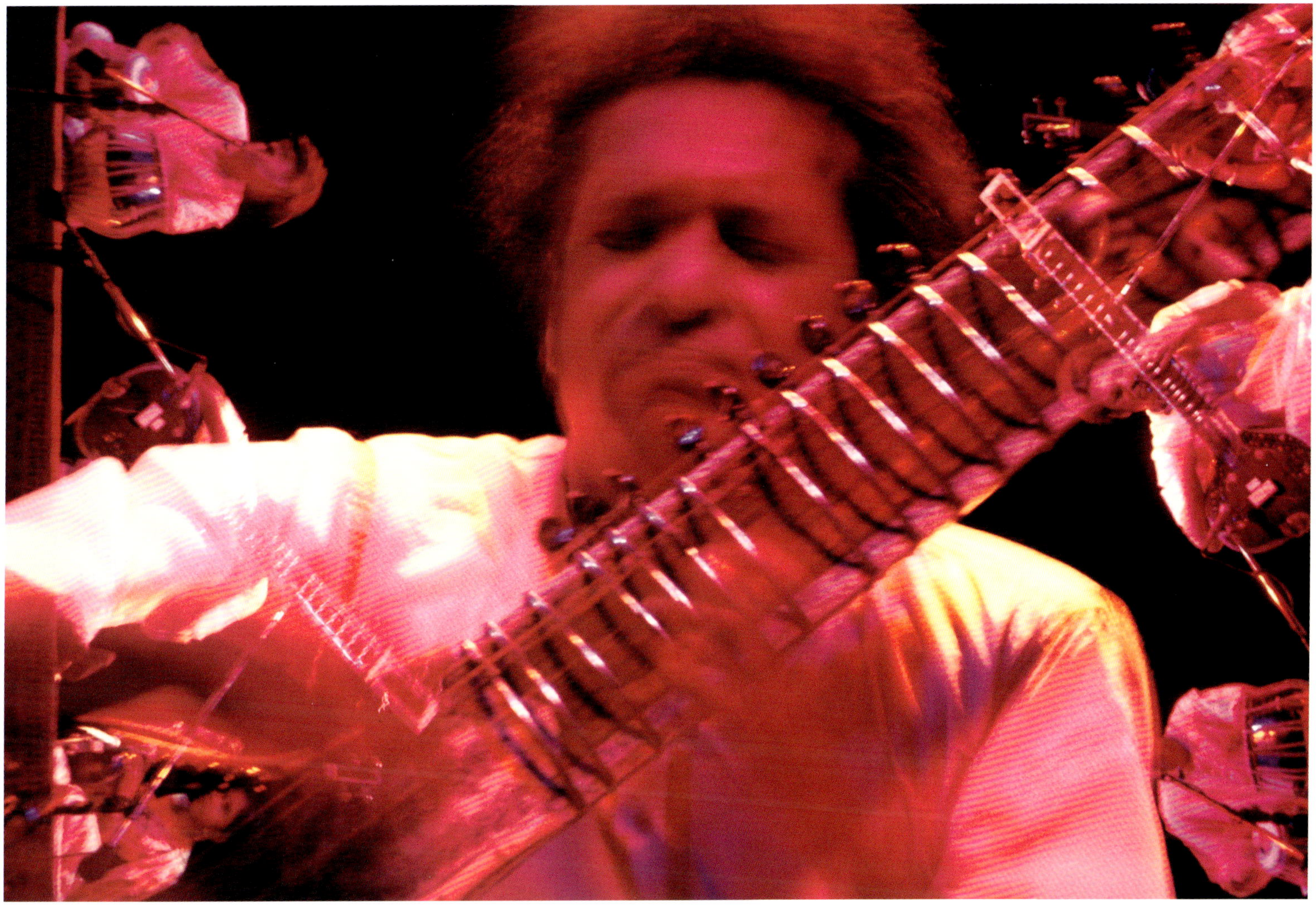

Ravi Shankar, Fillmore East, New York, March 1970.

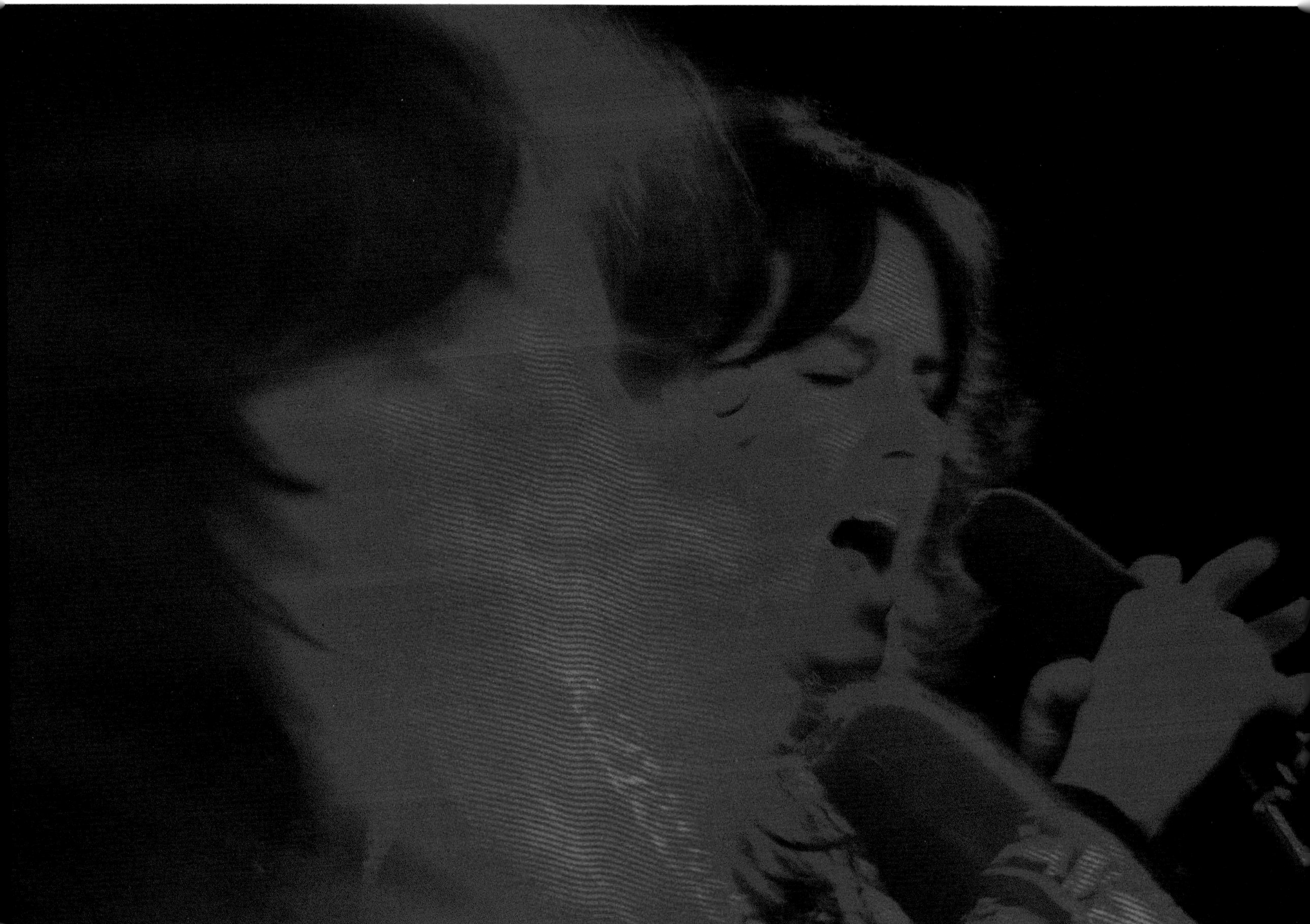

Grace Slick of Jefferson Airplane, Gaelic Park, Bronx, New York, August 1971.

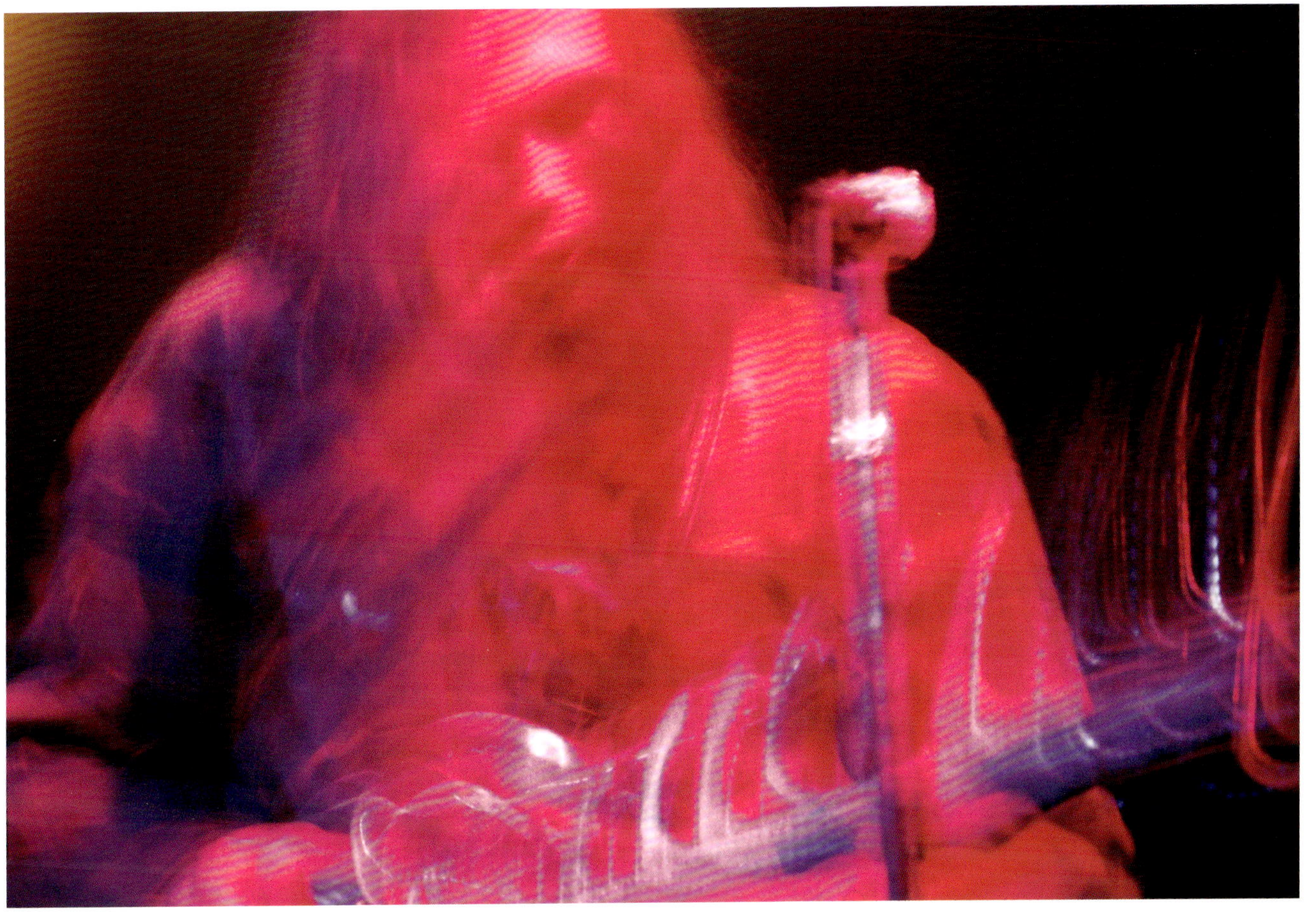

John Cipollina of Quicksilver Messenger Service, Fillmore East, New York, April 1970.

I set out to capture the intensity of the sound, which at times would propel one to a higher state of consciousness. . . . As the music I listened to became more abstract, my own work became more abstracted as well.

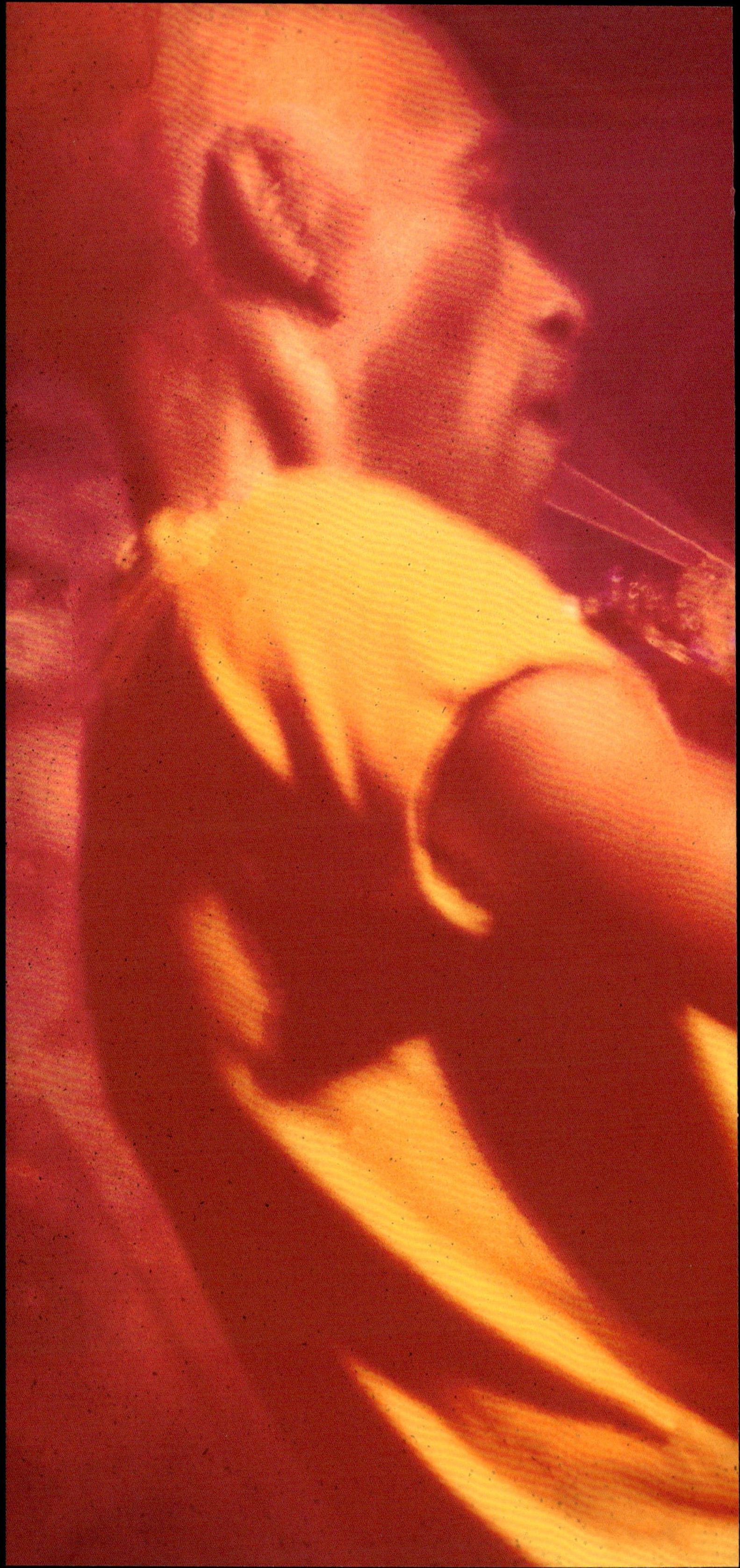

Papa John Creach and Jack Casady of Jefferson Airplane, Gaelic Park, Bronx, New York, August 1971.

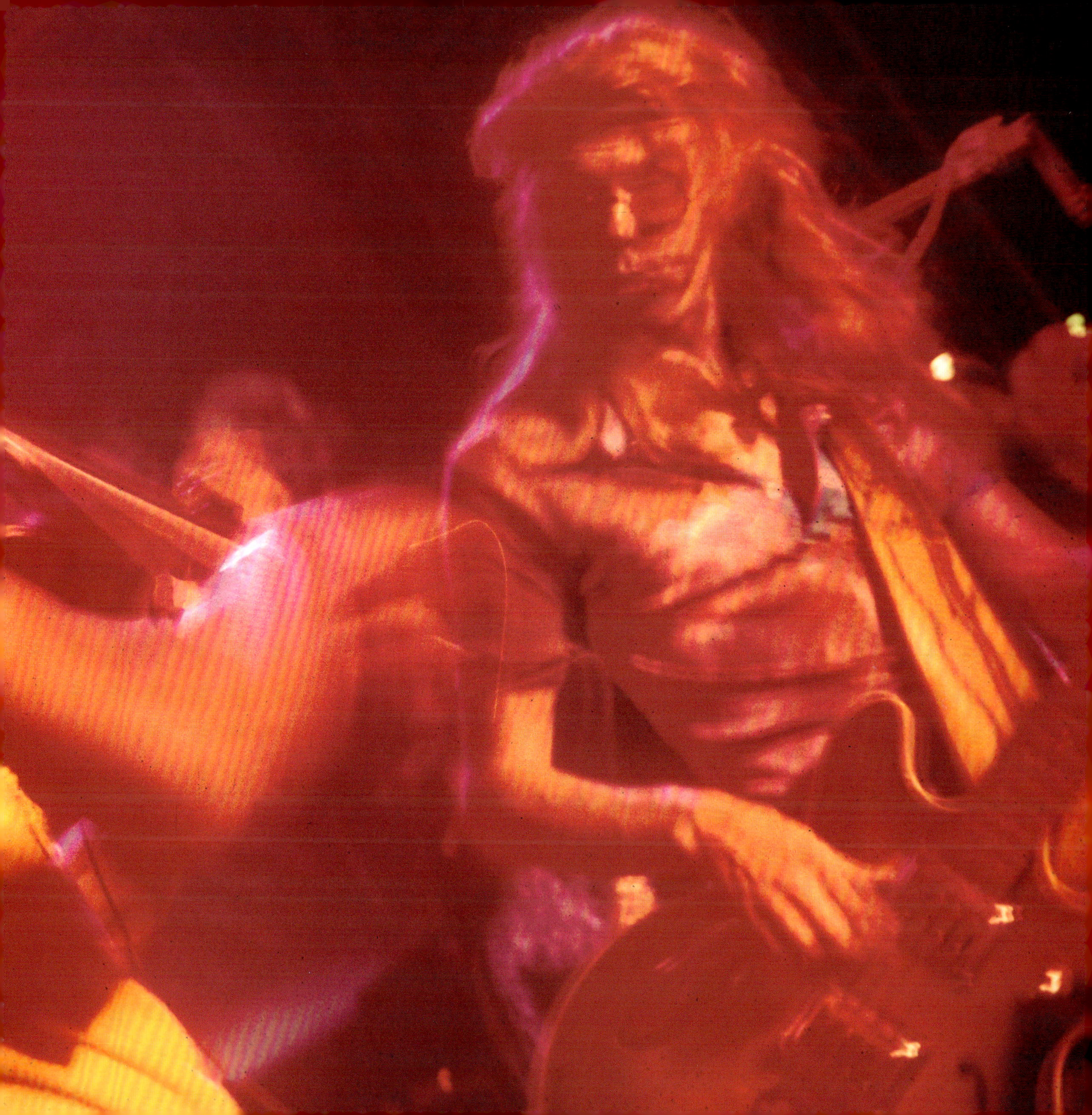

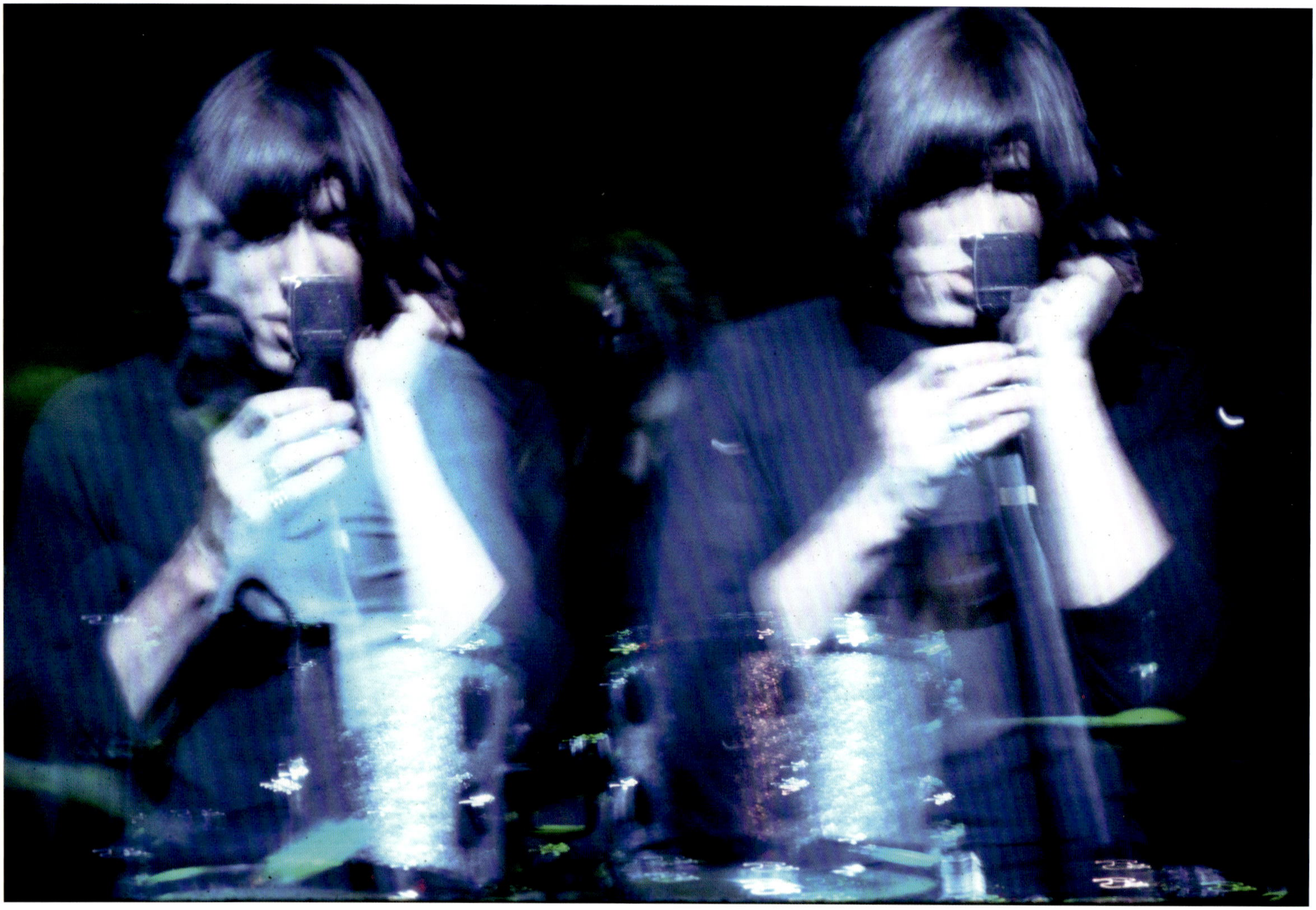

Richard Wright, Roger Waters, and Nick Mason of Pink Floyd, Fillmore East, New York, September 1970. *Opposite*: Frank Zappa, Fillmore East, New York, May 1970.

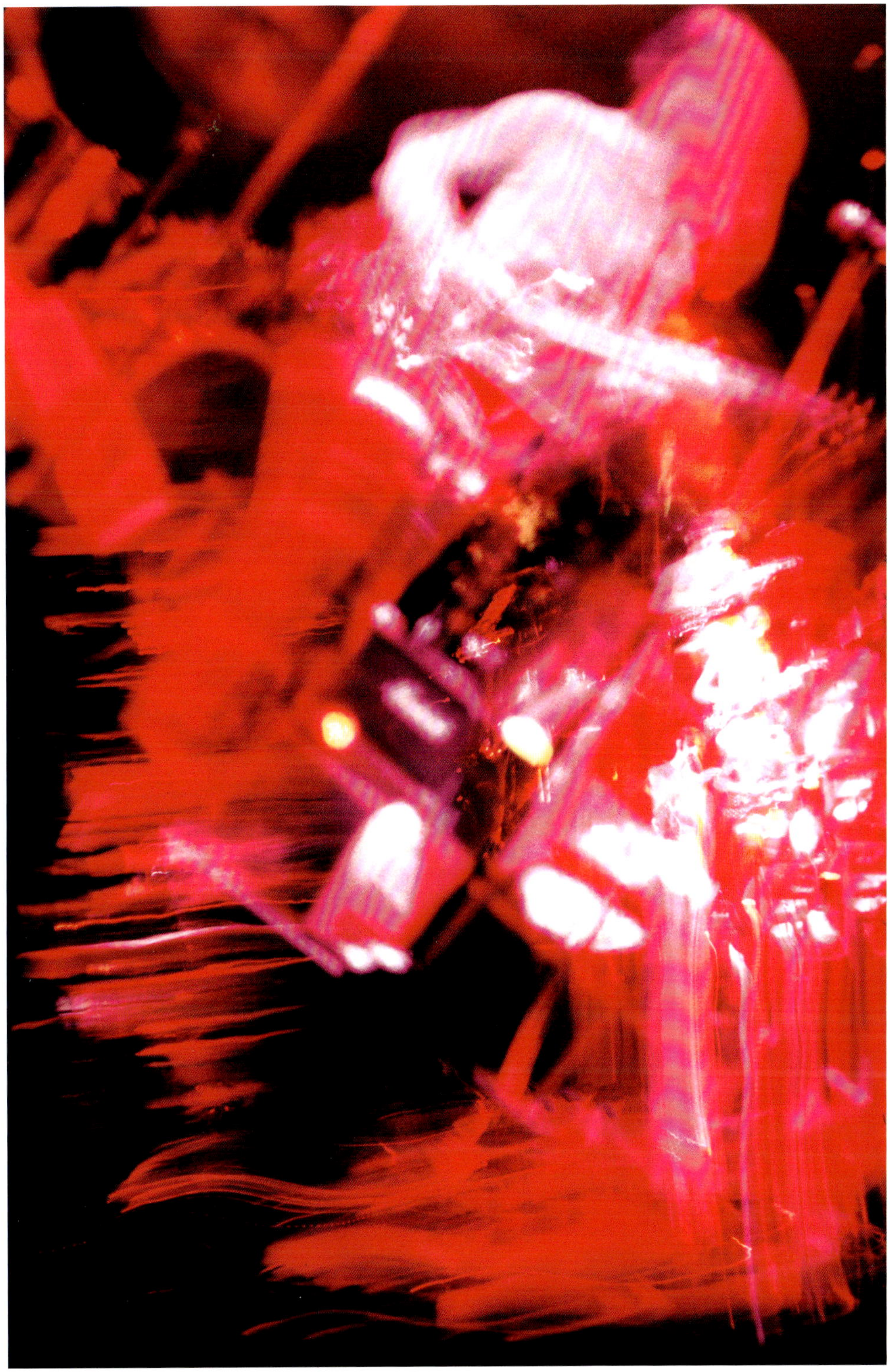

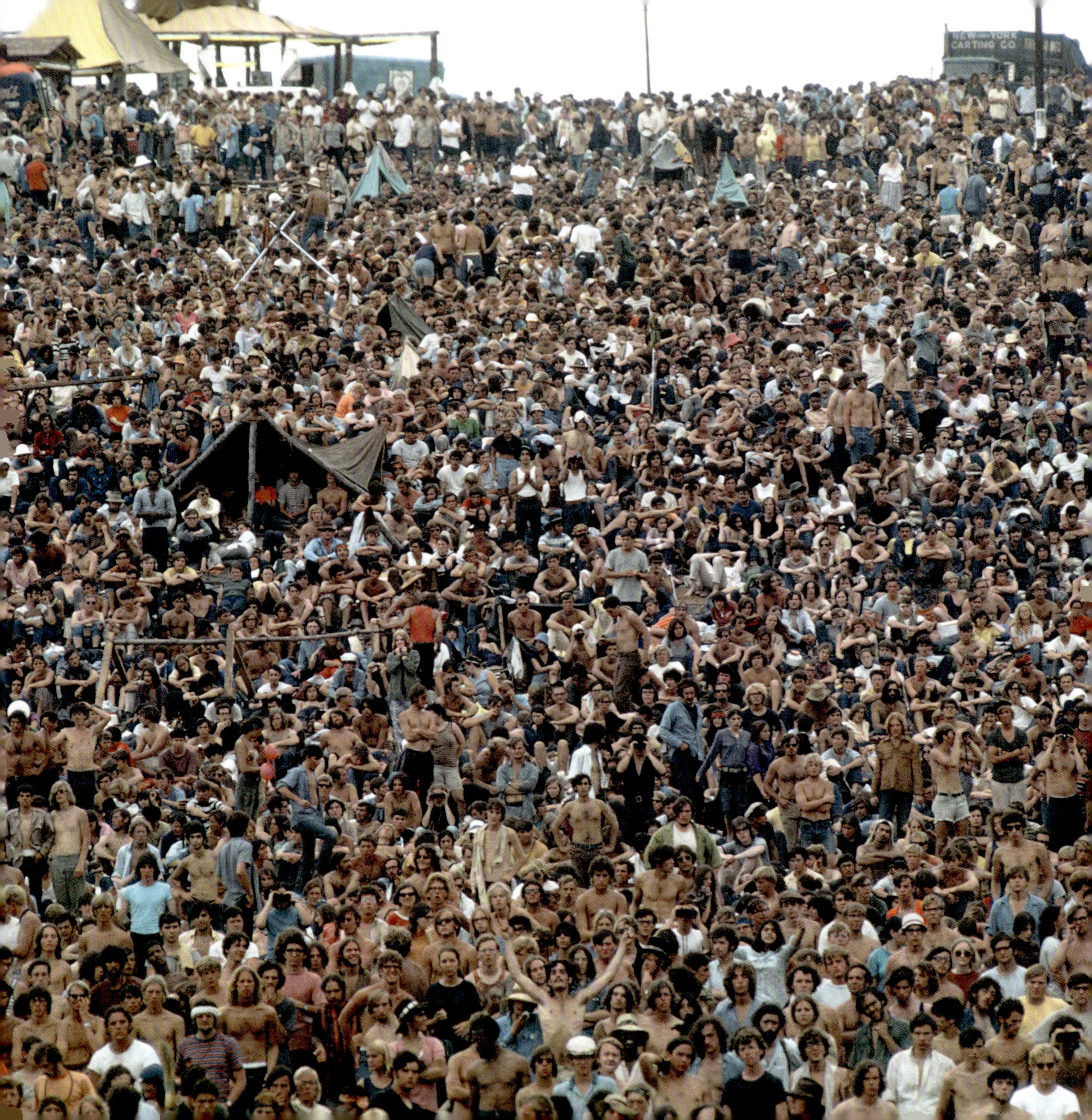
CARTING CO.

5

Woodstock

Boom! There I was. In the unrelenting midafternoon New York heat, August 16, 1969, on stage at the Woodstock Music and Art Fair. All of twenty years old, dazed and dazzled by the events that led up to my charmed position now swimming in my head. It was the second day of the festival, and I was there to photograph Jefferson Airplane, who had asked me to capture them under the full-stage lighting, using what was by then my signature style. My work now featured multiple images, motion, wild in-camera effects, and a psychedelic feel, which fit the band's equally wild, experimental, and highly psychedelic music.

I set off for Woodstock on Friday, August 15, with no thought that it would be much different from the several other festivals that had already taken place that summer. After a hot ride up to Bethel from the somewhat cooler Jersey Shore, I arrived at the scene. Making my way through the tangle of traffic, I was able to park my car on the side of the road without too much trouble. I got out and walked among the crowd, just in time to see Richie Havens, the opening act, and several other bands from the vantage point of the growing masses. There was an excitement that was palpable even in these early hours of the event, and the crowd was immense, but I encountered no trouble navigating the scene. I took a couple of faraway crowd shots, ever stewarding my film for the events to come. The Incredible String Band began their set, and their transcendent, otherworldly sounds resonated across the grounds. After listening for a bit, I left for my hotel.

The Airplane and some other bands were staying in the town of Liberty at the Holiday Inn. When I arrived in the early evening, I located several of the band members. We huddled in Paul Kantner's room, and I

Crowd from the stage at Woodstock, August 1969.

broke out my slide projector, which I always had with me. The images, blown up on the wall, had a powerful impact. The assembled crowd, including drop-in guests Jerry Garcia and David Crosby, reacted positively while I pointed out many of my influences. I was gratified that my audience knew many of them and could see how these "nonchemical" inspirations affected my work. After a full evening of refreshments as only the Airplane could provide, everyone seemed to appreciate the visual entertainment I provided, except perhaps for Crosby. Though at first I noticed that he reacted enthusiastically to my work, at one point he asked me where I was from; after I answered New Jersey, he oddly he got up and left the room. I couldn't help but feel slighted in the moment, but by the end of the evening my spirits and confidence were high.

Heading to my room that night, I passed other musicians and roadies, I sensed that this festival was going to be different from all the rest. The Airplane was scheduled to play around midnight on Saturday, headlining the day as they always did. Little did we know that things would not go as planned.

By early Saturday afternoon, when it was time to go to the festival site with the band, there was most certainly a buzz about the show. I piled into one of the cars that made up a caravan of the band members, road crew, and the ever-present entourage. There was an air of excitement accompanied by a definite feeling of venturing into the unknown. The drivers knew the back roads through the heavily treed landscape and delivered us to the back of the ever-burgeoning festival site around 2:30 p.m., with everyone now intoxicated by both the many and varied substances being consumed and the apprehension of things to come.

From the car, I could see scores of people trying to execute the many tasks associated with making a festival run under increasingly chaotic circumstances. The stage at Woodstock was elevated and was probably about twenty to twenty-five feet above the crowd; as I emerged from the car, in quite the altered state, I could hear the unfamiliar sounds of a band onstage. They were deep into an intense instrumental jam completely unknown to me. Someone mentioned that the band was managed by Bill Graham, who demanded that they be part of the festival in return for his help. They were little known outside of the San Francisco Bay Area, and this was their first East Coast performance.

The band was Santana, and they were finishing their set with what was to become their signature instrumental, "Soul Sacrifice." Jorma Kaukonen, Jefferson Airplane's lead guitarist, his then wife, Margareta, I, and a few other brave souls took on the daunting task, in the state we all were in, of climbing a series of switchback ramps that led up to the scaffolding at the back of the stage. By accomplishing this, we knew we would see the true nature and size of the crowd. As we made the trek, zigzagging across the broad sweep of ramps, the music continued to grow in intensity and impact; all the while we were getting dizzyingly higher, in both altitude and attitude. As the music swelled to its final crescendo, a sight was slowly and surely revealed that none of us would ever forget.

By the time we arrived at the top, we were profoundly stunned at what was now fully visible, and we stood dumbfounded and silent as Santana brought the tour de force that was "Soul Sacrifice" to its epic, cataclysmic conclusion. There was, before us, a sea of bodies as far as one could see ahead, to the side, and as wide as 240 degrees surrounding the stage. Aghast at this totally unexpected sight, and attempting to process this overwhelming vision, we encountered the Grateful Dead's Bob Weir, who turned, gave a complicit high stare, and turned back silently pointing to the crowd with an utterly befuddled yet reverential look.

I made my way down to the stage and began to reconnoiter where to set up camp, to ensure that I would be able to take full advantage of the events to come. I sat down next to John Sebastian and Country Joe McDonald, observing and respecting their space and whatever they were experiencing. I gladly partook of the joints being passed back and forth between the two, and in a somewhat stoned stupor observed, slack-jawed, the seemingly nonstop, ever-growing, overwhelming sea of people gathering beyond the stage. I then clammed up and made myself as comfortable as I could on the hard, unfinished bare wooden planks of the temporary yet hopefully sturdy stage. Even as I was amazed and confused by the music, the crowd, the personalities, and the smell of the ever-present patchouli oil in the air, I began to wonder at how I, barely twenty years old, came to be at ground zero of what was to become one of the most memorable events of the twentieth century.

As I was on the stage at Woodstock, I tried to take in the spectacle, processing it as best as I could. I did not leave the stage for over twenty hours, not even to go to the bathroom (which would be impossible now that I can barely hold things for a few hours, at my advanced age!). During that time, I chatted with many of the artists coming and going as they roamed the stage in awe of the growing scene surrounding them. As I strolled about freely, I spent some time with and photographed Grace and Paul as well as Spencer Dryden and his soon to be wife, Sally Mann. As the hours passed there was much weed smoking and conjecture as to whether there was any chance of the Airplane performing close to the scheduled midnight time slot. No one knew that their performance wouldn't begin until 8:00 a.m. the next morning. Meanwhile, as the night wore on, I nearly tripped over an overserved and comatose Ron "Pigpen" McKernan from the Grateful Dead lying supine backstage in the dark. I also ran into the always gracious Janis Joplin, whom I had photographed in New York and met a year before at a Philadelphia concert with her original band, Big Brother and the Holding Company. She was very talkative and said she remembered me, but she may have been just being polite. Either way, we chatted about how excited she was to bring her new band to Woodstock, which would expose them to a huge new audience. I told her that Woodstock could be their breakout performance, perhaps like the Monterey Pop Festival had been for her two years earlier.

We toasted to the possibility that it would indeed be a significant night for her and the new band.

After listening to and photographing some of the other scheduled bands (while trying to save most of my film for the Airplane), the Who took the stage just before daybreak. During their set, I witnessed their stirring rendition of "Pinball Wizard" as well as, from mere feet away, the infamous Abbie Hoffman incident where he attempted to hijack the microphone in the middle of the band's set only to be met with a harrowing smash of a guitar by a visibly angered and rightly outraged Pete Townshend. I was shooting right up to and at that moment of quickly resolved chaos.

The time-stretching performances by band after band thwarted my plans to photograph the Airplane in my signature style. I had to adapt to the conditions, producing up-close, sun-drenched images of the band, yet I feel the shots are still extremely dynamic, powerfully portraying the intensity of the performance on that historic early morn. Contrary to some critics, who over the years have dismissed the Airplane's music that day as uninspired, I continue to maintain that their set was well performed and transformative, uplifting to not only myself but the hundreds of thousands of spirits in the audience, either just waking or having survived enough to be somewhat conscious after the chaotic night. Grace greeted them with the invocation: "Alright friends, you have seen the heavy groups, now you will see morning maniac music, believe me, yeah. . . . It's the new dawn." And a new and blazing dawn it was.

By the time of Woodstock, the Airplane's music had gotten deep into politics, and they possessed a mighty arsenal of songs, like no other band of the day, challenging the Establishment, the Vietnam War, and conventional behavior in general. A lot of their music was disturbing, thought-provoking, and iconoclastic but mixed with outright pleas for love and tolerance of their fellow humans. The music was delivered with a combination of Jorma's powerful guitar, Jack's thunderous bass, guest British artist Nicky Hopkins's subtle but strong piano, and Spencer's always dramatic yet finessed drumming. The vocals of Grace, Paul (who always provided twelve-string guitar rhythm), and Marty generated breathtaking anthemic singing. The songs were wielded with ferocity, transmogrifying the band into a formidable weapon of freedom—no less than the electric embodiment of the message scrawled on Woody Guthrie's acoustic guitar, "This Machine Kills Fascists."

At the end of what was a long but beyond satisfying day, night, and day again, utterly sleep deprived, we all miraculously assembled somehow back at the caravan of cars, which returned us to the Holiday Inn. I had to be back at work on Monday morning, in the salt-mine darkroom, so I had to miss the Sunday night and Monday conclusion of the festival. With my head spinning I poured myself into my car, made my way through the backwoods of Upstate New York, and headed back to Jersey, changed forever by the once-in-a-lifetime experience of Woodstock.

It's important to say here that the Vietnam War was the ten-thousand-pound gorilla in the fields at Woodstock. During just that weekend, 109 Americans sacrificed their lives while so many of us reveled and celebrated the freedoms that they were giving their lives for. The war touched virtually everyone in the country. There were those who were well connected and influential and got out of service for whatever reason, legitimate or otherwise. My situation was somewhat complicated and mysterious. Through a series of changes in my draft status due to school and some arcane system of classification, I was not drafted even though my draft number was ninety-three. The lower the number the more chance one had of being drafted. I benefited from an anomaly or a bureaucratic glitch and there was a three-month period that the government had to draft me. I survived the wait and was reclassified "not to be drafted" (1-Y) for the rest of the war. I considered myself more than lucky, though I also feel guilty to this day that I was able to escape the peril of the war and was somehow allowed to pursue my life uninterrupted.

I sometimes say jokingly, but with more than a modicum of truth, that my life and career peaked that weekend, but there were many more adventures on the horizon. Woodstock was a brilliant step, not the culmination of my odyssey.

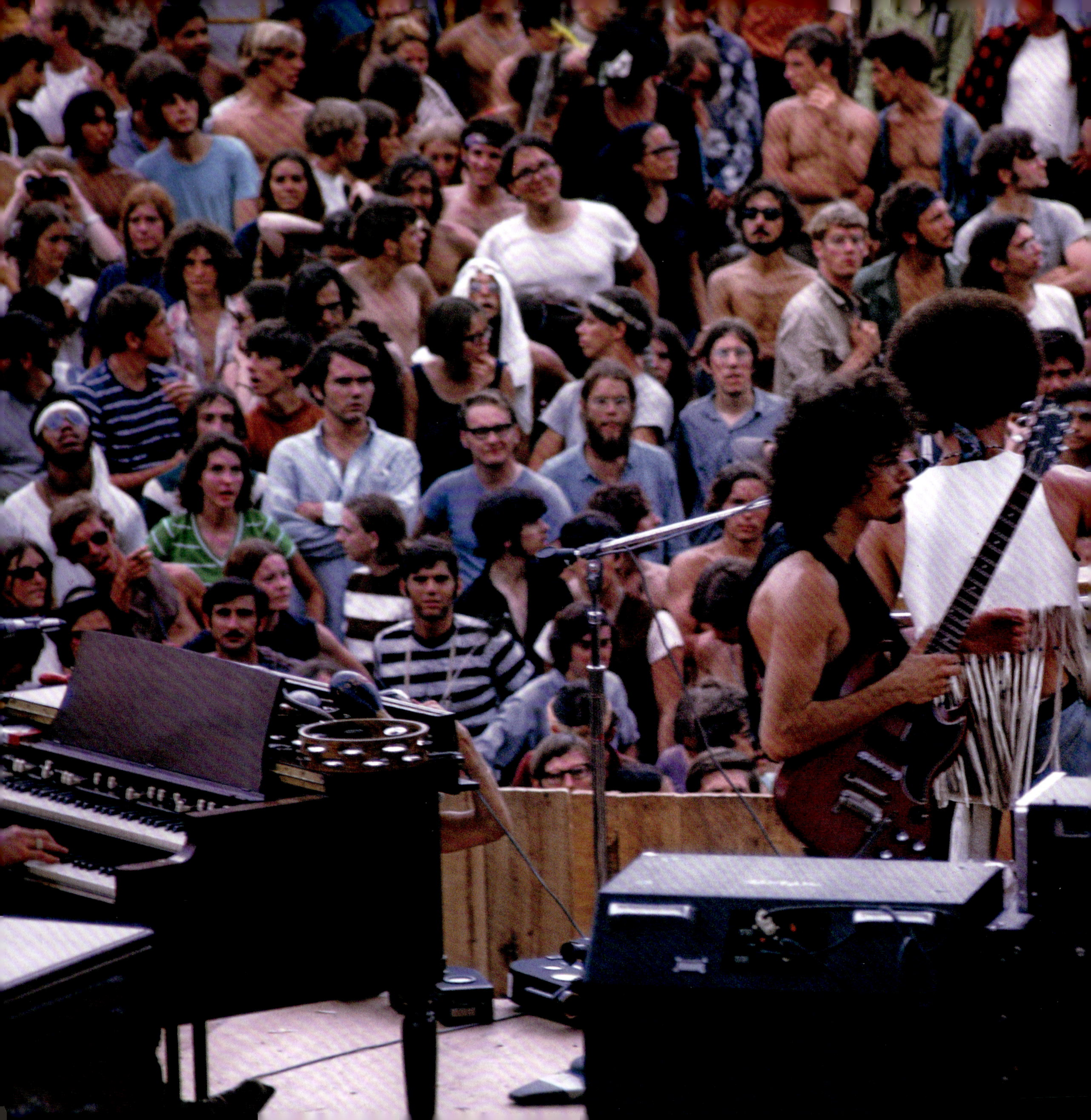

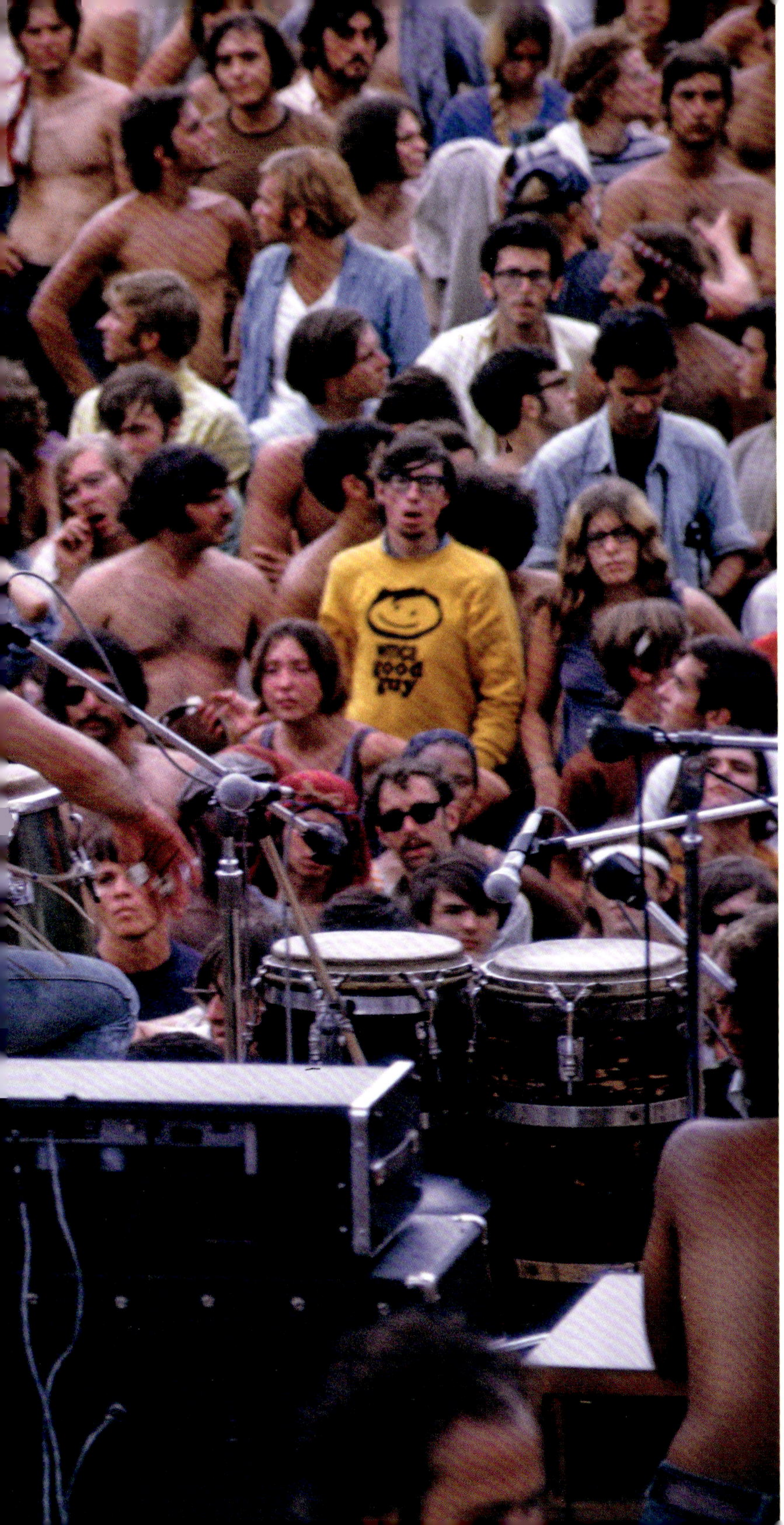

Carlos Santana at Woodstock with crowd.

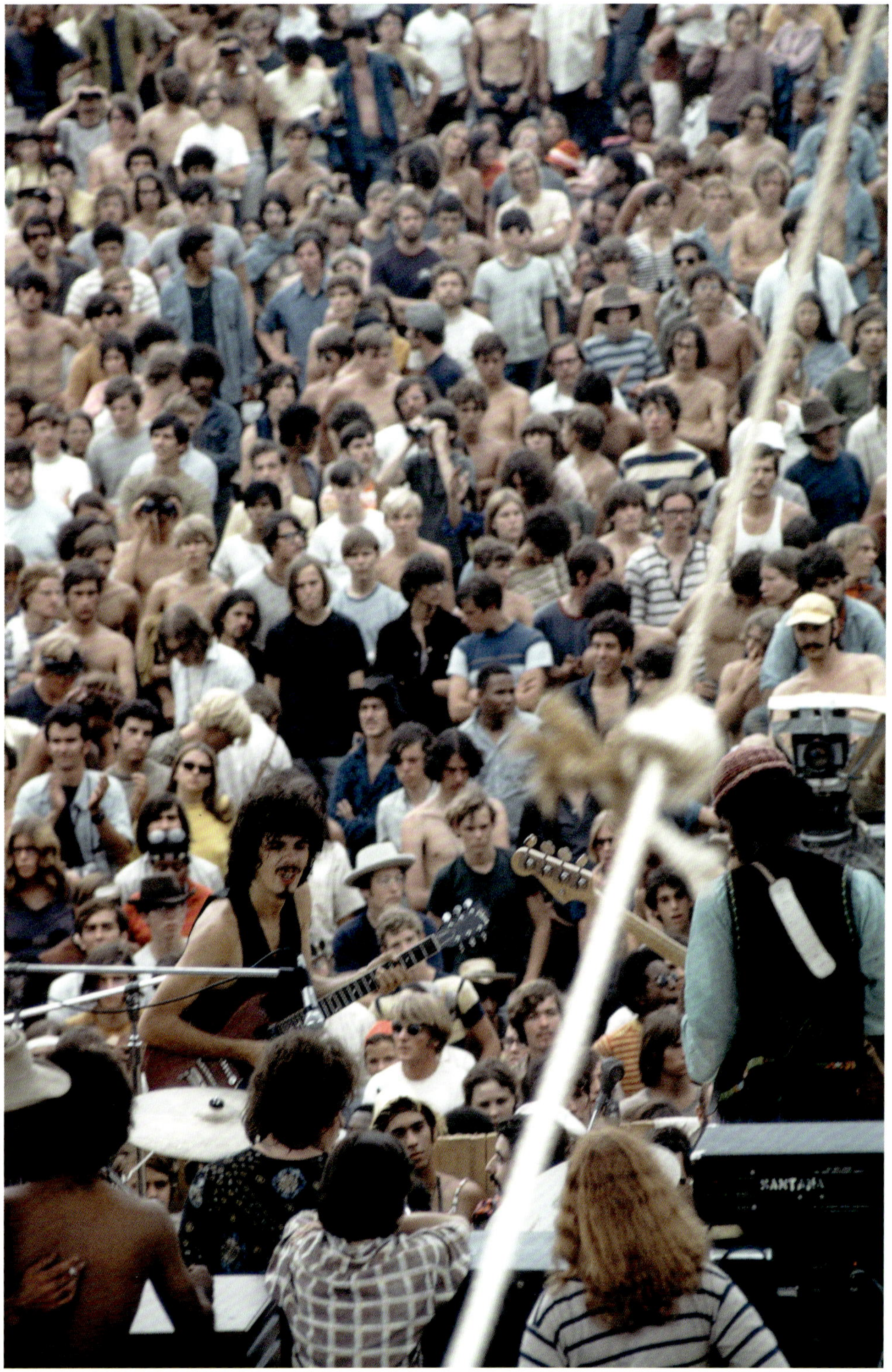
SANTANA

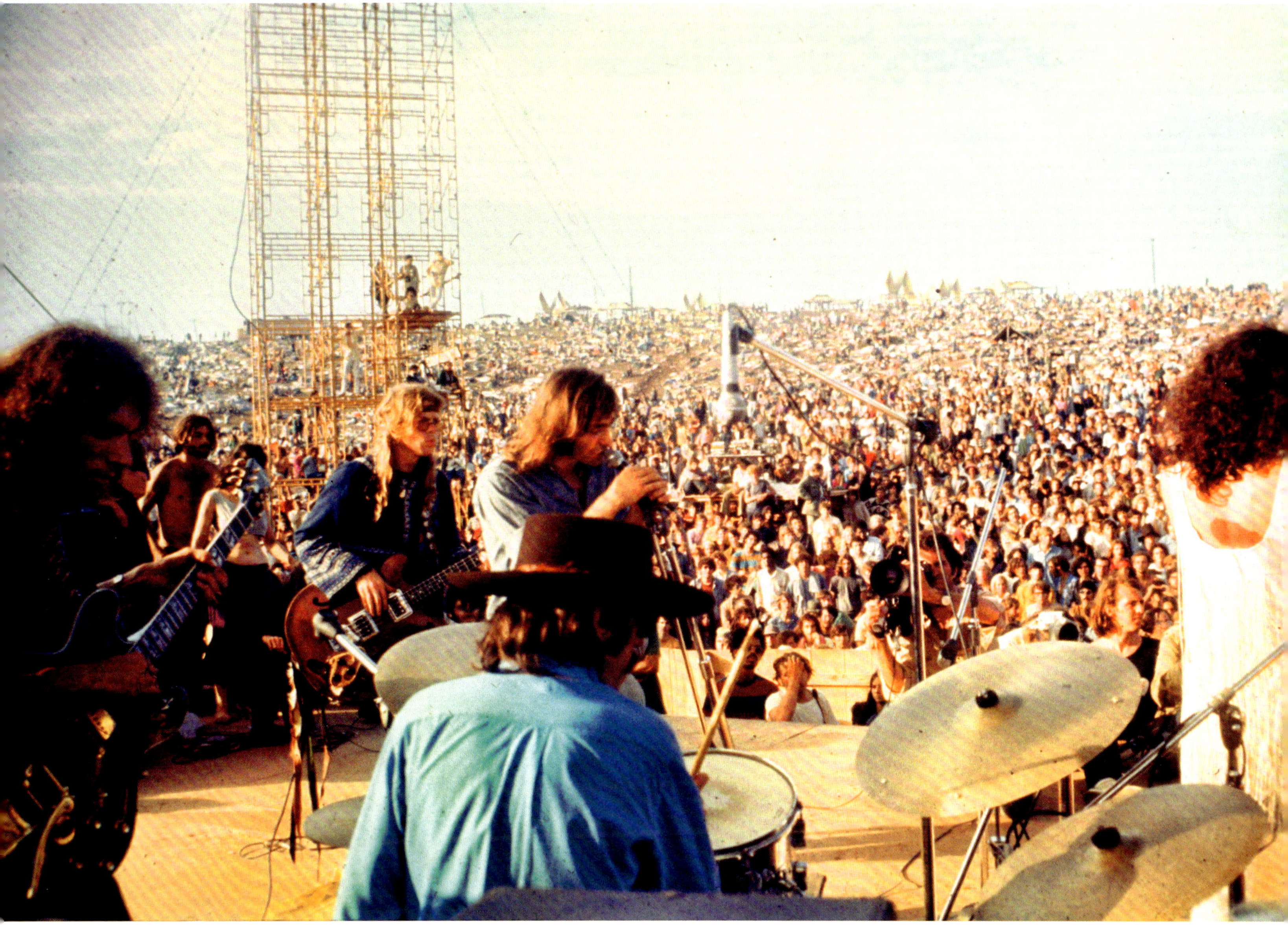

Jefferson Airplane, Woodstock. *Opposite*: Carlos Santana, Michael Shrieve, and David Brown from backstage, Woodstock, August 1969.

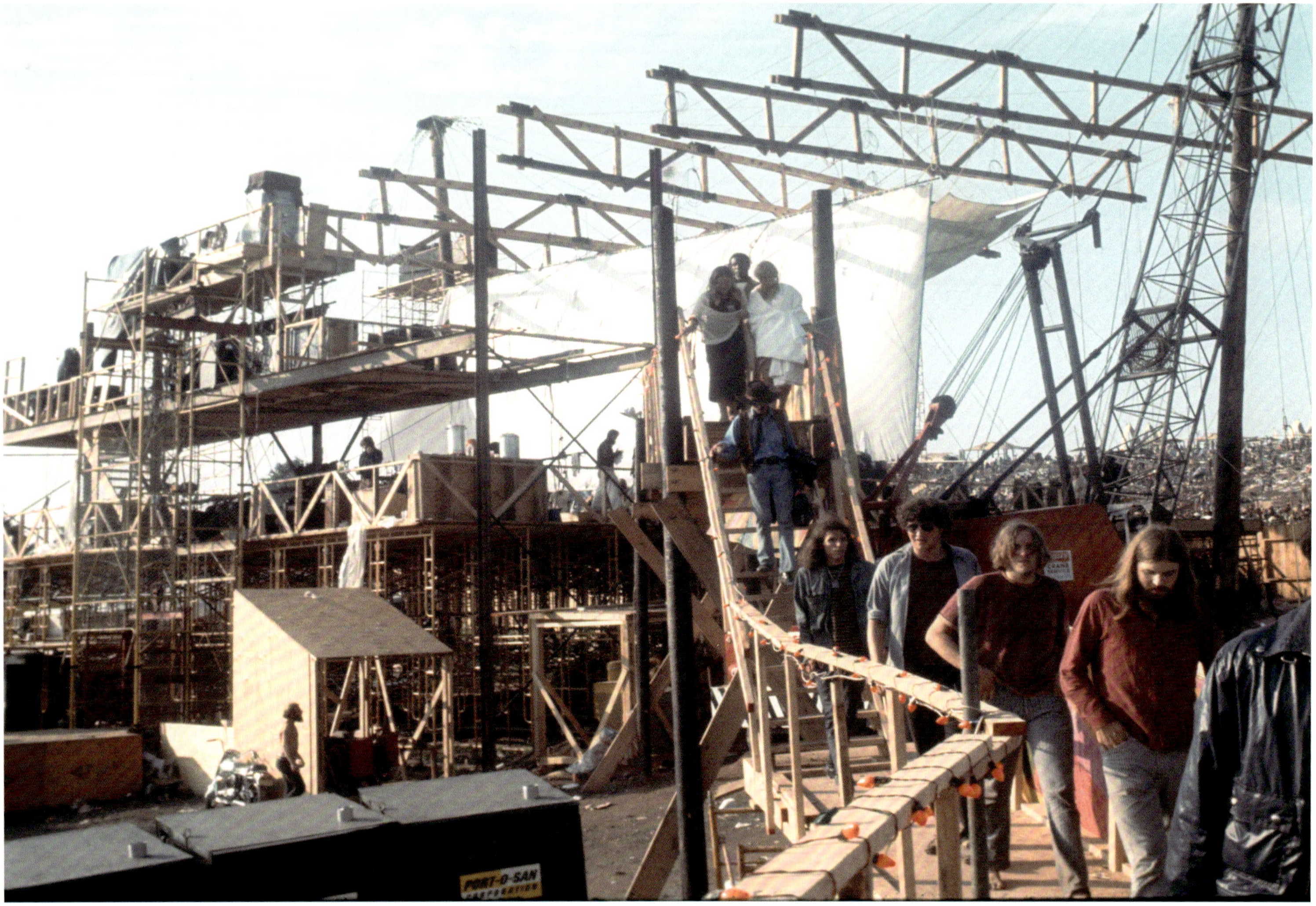

Backstage scaffolding at Woodstock Center Spencer Dryden and Jorma Kaukonen of Jefferson Airplane, August 1969.

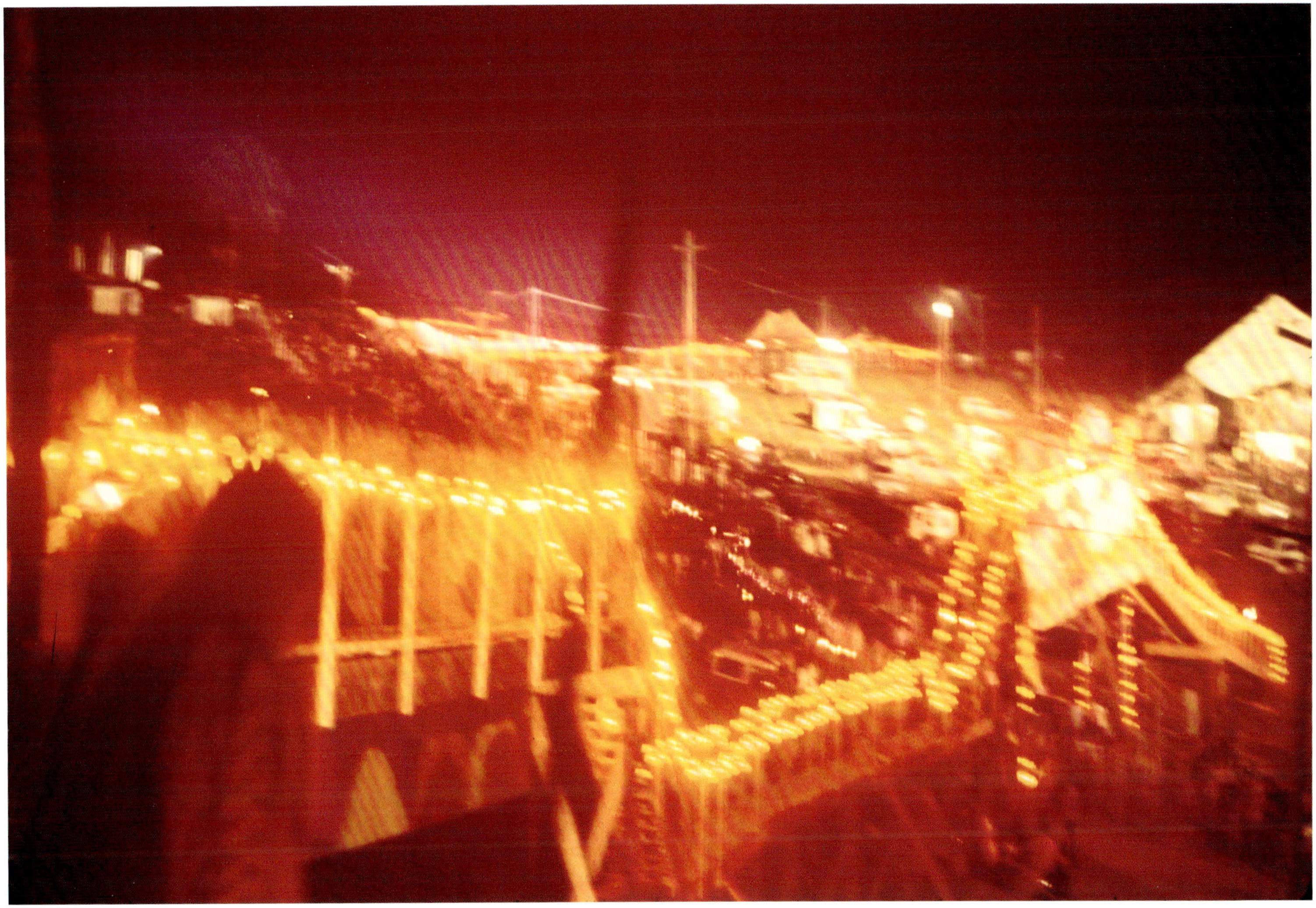

Impressionistic night view of bridge in back of Woodstock, August 1969.

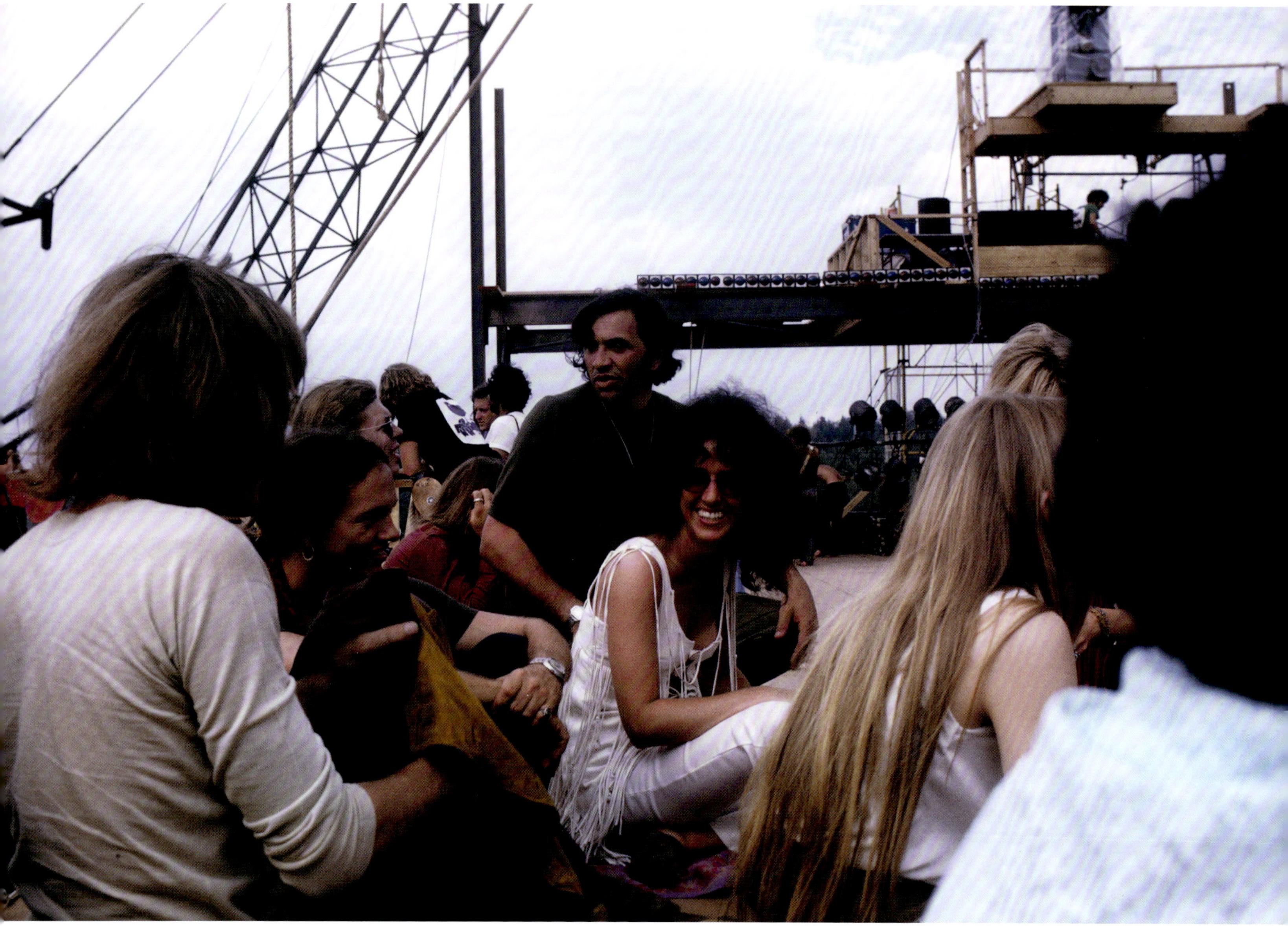

Grace Slick and Bill Graham, Woodstock, August 1969.

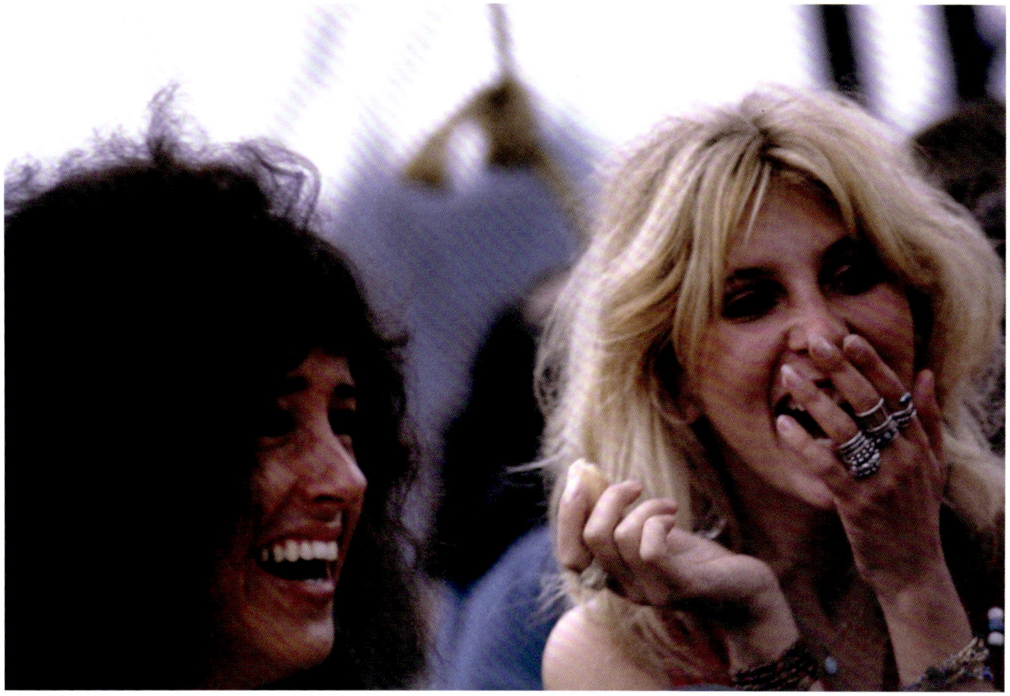

Grace Slick and Sally Mann, Woodstock, August 1969.

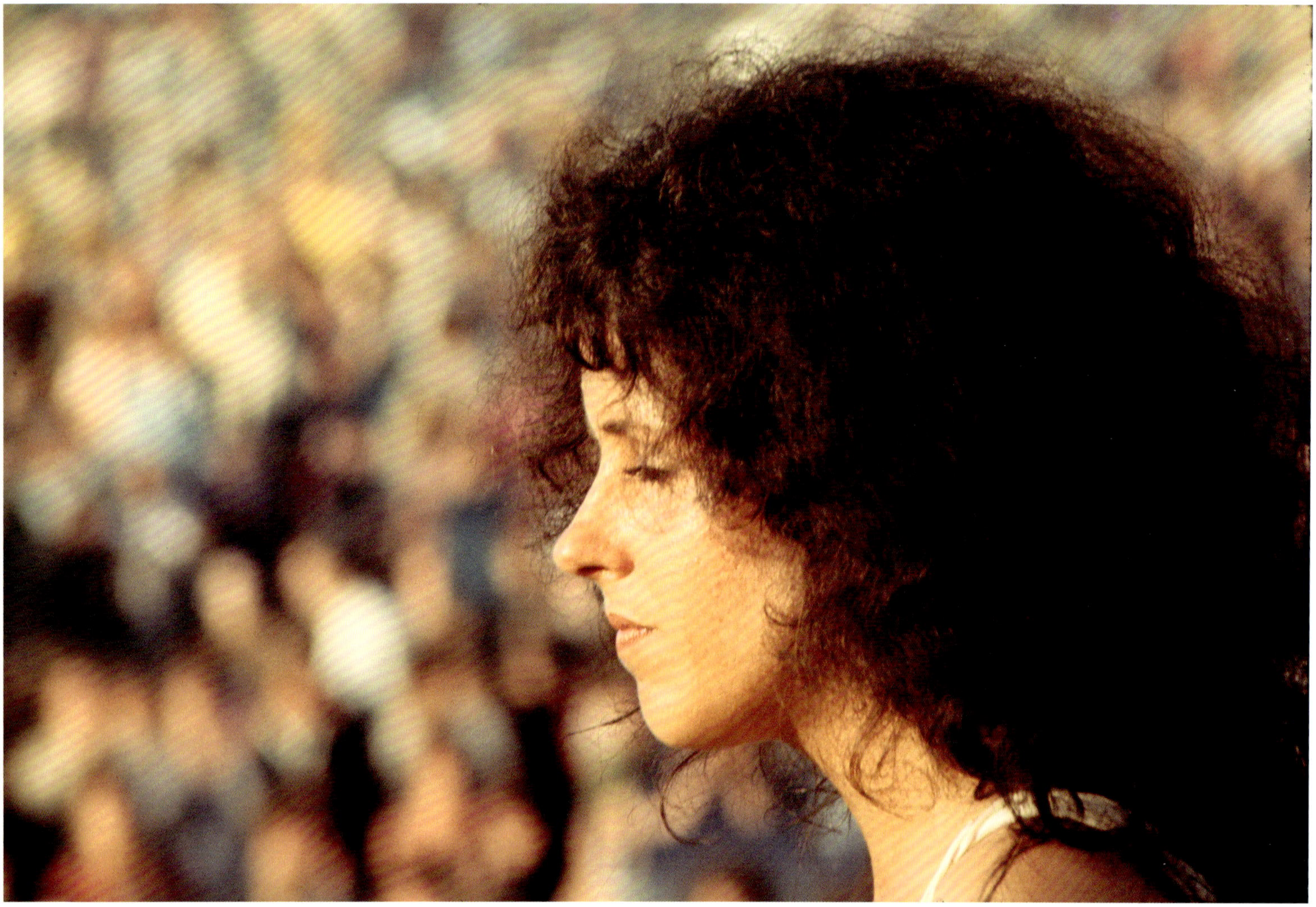

Grace Slick of Jefferson Airplane, Woodstock, August 1969.

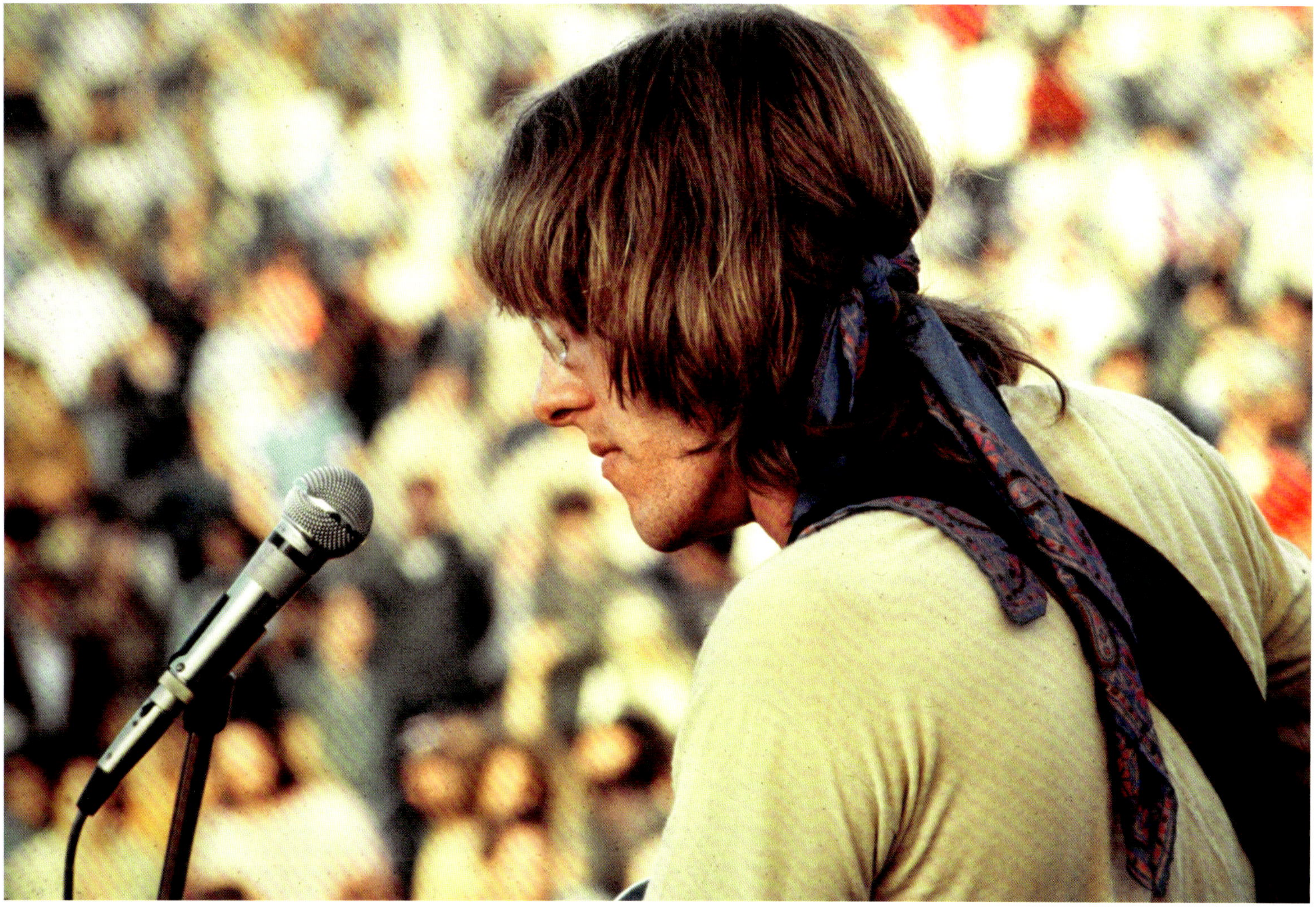

Paul Kantner of Jefferson Airplane, Woodstock, August 1969.

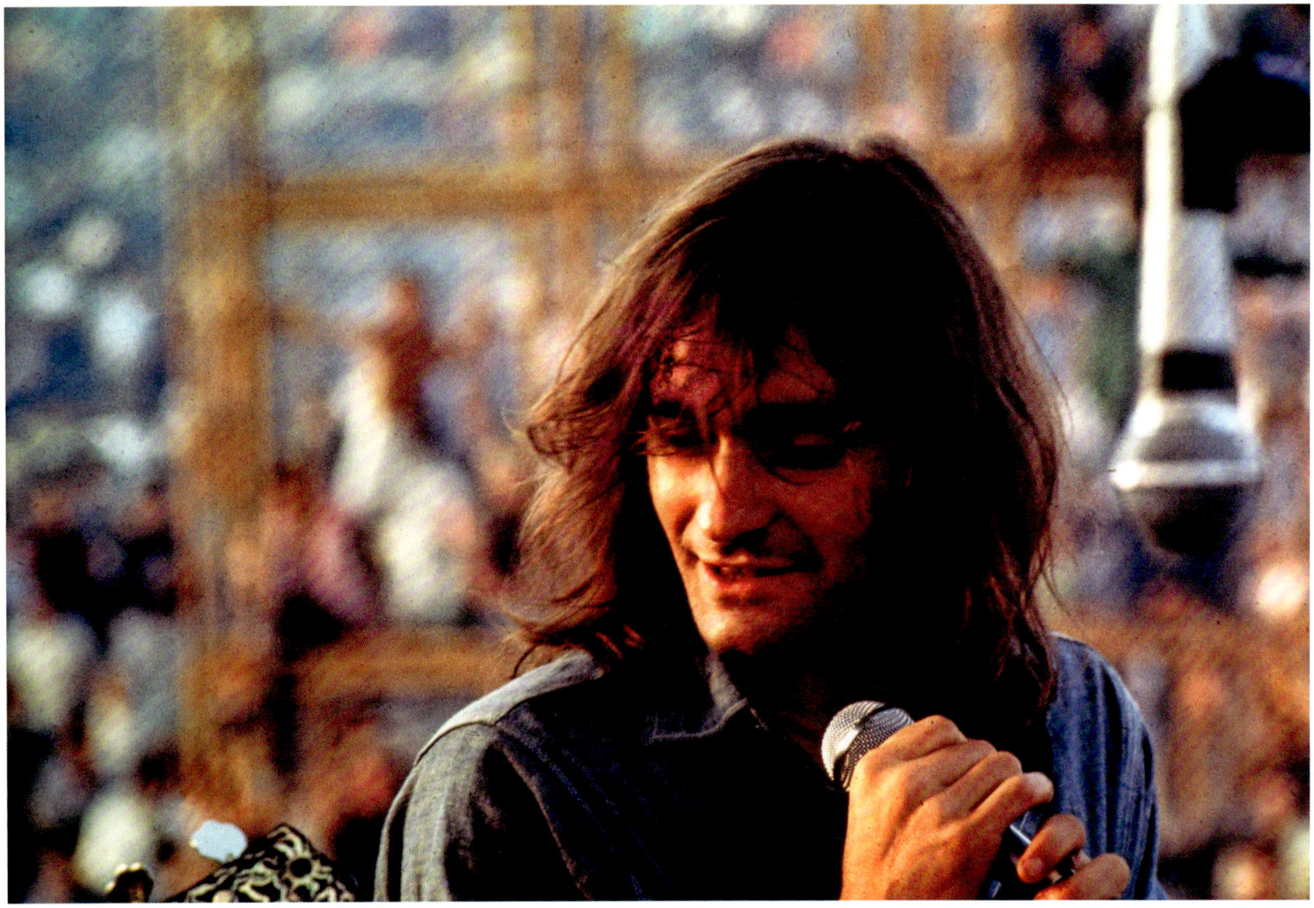

Marty Balin of Jefferson Airplane, Woodstock, August 1969.

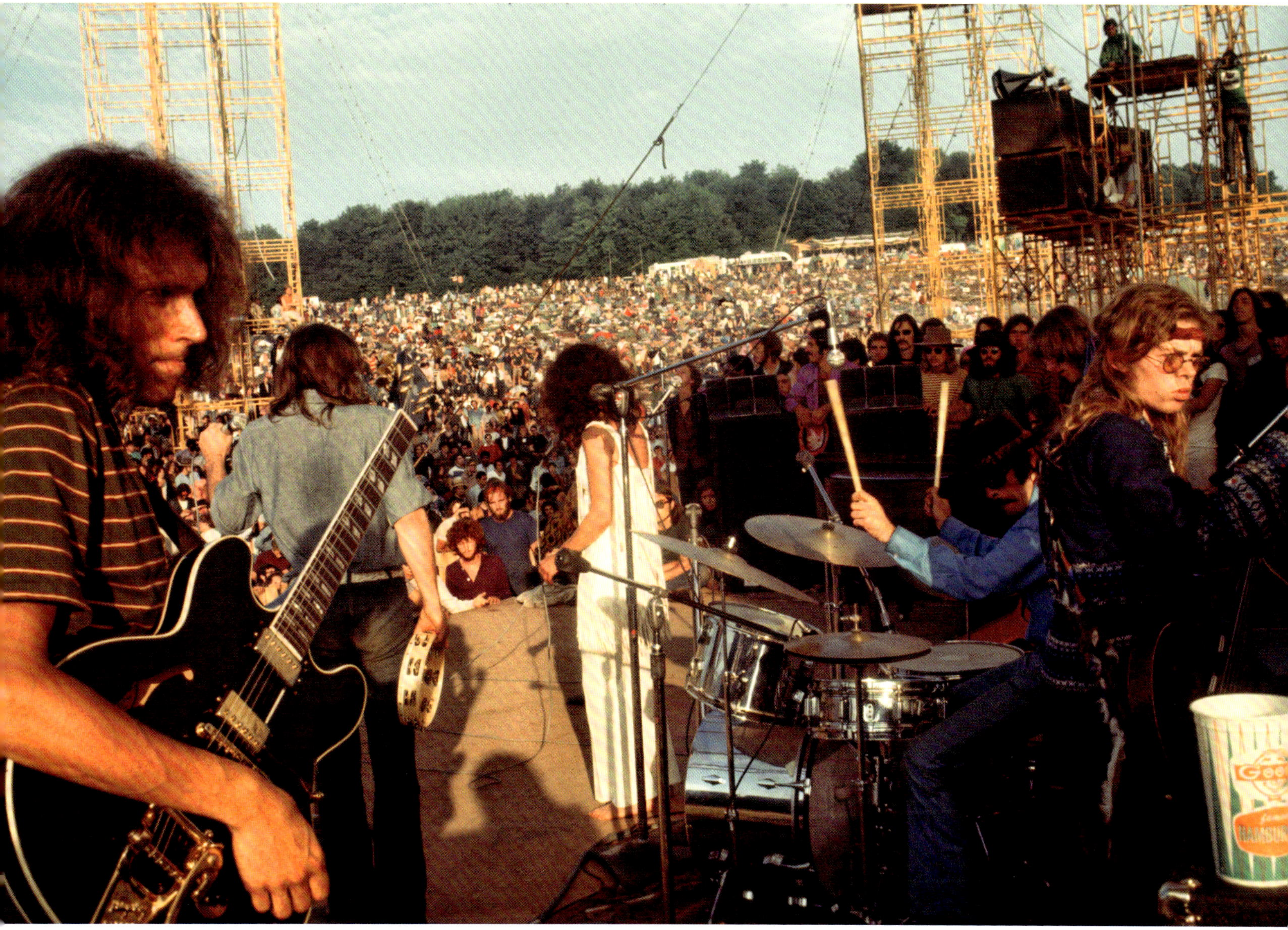

Above and overleaf: Jefferson Airplane, Woodstock, August 1969.

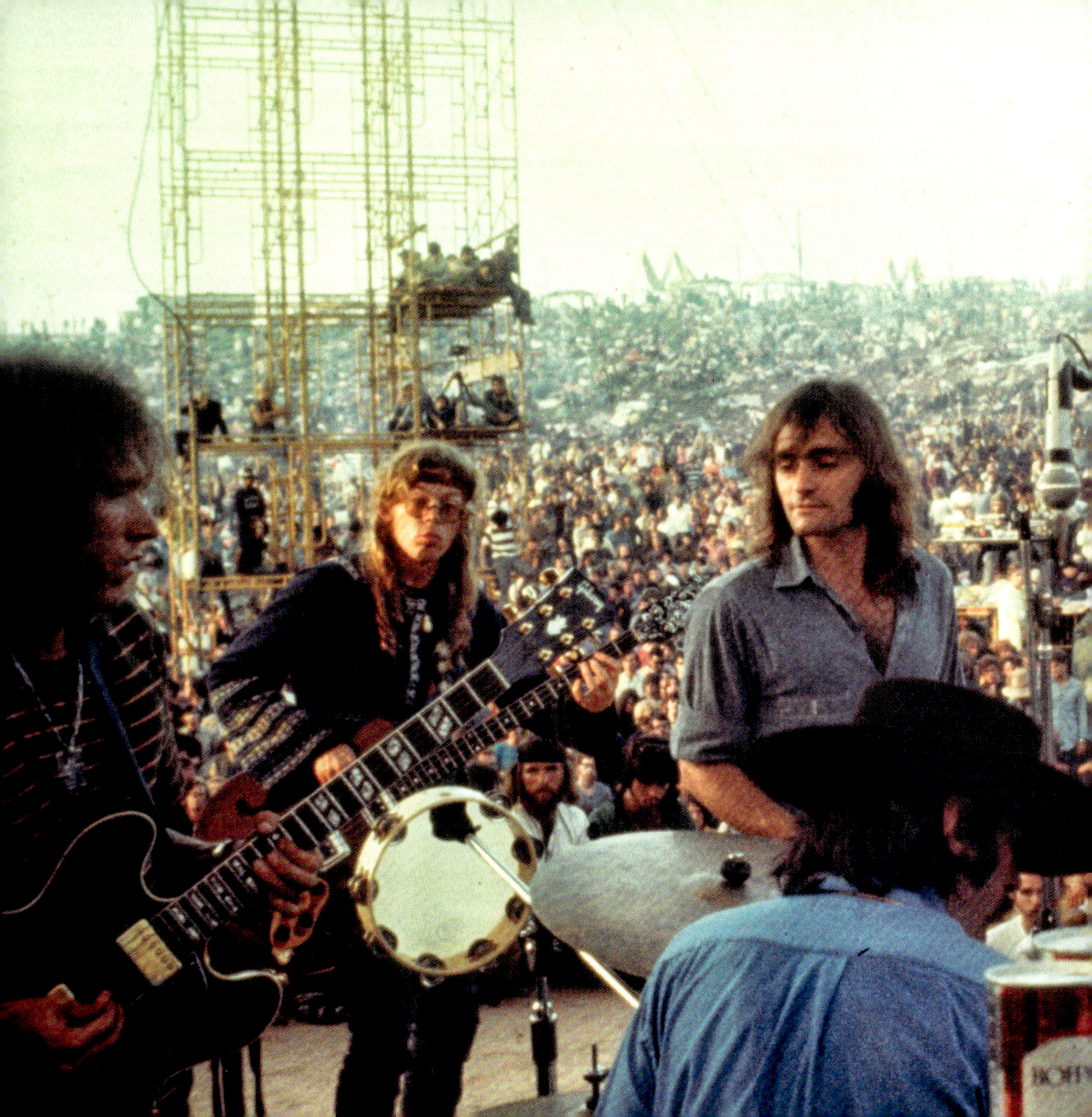

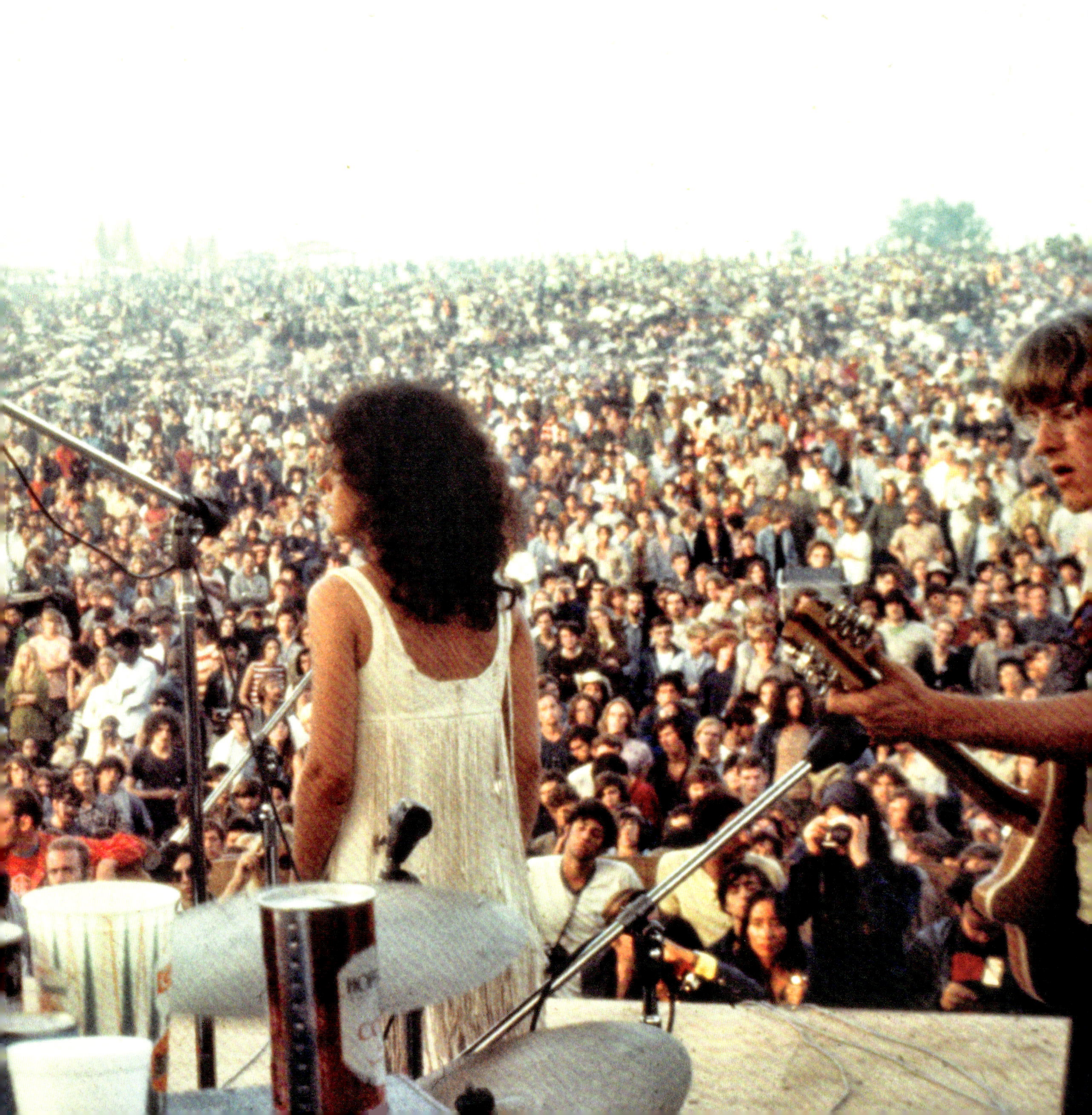

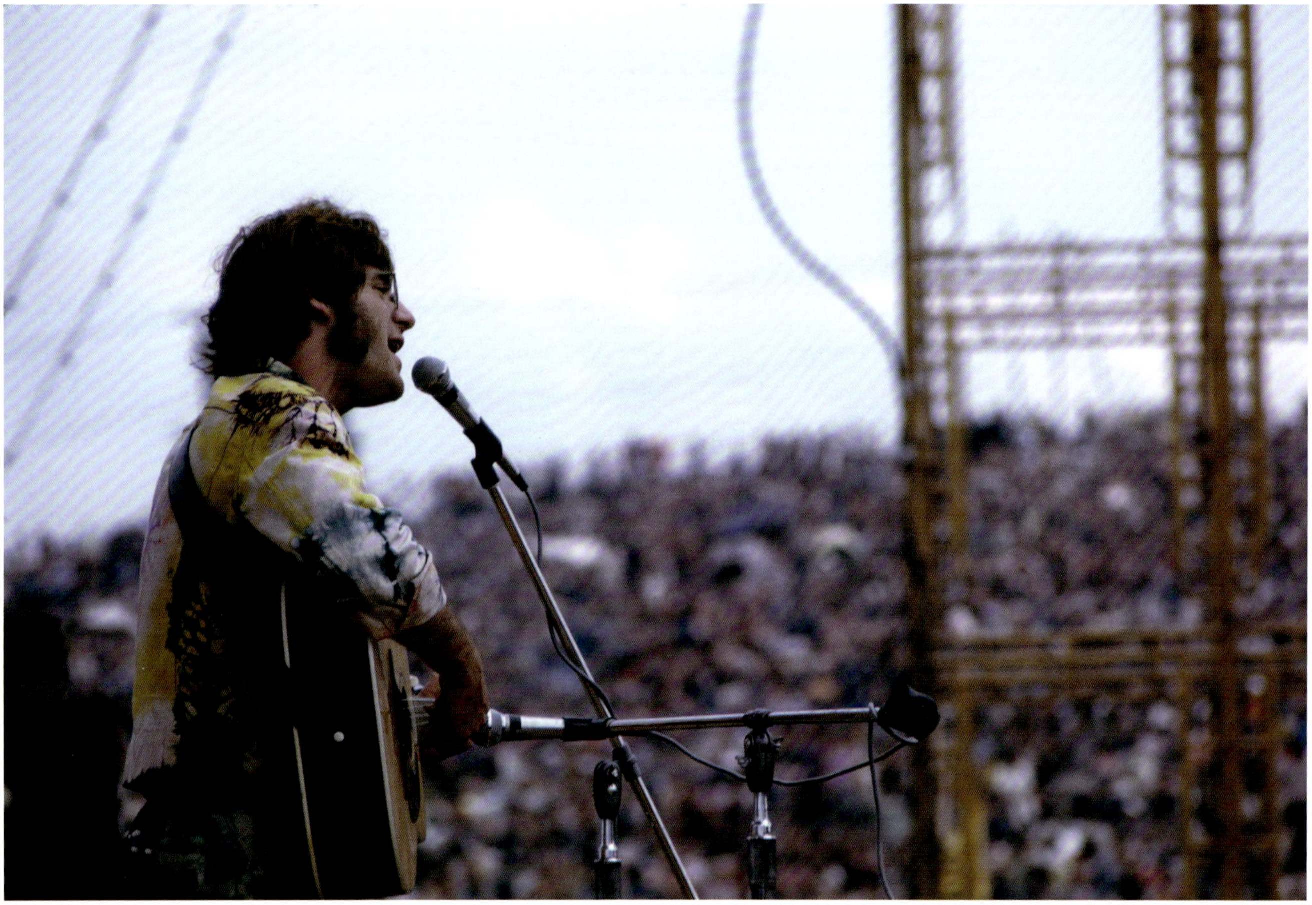

John Sebastian, Woodstock, August 1969. *Opposite*: John Sebastian being filmed, Woodstock, August 1969.

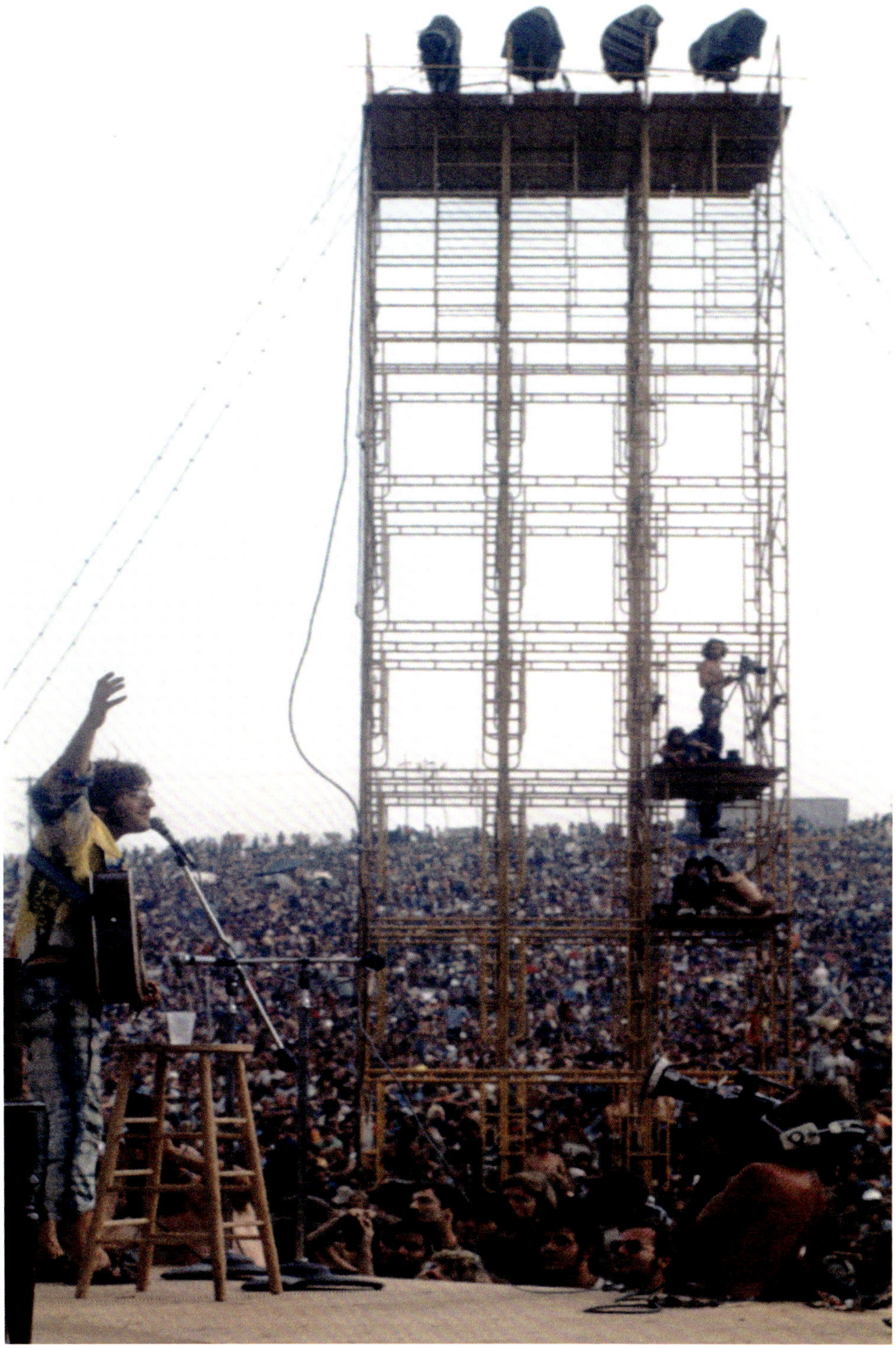

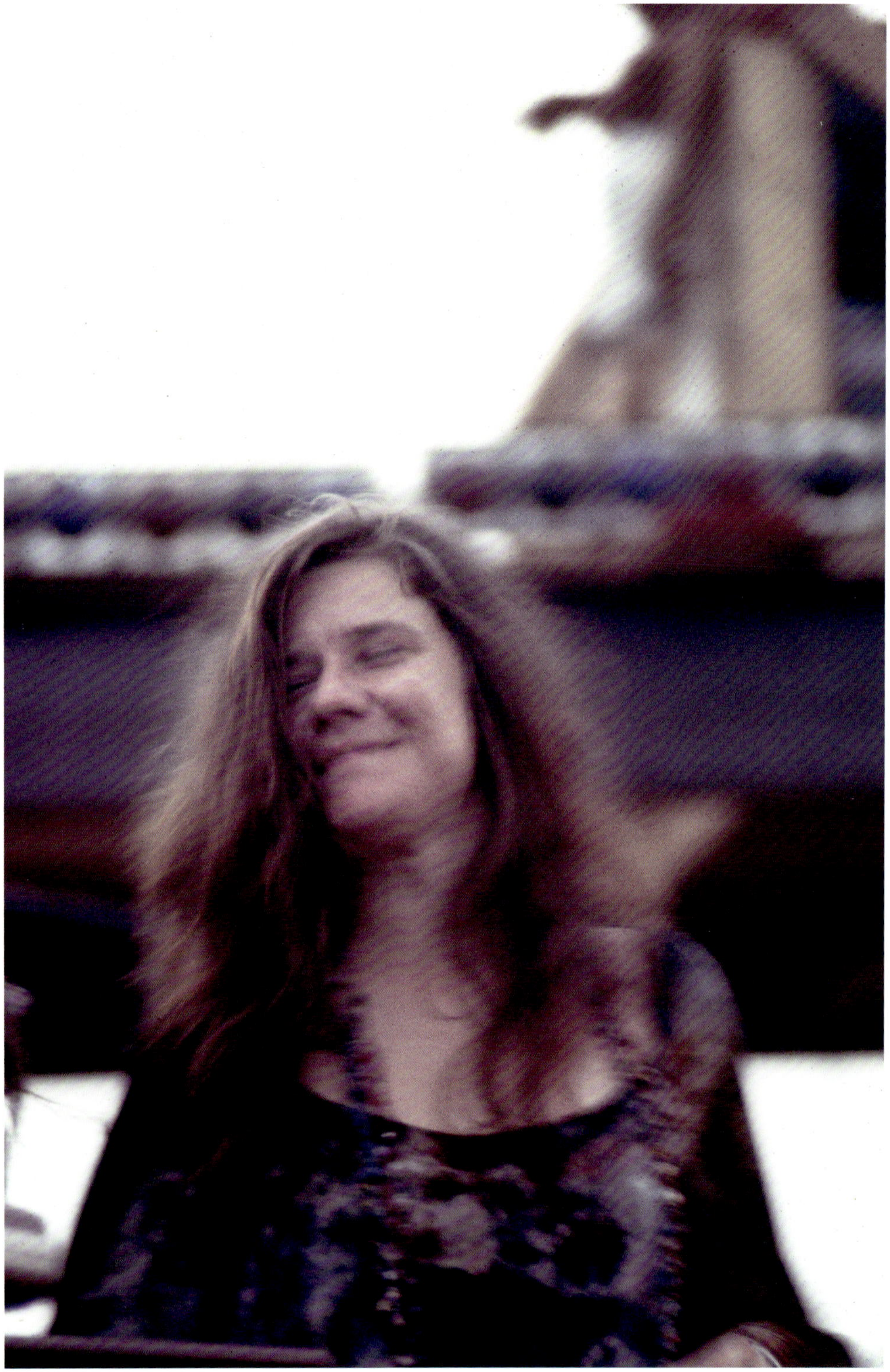

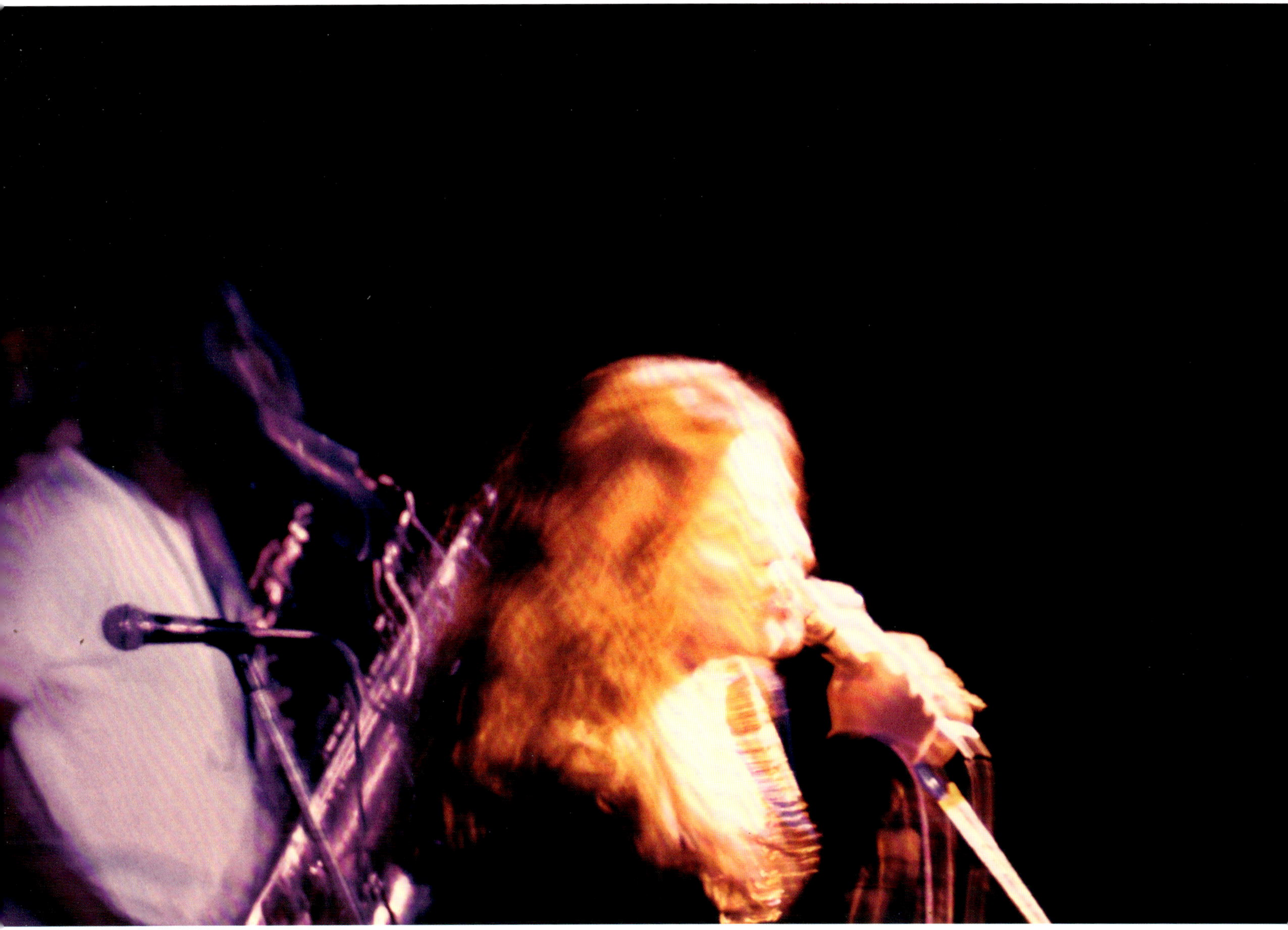

Snooky Flowers and Janis Joplin, Woodstock, August 1969.
Opposite: Janis Joplin, Woodstock, August 1969.

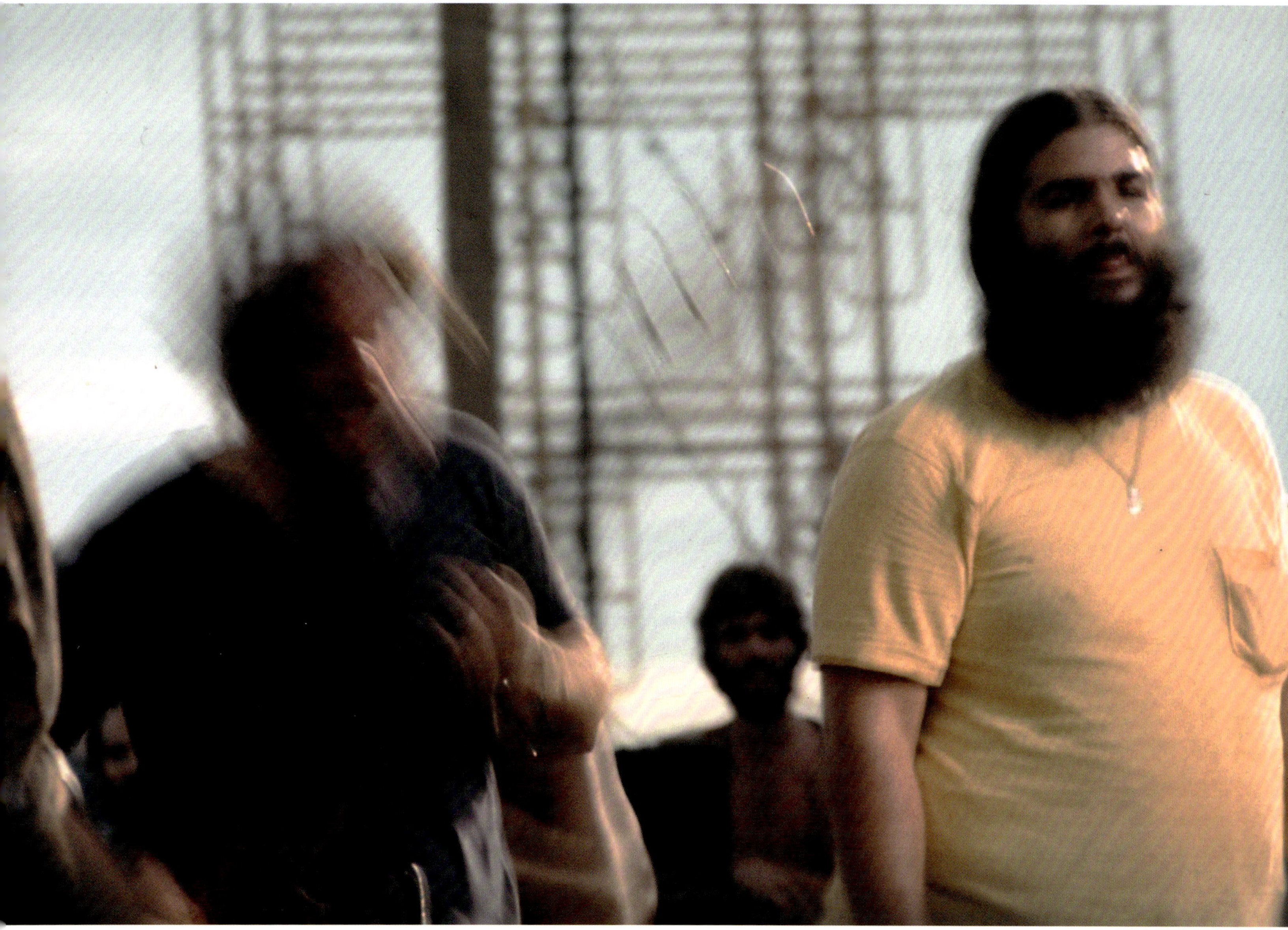

Larry Taylor (left) and Bob Hite (right) of Canned Heat,
Woodstock, August 1969.

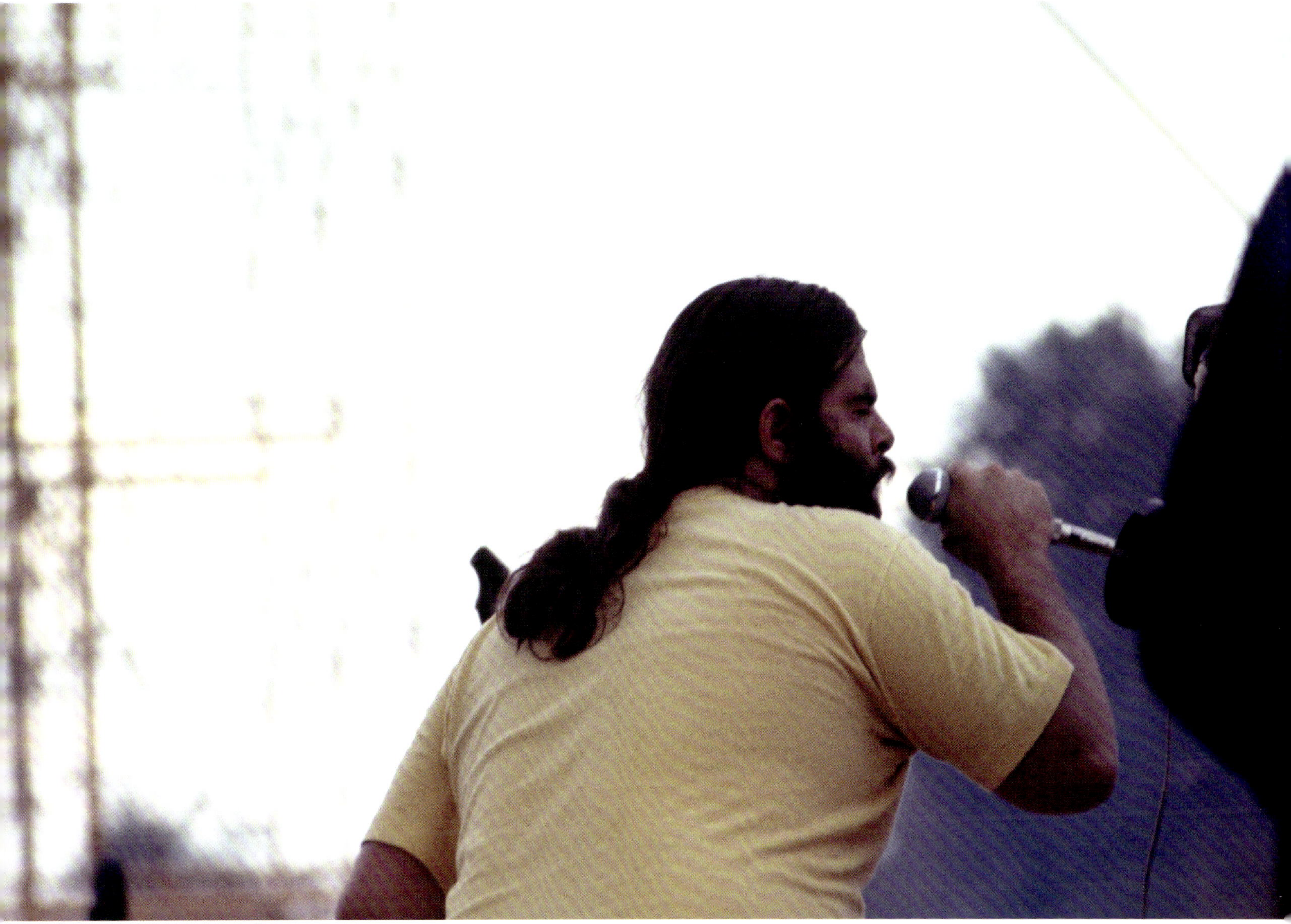

Bob Hite with Canned Heat, Woodstock, August 1969.

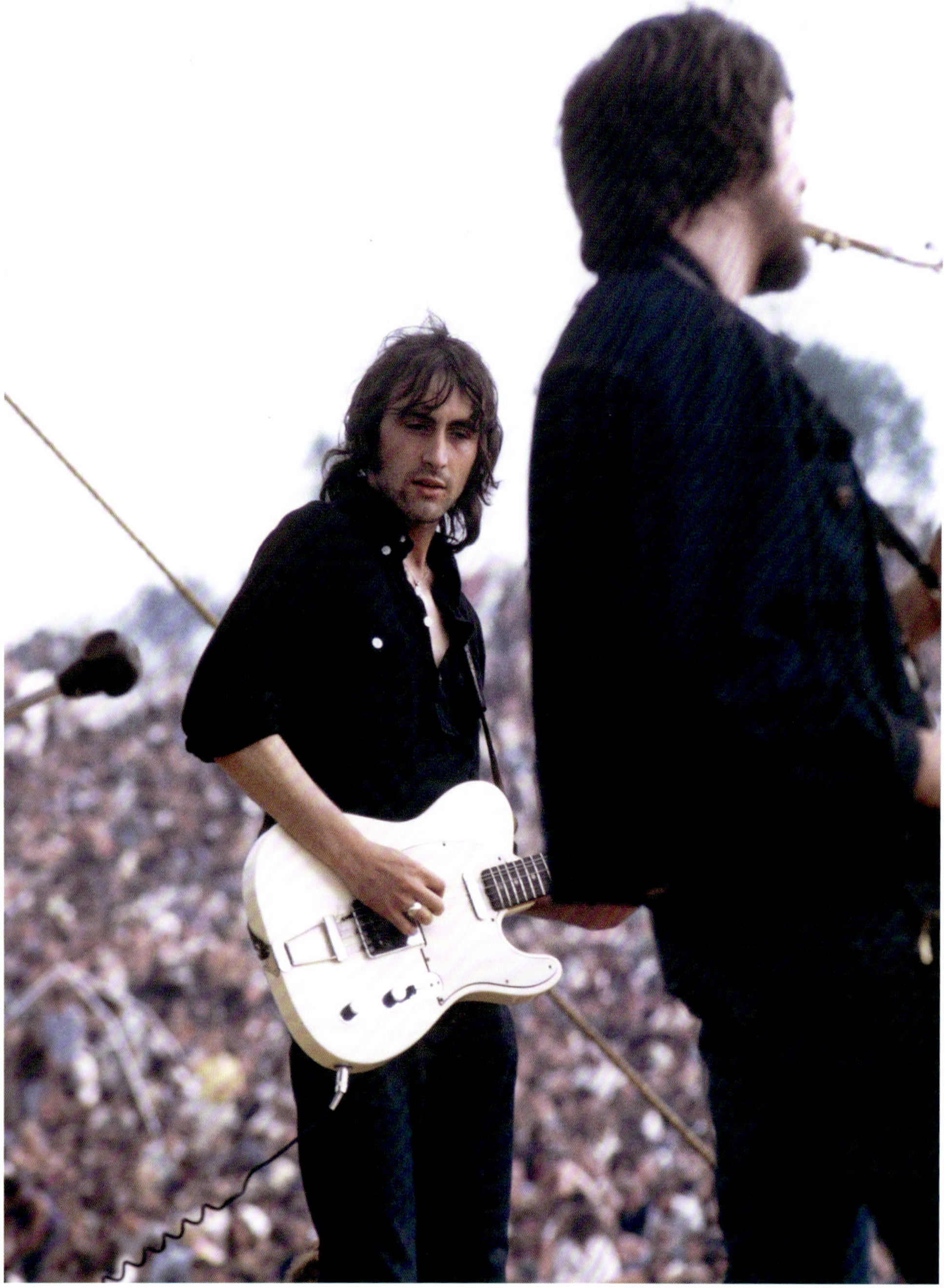

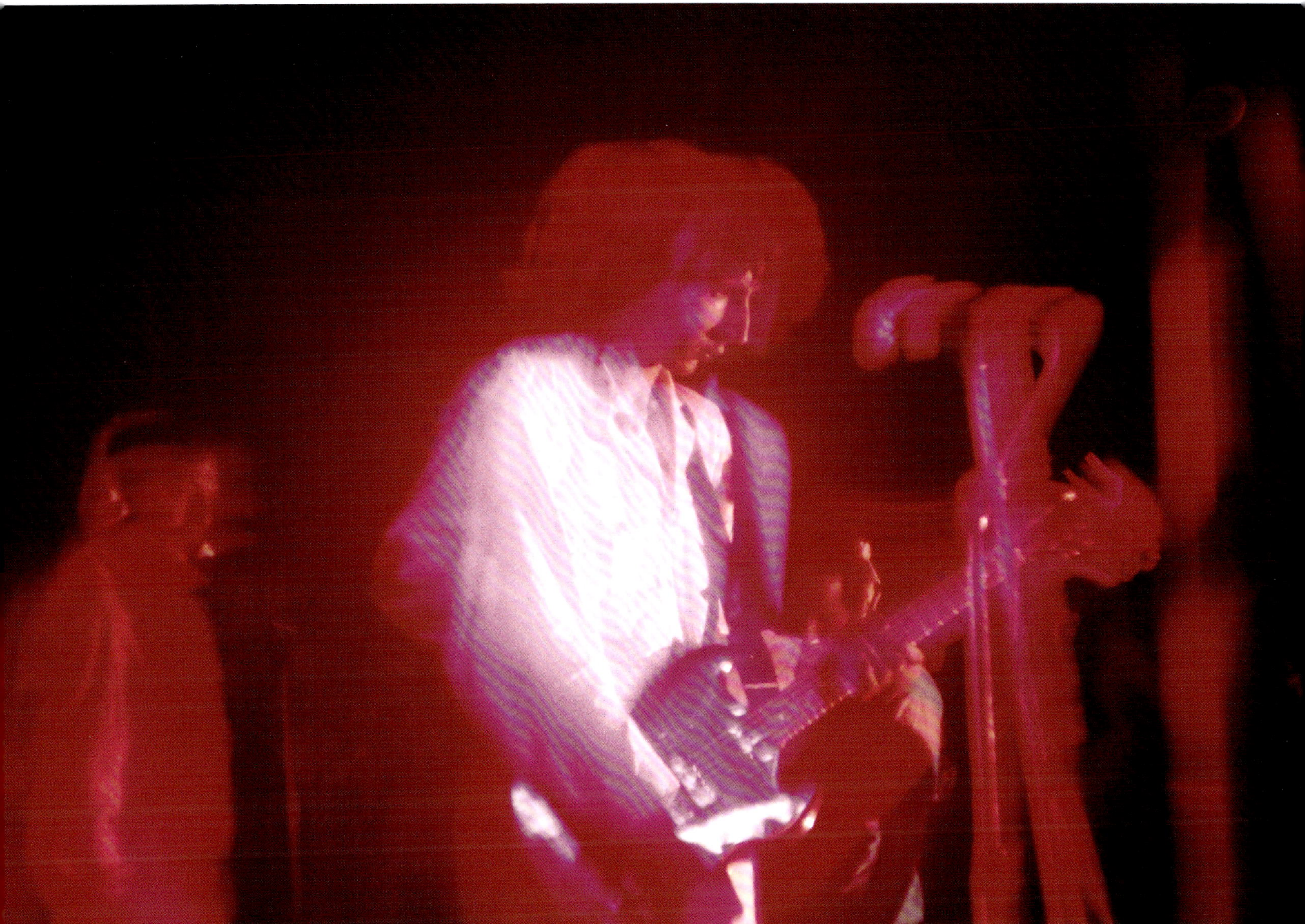

Pete Townshend of the Who, Woodstock, August 1969.
Opposite: Miller Anderson (left) and Jimmy Jewell (right) of the Keef Hartley Band, Woodstock, August 1969.

We were profoundly stunned at what was now fully visible. . . . There was, before us, a sea of bodies as far as one could see ahead, to the side, and as wide as 240 degrees surrounding the stage.

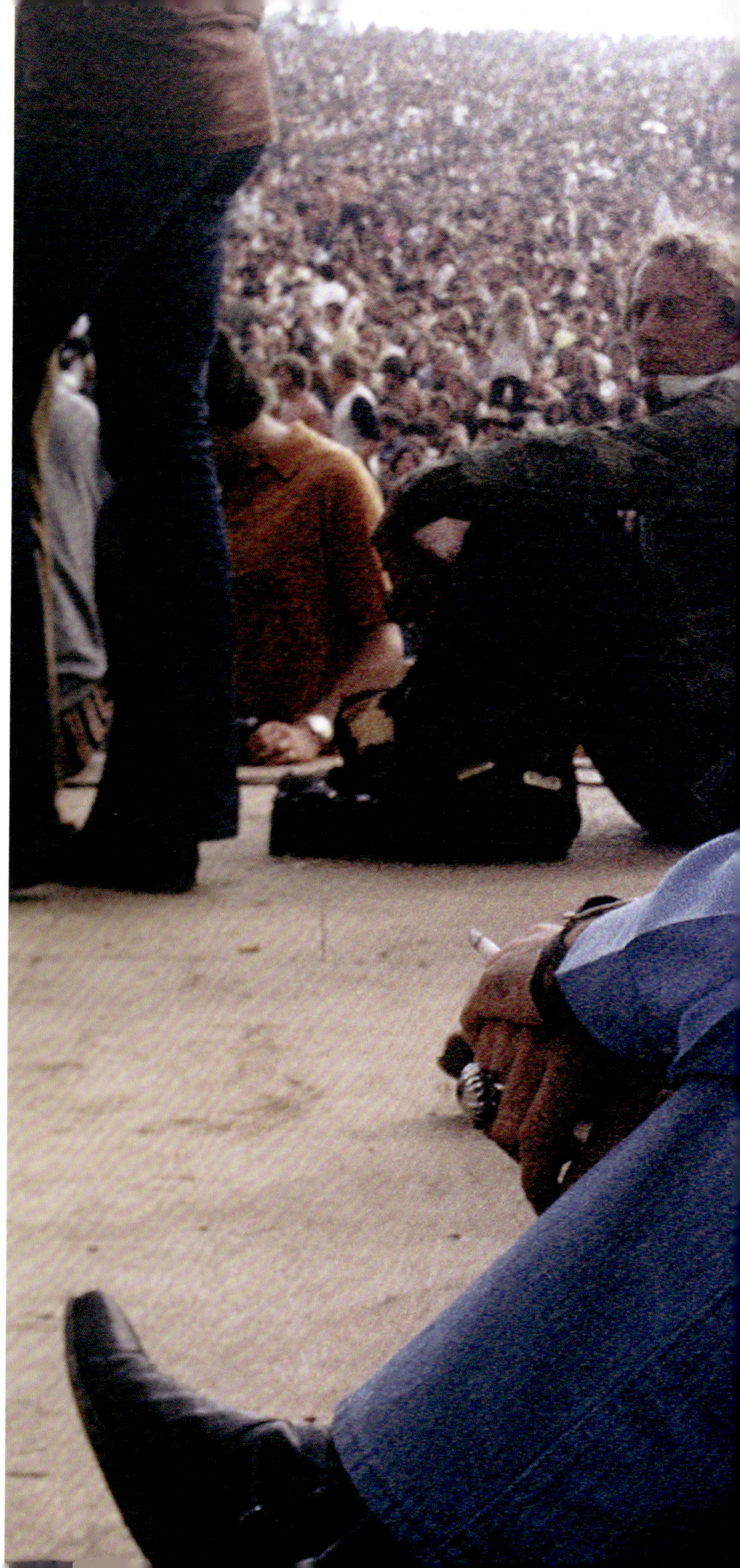

Spencer Dryden, Grace Slick, and Country Joe McDonald, Woodstock, August 1969.

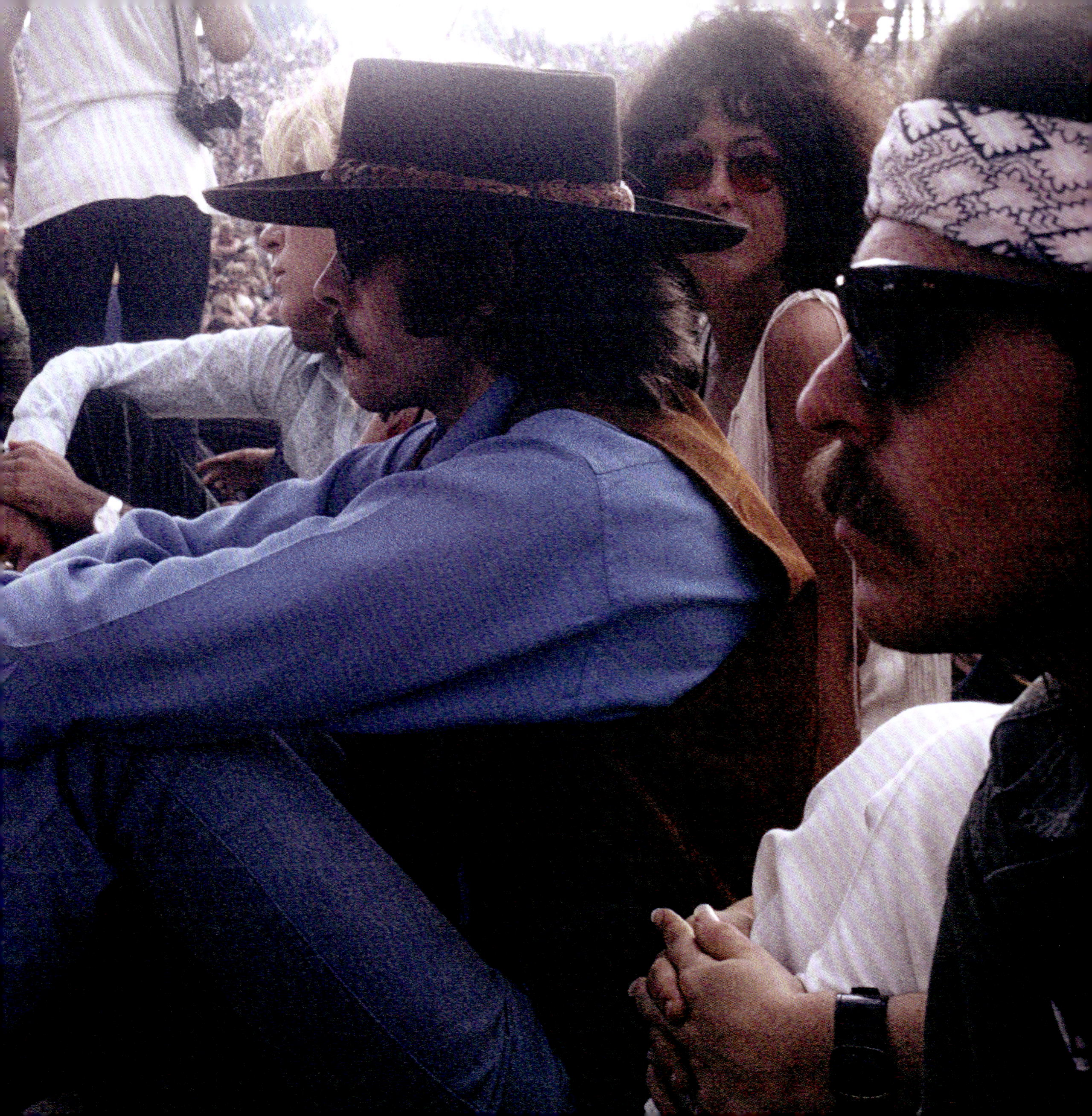

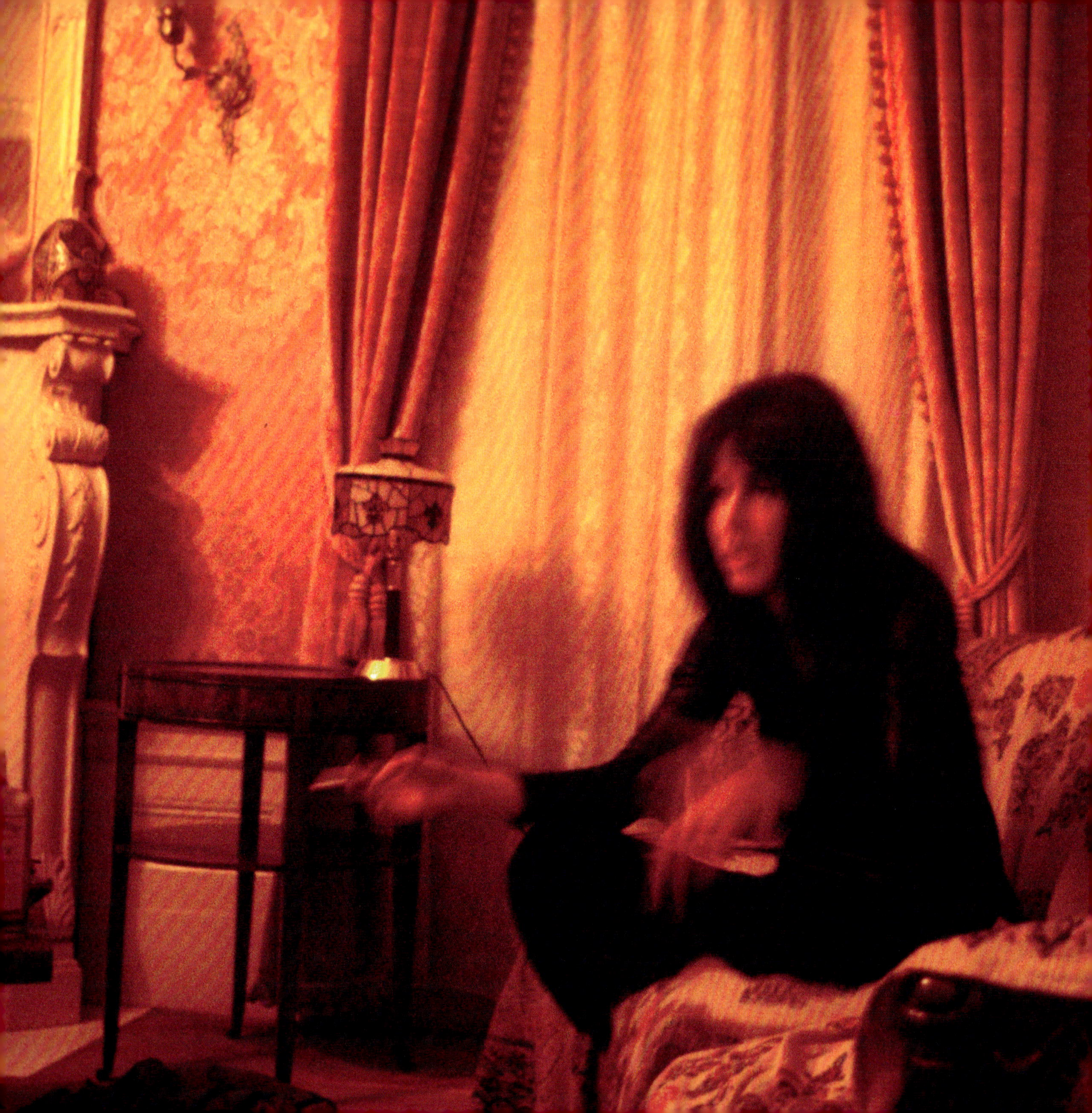

6

Jefferson Airplane World Headquarters

I capped off the year with a visit to San Francisco, spending the holidays at 2400 Fulton Street, the world headquarters of the Airplane. I flew out intending to photograph the band and the nascent Hot Tuna on December 31 at the famed Winterland, whose New Year's Eve concerts were always epic and unforgettable, lasting all night. I was excited to finally see the band in their native environment. I also saw this as a chance to solidify and expand my relationship with them and was wildly enthused about what the adventure might hold.

I was overwhelmed by the kindness and hospitality of Jorma and his then wife, Margareta. They made me feel like part of the band; even though I was still quite young they treated me as an adult. Some evenings Jorma would invite me for dinner at his home, and we would have stimulating conversation over many types of refreshments late into the night.

At 2400 Fulton I was privileged to stay in Grace's room since she and Paul were absent much of the time. Though when they were there it was quite an experience, with Grace often holding court downstairs in the spacious living room on such widely varied subjects as music, literature, and popular culture in general. I was of course enchanted and enthralled on these occasions, and the insights on the workings of Grace's mind enhanced my knowledge of both the subject and the subjects. Grace's room was surprisingly small yet intimate and beautifully decorated. I must admit to having a strange feeling as I slept in the bed of someone I so admired.

When Paul was there, he was usually upstairs in the "Poet's Room" as Grace put it in the song "Mexico," entertaining varied Bay area characters. Many came to the house seeking his guidance, often delivering

Grace Slick, 2400 Fulton Street, December 1969.

mind-enhancing substances for his exalted highness. Others came to just hang out while soaking up the scene.

2400 Fulton Street was a counterculture wonderland. It was appointed with a combination of antique furniture and other décor that I imagine today would be called "hippie chic." There were so many rooms, nooks, and crannies to explore, but one standout feature of the house was a wall full of live Airplane recordings on 7" reel-to-reel tape. It was a treasure trove of concert recordings that showcased their true sound in ways the studio recordings couldn't. From what I've heard, many of these recordings may have been lost, which is a huge loss for American music history. To this day there are too few live Airplane recordings in circulation compared to their peers (e.g., the Grateful Dead).

The kitchen presented a cautionary tale in psychedelia, as confirmed by a large sign on the refrigerator saying that any liquid ingested there may produce "a prolonged bout with an altered state of mind . . . so beware!" And I most certainly did proceed with caution.

One day the band assembled in their basement rehearsal space and was filmed for a promotional video of "We Can Be Together." I never knew what became of this footage until I saw snippets of it in the 1972 film *Fillmore: The Last Days*. The shoot was quite the riot, and in the film Grace can be seen clearly with the delivery tube of a large and quite active canister of nitrous oxide by her mouth, held tightly against a microphone as she lip-synched to the musical track that played. I photographed the band during that event and several other basement rehearsals, along with Hot Tuna, as both prepped for New Year's Eve.

The show went on and on at 2400 Fulton. Throughout the day there was a stream of supplicants and Haight (as in Haight-Ashbury) "freaks," Hells Angels, and drug devotees. During my stay, whoever answered the door (and it was me at times) would just take in any "contributions" with a smile and put them in a pile for later review before they would filter out to the band and their close entourage.

The inseparable Spencer and Sally were in and out of the house at various odd times. I encountered them in the basement rehearsal space putting the finishing touches on a diorama, one of several that Spencer (inexplicably, to me) spent much time on. The diorama was some farm-like, bucolic scene, and Spencer was attending to some detail he felt required great attention. I guess even rock stars need a hobby.

Sally was and continues to this day to be a fearsome force, yet she was also one of the kindest and most friendly members of the Airplane family I encountered. She even rescued me one time on stage at a concert when an uninformed security guy tried to throw me off. She intervened and in short order dispatched the guard, telling him, "He is with the band—don't harass him!" I never forgot that meaningful gesture, and I have resumed our friendship in recent years through social media. Sally became a lawyer in her post-rock life, and time has not diminished her empathy. She shares her Texas ranch with a plethora of beloved rescue animals, which warms my animal-loving heart to no end.

Underlying all the dazed daily goings on at the house was darkness. My stay at 2400 Fulton coincided with the immediate aftermath of the much-recounted Altamont disaster. I had a foretaste of the events at Altamont when, at a Rolling Stones Thanksgiving concert at Madison Square Garden just a few weeks prior, I saw how Mick Jagger could whip a crowd into a frenzy (though without the deadly outcome that would play out barely a week later). The story of Altamont has been well documented in other places, so I will just say that all the band members were visibly disheartened in the wake of the Hells Angels knocking Marty Balin out cold during the Airplane's set and the motorcycle club's ensuing murder of a gun-wielding audience member. During my stay, Marty was still feeling the effects of the tragic incident; suffice it to say, he was heavily self-medicating and was far from any good frame of mind.

To their credit, the band always came together to rise to the musical occasion, and on New Year's Eve they played an extended, incredible show along with Quicksilver Messenger Service, Hot Tuna, and the Sons of Champlin All the sets and jamming lasted well into the wee hours of the New Year, concluding near dawn. This was one of the high points of the trip, and I reveled in not just photographing the festivities but being a part of them and taking part in the refreshments that were offered up liberally all night without interruption.

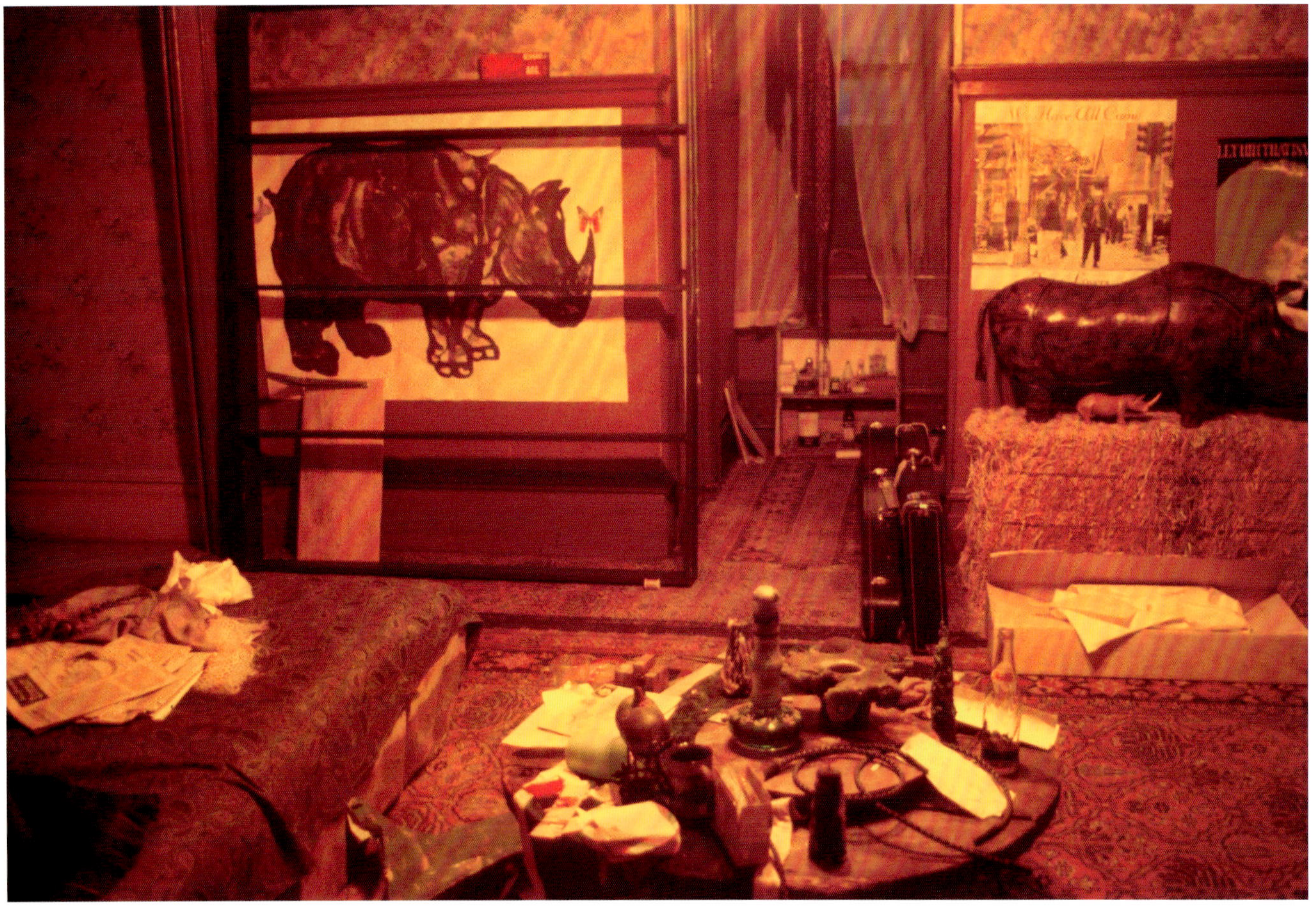

Common area, second floor, 2400 Fulton Street, December 1969.

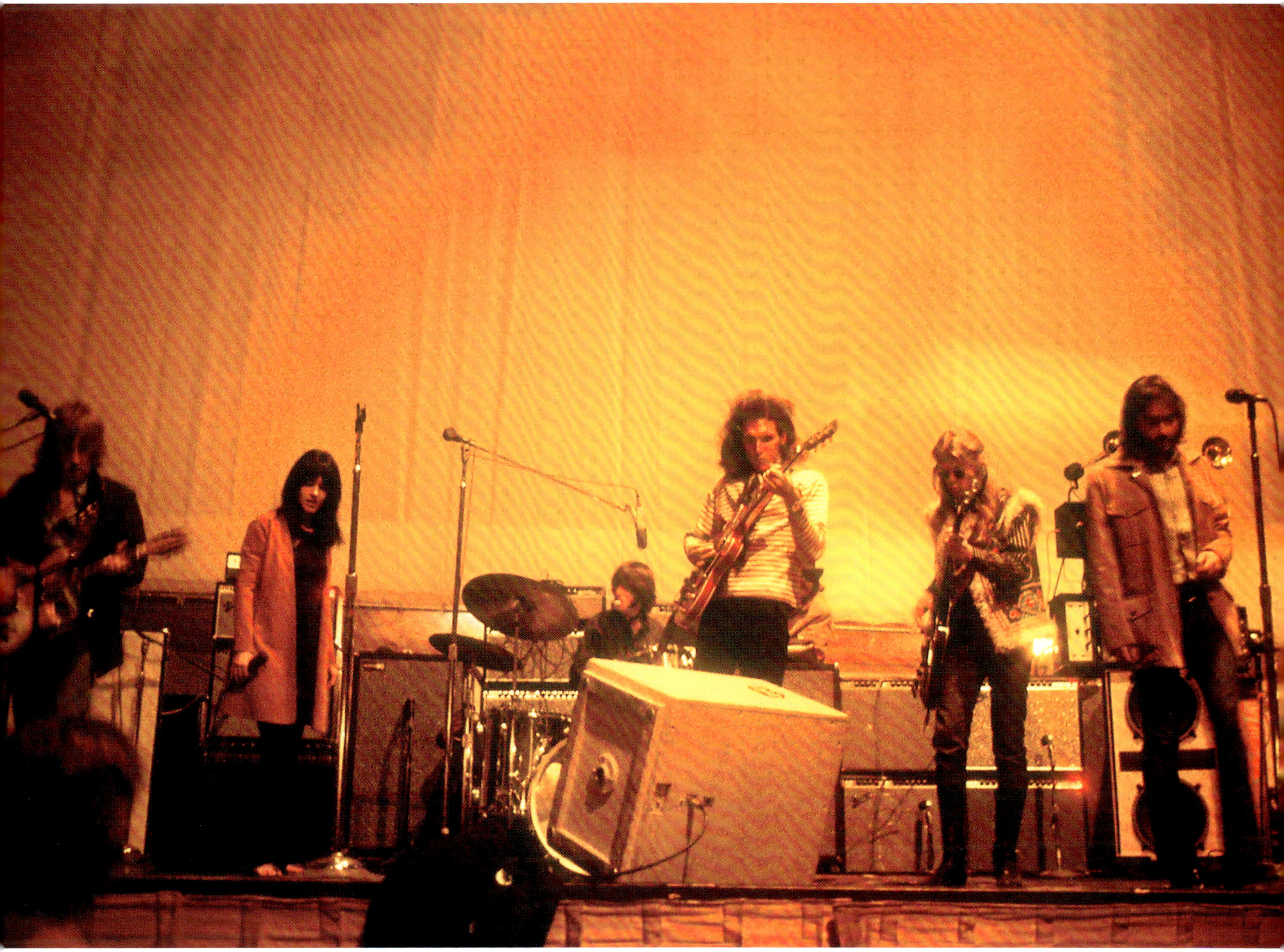

Jefferson Airplane, rehearsal, Winterland, San Francisco, December 1969.

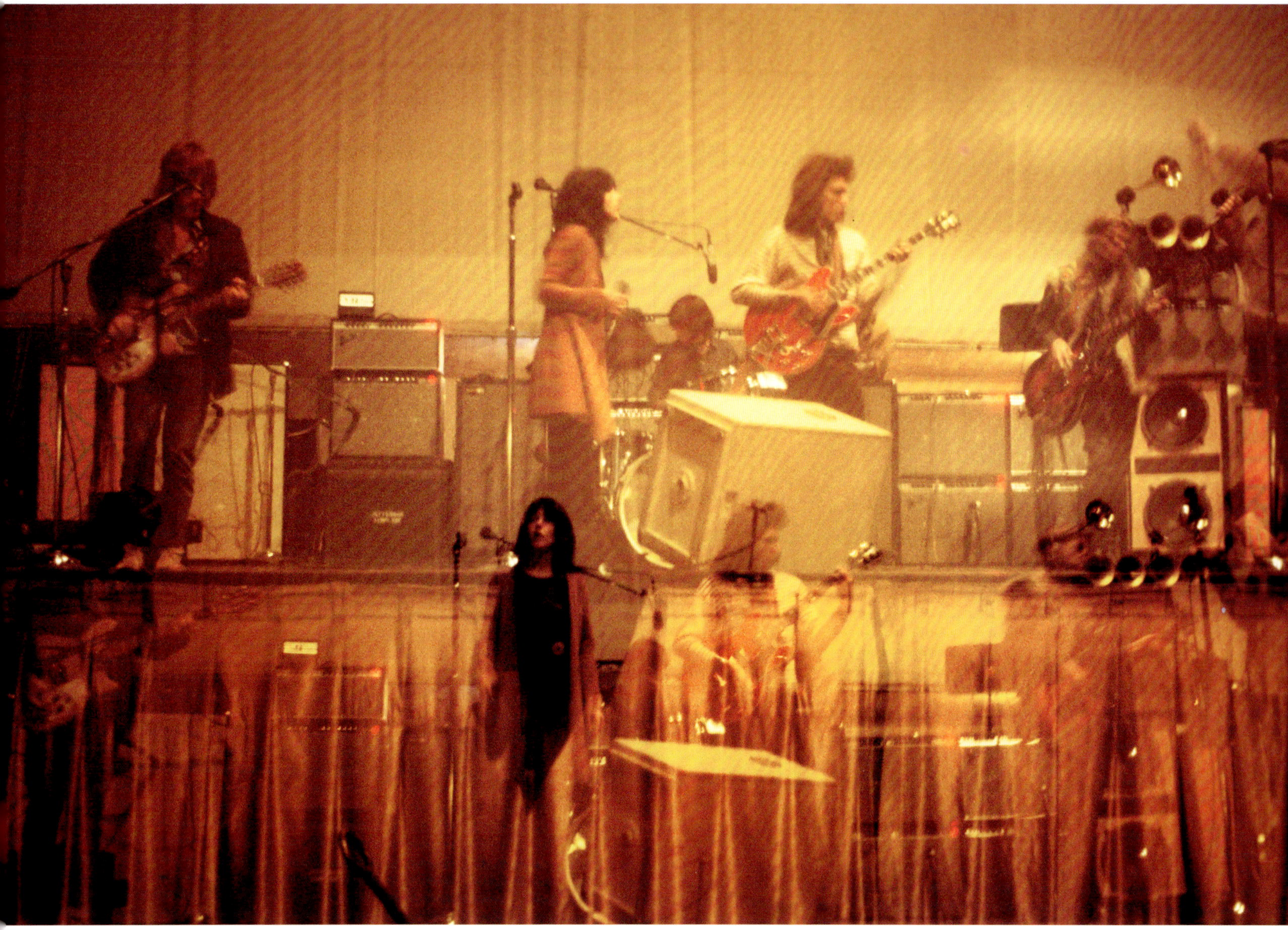

Jefferson Airplane, rehearsal, Winterland, 1969.

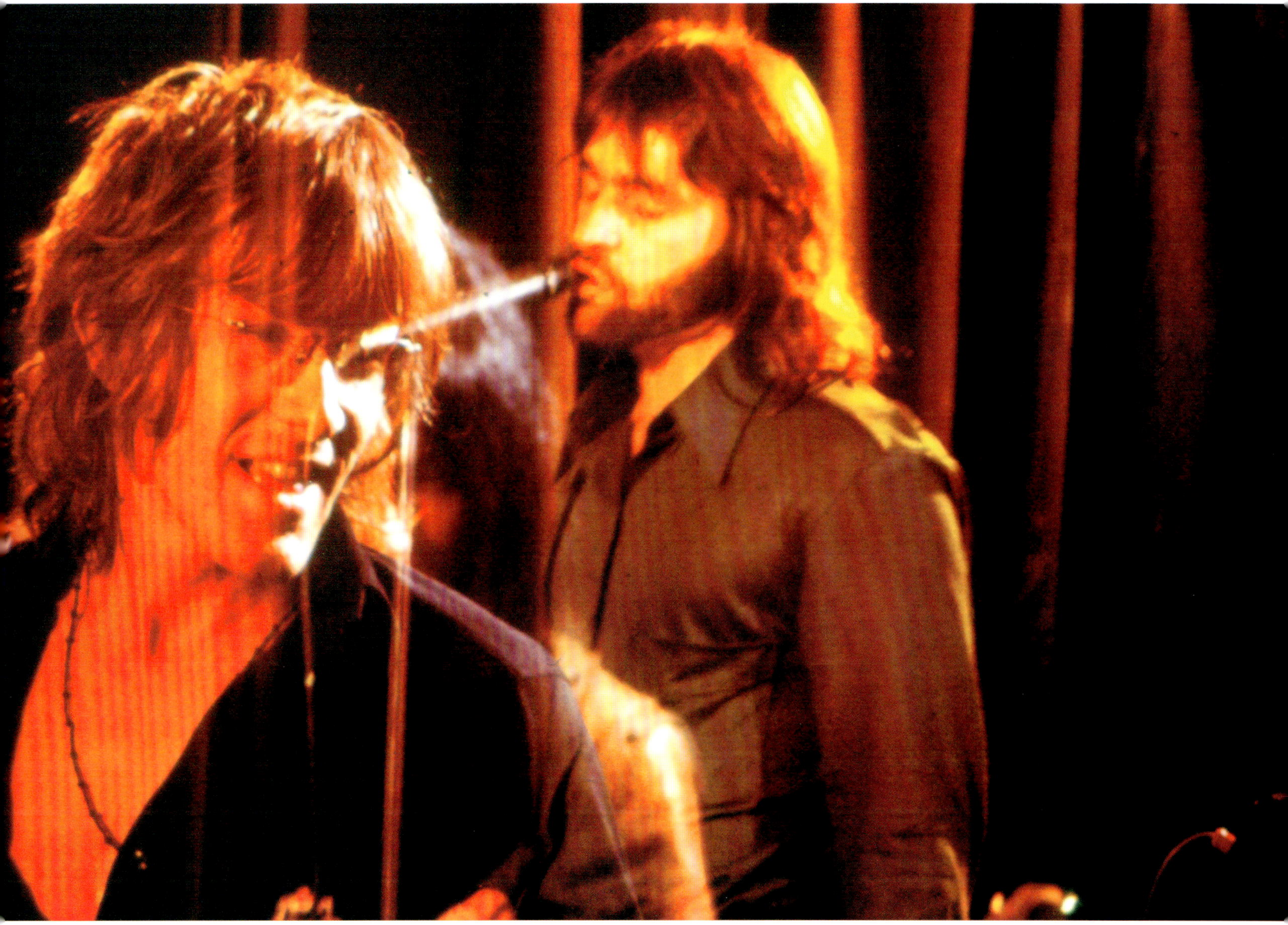

Paul Kantner and Marty Balin of Jefferson Airplane, rehearsal space at 2400 Fulton Street, December 1969.

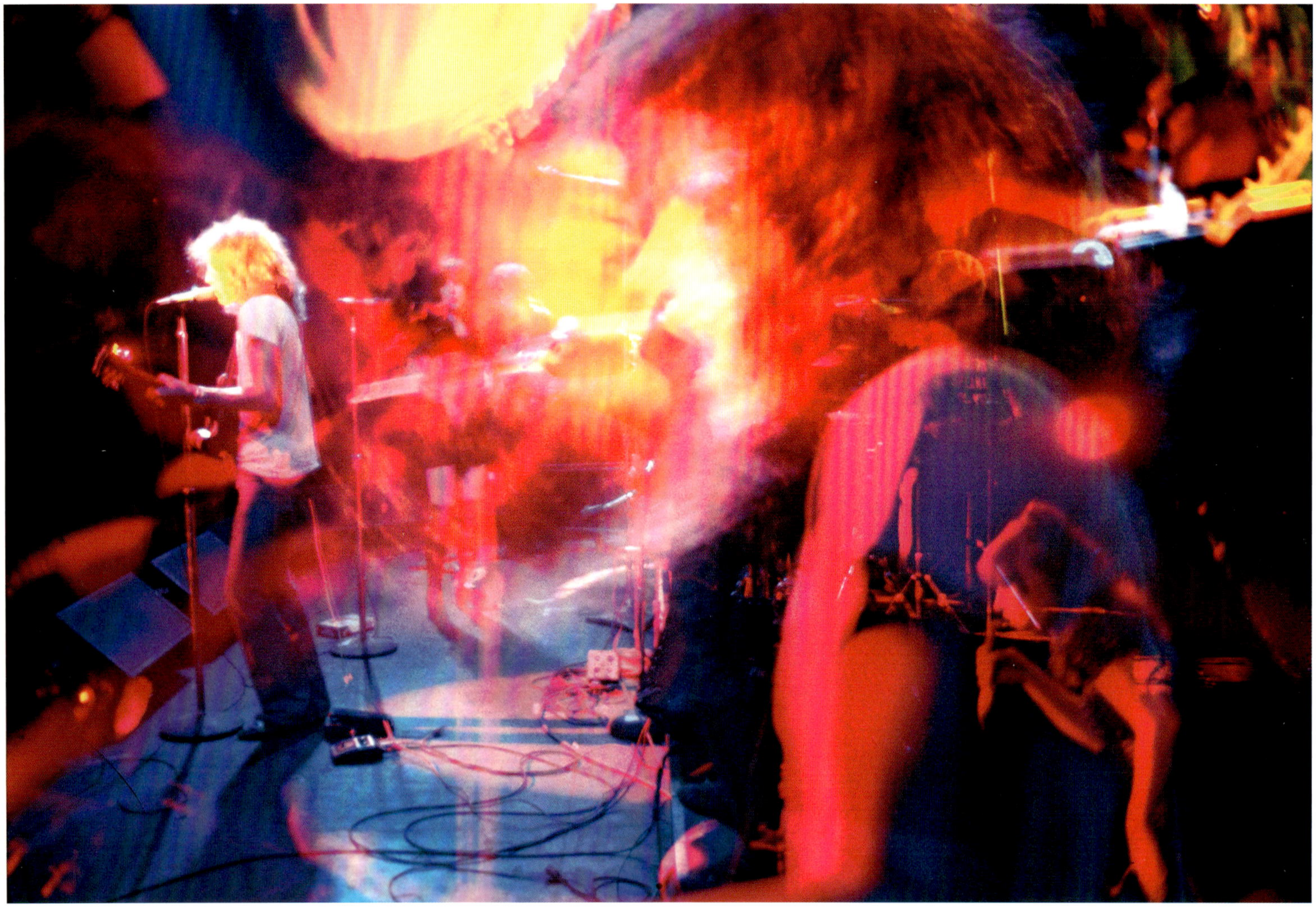

Jefferson Airplane, Winterland, December 1969.

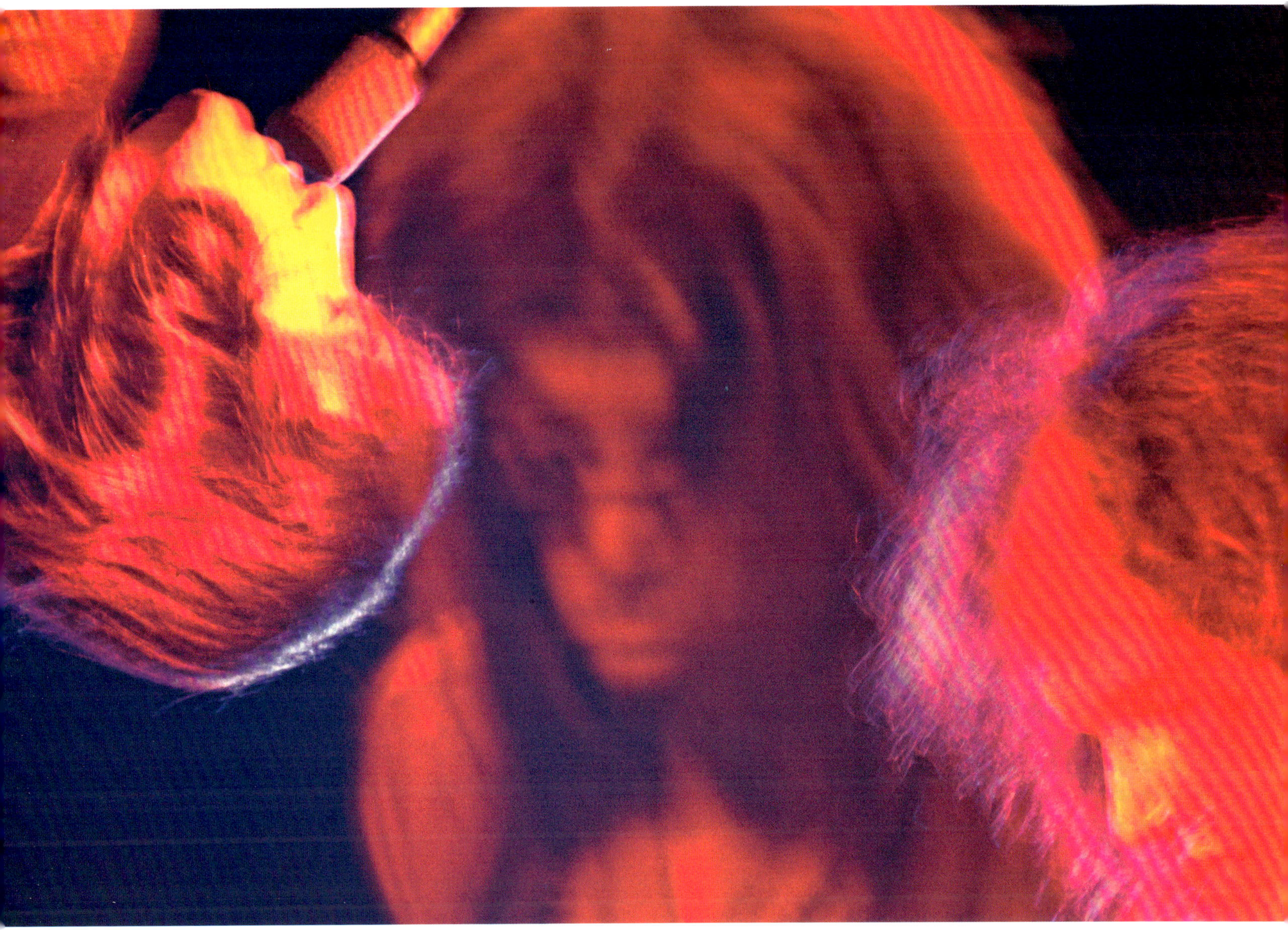

Marty Balin (left), Jack Casady (center), and Jorma Kaukonen (right) of Jefferson Airplane, Fillmore East, New York, October 1970.

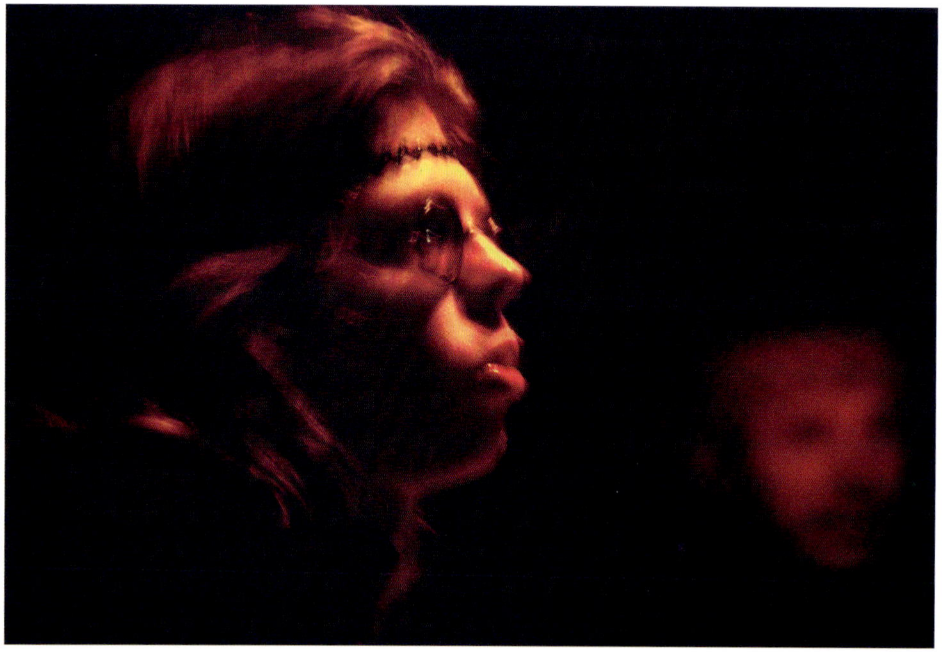

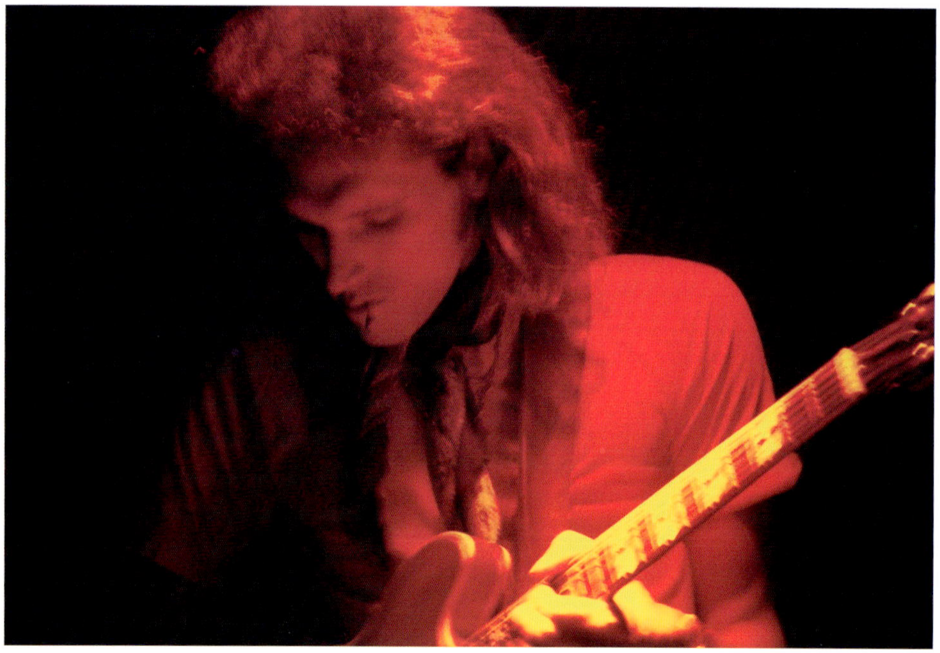

Top: Jack Casady and Joey Covington (background) Hot Tuna, rehearsal space at 2400 Fulton Street, December 1969. *Bottom*: Jorma Kaukonen of Jefferson Airplane, rehearsal space at 2400 Fulton Street, December 1969.

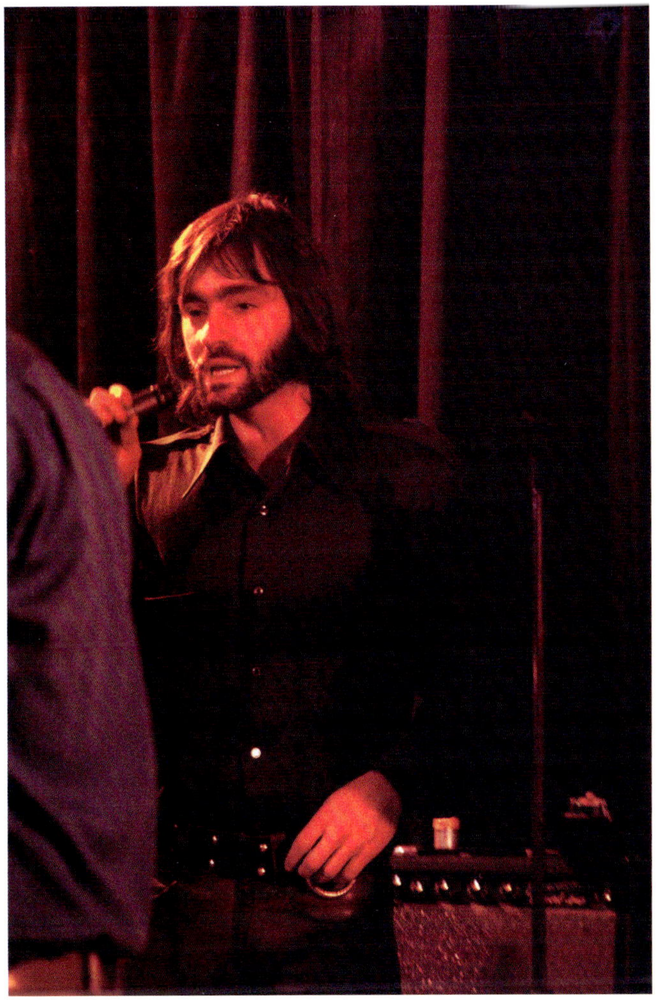

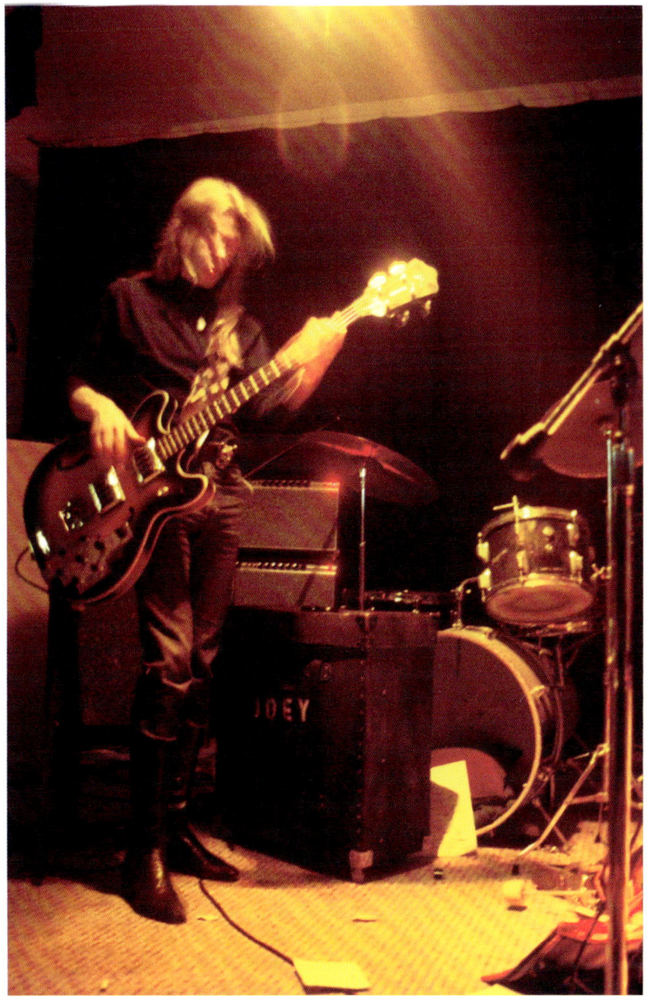

Left: Marty Balin of Jefferson Airplane, rehearsal space at 2400 Fulton Street, December 1969. *Right*: Jack Casady of Hot Tuna, rehearsal space at 2400 Fulton Street, December 1969.

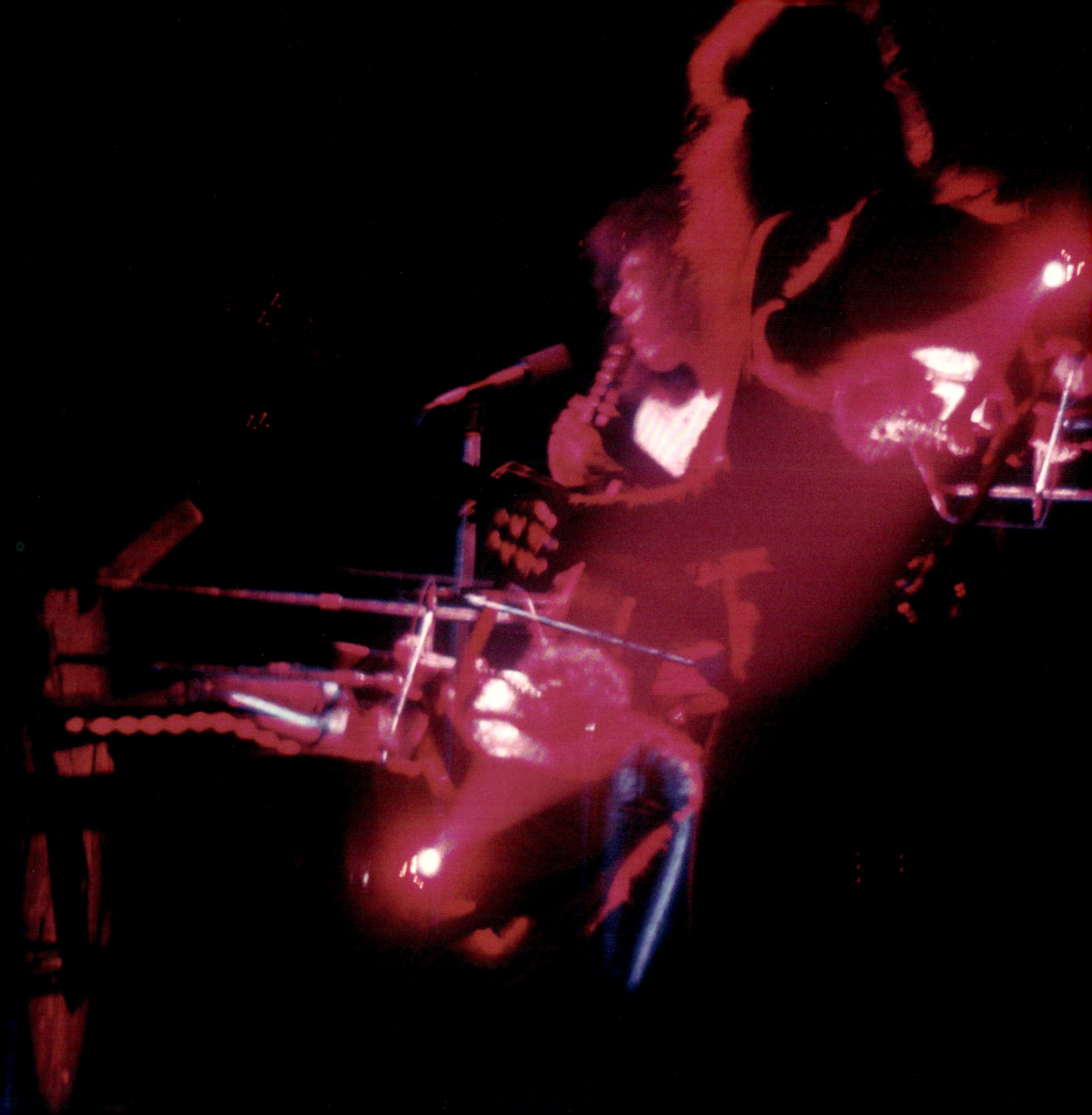

7

The Arrival of Hot Tuna

During the years around Woodstock Jorma and Jack had been warming up for their duo by performing a few songs together during the full band's sets.

Jorma had a long and extensive acoustic guitar background and was a complete master of the instrument, having created his own style inspired by his own blues heroes. Jorma, along with Jerry Garcia and the underrated John Cipollina formed the San Francisco triumvirate that produced some of the most stunningly spectacular sounds that were ever produced in any musical format anywhere.

Jack has owned for decades the unchallenged mantle of being the greatest rock bassist, in my humble opinion. He transformed the conventional role of the bass guitar from a supporting position to producing soaring, complex lead lines, which at the time was virtually unheard of, and he continues to innovate to this day along with Jorma, his partner in musical crime for almost sixty years now.

In the Airplane Jorma and Jack wielded their electric weapons, loading their power into the wide bore barrel of the megawatt amps of the day and unleashing a barrage of intense sounds, which ferociously drove the band's full-frontal aural attack. But neither left their acoustic roots behind, so Hot Tuna was a perfect vessel for expanding on that tradition in a never heard combination of acoustic guitar and amplified bass. What began as a subset of the Airplane's music at concerts became a separate band mainly because their unique acoustic and eventually electric approach thrilled their ever-growing fan base.

I must admit to being stunned when I was informed in early 1970 that Jorma and Jack wanted to use some of my images for both the cover and inner sleeve of their

Hot Tuna, Fillmore East, New York, May 1970.

upcoming first Hot Tuna record. They had me contact their manager Bill Thompson and an art director at RCA Victor Records, Acy Lehman, who was to be my point of contact at the label. I began the process of transmitting my work to RCA in New York and, owing to my naivete in believing I would receive my originals back, I sent them around 150 35mm slides by special delivery (It took decades and a lawyer to get some of them back). I did not have input in the artistic direction of the project, which I attributed to my tender, unexperienced age of twenty. Though I was blown away with what was done with the cover, I really have to say that the collage work of my pictures on the inner sleeve—done by an artistic Hells Angel by the name of "Gut"—disappointed me. The composition was crude and not thought out in the least. It looked like the pictures were cut out with scissors and slapped together without much creativity behind it. I was nonetheless thrilled to have so many of my images reproduced, and the cover has stood the test of time.

I received my advance copy right around my birthday in April 1970, shortly before its general release the following month. There could not have been a better present to commemorate my twenty-first year on earth. I was truly gobsmacked and proudly showed it to my beaming parents and close friends, but it took weeks to fully process and grasp.

Shortly after *Hot Tuna* was released, I was informed of the plans for a second, electric record, and again to my youthful amazement Jorma and Jack wanted one of my images to grace the inside of this sleeve. The early '70s was the golden age of the gatefold 12" LP. When I held in my hands *First Pull Up, Then Pull Down* (the name inspired by a phrase seen in public restrooms across the land) and opened it up to reveal my glowing, bright image introducing the electric version of the band, I felt that another milestone in my life had been achieved.

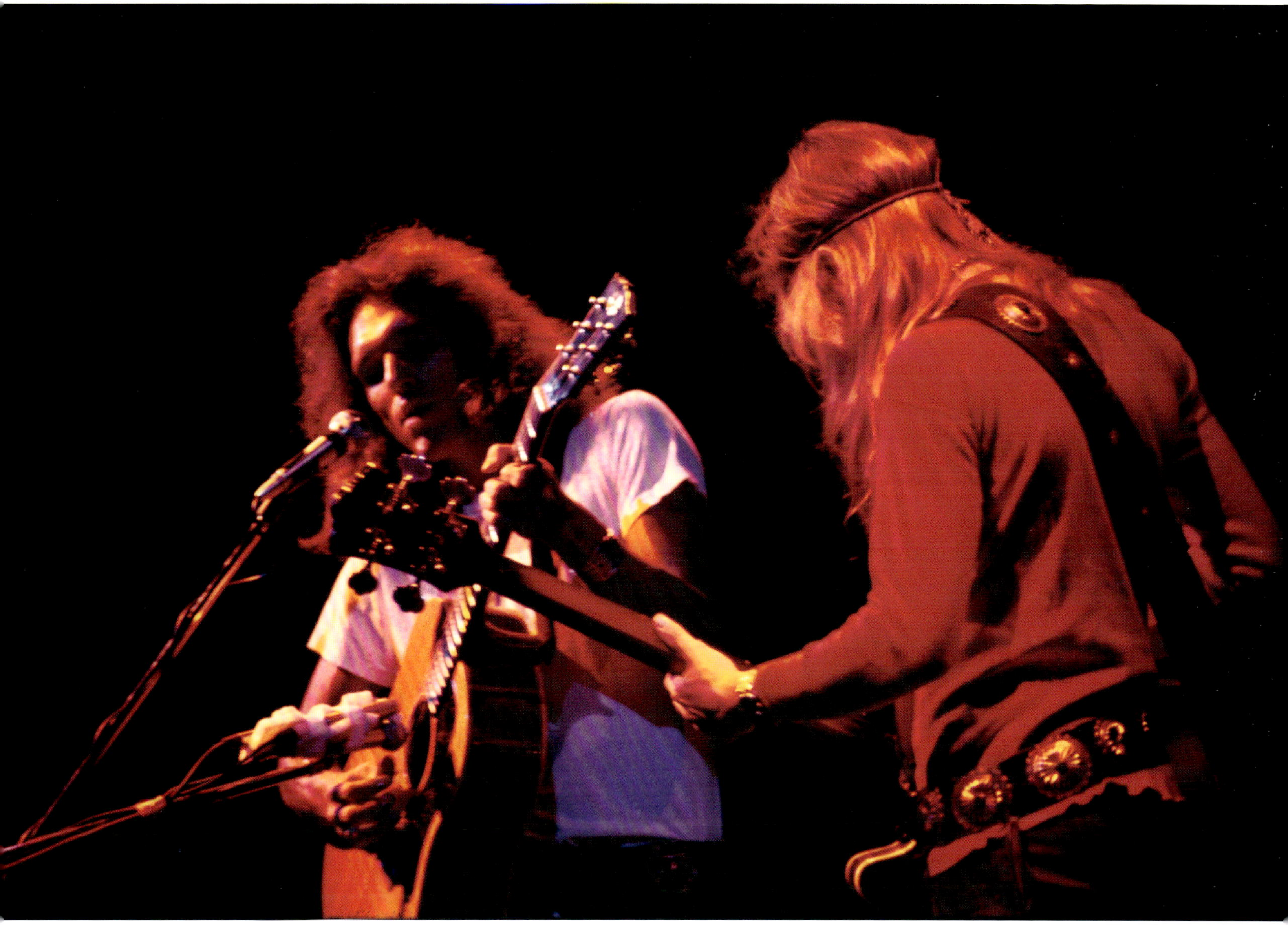

Album cover photo for the fortieth anniversary alternate evening recordings of the first Hot Tuna record, Fillmore East, New York, July 1970.

Overleaf: Jorma Kaukonen (left) and Jack Casady of Hot Tuna, Fillmore East, New York, July 1970.

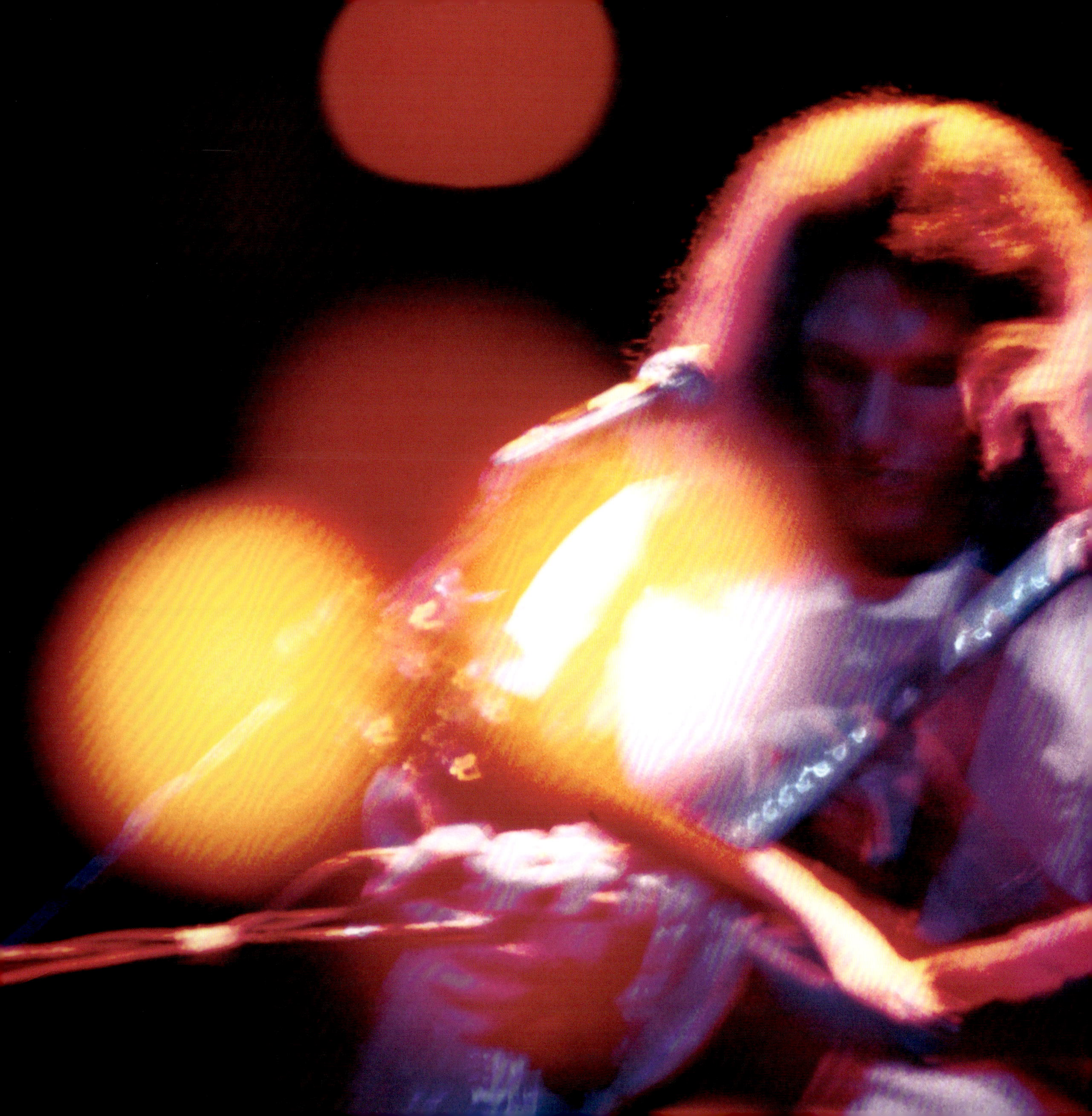

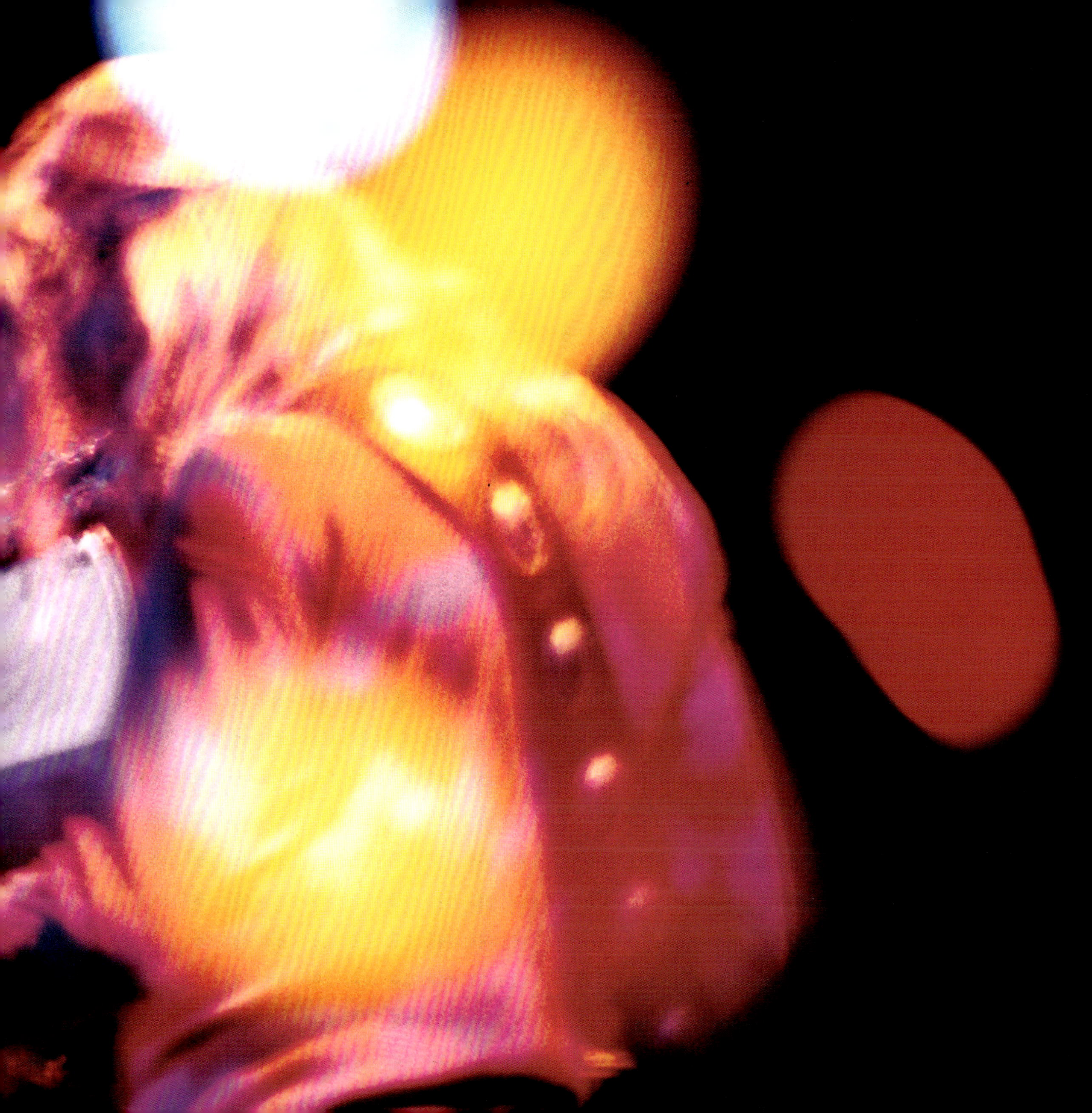

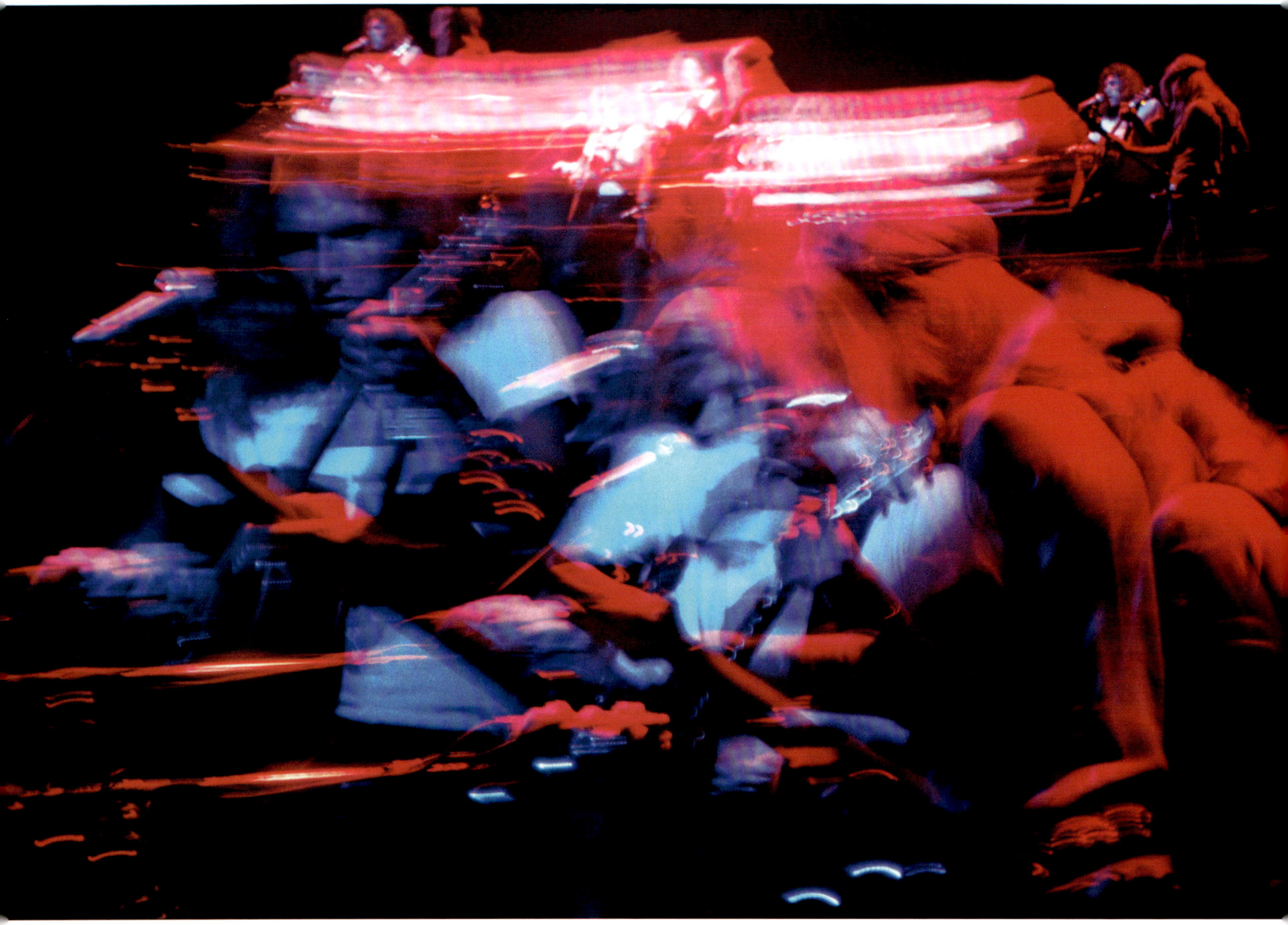

Jorma Kaukonen (left) and Jack Casady of Hot Tuna, Fillmore East, New York, July 1970.

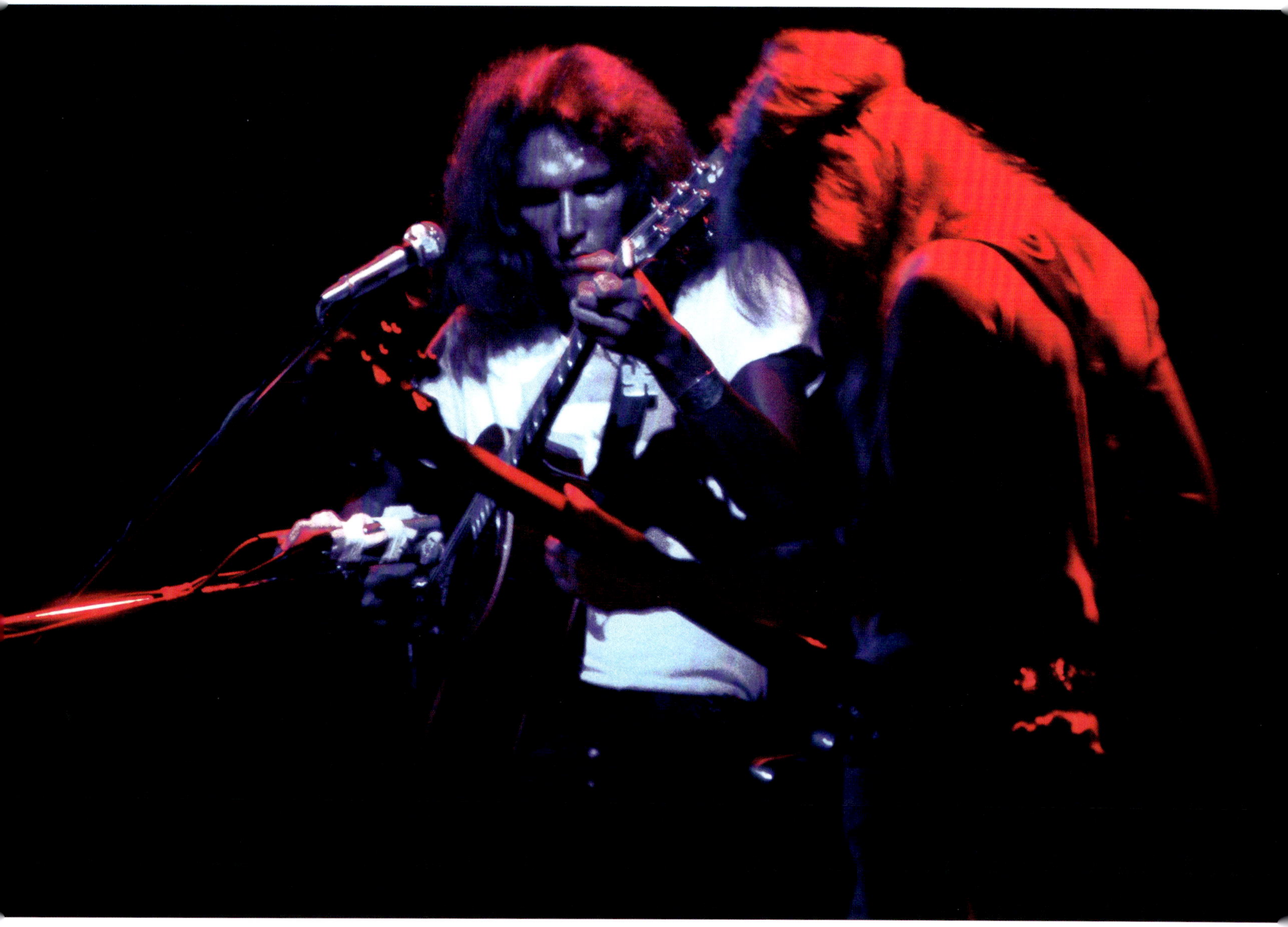

Hot Tuna, Fillmore East, New York, July 1970.

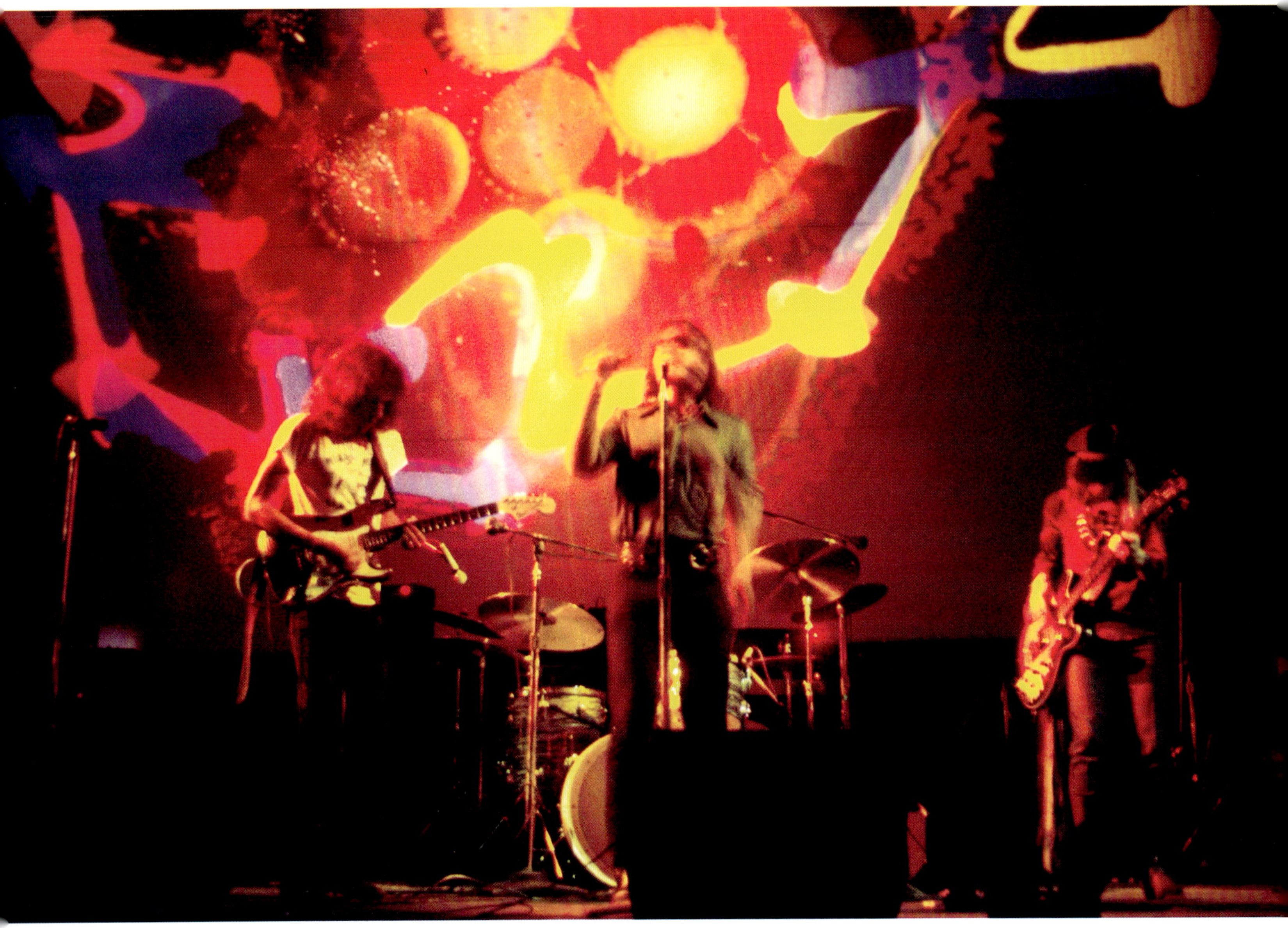

Jorma Kaukonen, Marty Balin, and Jack Casady of Hot Tuna,
Fillmore East, New York, May 1970.

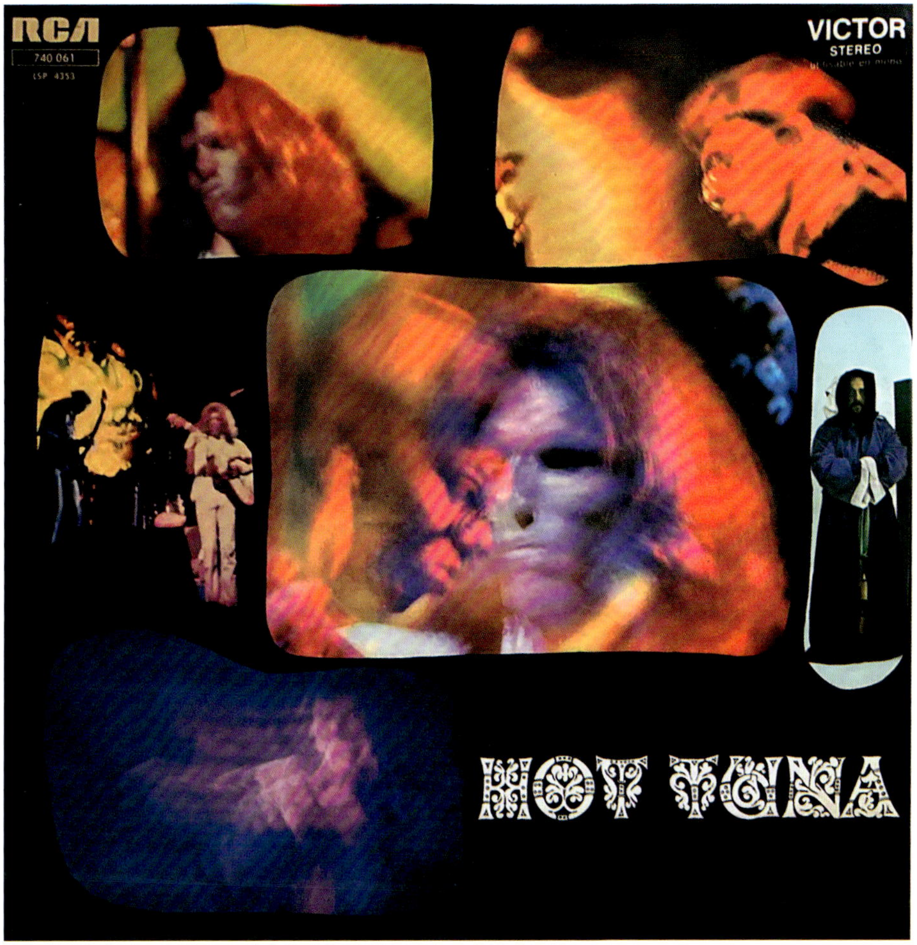

French cover, Hot Tuna, 1970.

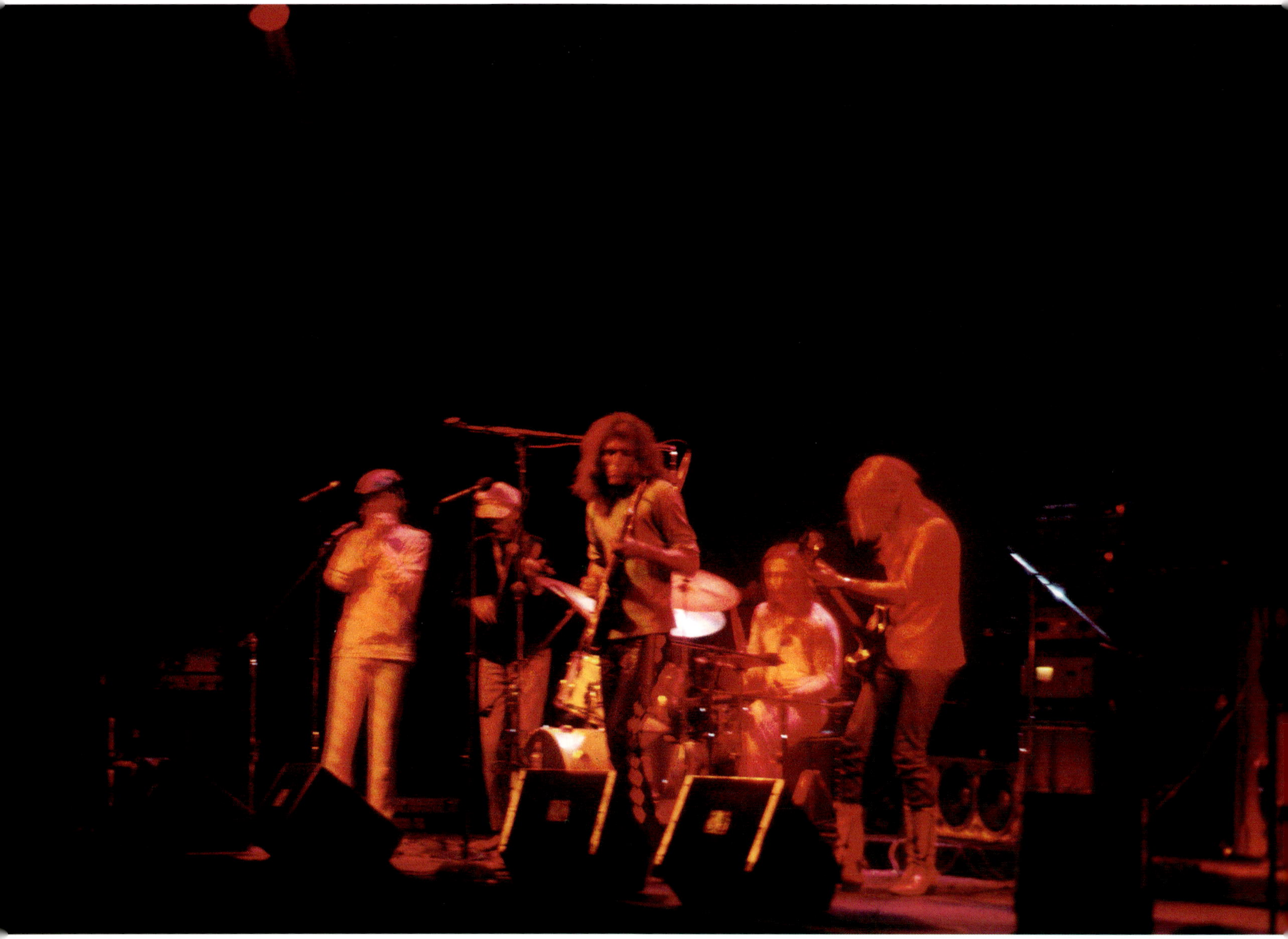

Hot Tuna Fillmore East, New York, July 1970. Used for inside gate fold on the second Hot Tuna record, First Pull Up, Then Pull Down. *Opposite*: Jorma Kaukonen and Jack Casady on the cover of the first Hot Tuna record, 1970.

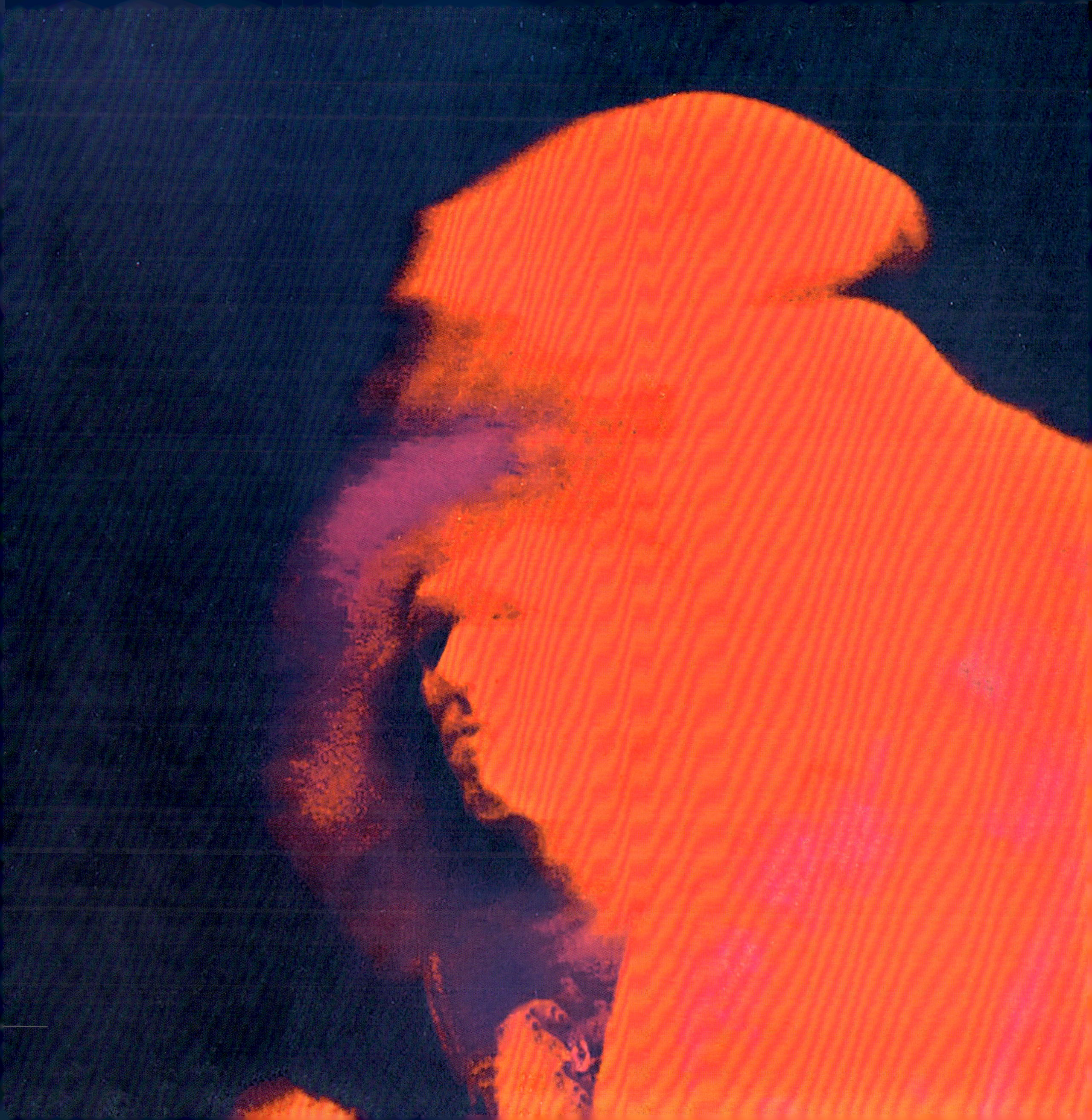

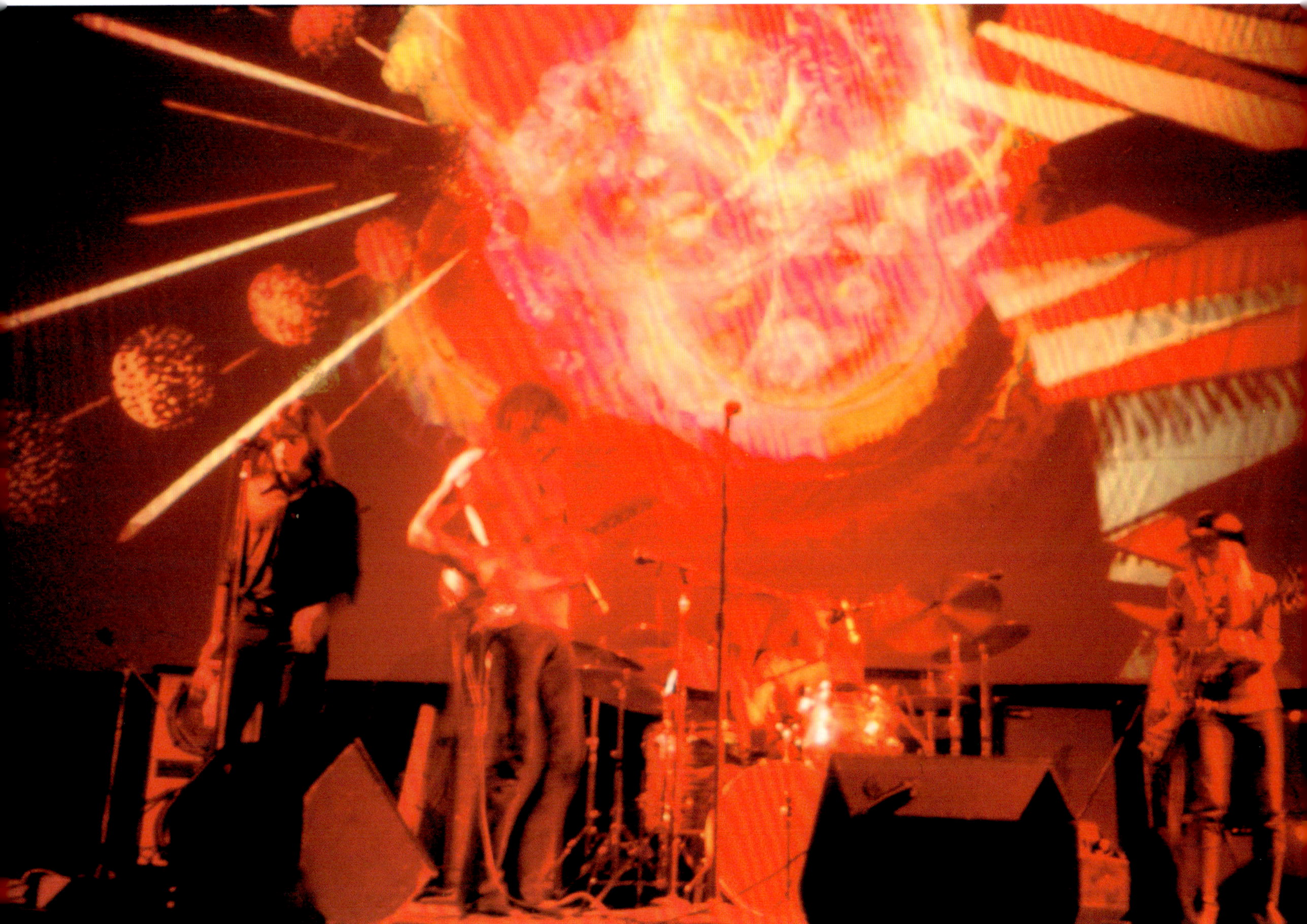

Marty Balin, Jorma Kaukonen, Joey Covington, and Jack Casady of Hot Tuna, Fillmore East, New York, May 1970.

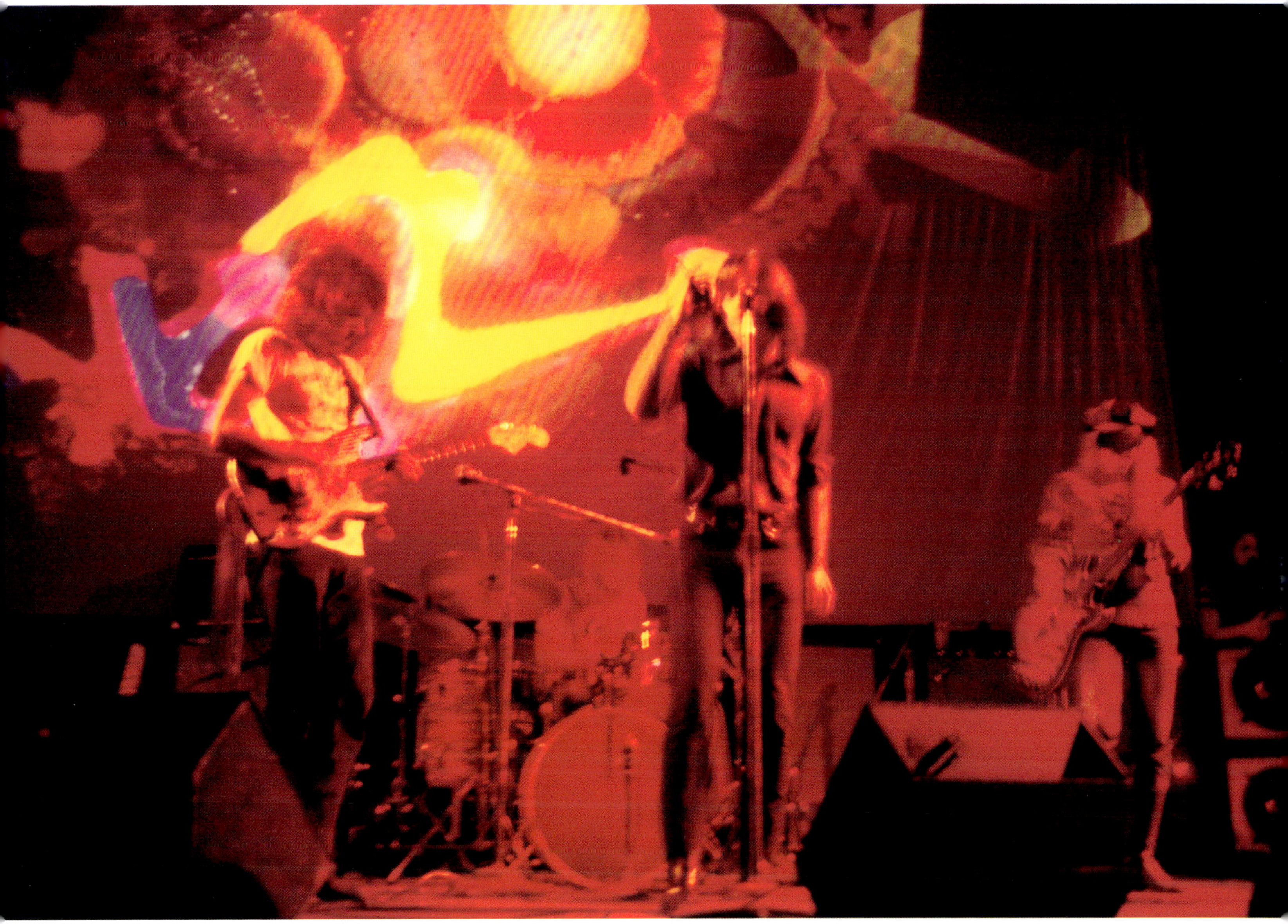

Jorma Kaukonen, Marty Balin, and Jack Casady of Hot Tuna, Fillmore East, New York, May 1970.

Overleaf: Jorma Kaukonen and Jack Casady of Hot Tuna at the Fillmore East, New York, July 1970.

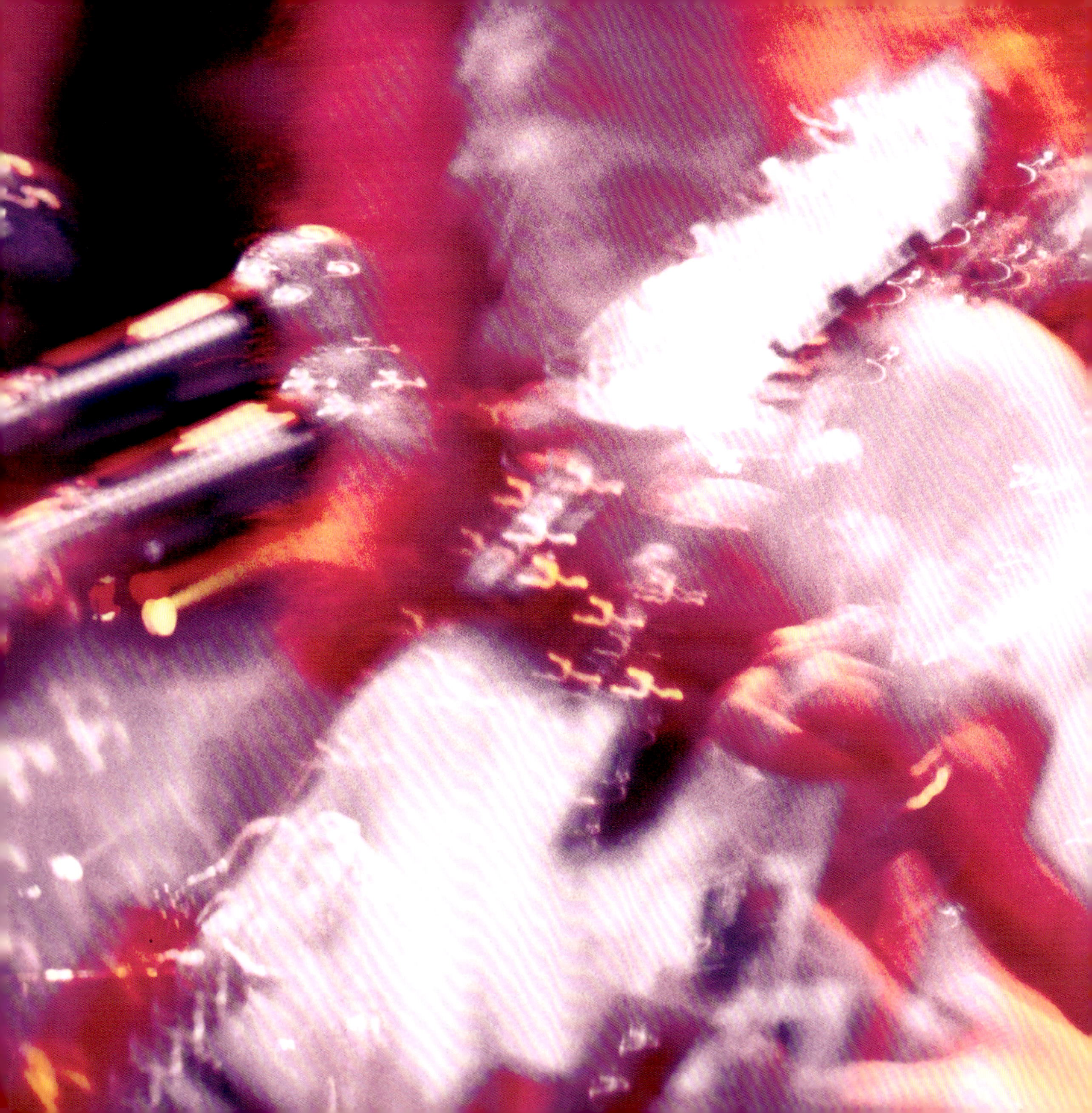

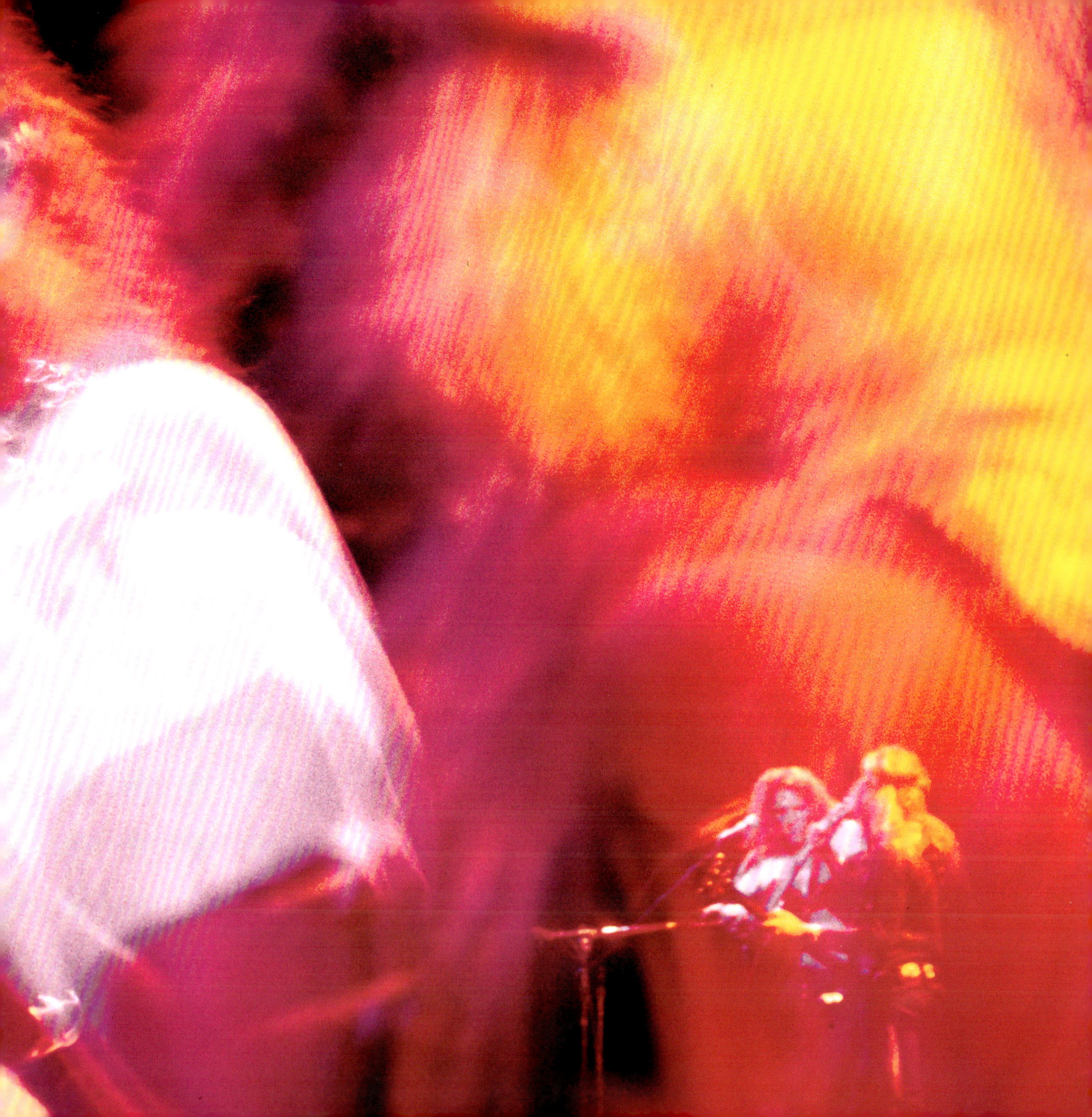

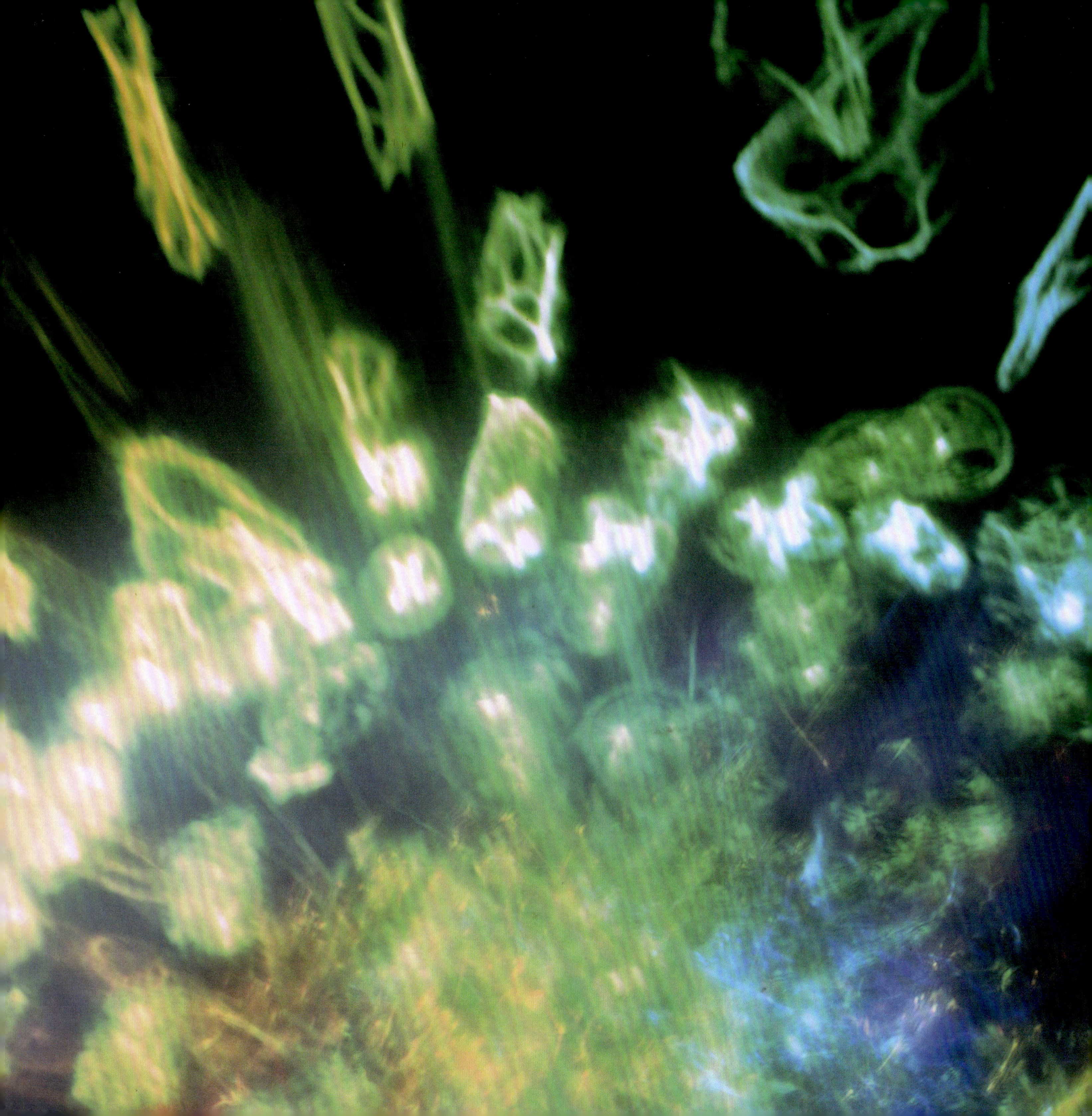

8

Holograms, Lasergrams, and Heliographs

From the time I first set my eyes on a ray gun, either in a comic book or a Flash Gordon movie serial, I was fascinated by the thought of such a weapon and the force it could deliver. This led me to become obsessed with the invention of the laser in the late 1950s. I had already read about the maser, a microwave version that seemed to have only military and communication applications, but the laser was a fevered fantasy of my science fiction dreams come true. Seemingly a laser could blast through walls and transmit data as fast as light (of course much of that promise was decades away and still not fully implemented with fiber optics). Then, in the June 1965 issue of *Scientific American*, I read about the creation of true holograms, which were first theorized and very crudely created in 1947 by physicist Dennis Gabor but could not be truly achieved until the laser was invented in 1958 by Theodore Maimon (holograms needed an actual source of coherent light to produce them). The article triggered a fascination with holography, recalling 3D movies I had seen when I was a kid during the tail end of their first wave of popularity. My obsession was cemented when in the 1967 *World Book Science Annual* I saw my first real hologram, which depicted chess pieces. Later in 1970 I built my first laser from a kit from Edmund Scientific fortuitously headquartered in southern New Jersey, just an hour or so drive from me. I began to imagine new photographic experiments and even more intriguing holographic experiments, which I threw myself into furiously.

After I built the laser, named "Dinginthall" in honor of one of the scientists who worked at Edmund Scientific, I did some small experimentation with holography. Because I didn't have a much-needed iso-

"Heliograph 33," Mike Frankel, April 1972.

lation table to shield the laser from vibrations, I had to improvise by putting my laser on a very heavy washing machine in a friend's basement to make my first holograms of chess pieces, coins, and other small objects. At the time, by happenstance, my laser hit a drinking glass made of patterned glass, which produced curious and intriguing results: on the wall were projected stunning, abstract images the likes of which I had never seen. I began to shine the laser through and off as many different and varied types of glass, mirrors, lenses, and objects as I could get my hands on, to shape and distort the laser beam into a myriad of unique shapes and figures.

I began thinking about how I could capture and record on film the results of my experiments. I tried taking the lens off my Nikon F and imprinting the red laser light directly on film, filtered through my growing arsenal of glass, which created stunning crimson images that were controllable and configurable into many otherworldly, intergalactic-looking shapes, sizes, and complex structures. To vary the colors, I used infrared film, shifting the reds to greens, yellows, and subtle blues, which expanded the range of colors I could manipulate.

This expansion of my palette still wasn't enough, so I begin thinking about how to get full colors to project through my image-creating and -transforming devices. It was when I was working with a prism that I had my epiphany of how to solve this vexing problem. The prism accidentally caught the sunlight as all the spectral colors spread momentarily across a far wall; in a flash, the answer became abundantly clear to me.

I devised a way, when the sun was in the right position streaming into my room, to direct its beam into a cardboard box with a prism affixed to the entrance aperture of the crude device I had fashioned. And just as I had done with the laser beams, I imprinted the light, now fully ablaze with the most intense spectral colors, directly onto 35mm film sans lens, through the same elements used for the lasers, now employing the slowest speed film I could find because of the intensity of the light being captured. I had called my laser images "lasergrams," and so I dubbed these amazing new multicolor images "heliographs," inspired by the Greek name for the sun, Helios. All this fevered activity—executed in a somewhat crazed, mad scientist–like manner—led a science fiction writer and friend William Jon Watkins to fictionalize my experiments when he based a character in his 1973 book *The God Machine* on me.

I then began to combine the abstract images I created with lasers and sunlight with images that I took of rock and roll performers, once again using my multiple-image technique, but this time hours and sometimes days apart. I executed this effect with many of the bands, most prominently Jefferson Airplane and Hot Tuna, but also Humble Pie, Pink Floyd, and Emerson, Lake & Palmer.

Many of my most outlandish multiple-exposure rock images were previsualized to be viewed at any angle, and I called these "spinners." It was not until 2019 that they were finally displayed in this way at my Monmouth University exhibition, after I mounted the works so they could be "spun" by the viewers and seen from all 360 degrees. These experiments also led to other wild ideas, including putting my slides under a microscope and rephotographing them, enhancing and emphasizing the film grain in a pointillist-influenced image. Some of my photographic work at the time became completely abstract, merging completely with my lasergrams and heliographs.

Perhaps the pinnacle of these multiple-image experiments occurred on March 7, 1970, during a 90 percent partial eclipse, which I photographed in the afternoon. I then rewound the film and photographed Neil Young over the eclipse images that night at his first solo appearance at the Fillmore East. At the concert, I also produced the greatest number of multiple exposures on one frame of film, with ten separate images of Neil on one frame. This necessitated, in addition to rewinding the film ten times, employing my method of masking off the lens with my hand to make sure the rest of the images were not overexposed. This technique worked well and became easily repeatable, even though I had to focus my concentration on this complex, multipronged execution, no matter what my state of mind or the surroundings were at the time, which often could be quite intense and chaotic.

Later that year my lifelong friend Joe Rubin helped to promote my work on a national level. He arranged for me to attend as an invited guest a new media conference at Syracuse University where he was doing undergraduate work. So I displayed to hundreds of attendees my rock and roll images along with the experimental work I was doing with lasers and holography. I even shared the stage in a discussion of new media with the world-famous media theoretician Marshall McLuhan, whose visionary ideas were just then beginning to be recognized.

It was during this visit to Syracuse that I had access to some early half-inch black-and-white video equipment for a recording of my abstract laser images in motion. I was able to use the equipment for an afternoon and employ the various lenses, mirrors, and twisted glass that I brought with me for my demonstration and lecture. I used all this and the home-built laser I had brought to capture on video my abstract laser patterns for the first time in motion. I later incorporated this black-and-white footage into the predominantly color short film I completed with the help of the grant of $1,000 from the New Jersey State Arts Commission in 1972. I was amazed and overjoyed when I received the grant—this being the one and only time that any entity in New Jersey recognized my work. I felt these captivating moving images needed their own specifically composed music, unlike Laserium's later efforts, which used existing rock music. I collaborated with my good friend and guitarist-composer John Thorpe, along with the late percussionist Dave Patt; together they composed perfectly complementary music to my images. The film, which I named *Psycostar*, was to my knowledge the first film of abstract laser images in history.

Another unique venture consisted of an attempt in the late 1970s to commercialize my early work with holograms by creating and marketing the first Marvel superhero holograms as well as holograms of the great Ray Harryhausen's fantasy creatures. This endeavor met with moderate success and led to—and was eventually funded by—my operation of the Man Ray Cinema, a movie theater I ran in Belmar, just south of Asbury Park, the likes of which no one had seen at the Jersey Shore before or since. But tales of those adventures must wait for another day.

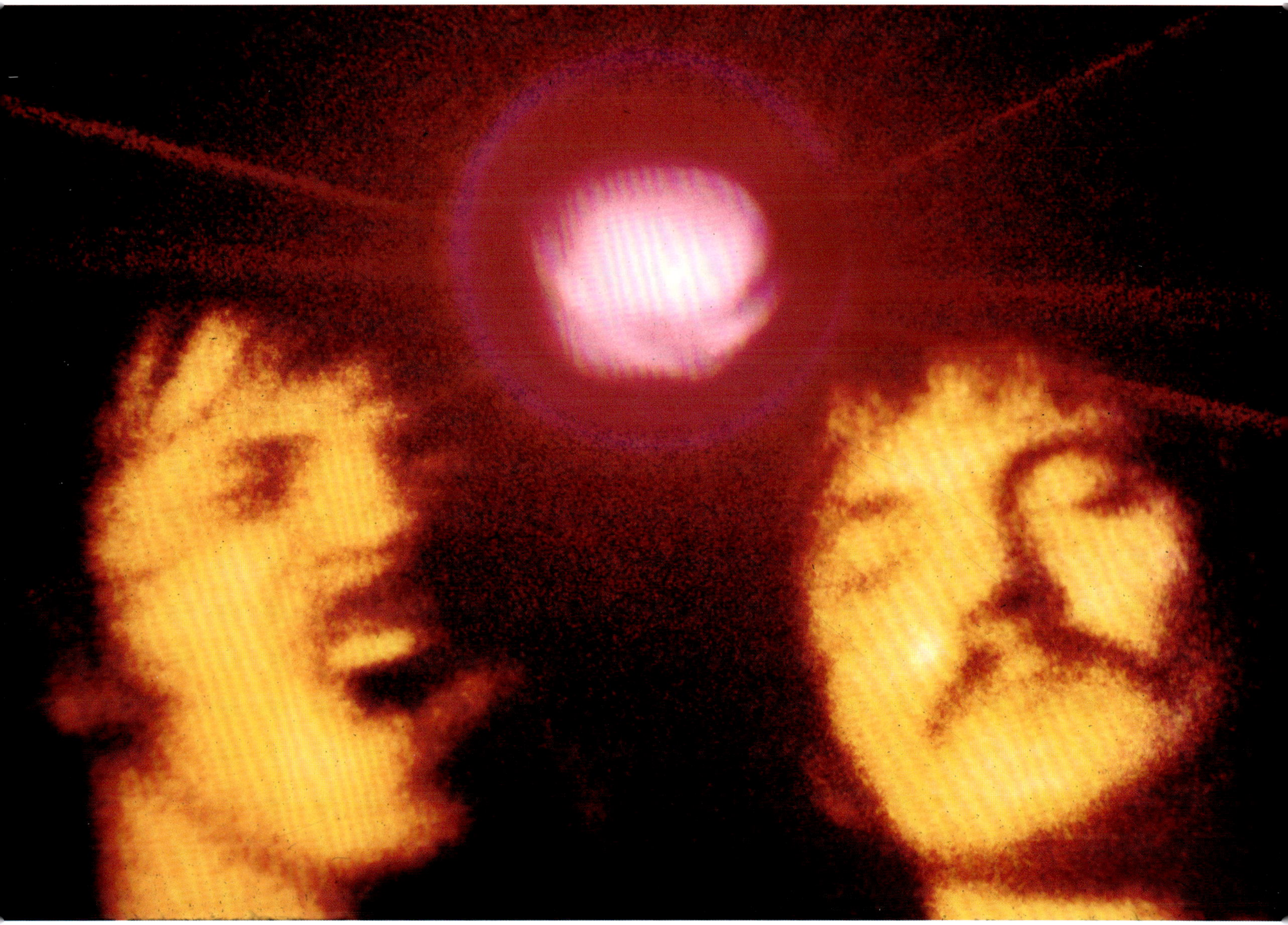

Steve Marriott of Humble Pie, microscope laser image, Fillmore East, New York, October 1970.

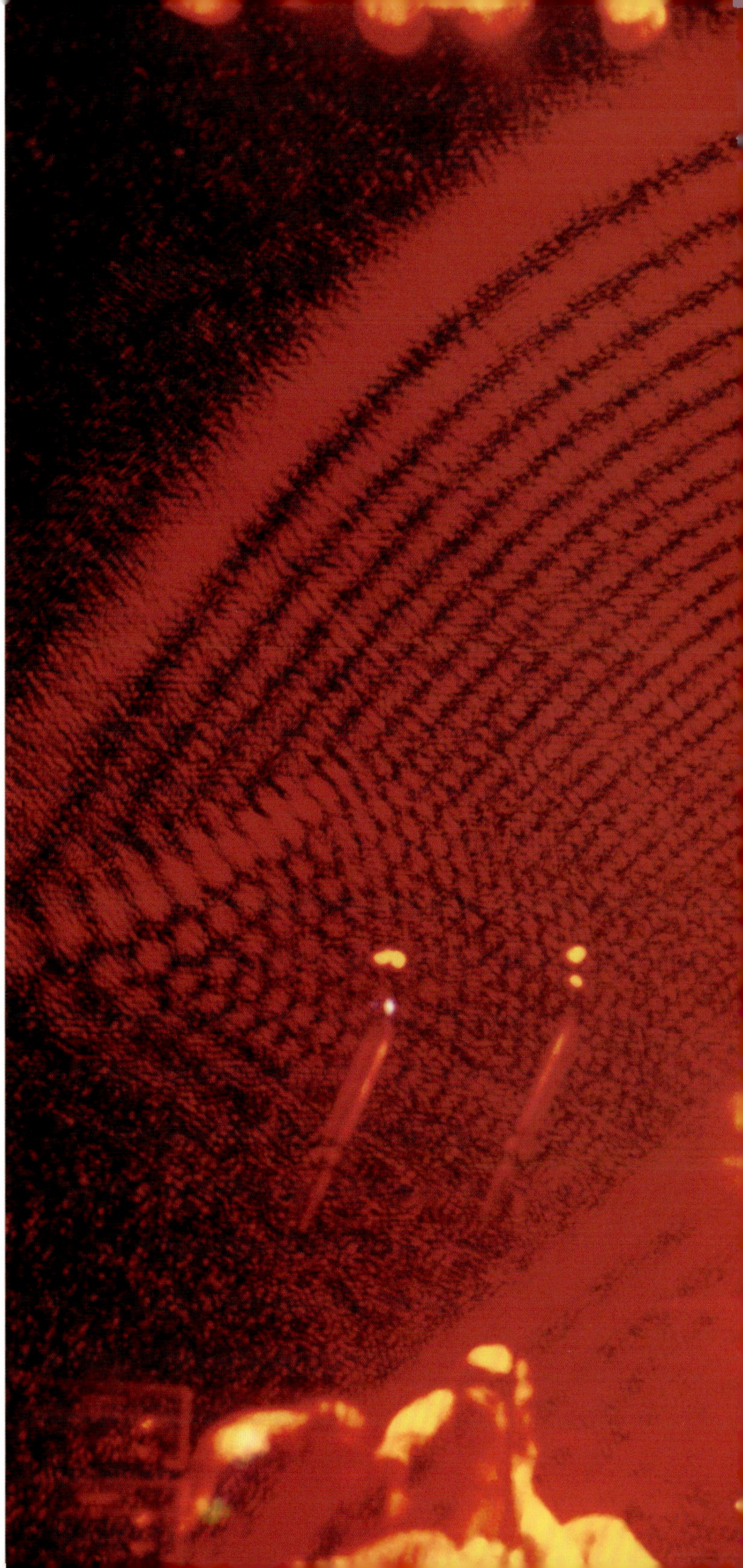

Pink Floyd with laser image, Fillmore East, New York, June 1971.

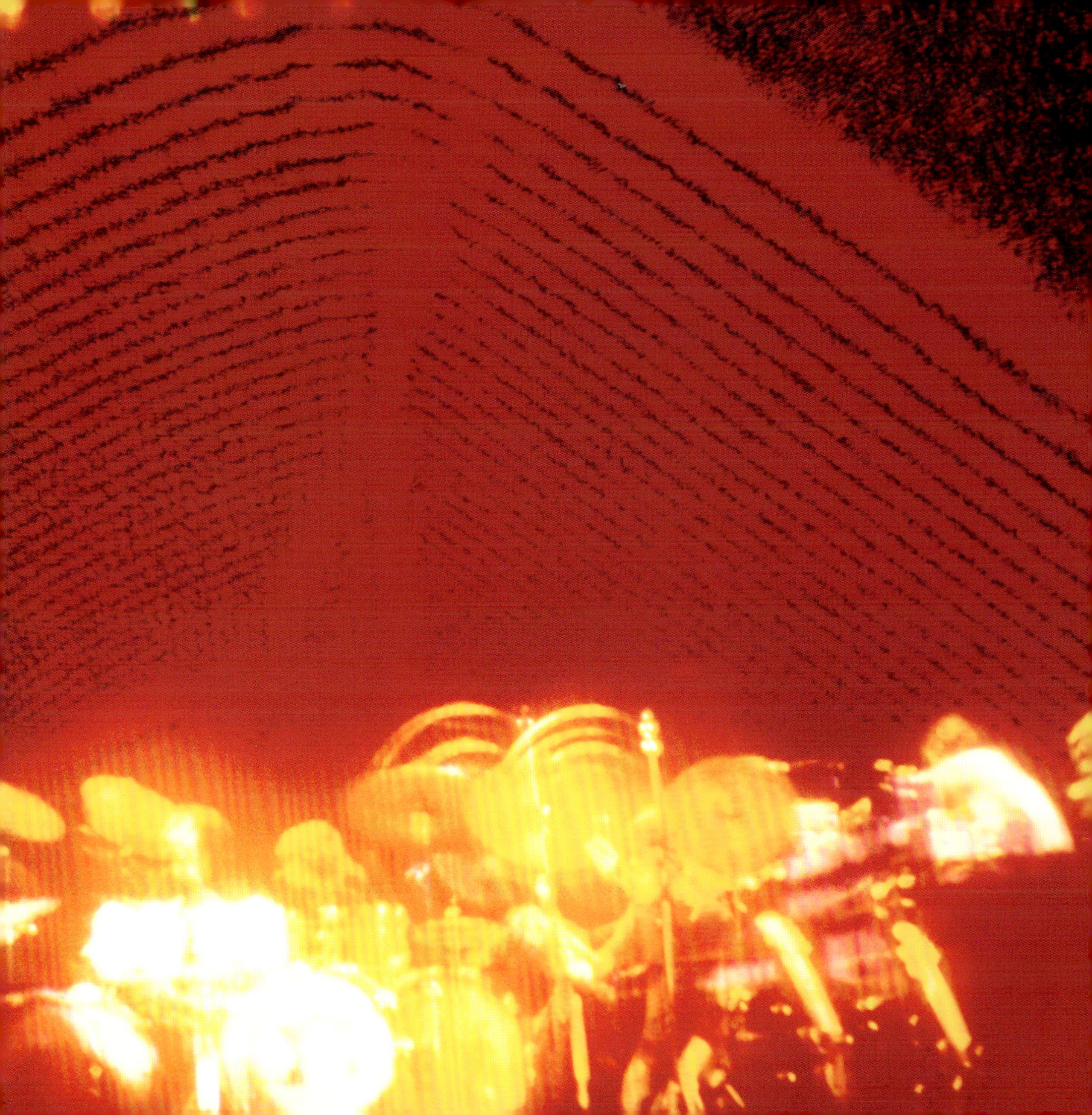

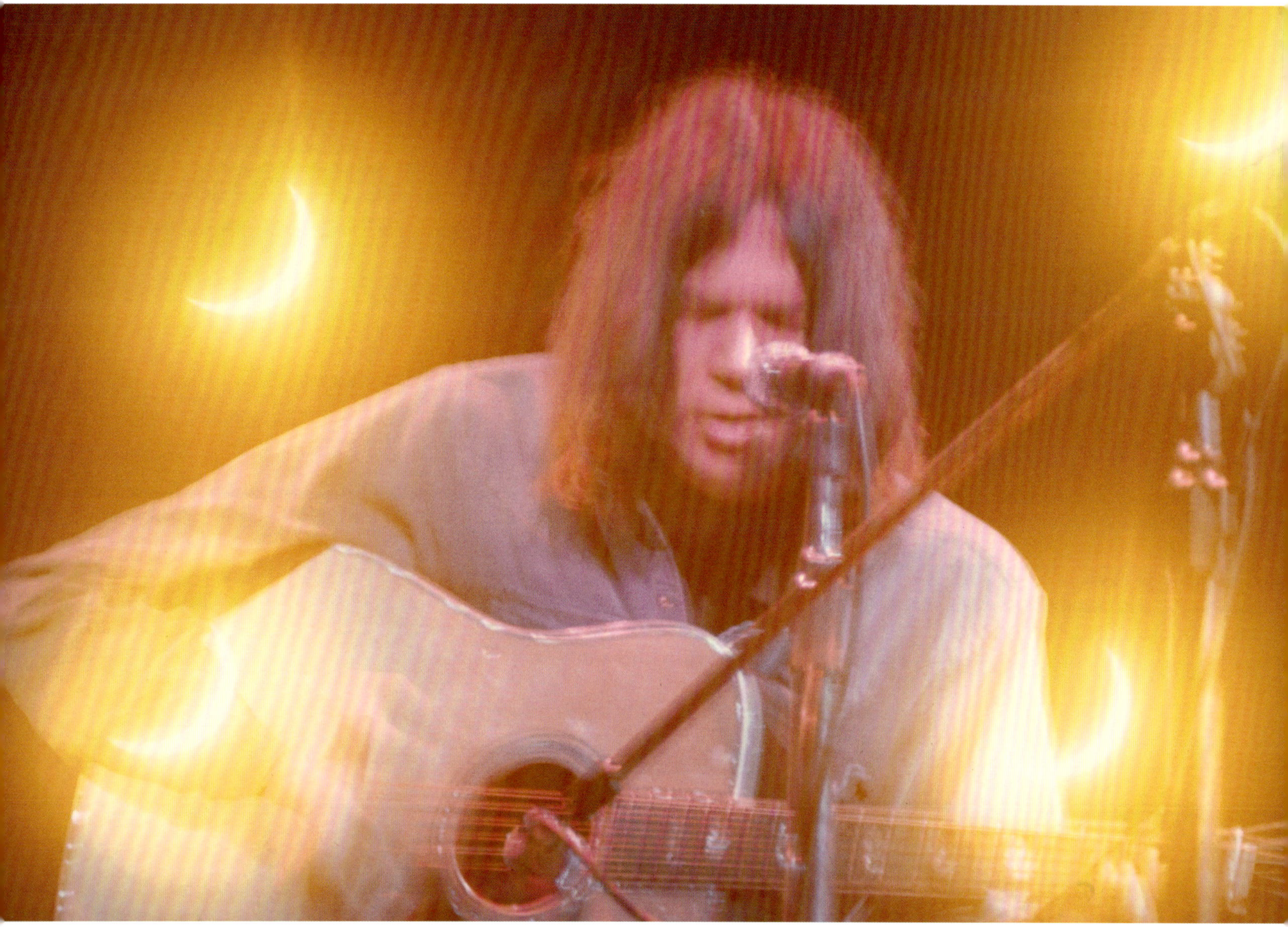

Neil Young with Eclipse of the Sun, Fillmore East, New York, March 1970.

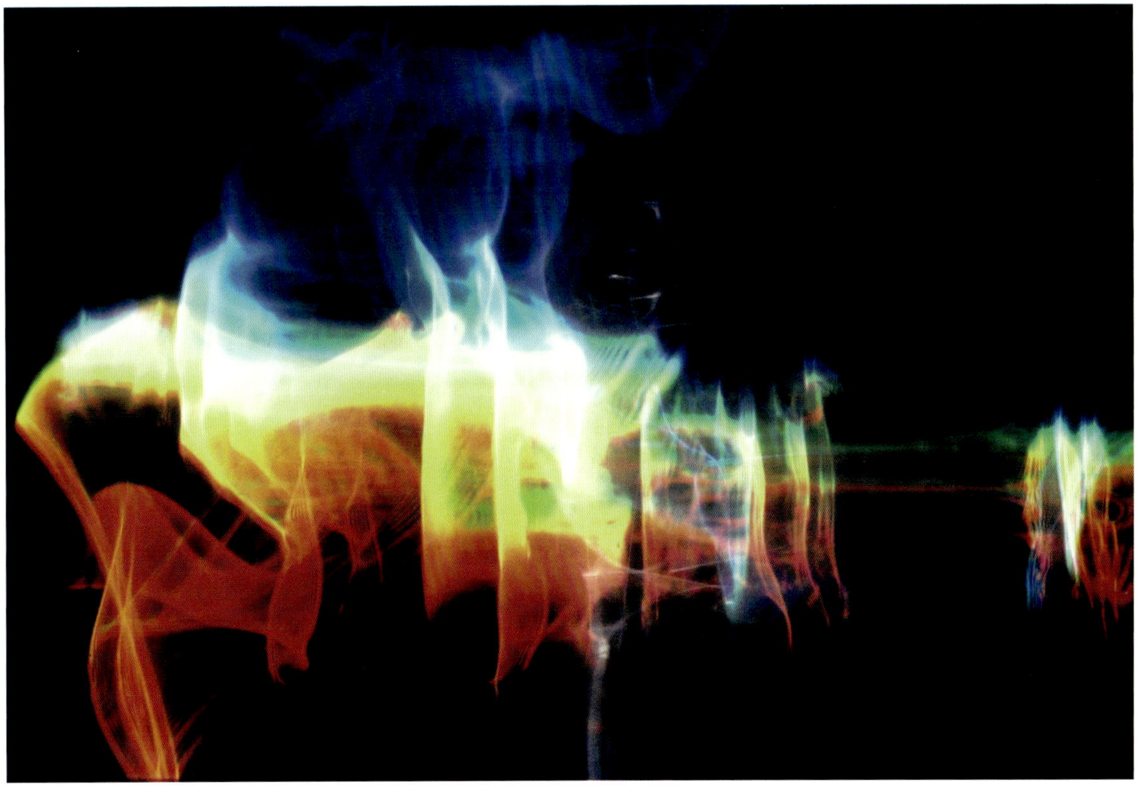

"Heliograph 21," Mike Frankel, June 1971.

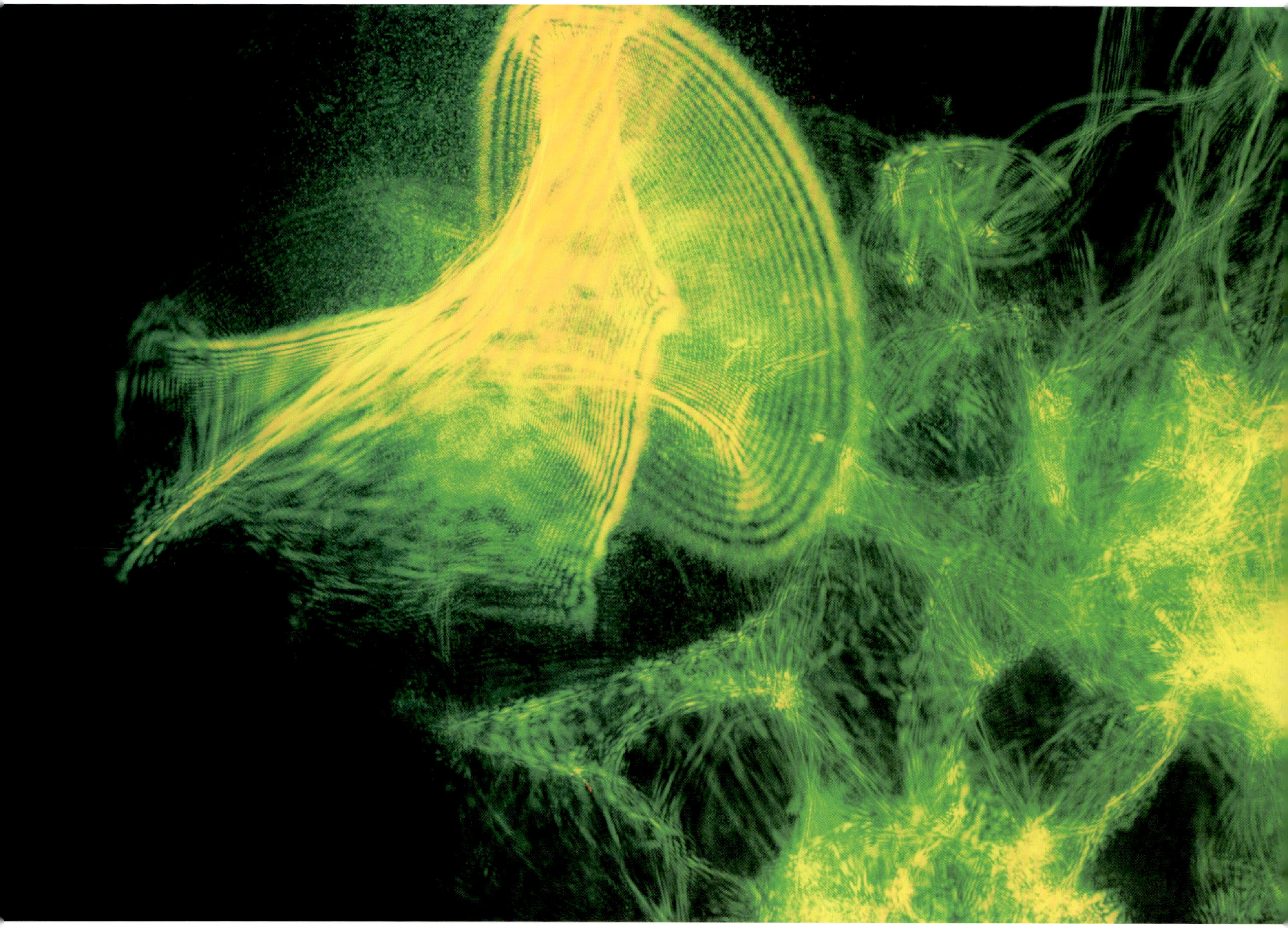

"Siderial," infrared lasergram image, Mike Frankel, June 1971.

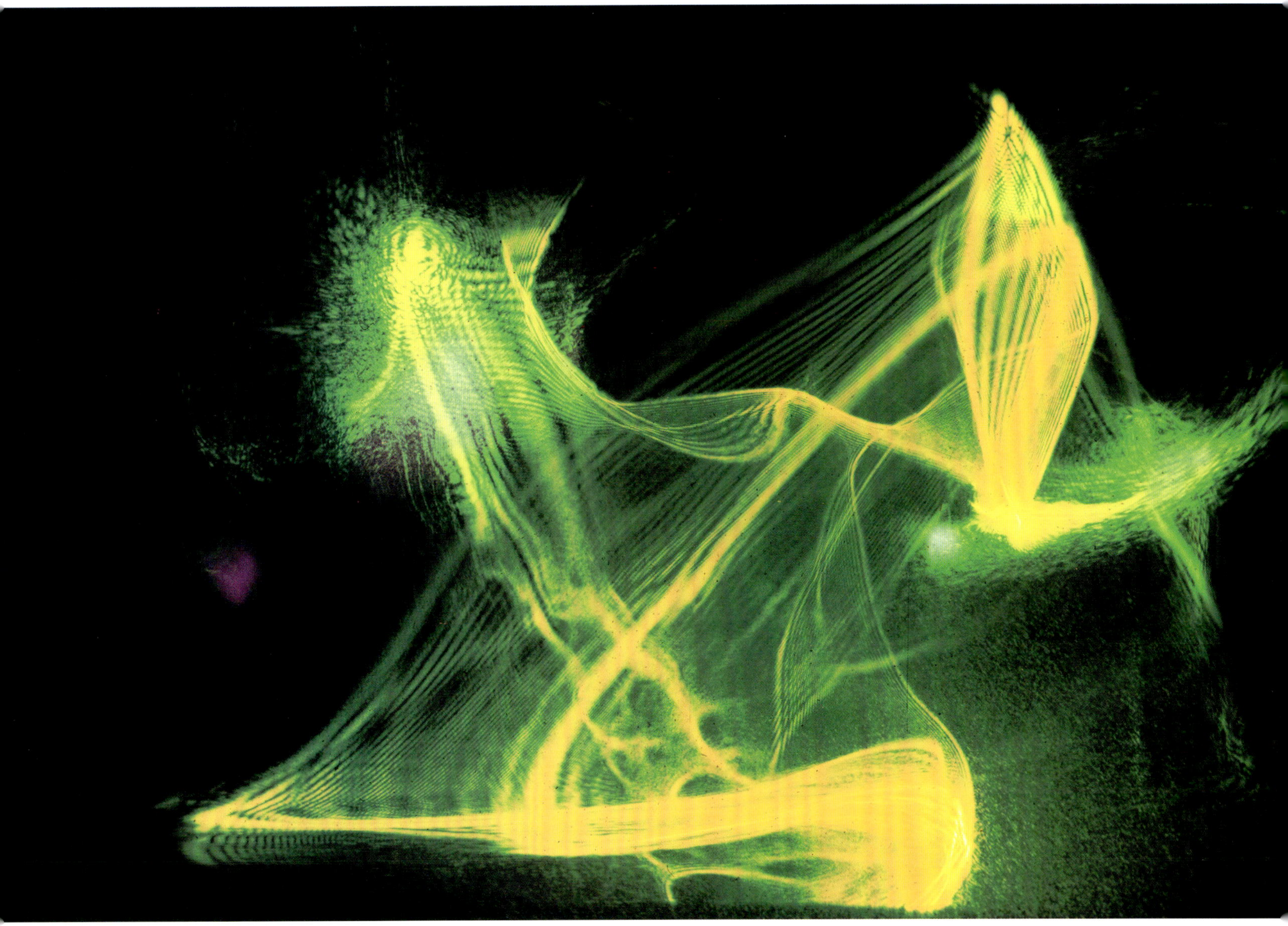

"Butterflyee," infrared lasergram image, Mike Frankel, June 1971.

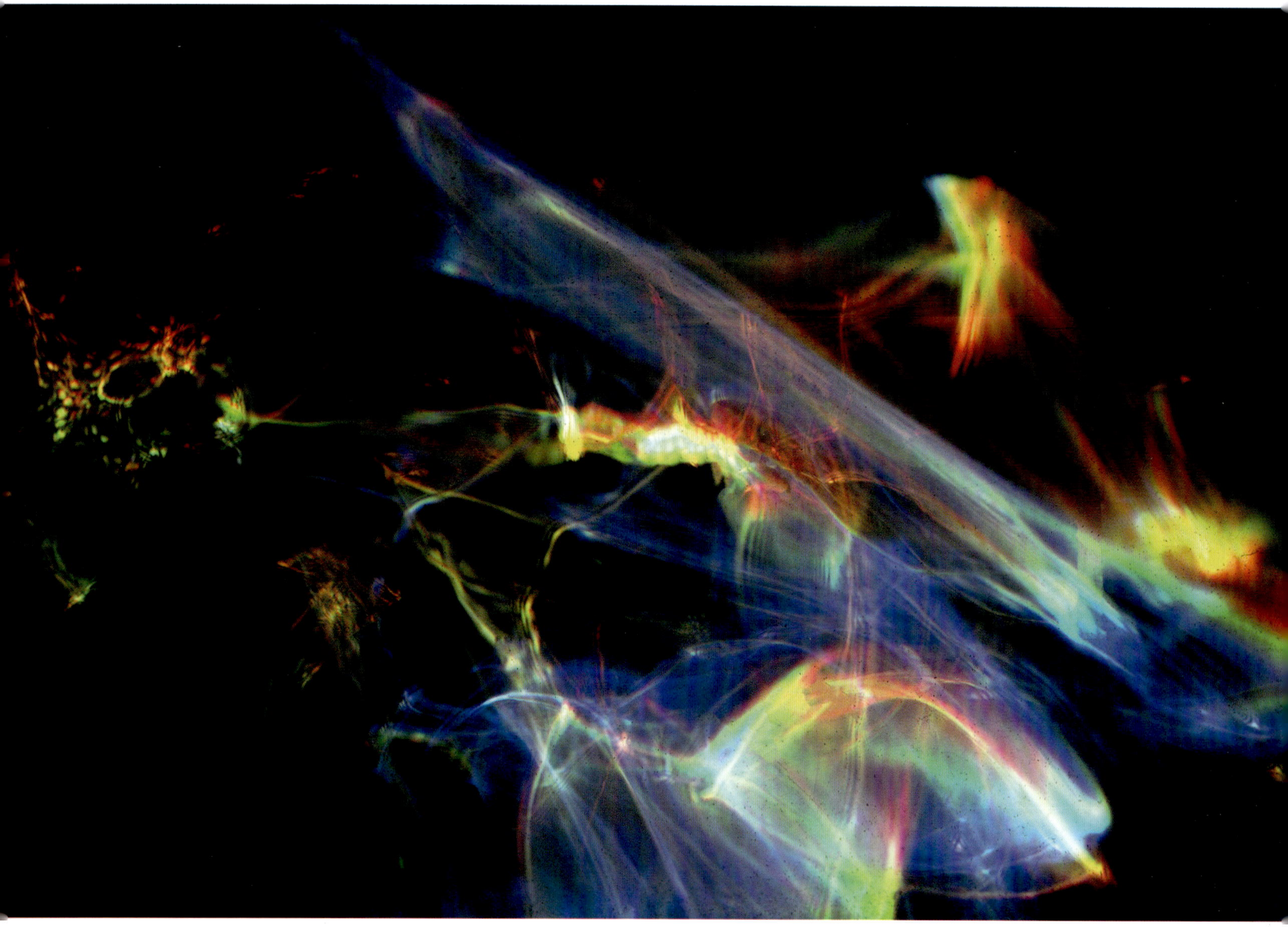

"Heliograph 14," Mike Frankel, June 1971.

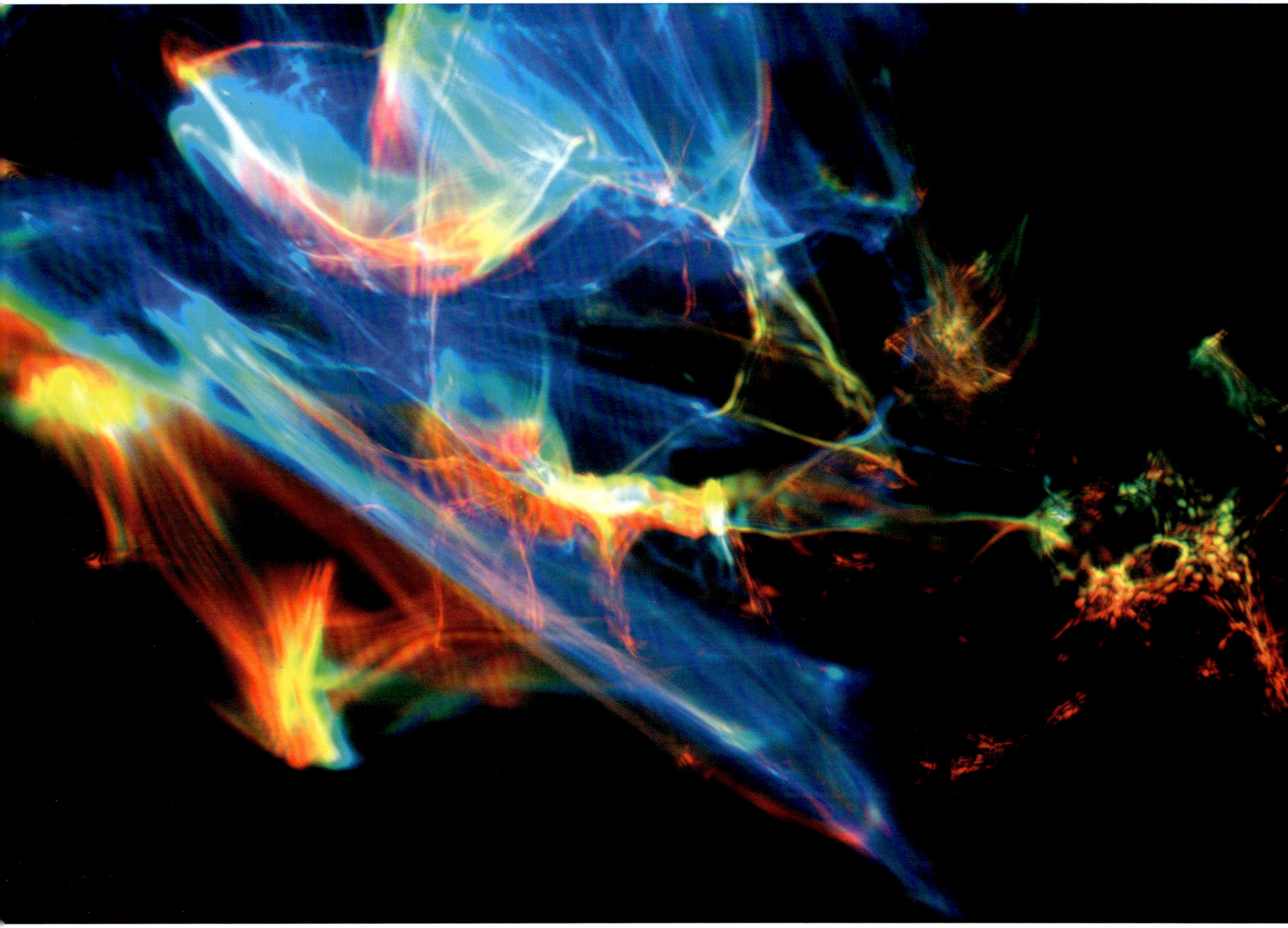

"Heliograph 28," Mike Frankel, June 1971.

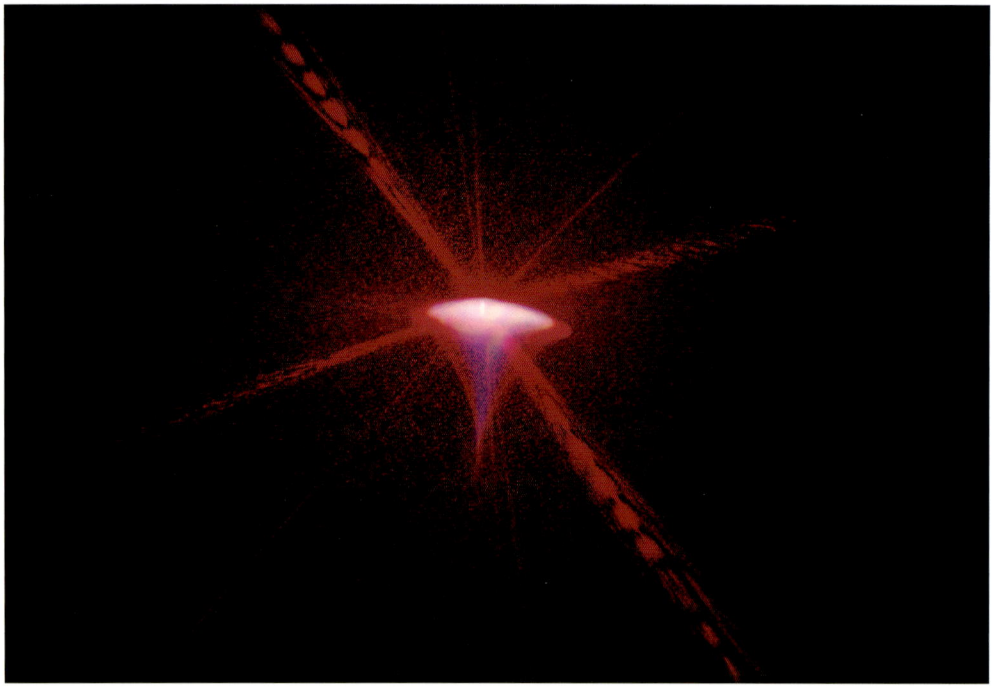

“Mindbender,” lasergram, Mike Frankel, September 1970.

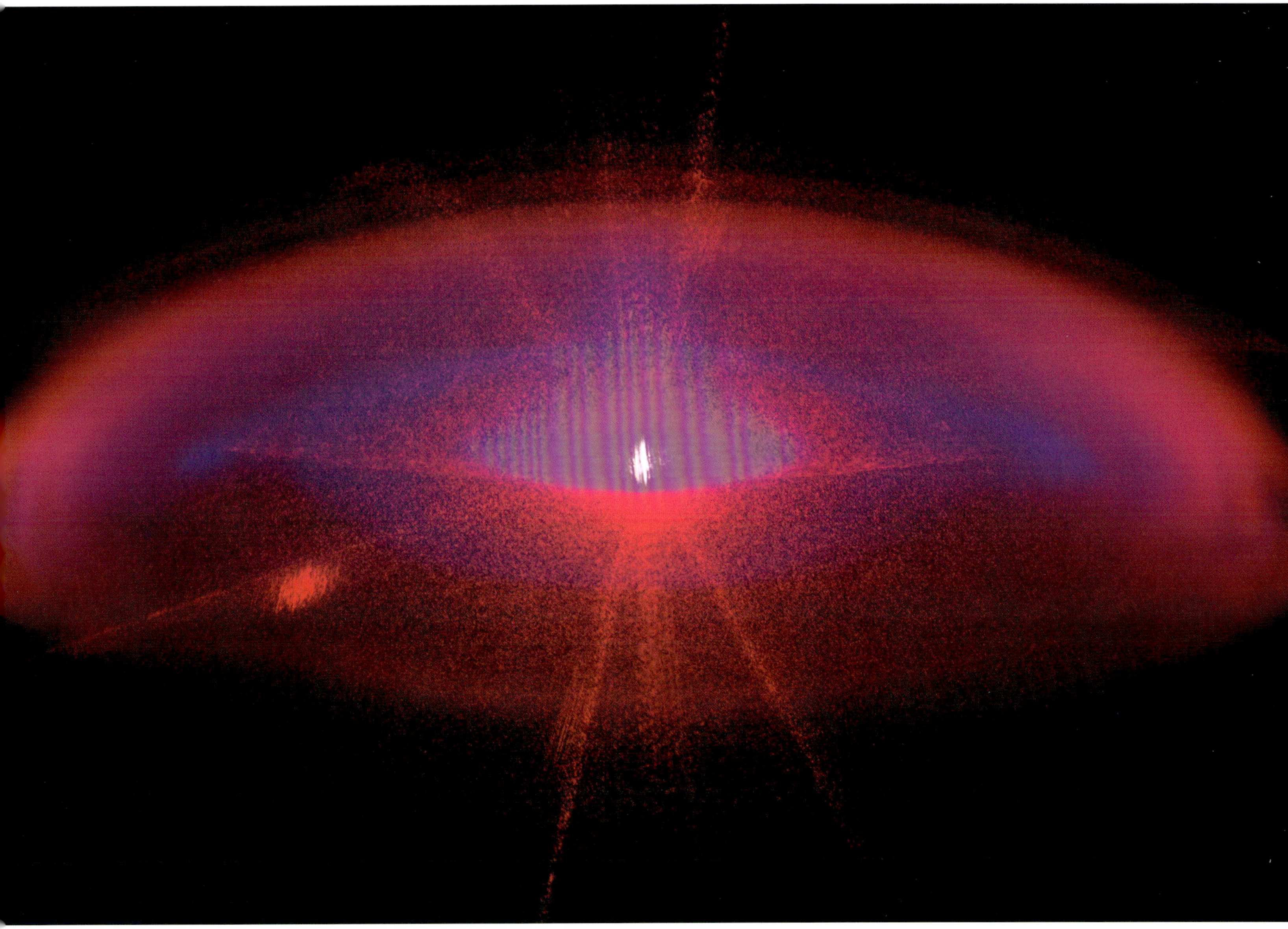

"Frequency Dome," lasergram image, Mike Frankel, September 1970.

Overleaf: "Altitude Leverage," lasergram, Mike Frankel, April 1970.

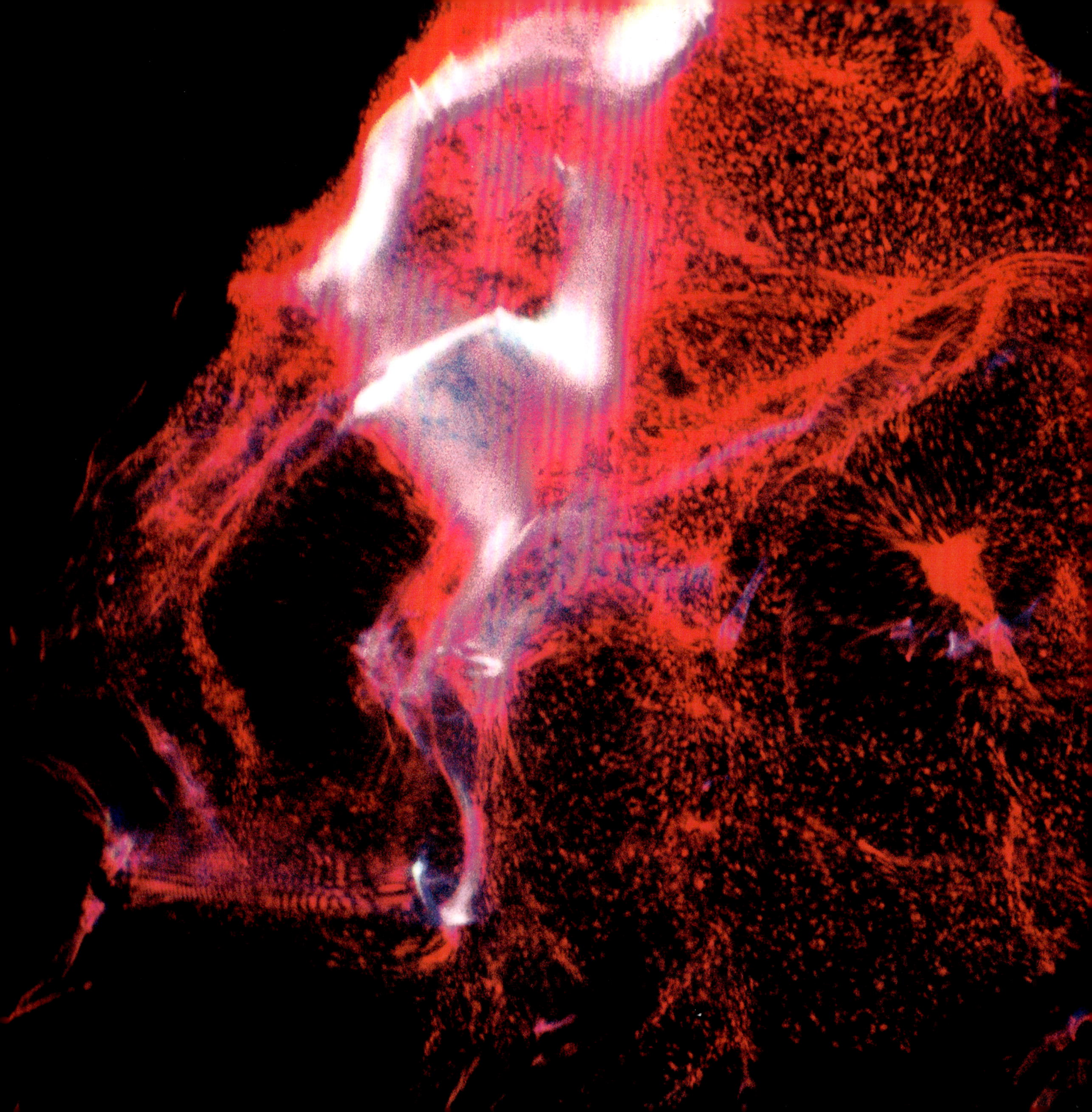

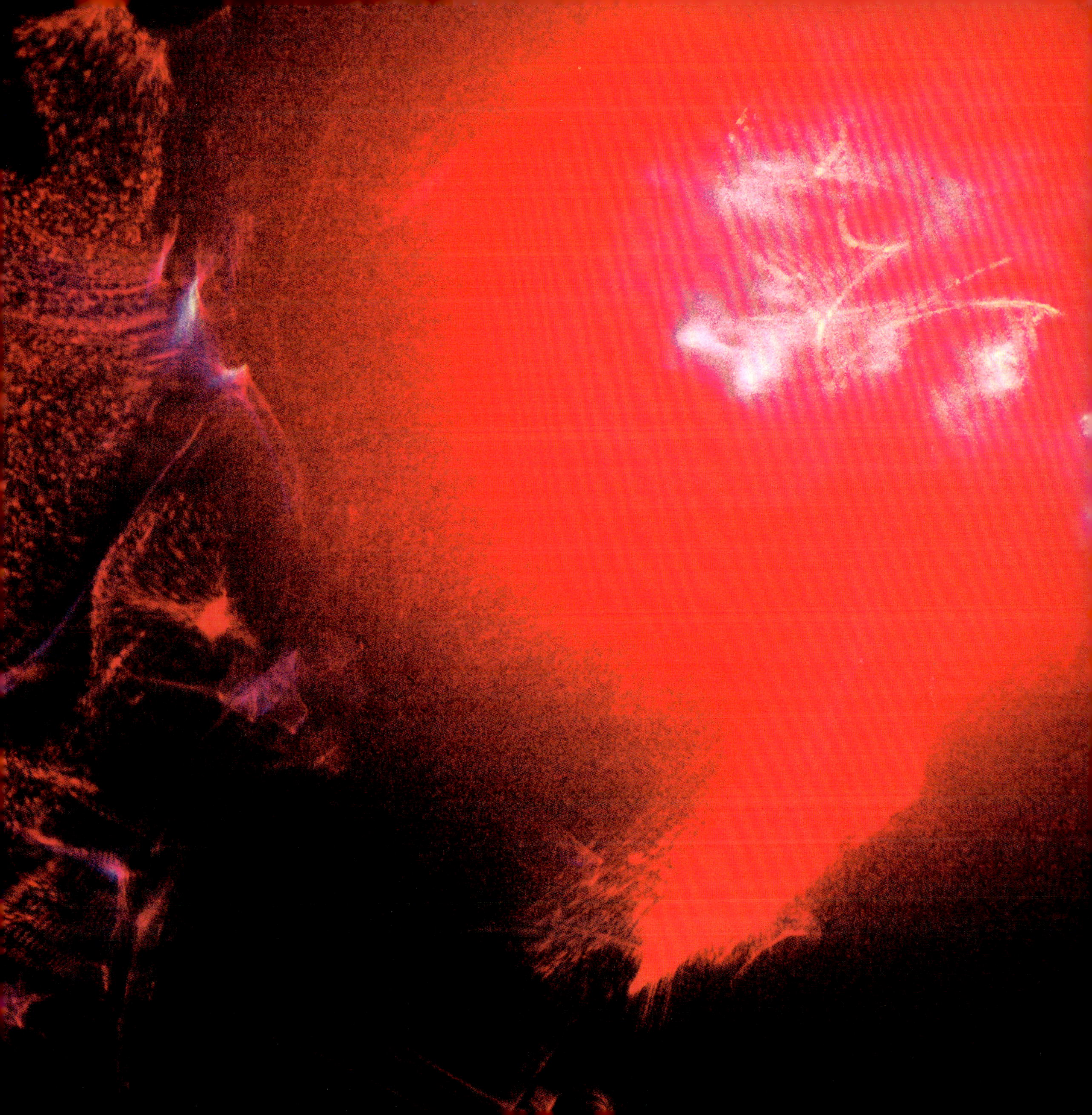

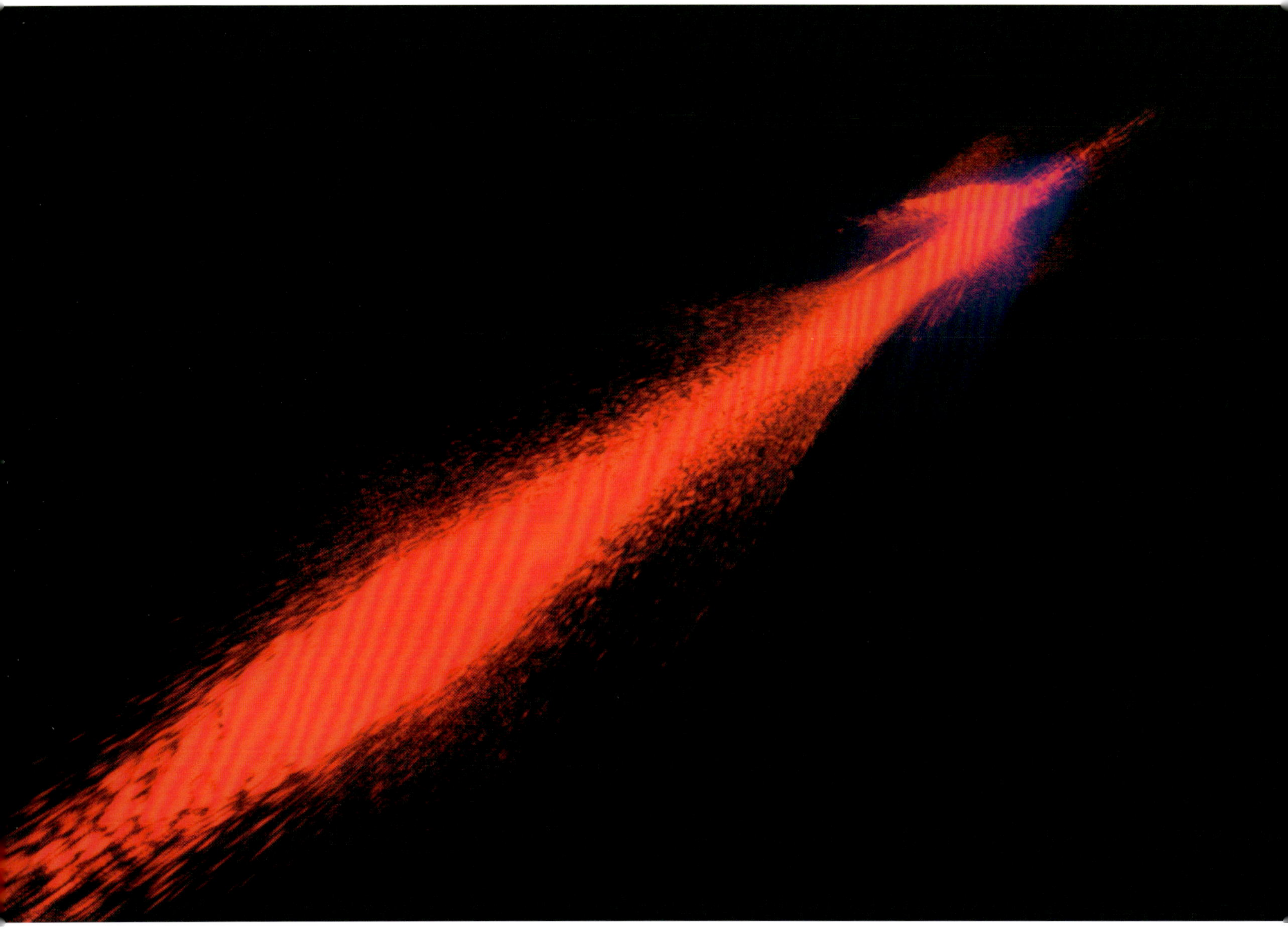

“Full Throtle,” lasergram, Mike Frankel, April 1970.

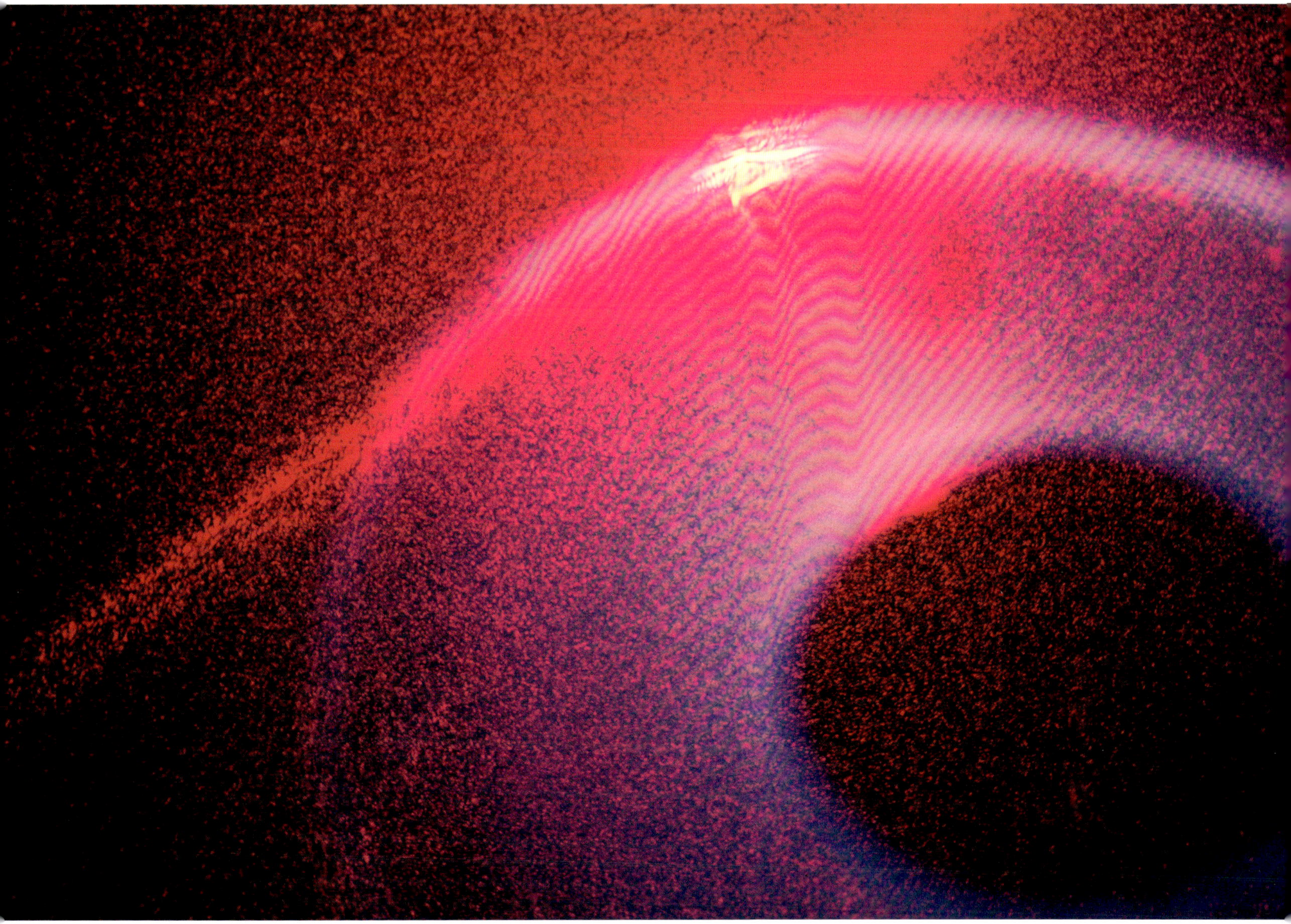

"Mercatorum IV," lasergram, Mike Frankel, February 1970.

Wilderness is not a luxury but a necessity of the human spirit, and as vital to our lives as water and good bread. . . . There are some places so beautiful they can make a grown man break down and weep.

—EDWARD ABBEY, *Desert Solitaire*

Conclusion

Struggles and Success

I grew up and spent my first fifty-three years in New Jersey, a unique state. It is of course the butt of many jokes, which it both does and doesn't deserve. But the New Jersey of the 1960s was no doubt a tough place for somebody experimenting in art or music. My artwork was highly stylized and abstract in extremis. As I showed it around to galleries in the area, they just wanted to see images of lighthouses and seagulls, which was a debilitating revelation for me. And for whatever reason, these lighthouses and seagulls were what the public seemed to want at the time, making it nearly impossible for me to show my work locally.

When I went to New York City, where I believed the work would be more welcome. Getting in the door of any gallery there was difficult if you didn't know someone with connections, have an agent (which I could not get), or already have an established name. My work with the Airplane and Hot Tuna seemed to count for nothing in the eyes of the gallery owners in both New Jersey and New York.

One particularly telling experience took place at the OK Harris Gallery, one of the most prestigious at the time. I arrived with a black portfolio case containing some of my best work and hoped to be at least politely received. I was quickly disabused of that notion. The officious person in charge blew me off at first sight of the portfolio, before I could even get out of my mouth any semblance of an introduction or description of my work. I was told abruptly and with extreme prejudice that "we don't receive or interview any aspiring artists without knowing them personally or without a referral from an agent." As the door slammed on my hopes, it dawned on me what a little fish I was with much more to learn about "getting in the door." After many similar experiences with other galleries, I returned to Jersey that day humbled and belittled like no other time in my artistic life.

All my work in rock and roll had been at the behest of my band contacts and friends I had made at various venues across the country. That's how I worked. And so the first time I was asked to produce a press pass in order to take photographs, I told the security person demanding to see my credentials to "fuck off" and walked away from that photography work, basically never to return. There are exceptions of course, those being for artists I have become fond of and for friends who ask me to photograph their bands. For example, I photographed Fatal Rage in 1983 for my good friend and leader of the punk scene in Central New Jersey, Jack "Jacko" Monahan. I've also managed to smuggle a camera into a concert or two to take photographs of bands I enjoy, just for my own edification.

Over the years, I have also provided archived images for various bands, some internationally known and some local to New Jersey. In 1971, I sent quite a few duplicate slides to the management of Emerson, Lake & Palmer, at their request, only to be told later that they had not used any of my photographs. However, several months later I bought a copy of *Melody Maker*, a British music periodical, and I found an ad using one of my images! I was ultimately compensated after pressing the management, but had I not seen it I would have been in the dark about the unauthorized use. This event presaged a far more extensive "appropriation" of my work in the 1990s by the late manager of Jefferson Airplane. After I had contributed, and was compensated for, thirty-five images for the *Jefferson Airplane Loves You* box set, dozens of my photos were used by this individual in a Hot Tuna box set without my knowledge. As it turned out, these were the "lost" images that RCA never returned to me some twenty-six years ago! I enforced my ownership and was eventually compensated, but it was true betrayal from someone I had trusted and had always seemed to have supported my work in the past. I did work with RCA again after the Hot Tuna incident, and several other labels, providing never-before-seen photos for remastered versions of several Airplane records including *Volunteers*, *Bless Its Pointed Little Head*, and a limited-edition CD that one received when one purchased both.

One release I took particular delight in was that of alternate-night recording from the sessions that composed the first Hot Tuna record. This "new" recording was released in conjunction with the fortieth anniversary of that debut release. Both featured my work on the cover, making for fitting bookends to my forty years of work with the band.

Alongside my work with lasers and holography, from the 1970s onward I turned to assemblages created with "odd" found objects and collages inspired by my heroes Max Ernst, Man Ray, and their fellow surrealists. I began employing old engravings found in used books and magazines from the nineteenth century, featuring watch images and strange mechanical devices, which presaged the steampunk movement. I also had the fortune to do book covers for the Swedenborg Foundation and textbooks that featured both my abstract lasergrams and my full-spectrum heliographs.

In 1974 I attempted to singlehandedly save a historic 1920s movie palace in Asbury Park called the Mayfair Theater, an absolute architectural treasure. But it was destroyed by the wrecking ball despite my success at having it declared a US National Historic Site. Opportunities arose to do product and food photography and "forensic" photography for law firms representing injured people and clients in industrial settings. Some of the scenes I photographed were quite horrific but needed to be documented for trial. I had a stint in real estate sales, easily achieving the status of million-dollar salesperson several years running, when a million meant something more than it does today. However, this was the nadir of my employment because it was so far from my ongoing artistic goals—but hell, it paid the bills and allowed me time to pursue my artwork. My longest employment was as a partner in a computer company founded by a friend in the late '80s, where I was finally riding the crest of a wave rather than being ahead of it. That time was most profitable to me financially and taught me all I needed (usually by the seat of my pants) to keep up with tech to this day.

Even during these times I continued to produce art. In 1985 I created a video called *24 . . . 24*, which was an examination of the state of television programming at the time. The video was recorded over a twenty-four-hour period with ten-second increments every half hour of TV from twenty-four television channels. I wanted to highlight the vast amount of mindless garbage that was broadcasted during a time of growing choice in media. The piece very much presaged the hundreds of channels now available with not much improvement in content. In 1995 I produced the prototype of what I called a "laser kaleididome," which I believe was the first small-scale, portable, self-contained abstract laser light show projector. I utilized all the techniques I had developed producing my earlier lasergrams to present the abstract images in real multicolor movement.

One of the more interesting highlights of my work was participating in arguably the first internet collaborative hypermedia art projects in the mid-1990s. "Deconstructing Duchamp" was a series of twenty-five interlinked webpages interpreting in depth all the elements of Marcel Duchamp's influential artwork from the early twentieth century, most commonly known by the English titles *The Bride Stripped Bare by Her Bachelors, Even* or *The Large Glass*. The project spanned the globe, and I was one of the only participants from the United States. This pioneering "virtual" artwork was live on the web for many years, with interaction from thousands of viewers.

The years 1996 through 2002 were some of the most challenging in my life. Within a span of four years, I lost both my mother and father, quite suddenly and without warning. It was as if the sun, moon, and all the stars had been extinguished and fell from the sky. I never had a chance to say farewell to either of them, which shattered my heart. A veritable orphan at fifty years old, I was severely depressed and all but nonfunctional. This led to a time of deep introspection and examination of not only my life but my work as well. The loss of Mom and Dad made me want to continue even more intensely the quest to have my artwork seen and to produce even more. Though I wished they had seen my work receive more recognition, I knew how proud they were of my modest accomplishments, and I am sure they know that I continue to share my creativity with the world. I rededicated myself to that goal. And so I scraped myself off the floor, with the aid of some all too necessary medications; put my parents' and my affairs in order; and sold their house. It was now time to move on and to seek out other worlds, realize new destinies, and leave New Jersey behind.

As a child I came across a book from *Look*, a biweekly magazine that was a competitor of *Life* during the mid-twentieth century. *Look at the USA* afforded me my first look at the Grand Canyon and Monument Valley. Seeing these images lit a fire in me that culminated with my moving to Flagstaff, Arizona, less than one hundred miles from the Grand Canyon. Of course, as a kid living in a densely populated urban area in Central Jersey, I had no clue about the real West. My ideas came from John Ford westerns, in both black-and-white and in color; in all honesty, I long believed that the background scenery of the West was all special effects, even when I saw the pictures of the Grand Canyon. I could hardly believe it was a real place; little did I know what a large presence it would have later in my life.

I already had a lifelong obsession with my "mythic West" (as I came to refer to it), and in 1989 I took a fourteen-day trip encompassing sixteen national and state parks. As I traveled around the region, I felt a sense of home, and my soul was set on fire. I had finally found where I physically and spiritually belonged.

My trip included a stopover in Flagstaff, Arizona, a locale I was familiar with from the litany of towns recited in the oft-covered Bobby Troup song "Route 66." I was duly impressed with my brief exposure to this mountain town and filed the experience away for later thought. After that dizzying trip I was hooked, and I returned year after year, exploring further the magnificent Grand Canyon and my personal favorites, the Arches and Canyonlands national parks near Moab, Utah. When in 2002 it came time to decide where to move, I determined that Flagstaff checked all the required boxes in bright red, like the rocks surrounding it.

I left New Jersey, nearly filling a fifty-foot truck with a lifelong accumulation of stuff, and headed to Arizona. In Flagstaff, I found that my work, both my early rock and roll photographs and my experimental art, was embraced with excitement and praise. To many in New Jersey, my work seemed radical; in Flagstaff it was welcomed, even my most politically provocative pieces.

To top it off, I discovered an art group, the Artists' Coalition of Flagstaff, which made me their president after only a year and subsequently executive director. I've led the group now for over twenty years. During my tenure it has grown from a sleepy organization, presenting only one event a year, to the one of the largest and active nonprofit art groups in northern Arizona, with multiple yearly events, educational programs, and community outreach, including building one of the largest and longest running recycled art exhibitions in the country. In my work with the group, I mentor emerging artists, young and old, and get to see their work evolve and their careers flourish. The Coalition also partners with the Hozhoni Foundation, a nonprofit that specializes in providing social services to Native American artists as well as "challenged artists" in Flagstaff, and provides extensive studio and gallery space for the artists at their facility. And I collaborated, in 2013, with fellow artists John Rogers and Tom Williams on an interactive sculpture, *The Mars Kaleidisphere*, which is permanently installed at the internationally famed Lowell Observatory in Flagstaff. My work with the artists at Hozhoni and on the *Kaleidisphere* collaboration stand out among the proudest and most inspiring moments in my life.

The validation in Flagstaff of my art peaked when, in 2007, a gentleman came into my life named Joseph Crownover. He opened a gallery on the south side of Flagstaff and became a champion of many artists in my group, including myself. Joe's Tanglewood Fine Arts gallery was first class all the way. It was beautifully appointed with the artwork impeccably displayed in custom frames. Joe immediately took a liking to my work, and in October of 2007 he went full bore on an exhibition of my work, presenting over fifty 20 × 30 prints, which he called *Rock of Ages*. It was by far the largest retrospective of my work to have been mounted at the time, and due to Joe's prowess in promotion the exhibition was a major event in town, producing outstanding sales. The event and the people I met there led to another exhibition in Modesto, California and to some of my work being featured in the Beat Museum in San Francisco.

Joe left Flagstaff after a few years and I didn't hear from him for a long time, but in 2019 he contacted me out of the blue with the news that he had opened a new gallery in Independence, Missouri, close to Kansas City, and wanted to take up where we left off years earlier, promoting my work to the world. I am honored and delighted to have Joe representing me once again, and since 2019 his gallery has exhibited and sold my work for a second time.

After the *Rock of Ages* show in Flagstaff, and at the urging of my longtime best friend Michael Green, the two of us embarked on a journey to various Los Angeles art galleries with the intent of finding more opportunities for exhibiting my work. Armed with copies of a twenty-five-page full-color book featuring my most dynamic rock images, which I had created with an online publisher, we set out on our quest. Our first stop was in Santa Monica at the Bergamot Station Arts Center, where we could visit many resident galleries, all in one locale. The first place we tried was the Robert Berman Gallery. We had been informed that this was *the* leading LA area gallery, so we figured we might as well start at the top. Mr. Berman happened to be on site on that day, and he took my book and reviewed it right on the spot. Without hesitation, he offered me a place in his upcoming *Month of Photography Los Angeles* group exhibition. Holy shit! We had hit unexpected pay dirt on the first attempt, unlike my earlier New York gallery experiences. I left stunned, turned to Michael, and said that perhaps the tide may be changing thanks to his never-ending persistence. So, for the month of April 2012, four of my images were on display at the premiere gallery in Los Angeles. The photos represented both my representational portraits (Grace Slick) and some of the most wild experiments (Country Joe MacDonald, Jerry Garcia and Bob Weir, and a Pink Floyd eight-image stunner).

I sure wasn't in New Jersey anymore. There was not a lighthouse or seagull on any canvas in the exhibition. My work was received enthusiastically, and the biggest thrill of the event was that I was in the company of—and listed in the program and poster alongside—the late Man Ray, one of my heroes and inspirations.

One evening in Flagstaff I attended a film screening and met a local filmmaker and editor named Darren Rudy. Darren has a youthful enthusiasm, ambition, and energy reminding me of my younger self, and we became fast friends discovering all the films and genres that we were mutually passionate about. This has led to the resurrection of a long dormant film project of mine, the first feature-length documentary on the life and toweringly influential career of another of my lifelong inspirations, the master film director of *Metropolis* Fritz Lang. The film is in the planning and preproduction stage now and hopefully will appear by the hundredth anniversary of *Metropolis* in 2027.

In September 2019, after a seventeen-year self-imposed exile, I returned to New Jersey. A year or so prior to that, Michael Green, always on the lookout to promote my work, told me of a new acquaintance of his, Gregory Schwartz, known as the "Poet of Asbury Park." Greg was in turn connected with the then dean of humanities at Monmouth University, Kenneth Womack, himself a world-class Beatles scholar and author of numerous books on the Fab Four, including the definitive biography of their producer George Martin. After seeing my work on my website, Ken was more than interested, and this led to several phone calls in September 2018 about mounting an exhibition of my work. The exhibition opened in late September 2019 at the university's art gallery and continued for three months. I worked with Vaune Peck, the gallery's director, to present the work in stunning metal prints, including several of the "spinners" I had envisioned decades ago, allowing viewers to turn the photographs and view all the layers of multiple images from all 360 degrees. The exhibition also featured a 40 × 60" image of David Bowie that Michael had printed and framed for the event.

Concurrent with this exciting turn of events, Michael and Greg ran into Alberto Engeli, a filmmaker living in Asbury Park and working on a documentary to commemorate the fiftieth anniversary of Woodstock. They told Alberto about my work at the festival, and he contacted me shortly thereafter. We had a long conversation during which he concluded that my stories were well worth inclusion in his film. So he flew out to Flagstaff in October 2018 to lens the interview. I was honored and thrilled that, as a part of the film, I would be in the august company of Jorma, Jack, John Sebastian, and one of the organizers of the festival, Ticia Agri, along with several key surviving attendees.

The premiere of *Looking Back: Woodstock 50 Years Ago* was scheduled to coincide with my appearance and lecture at the opening reception of the exhibition at Monmouth in 2019. To say that I was apprehensive to travel back to New Jersey is an understatement. This onetime "stranger in a strange land" was returning in modest and humble triumph, proudly accompanied and supported by the newfound the love of my life Kathleen Leatherwood.

At the opening reception of my exhibition, *Woodstock and Beyond: The Visionary Art of Mike Frankel*, there was standing room only. Old friends, new friends, and the curious listened to me discuss my life and work. Standing there, in Jersey, at my alma mater, well over sixty years removed from when I picked up my first camera, I felt an overwhelming sense of redemption.

As I stood before the crowd of lifelong friends and family who had come to share the moment with me, wonderful memories of my work and life flooded my thoughts. The memories of events separated by so much time are powerful, giving one perspective. I was moved to my core and thought of my wonderful parents and the fact that they could not be with me.

This book is a culmination of a half century of many stop-and-go, incremental attempts to have the world see my vision and my art, something I had desired for so many decades. It is proof positive in my mind that my mom was right: things do happen for a reason.

My future is blindingly bright, and I am busier at the ripe old age of seventy-five than I have been in a long time. I'm in perfect health and roaring to bring to fruition many more projects before I shuffle off this mortal coil.

As I look back on my life's work, I find that it instilled confidence in me when I had little clue about how or what I was put on earth to do. Through my art I was able to attain self-esteem, and I think my story of early success, subsequent disappointment, and final triumph is one that should inspire anyone out there struggling with their own work.

And having passed along that bit of wisdom, I have now arrived not the end, but at yet another beginning . . .

SELECTED WORKS AND EXHIBITIONS

IMAGES FOR LPS AND CDS

Fatal Rage. *Fatal Rage*. Mutha Records, 1983. Live action photographs.

Hot Tuna. *First Pull Up, Then Pull Down*. RCA Victor, 1971. Gatefold interior art.

———. *Hot Tuna*. RCA Victor, 1970. Numerous worldwide editions and variant covers and interior art.

———. *Hot Tuna in a Can*. RCA, 1996. Back cover and book art for box set.

———. *Live at New Orleans House: Berkeley, CA, 09/69*. Collectors' Choice Music Live, 2010. Cover art.

Jefferson Airplane. *Bless Its Pointed Little Head*. RCA / BMG Heritage, 2004. Interior art.

———. *Jefferson Airplane Loves You*. RCA, 1992. Book art for box set.

———. *Live 1967*. Collectors' Choice Music Live, 2010. Cover and back art.

———. *Return to the Matrix: 02/01/68*. Collectors' Choice Music Live, 2010. Cover art.

———. *Volunteers*. RCA / BMG Heritage, 2004. Interior art.

MAGAZINES AND BOOKS

Goldmine, October 1992. Magazine cover image.

Melody Maker, 1970. Magazine advertising image of Emerson, Lake & Palmer.

The Noise, 2012. Magazine cover images.

Perry, John A., and Erna K. Perry. *The Social Web: An Introduction to Sociology*. Harper and Row, 1983. Cover art.

Plunkett-Powell, Karen. *Remembering Woolworth's: A Nostalgic History of the World's Most Famous Five-and-Dime*. St. Martin's Griffin, 2001. Interior photo illustrations.

Tamarkin, Jeff. *Got a Revolution! The Turbulent Flight of Jefferson Airplane*. Atria Books, 2003. Interior images.

Van Dusen, Wilson. *The Presence of Other Worlds*. Swedenborg Foundation, 1981. Cover art.

FILMS

Fritz Lang: Cinematic Oracle. Documentary film in preproduction. 2018–. Producer and codirector.

Psycostar. 25-min abstract laser film. 1970/72. Producer and director.

24 . . . 24. 240-minute experimental film. 1985. Producer and director.

Looking Back: Woodstock 50 Years Ago. 62-minute documentary directed by Alberto Engeli. 2019. Interview subject.

MAJOR EXHIBITIONS

Psychedelic Solution, New York, New York, 1988.

Tanglewood Fine Arts Gallery, Flagstaff, Arizona, 2007.

Beat Museum, San Francisco, California, 2008.

Robert Berman Gallery, Santa Monica, California, 2012.

Monmouth University Art Gallery, West Long Branch, New Jersey, 2019.

Four Corners Framed Art, Independence, Missouri, October 2019–.

For updates, new work, ordering of prints, and contact information, visit mikefrankel.com.

ABOUT THE AUTHOR

I consider myself extremely lucky. I was adopted at four days old by the two most wonderful, kind, and encouraging people, Dr. Noah Nathan Frankel and his wife, Lillian. Their influence and impact on my life can never be understated or minimized, and I will cherish this fact until I draw my last breath. “Nate” and “Lil” could not have children. Through their association with Zimel Resnik, the “Jewish Godfather of Asbury Park,” as I dubbed him, they found a woman in New York City who was putting her baby up for adoption. This set me up to hit the “adoption jackpot”!

For seventy-three years I off and on wondered about my biological mother to no avail. In August 2022, though an amazing set of circumstances, I discovered the identity of my birth mother and that I had three half siblings. It has been joyous to connect with Alan and Rick Esner and Beth Mason and learn about my birth mother, Ruth Taxier. And to put the icing on the cake, in May 2023, I found the identity of my birth father, Joseph Braham, and another half sibling, Danielle Furci, in England. All this is thanks to Karen and Scott Miller and Marlise Gross, my “Search Angels,” and the amazing DNA technology of today.

After high school, having long decided that my idée fixe was photography and art, I applied to my father’s alma mater, the University of Maryland. I signed up for liberal arts courses, but when I showed up these classes had been closed out. Placed in a business program and told I was too late to get any housing, I went home humbled and disappointed. But I decided to check out Monmouth University (then Monmouth College), right in my backyard. To my amazement, I was offered a full scholarship—an offer I couldn't refuse. This singular turn of events led to my ability to work with Jefferson Airplane and Hot Tuna and to witness and document so many popular music artists of the day: I simply could not have accomplished this had I not had access to the New York concert scene and beyond.

Early in the '90s I bought a home just six houses away from Mom and Dad. They were well into their eighties and needed attention and support. I cherished the opportunity to repay the lifelong love I received from them both. Sadly, on a winter day in 1996, a second heart attack felled Mom, just minutes after I had seen her for lunch. After she passed, I went into high gear taking care of Dad. In 1998, Nate was diagnosed with an abdominal aortic aneurysm, which took his life two years later. The only way I have come to live with their untimely deaths is to believe that both of them unconsciously wanted to spare me the pain and heartache of saying goodbye if they were failing from disease, perhaps incapacitated and uncommunicable.

In 2002 I moved to Flagstaff, Arizona, and ever since have been able to expand my work as an artist while surrounded by some of the most magnificent scenery on earth. This book recounts my "odyssey" as an artist. Thanks for coming along for the ride!

AMERICAN ★ MUSIC ★ HISTORY ★

Music shapes our world more powerfully than any other cultural product. To fully understand America, we must learn the complex, diverse history of American musical life. The books in this series tell the stories of the artists, forms, and innovations that define the musical legacy of the United States and fashion its ideals and practices.

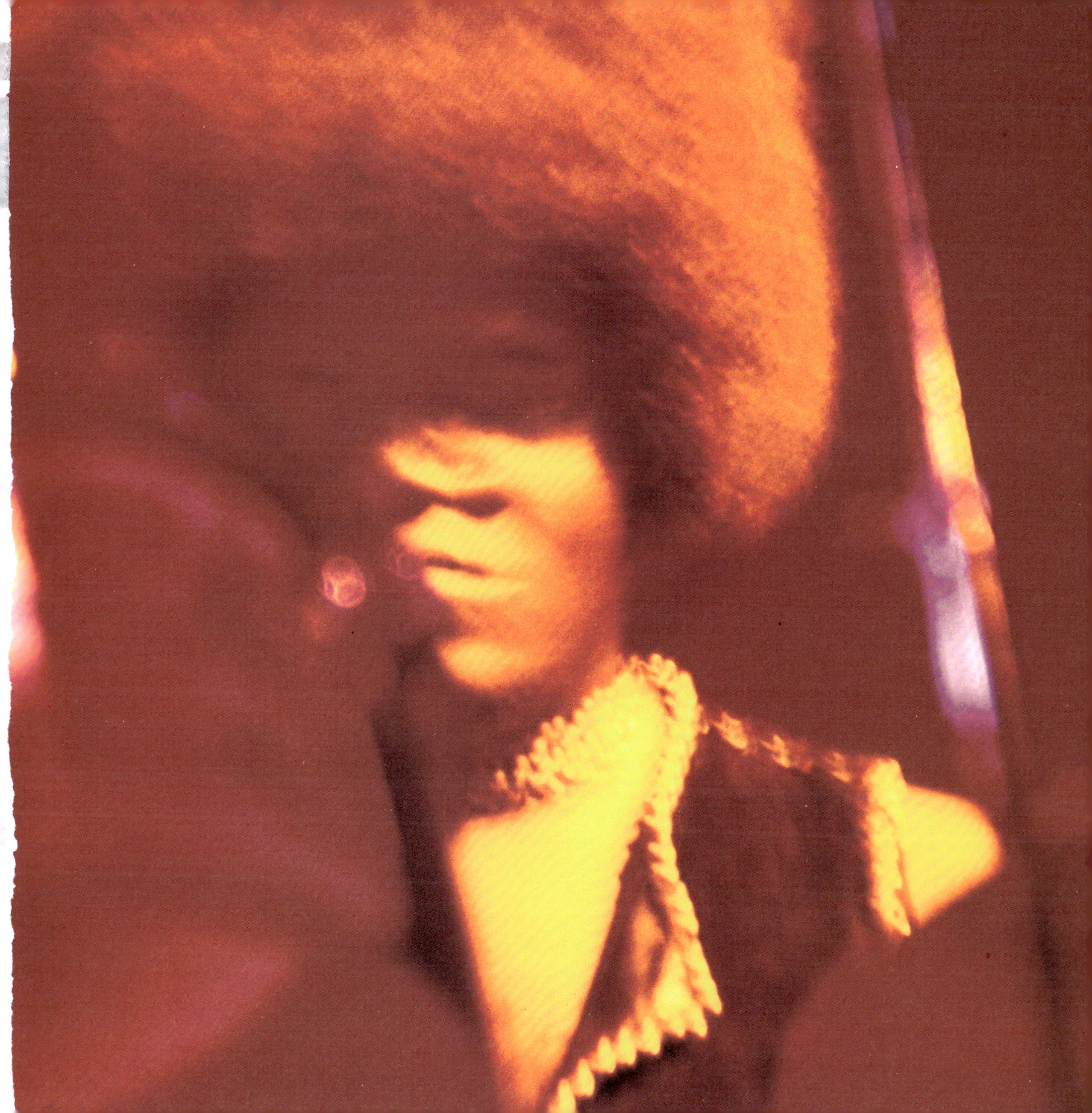

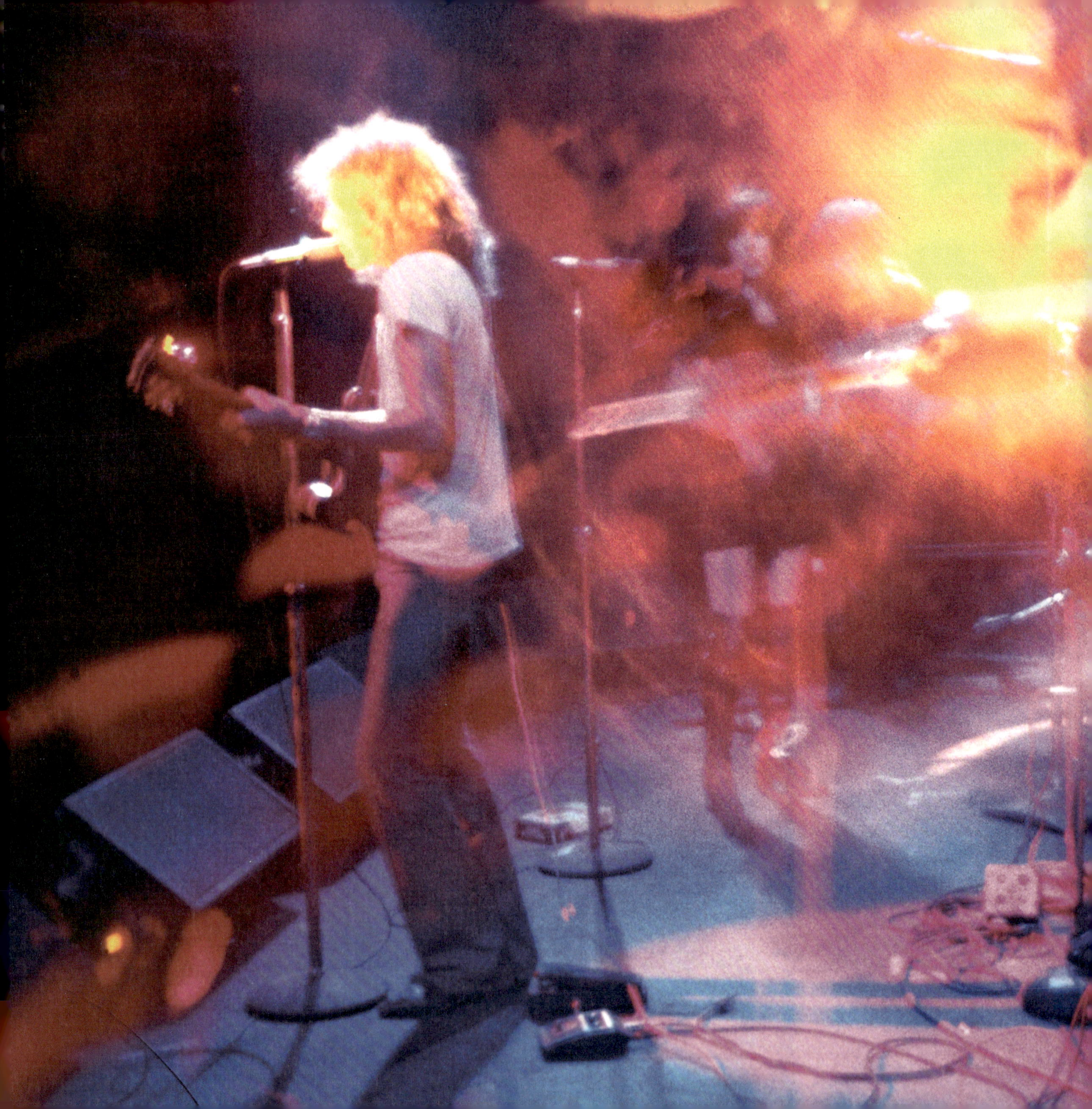